DATE DUE

NO 1 1 '08			

DEMCO 38-296

WORK-*PLACE*

A GUILFORD SERIES

Perspectives on Economic Change

Editors

MERIC S. GERTLER
University of Toronto

PETER DICKEN
University of Manchester

Work-*Place:*
The Social Regulation of Labor Markets
JAMIE PECK

Restructuring for Innovation:
The Remaking of the U.S. Semiconductor Industry
DAVID P. ANGEL

Trading Industries, Trading Regions:
International Trade, American Industry,
and Regional Economic Development
HELZI NOPONEN, JULIE GRAHAM, *and* ANN R. MARKUSEN, *Editors*

Forthcoming

The Golden Age Illusion:
Rethinking Postwar Capitalism
MICHAEL J. WEBBER *and* DAVID L. RIGBY

WORK-*PLACE*
The Social Regulation of Labor Markets

Jamie Peck

THE GUILFORD PRESS
New York London

©1996 The Guilford Press
A Division of Guilford Publications, Inc.
72 Spring Street, New York, NY 10012

Marketed and distributed outside North America
by Longman Group UK Limited

Printed in the United States of America

This book is printed on acid-free paper.

Last digit is print number: 9 8 7 6 5 4 3 2 1

Library of Congress Cataloging-in-Publication Data

Peck, Jamie.
    Work-place : the social regulation of labor markets / Jamie Peck.
      p. cm. — (Perspectives on economic change)
    Includes biographical references and index.
    ISBN 1-57230-043-4. — ISBN 1-57230-044-2 (pbk.)
    1. Labor supply—Social aspects. 2. Industrial sociology.
    3. Labor policy. I. Title. II. Series.
    HD5707.P425 1996
    331.12—dc20   96-1005
                                                        CIP

for Bryony and Holly

CONTENTS

LIST OF FIGURES
AND TABLES

PREFACE

During a recent taxi ride in Vancouver, the driver shared with me his analysis of Canada's twin problems of mass unemployment and burgeoning public indebtedness: there is work to be done, but because of the overly generous welfare system, the unemployed are not motivated to work; in order to solve the problem, women should be excluded from welfare and all but the most menial of paid work, which would result in full employment (for men) and renewed commitment to the sanctity of marriage (on the part of women). Never before, it is probably fair to say, has this taxi driver been so in tune with the thinking of employment ministers in Canada and elsewhere in the "advanced" industrial world.

While the problem of unemployment is certainly not new, what *is* new is the way in which analyses of and remedies for the employment crisis are being formulated. In the 1960s, labor market policymakers focused on the social distribution of "good" and "bad" jobs, concerns reflected in theories of labor market dualism and segmentation. In the 1990s, however, the prevailing ethos of neoliberalism is associated with an indiscriminate scramble for any jobs—a concern, first and foremost, with the geographic distribution of jobs (the need to bring more *here*) irrespective of their quality. These changed conditions have been paralleled by a return to orthodox, market-based theories of the labor market, which not only endorse but make a virtue of income polarization, employment insecurity, and deunionization.

Fashionably to scorn connections between theoretical shifts and material/political conditions would be to overlook a vital link between the new realities of job shortage and insecurity and the new orthodoxies of flexibility and deregulation. It is hardly an exaggeration to say that the current labor market crisis is, *at the same time*, a crisis in the quantity and quality of jobs, who gets them and where, *and* a crisis of how we think about, analyze, and theorize the labor market.

To write a book like this one, seeking to establish an analytical purchase on the labor market in its many local forms, is not to duck the material issues of jobs, pay, and unemployment, but rather to confront them in a different way. The battles waged in the 1960s and 1970s between orthodox and nonorthodox approaches to the labor market seem to have been won by the latter in theory but lost in practice. They need to be fought again, though on somewhat different terrain. In the context of a globalizing economy, as national and local states have been induced (either willingly or unwillingly) to resort to supply-side and monetarist measures, labor market policy has assumed inordinate significance just when labor market theory has given way to a feeble and permissive new classicism. The alliance between market-based theory and market-based politics has proved strong. Recourse to such theories is supposed to reassure us that attacks on the low-paid and welfare mothers are not motivated by spite or fiscal austerity, but in fact are driven by high-minded concerns for economic efficiency, flexibility, even equilibrium. As labor market rhetoric and practice threaten a return to the nineteenth century, it is perhaps fitting that there be a parallel return to nineteenth-century theorizing and moralizing.

Somewhat perversely, it has been the right which has been more successful in connecting economic theory and political praxis in recent years. Perhaps the tide is beginning to turn; programs of neoliberal deregulation in the labor market continue to unravel while evidence mounts that labor-inclusive approaches, based on social protection and negotiated worker involvement, present a coherent and sustainable, as well as desirable alternative. It remains to be seen whether alternative labor systems can stave off the challenge of neoliberal models which, despite their internal flaws, have the "advantage" of short-term cost-efficiency and the capacity to undercut and undermine systems constructed through a social compromise between capital and labor. It is imperative to halt, then reverse the current dynamic of regulatory undercutting which is ratcheting down working conditions, trading away workers' rights and benefits, and leading a race to the bottom in labor standards.

Essential to this challenge is an understanding of the uneven and unstable terrain on which labor markets are being remade. An alternative regulatory, rather than *de*regulatory agenda must build from an appreciation of how labor markets work in all their diversity and how they relate to one another. This book is written as a modest contribution toward that goal, seeking to construct a conception of the labor market which is sensitive to the variability of labor market experiences and processes and which takes account of the tensions between globalizing and localizing tendencies in labor market organization. In large part this is a theoretical project, and unashamedly so. The book seeks to build from a set of fundamental ideas drawn from theories of segmentation and regulation (sites of considerable innovation over recent years), and at the same time to draw on more practical experience of policy-oriented work on labor market programs, training systems, and local employment strategies. In other words, there is an attempt to "ground" the book's argument both in theoretical terms and in the real-life experience of labor market policies and practices.

Work-Place: *The Social Regulation of Labor Markets* argues for an approach to labor market analysis which is sensitive to both their institutional embeddedness and geographic differentiation. Labor markets, it is argued, *work* in different ways in different places. This is not an excuse to wallow in the differences of labor market structures, dynamics, regulatory regimes, and so on, as if, somehow, they were so differentiated as to defy explanation. Instead, it represents an attempt to confront questions of labor market (de)regulation and institutionalization, uneven development and path-dependence, in a systematic and theoretically situated fashion. The foundations for this project lie in four decades of theoretical work on labor segmentation and the structuring of labor markets, and, while it does not need to be reinvented, it does need to be sensitized to the spatiality of labor market processes. That is the task of this book, clearly in large measure a theoretical one but also concerned with how labor market theory may be applied in concrete research. The first half of the book makes a theoretical case for spatializing labor market theory, and the second illustrates some of the ways in which this approach can be put to work.

Needless to say, a great deal of the work behind this book has been collective rather than individual. This is no way to repay the debts I owe to the numerous friends and colleagues who have helped shape the book and its arguments, yet who really cannot be roped into sharing responsibility for its remaining flaws and shortcomings. I hope they will accept this as a kind of down payment: Ash Amin, Peter Baker, Huw Beynon, Peter Bibby, Iain Campbell, Diane Elson, Bob Fagan, Ruth Fincher, Harry Hall, Graham Haughton, John Holmes, Ray Hudson, Bob Jessop, Andy Jonas, Martin Jones, Roger Lee, Peter Lloyd, Phil Morrison, Phil O'Neill, Jill Rubery, Nigel Thrift, Adam Tickell, Michael Webber, Frank Wilkinson, Jane Wills, Ian Winter; and Richard McArthur, who would have had a chuckle. Thanks also to

Dave Carter, Dan Finn, Mike Emmerich, Bill Sheppard, and John Shutt for showing that policy work is never *just* policy work. The staff at Guilford Publications have helped enormously too, particularly Peter Wissoker, editor, and Jackie Southern, copy editor. I am especially grateful to Peter Dicken and Meric Gertler for their always incisive, often tricky, but never less than constructive editorial comments. I hope that I have done them justice. And never least, I thank Bryony and Holly, for their tolerance and generosity with my regular claims for weekend "research leave."

Glossop
June 1995

Chapter 1

INTRODUCTION
Places of Work

The *value,* or worth of a man, is as of all other things, his
price; that is to say, so much as would be given for the use
of his power. . . . And as in other things, so in men, not the
seller, but the buyer determines the price. . . . Their true
value is no more than it is esteemed by others.

> —Hobbes, *Leviathan*

Labor markets are not working. These fundamental institutions of
capitalist societies—bringing together workers in search of a wage and
capitalists in search of employees—no longer seem up to the job. For
some time the problems have been evident. Since the 1970s, in most
of the leading capitalist countries, unemployment has risen inexorably,
real wage growth has slowed, and labor market inequalities have
widened. In much of Europe and North America today, it is not
uncommon to find, among those who want and *need* a job, one in six
out of work; while, of those in jobs, around one-third find themselves
in various forms of precarious employment.

There has been a search for scapegoats. At the institutional level,
labor unions, schools, and welfare systems have fallen under attack.
At the individual level, the finger has been pointed at the "work-shy"
unemployed, "feckless" youth, and "irresponsible" single parents. The
neoliberal response to labor market failure has been to seek "flexibility" through strategies of "deregulation." From this perspective, fail-

ure is seen as having occurred *in* the market, not *because of* the market. On the contrary, the neoliberal solution is to liberate the labor market from "external interferences" in order to give market forces their head. If, the argument goes, the labor market can be made to behave more like other commodity markets—in which there is unfettered competition and prices fluctuate in accordance with the balance of supply and demand—then its problems will be solved. For example, the way to tackle unemployment is to allow wages to fall so that employers will be induced to create more jobs and thereby absorb the excess supply of labor.

Although couched in the ostensibly apolitical discourse of free markets, competition, and flexibility, neoliberal attempts at deregulating the labor market have been associated with an unprecedented attack on the social and working conditions of labor, which Harrison and Bluestone (1988) have called "zapping labor." Along with the commodification of labor have come the weakening of labor unions, the erosion of social protection in the labor market, the withdrawal of welfare entitlements, and the widening of inequalities. Contrary to the nostrums of neoliberal ideology and neoclassical economics, the hidden hand of the market is not an even hand: the imposition of market forces is associated with the degradation of labor. As if to add insult to injury, it also became clear in the 1980s—most notably in the United States and the United Kingdom, where neoliberal strategies were pursued with missionary zeal—that attempts further to commodify the labor market were manifestly failing to solve the problems of the 1970s. On the contrary, "new" and more intense problems of long-term unemployment, job insecurity, and pay inequality were created.

The problems of neoliberal deregulation are not simply those of ineffective policy prescriptions. Fundamentally, they are problems of *analysis,* resting on an idealized notion of a competitive labor market. Contrary to the ideal, real-world labor markets are not like commodity markets: prices do not coordinate supply and demand, participants do not enter the market as equals, and commodities do not pass—in the absolute sense of legal ownership—from seller to buyer. Before wielding her scalpel, the neoliberal surgeon must first ask us to believe that the patient is something it is not. Little wonder that the patient has been unable to make a recovery.

As Marx and Polanyi argued, to construct the labor market as a commodity market is to deny the *social* nature of human labor and productive activity. Moreover, according to Polanyi (1944), "the idea of a self-regulating market implied a stark utopia. Such an institution could not exist for any length of time without annihilating the human and natural substance of society; it would have physically destroyed man and transformed his surroundings into a wilderness" (p. 3). While Polanyi recognized that labor markets qua markets exhibited a certain "satanic efficiency," he also pointed to their enormous destructive capacities for both communities and, in the long term, business.

Yet, if the reading of the labor market as a commodity market is a fiction, it is a powerful fiction. The competitive model performs a fundamental ideological function, justifying rewards to those thought to have earned them and issuing penalties to those who have not. "What the theory is really trying to say," Barbara Wootton (1955) has argued, "is that in a fully competitive labour market people tend to get out of the productive process just about what they put into it" (p. 14). In other words, the market gives people what they deserve—no more, no less. According to the model, success in the labor market is secured through investments in education and training (which Becker, 1975, terms "human capital") while failure follows from the individual inadequacies of workers. In perhaps the most blunt and infamous statement of this orthodox position, Hicks (1932) once claimed that low-paid labor is "often badly paid, not because it gets less than it is worth, but because it is worth so appallingly little" (p. 82).

It is difficult to reconcile the claim that labor markets reflect, as in a mirror, the human capital endowments of the labor supply with the persistent and chronic inequalities characterizing the distribution of work. The burden of labor market risks (such as vulnerability to unemployment or low pay) continues to be borne by ethnic minorities, women, the disabled, the old, and the young. The orthodox response is that these groups suffer discrimination *before* entering the labor market (i.e., in the education and training system); subsequently the evenhanded labor market merely reflects those wider inequalities. This represents both a willful misconception of how labor markets *really* work and a misreading of the facts. The evidence suggests that patterns of inequality are not simply inherited but in fact are *magnified* in the labor market. First, individuals of equal human capital endowments continue to experience different levels of exposure to labor market risks, and second, the magnitude of income inequalities in the labor market continues to exceed those associated with virtually all measures of human ability (Thurow, 1975). Thus, labor market allocation processes *themselves* need to be questioned, especially the possibility that inequalities (for example, of gender and ethnicity) not only pervade the labor market, but are in part created by it and shape the way that it works.

Yet still orthodox economists will try to claim that it makes sense to conceive the labor market as a commodity market. We are implored to accept that market-like features will prevail in the long run, that the motive force of the market would be clear to see if only this institutional fog would lift, that market rules are really the only ones that count even if the social actions of the workers and managers suggest otherwise. Faith in the market becomes just that, an article of faith. The manifest reality of the labor market as a contradictory, complex, social institution is not allowed to intervene. Instead, analytical faith is restored by resort to even more formal modeling and mathematical sophistry. But the problem remains: the labor market continues to function in unmarket-like ways.

The answer to this problem is not to return to the orthodox economist's laboratory and relax underlying assumptions of the competitive model so as to allow space for such institutional factors.[1] Rather, it requires a different starting point from a different set of premises. This may seem to some readers somewhat presumptuous, having only prodded at the foundations of the competitive model rather than dismantling it brick by brick. However, given that this latter task has been tackled comprehensively elsewhere,[2] the way is perhaps now open to those with more modest goals to pick over the ruins. Needless to say, this process of attempting to reconstruct labor market theory will at times be a dirty one, unlikely to produce an alternative with the same clean lines as its predecessor.

It is an inescapable fact that labor markets are more complex, and more institutionally variable, than orthodox theory would have us believe. Departing the algebraic world of neoclassical economics means abandoning the simplicity and purity of the competitive model. Confronting complex and indeterminate issues, such as the role of power relations and institutional structures in the labor market, means surrendering any hope of emulating the elegant symmetry of a demand-and-supply schedule.

Another casualty must be the idea that labor markets are governed by the single, all-pervasive logic of the rationality of the market; in fact, they are places where logics collide. What seems logical for an individual employer (for example, poaching labor from a competitor rather than undertaking work-force training) may be illogical for the labor market as a whole. What seems logical for one group of workers (for example, forming a labor union in order to bargain collectively over wages and working conditions) may be illogical for other groups of (excluded) workers and for employers. The conflicting motivations, goals, and strategic practices of different groups in the labor market—which divide not only capital and labor but also social fractions within these aggregates—call for a conception of the labor market as a *socially constructed and politi-*

cally mediated structure of conflict and accommodation among contending forces (see Giddens, 1981). The tools of the trade in neoclassical economics—balanced equations and smooth curves—are singularly inappropriate for such an analytical task.

Rather than begin from the idealized construction of a perfectly competitive labor market, the starting point for this book is that labor markets are systemically structured by institutional forces and power relations. The task for theory is to analyze and explain these structures, not to assume them away. As argued by Wilkinson (1981a),

> there is absolutely no evidence that the atomistic labour market has ever been the general rule. The notion of a perfect market is derived from utilitarian philosophy rather than reality. Labour markets have always been structured, and the higher the skill and status of the workers the more organised and protected their position: professional associations are the most effective craft unions and have always been with us. Moreover, those parts of the labour market where workers are continually thrown into competition have been those typified by low pay and the most degrading working conditions. (p. x)

For more than four decades, research into the structuring of labor markets has drawn attention to the institutional bases of labor market processes, patterns of segmentation and stratification, and the contingent nature of labor market outcomes (see Kerr, 1954; Dickens and Lang, 1988). This rich body of work, which has begun to claim the status of an alternative paradigm[3] has produced persuasive analyses of historical transformations in labor market structures (see Edwards, 1979; Gordon, Edwards, and Reich, 1982), but it has been unusually silent on the question of geographic variability. This approach, variously labeled segmentation or structured labor market theory, provides the analytical bedrock for the following chapters, but a central argument of this book is that segmentation theory needs to be sensitive to both historical and geographic contingency. While work within this political economy tradition has recognized that labor markets are socially structured and institutionally mediated, it has so far failed to appreciate that spatial unevenness is also inherent in the ways that labor markets work. Political economists appear to be more comfortable with the lessons of history than with those of geography. It is argued here that political economy approaches to the labor market will remain truncated and partial as long as the roles of space and place are overlooked. There needs to be wider recognition that labor market structures and processes vary not only *over time*, but also *between places*.

A(NOTHER) PLACE TO START

Boston, Massachusetts. A report presented to the U.S. Department of Labor in January 1969 argued that the problem faced by residents of the city's ghetto areas was not so much a shortage of jobs—there were jobs aplenty—but a shortage of *good* jobs (Doeringer, Feldman, Gordon, Piore, and Reich, 1969). Jobs in industrial sweatshops, in hotels, and on construction sites were readily available to the disadvantaged, but without exception these were badly paid, under poor conditions, with little or no opportunity for job advancement. Black workers in particular found themselves trapped in a volatile "secondary labor market" in which workers moved frequently from one poor and insecure job to another, sometimes punctuated by short spells of unemployment. The problem involved not simply access to jobs, but access to meaningful employment opportunities in the "primary labor market." The authors, who visualized a dual labor market (Figure 1.1), argued for the need to "comprehend . . . the *structure* of labor markets when fashioning manpower programs" (p. i, emphasis added).[4]

Clearly, growth alone would not resolve such problems. Even under conditions of labor shortage, black workers continued to suffer employment discrimination and intermittent unemployment (Thurow, 1969). Thus, new policy questions were pushed onto the agenda, addressing not only the total number of jobs but also their nature and social distribution.

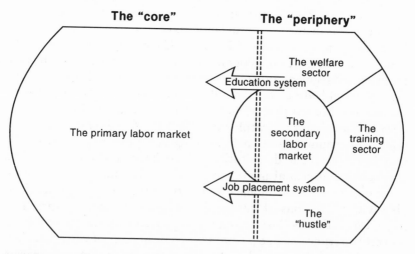

FIGURE 1.1. The Dual Economy and the Ghetto Labor Market. From Harrison (1972), p. 124. © 1972 by the Johns Hopkins University Press. Reprinted by permission.

For some workers, full employment and growth will be sufficient solutions to labor market disadvantage; for others, manpower and antidiscrimination programs will suffice; but for those who remain confined to secondary employment, the characteristics of this employment will need to be changed if labor market disadvantage is to be reduced. (Doeringer and Piore, 1971, p. 178)

However, changing the nature of secondary employment would be no mean feat. As Doeringer and Piore (1971) emphasized, the creation of secondary labor markets was not simply an exploitative act on the part of unscrupulous employers, but resulted from the complex interplay of job characteristics, discrimination, and the nature of the urban labor supply. The "style of life in low income neighborhoods" (p. 183) was seen as both cause and consequence of secondary labor market conditions. Absorbing disadvantaged groups into primary employment would require changing not only jobs and recruitment systems, but also the "street-corner" lifestyles held to be characteristic of the urban ghettos (pp. 175–177).

In *Internal Labor Markets and Manpower Analysis,* Doeringer and Piore raised issues that struck at the heart of the competitive model of the labor market. While continuing to insist that they were in the orthodox mainstream,[5] Doeringer and Piore already were bordering on the heretical. They identified fundamental institutional barriers to the clearing of labor markets through the wage mechanism. They showed how the character of jobs and labor market structures are shaped, through mutual interaction, by social and "non-market" influences. They exposed the extent to which bureaucratic and administrative rules, rather than purely competitive pressures, shape the allocation of jobs and setting of wages. They pointed to persistent labor market inequalities that could not be explained solely by reference to supply-side, human capital considerations, and they highlighted long-run trends for the institutionalization of competitive labor markets, such that the mechanisms of wage-setting and job-filling seemed to be largely insulated from market pressures in much of the economy. Thus, they delivered an inadvertent critique of fundamental neoclassical nostrums.

Although Doeringer and Piore did not consider the geography of labor markets in any explicit way, their book was casually punctuated with local case studies and spatial stereotypes. They drew heavily on their own research on low-wage labor markets in Boston, and they discussed entrenched and institutionalized practices of racial discrimination, which continued to be found after civil rights legislation, in southern states. They cited evidence of particular problems faced by inner-city workers, who tended to have lower educational attainment, higher unemployment, and more irregular work than "the average American worker," noting than an "increasing proportion of the central city laborforce is black and receives income from welfare or illicit activities" (Doeringer and Piore, 1971, p. 164). However, they continued to analyze the circumstances of inner-city workers in terms of their deviation from the supposed norm of the "average American worker," presumably a suburban white male in skilled and stable employment.[6]

What was especially perplexing was that this average American worker inhabited a labor market bearing no resemblance to the competitive model of neoclassical theory. Working in an internal labor market of some kind in which job advancement was secured by internal promotion rather than by movement through the market, from firm to firm, this worker was much more likely to be sheltered from competitive pressures than his inner-city counterpart. In their introduction to the second edition of *Internal Labor Markets,* Doeringer and Piore (1985) observed that subsequent research had highlighted considerably greater variation—in fact, a "significant and growing dispersion of prevailing practices across the country" (p. xiii)—in the structures of internal labor markets. In addition, international comparative research had revealed important differences in institutional practices. While some form of internal labor market was evident in "virtually every country studied . . . the rules associated with entry and exit and with internal labor market allocation and pricing tend to be nation-specific" (p. xii). For example, Maurice, Sellier, and Silvestre (1984) had uncovered significant differences between French and German internal labor markets which could not be accounted for by differences in technology or labor availability. Such research revealed that labor markets were institutionalized in a geographically specific manner.

Yet, years of reflection led Doeringer and Piore (1985) to grow "even more convinced" that the existence of internal labor markets was "basically an anomaly [which was not] understandable in purely neoclassical terms" (p. xvi). An anomaly maybe, but in no sense a small one. A large proportion of the total work force is employed in internal labor markets of some kind or another (Osterman, 1984). More anomalous, in fact, was the norm of the competitive labor market, in which demand and supply were regulated by price signals. On Doeringer and Piore's (1971) original calculations, fewer than one in five of the U.S. work force in the mid-sixties could be found in competitive, unstructured labor markets, the list including "general practitioners, street 'hustlers,' free-lance writers, some nonunion craftsmen, and the like" (p. 41). Drawing again on a regional example, they suggested that the "market for migrant labor in California is the paradigm of such a competitive system" (p. 4). Following Fisher (1949), they argued that the labor market experiences of migrant harvest laborers most closely approximated the postulates of competitive theory. Work was temporary and labor transient; payment was by piece rates, thereby relating labor costs directly to output; formal skill levels were low, making labor highly substitutable; and the short-term nature of the employment relationship meant that capital-labor relationships at the point of production were not normalized or institutionalized in the sense of forming durable social attachments.[7]

In seeking an exemplar for the competitive model, it is no coincidence that Doeringer and Piore should have selected such a dehumanized labor system, one which wrenches workers from the communities in which they live and constructs them for a period of time as *commoditized, placeless labor.* Fisher (1949) draws particular attention to the role played by labor contractors, intermediaries who undertake to organize the supply of labor to the farms and whose functions are explained in terms of bringing a commodity to the market; the contractor's role is to "recruit an adequate labor supply, transport it, supervise it in the field, make wage payments and maintain a camp at which the harvest workers can live" (p. 3). It is only in this "asocial" environment, where the routines of daily life and community existence are temporarily disrupted, that labor relations even begin to resemble those described in the textbooks of neoclassical economics and sought by neoliberal policymakers. Fisher contends that the market is of a "chaotic and uncertain nature," that it is "structureless," and that "there is literally no relationship between employer and employee upon which any claims to recurrent employment can be built" (pp. 5, 8).

To confer paradigmatic status on these idiosyncratic "competitive" labor relationships is not only perverse, it is fundamentally to misread the situation. In order to sustain this special case, the labor market relations of harvest workers must be abstracted from their social context. Although migrant labor may be purchased and employed *as if* it is merely a commodity, the fact remains that labor is not a commodity in the pure sense. Unlike genuine commodities, labor is not produced for the market or under the direct control of capitalists. Even the supposedly pure, unfettered market of the California harvest is structured by social and institutional forces. Fisher concedes that labor contractors performed a vital function in coordinating the labor market and reproducing the labor supply on a short-term basis, while employers' associations had been organized so as to regulate and minimize wage competition, and the labor supply was deeply structured along ethnic lines (Fisher, 1949).[8] This ostensibly unregulated, structureless labor market—the textbook case of commodified labor relations—was systematically structured and institutionalized by collective wage setting, ethnic stratification, and the presence of labor market intermediaries. As more recent work has shown, the harvest labor market is also regulated by a de facto immigration policy which

> is *not* to make the U.S.-Mexican border impermeable to the passage of "illegal" entrants, but rather to regulate their "flow".... A major contradiction in official immigration policy . . . results from the special nature of labor as a commodity that is embodied in persons and persons with national identities. Foreign labor is desired, but the persons in whom it is embodied are not desired. . . . The task of effective immigration policy is to separate labor from the jural person within which it is embodied, that is, to disembody the labor from the migrant worker. Capitalism in general effects the alienation of labor from its owner, but immigration policy can be seen as a means to achieve a form of this alienation that increases greatly in the age of transnationalism, namely the spatial separation of the site of the purchase and expenditure of labor from the sites of its reproduction, such that the locus of production and reproduction lie in two different national spaces.... Only in transnational "labor migration" is there a separation of the sites of production and reproduction. (Kearney, 1991, pp. 58–59)

Even the most "marketized" of labor markets are quite evidently social-political constructions. To treat harvest labor as a commodity is to ignore the wider social questions about how this labor supply is reproduced and socially regulated (Morales, 1984; Burawoy, 1985). It is only by defining out of existence such questions as the social reproduction of labor, and by turning a blind eye to the effects of institutional forces operating within the labor market, that neoclassical theory is able to operate on the assumption that labor is a commodity and that the labor market is a commodity market.

Work-Place: *The Social Regulation of Labor Markets* is about taking this social context seriously, indeed regarding it as integral to the way in which labor markets function. The key to understanding real-world labor markets is to grasp the social nature of labor and the institutional means by which it is reproduced, which implies a fundamental break with neoclassical orthodoxy.

> What makes labor a different commodity is in fact its process of reproduction, which is necessarily material and social and follows historically established social norms. [The] failure to recognize the peculiarity of the labour market is not due to naivety—or excessive sophistication—on the part of economists, but to the methodological foundations of neoclassical economics which assumes system-

atic relationships between prices and quantities, purged of all social and institutional processes. In the case of labor this method is fatal. (Picchio, 1992, p. 2)

Two implications of this statement are vital to the arguments in this book.

- First, if it is accepted that labor markets are not regulated by the price mechanism, how are they regulated? Labor markets, it will be argued, are *socially regulated.* Yet, the forms and functions of social regulation vary enormously, ranging from formal labor law to socially embedded work norms, from employer discrimination to union action. Coming to terms with this diversity of regulatory forms, and its implications for the differential structuring of labor markets, represents a major challenge for nonorthodox labor market theory.
- Second, if it is accepted that the analysis of labor markets must be concerned with a range of social and institutional processes, how do these processes shape the operation of different labor markets? Labor markets, it will be argued, are *locally variable.* Forms of social regulation, and by implication the structure and dynamics of labor markets themselves, vary over space.

As the following chapters discuss, this variability cannot be boiled down to a set of crude characterizations about different national systems of labor regulation, but in fact is much more complex and finely textured. The geographic distinctiveness of labor markets stems from variability in the social and institutional fabric that sustains and regulates capitalist employment relations.

A central objective of this book is the restoration and overhaul of the concept of the *local labor market,* which has been shunted into the sidelines in the debates over labor markets. Its theoretical status is negligible in orthodox, institutionalist, and radical economics. However, if social institutions matter in the functioning and reproduction of labor markets, then it follows that local labor markets matter, for this is the scale at which labor is mobilized and reproduced. It is also the scale at which considerable variability is evident in forms of labor market governance, acculturated labor practices, and labor qualities.

Local labor markets deserve special emphasis because of labor's relative day-by-day immobility which gives an irreducible role to place-bound homes and communities. . . . It takes time and spatial propinquity for the central institutions of daily life—family, church, clubs, schools, sports teams, union locals, etc.—to take shape. . . . Once established, these outlive individual participants to benefit, and be sustained by, generations of workers. *The result is a fabric of distinctive, lasting local communities and cultures woven into the landscape of labor.* (Storper and Walker, 1989, p. 157, emphasis added)

According to Storper and Walker, one consequence of the particular social conditions surrounding the mobilization and reproduction of labor is that labor itself becomes "idiosyncratic and place-bound." Following this logic, it has been argued that each local labor market is unique (Harvey, 1989b) and that labor markets are institutionalized and regulated in locally specific ways (Moulaert, 1987). However, this raises the question of *what it is* that is local about the local labor market. Do local labor markets function in locally specific ways? As Clark (1983) has asked, "How should local labor market form be understood theoretically?" (p. 1). Are universal theories of the labor market adequate to the task of explaining geographic variability in labor market outcomes and processes? Such questions go to the heart of the relationship between labor, place and the labor market. They also promise to push forward the agenda of political economy research on the labor market, by bringing to the fore the wider questions of how labor markets are regulated in different places.

LANDSCAPES OF LABOR

The rationale for the geographic perspective on labor markets advocated in this book is not a presumption that geography has all the answers. In fact, with but a few notable exceptions, geographers have been rather slow to appreciate the role of labor markets in economic restructuring. A geographic perspective is useful, however, in specifying the underlying forces behind local variability and uneven development in the labor market—phenomena which, despite their persistence, tend to be dismissed as quirky deviations from the universal competitive model by orthodox economists or as "noise" around a prevailing national model by political economists. The task is to *explain* these geographies of the labor market, not prematurely to write them off as theoretically trivial. Working out the difference that local difference makes is also a challenge for geographers, among whom according to Lee (1995) there has been "a tendency to accept 'local difference' rather than to offer a critique of it or to seek explanations at the level of social relations" (p. 1590). This, in turn, means not simply "importing" the concept of the local labor market, but reconstructing it—within a political economy framework—in such a way as to underscore the case that geography matters to the way that labor markets work.

Reviewing the U.S. literature on local labor markets in the post-war period, Rees and Shultz (1970) identified a "persistent theme that is puzzling for economists: an emphasis on the random, chaotic or purely institutional nature of wage structures and mobility patterns" (p. 3). Such findings are puzzling only to those with the a priori expectation that labor markets operate in a homogenous, spatially unvariegated way. From that perspective, durable and significant differences in local labor markets *are* paradoxical, the product of some form of institutional interference requiring suppression by ever more sophisticated, empirical reinterpretation.[9] Even writers more sensitive to the social and institutional bases of labor markets have found it difficult to make sense of local variation; Wootton (1955), for example, found herself confronted by a "thorough geographical muddle." An alternative view would be that geographies of the labor market require explanation (see Clark, Gertler, and Whiteman, 1986). As Clark (1983) has insisted, "local labor markets are man-made, not natural, and are structured according to power, not neutral rules of demand and supply" (p. 2), an approach favored here.

One of the most influential analyses of the inherent spatiality of employment and production is Massey's (1984) rendering of the spatial division of labor approach. For her, geographies of labor result from the way in which capital exploits prior spatial variation in its path of expansion. Particular rounds of accumulation (i.e., historically distinctive waves of investment) tend to be associated with particular geographies, as capital seeks the local conditions most conducive to profitable production. In turn, the economic structure of individual localities can be understood in terms of the succession of roles they have played in different rounds of accumulation. This framework renders systematic and explainable those geographies of labor which for many economists remain puzzling.

Massey's approach has informed those historical analyses stressing the *increased* importance of the "labor factor" in the location of production.[10] Central to this argument is the tension between globalizing capital and relatively placebound labor. As the locational capability of capital increases, it is able to exploit geographic variations in labor qualities in an ever more sensitive way. One manifestation of this posited general shift, fueled by the growth of transnational corporations and the progressive extension of the functional division of labor, is the tendency for different localities to be associated with different stages of the production process.

> In the 19th century, the economies of leading nations were based on geographical specialization, which was also predominantly a sectoral specialization. In the United States, major industries such as steel, textiles, automobile manufacturing, and so on . . . faced important geographical variations, including access to transport, raw materials, skilled labor, and markets. . . . [These industries responded] by concentrating all their capacity in the areas most propitious in terms of their requirements for production. . . .
>
> The economic landscape today, however, contains a spatial division of labor which is new. The spatial division of labor is no longer a sectoral one. Instead, it is an *intra*-sectoral one: one within the overall process of production of individual firms. . . . [In] the future, places will not be known . . . by *what* they produce as much as by *who* is employed there at certain stages of specific production processes. (Clark et al., 1986, p. 23)

Thus, distinct places are associated with sectoral and functional divisions of labor. In the United States, for example, "Pittsburgh meant steel, Lowell meant textiles, and Detroit meant automobiles" (Clark et al., 1986, p. 23), while in the United Kingdom, "one finds metal workers in the midlands, office professionals in London, miners in South Wales, and academics in Oxford" (Storper and Walker, 1989, p. 156).

The logic of Massey's account is that in its search for profitable locations capital is especially sensitive to the preexisting "map" of labor qualities. However, such maps are complex. Needless to say, South Wales has not only miners but office workers, academics, and metalworkers. While Massey is not blind to such complexity (indeed, she suggests ways it might be conceptualized through the local combination of layers of investment), her account is nevertheless somewhat ambiguous. Warde (1985) has suggested that recognition of the internal differentiation of labor markets is "potentially subversive" of her basic analysis: in segmented labor markets, "capital might be expected, in its search for spatial advantage, to consider only the character of the particular segment of the local laborforce which it seeks to employ" (p. 204).[11]

There is, then, a certain degree of tension between the notions of labor market segmentation and spatial divisions of labor, but there also is scope to render this tension creative rather than destructive, bringing the two notions together through reinterpretation of the local labor market. By holding together segmentation and localization, it is possible to explore geographic variation without resorting to a kind of theoretical parochialism. Places are different, but they also have shared features. Generalized processes tend to yield different concrete effects in different places, but generalized processes they remain. In Chapter 4, for example, it will be suggested that labor market segmentation is not a universal but a *locally constituted* process associated with a range of local effects. This is presented not as an empiricist challenge to the general claims of segmentation theory, but as a means of elaborating how processes of segmentation operate on the ground. The objective is not to displace a "segmentation matters" with a "locality matters" argument, but to insist that *both matter* and that they matter *together*. Notions of segmentation provide a way of enriching the concept of locality by pointing to divisions and cleavages in the labor market. Reciprocally, recognition of the importance of locality offers the possibility of a more nuanced treatment of labor segmentation. The nature of local labor markets is shaped by both "general" processes of labor segmentation and by "specific" local structures of labor reproduction and institutionalization. Geographies of labor are formed at this intersection, where flows of capital accumulation collide with the structures of community.

Although it would be a caricature to present capital as absolutely mobile and labor as absolutely static, these images do reflect an underlying reality. Capital is engaged in a restless search for more profitable sites of accumulation while labor continues to require the stability and support of community life. "Unlike other commodities," David Harvey (1989) has observed, "labor power has to go home every night" (p. 19). Reflecting on this, Beynon and Hudson (1993) have suggested a distinction between capital's use of space and labor's use of place:

> Locations that, for capital, are a (temporary) space for profitable production, are for workers, their families and friends places in which to live; places in which they have considerable individual and collective cultural investment; places to which they are often deeply attached. . . . As such, it may be helpful, terminologically and theoretically, to understand *space* as the domain of capital—a domain across which capital is constantly searching in pursuit of greater profits—and *place* as the meaningful situations established by labour.
>
> Within "places," people will have different orientations, commitments and understandings. . . . [Different] groups of workers (those with different skills, of different gender or ethnic group) may perceive their attachment to place in very different ways. Nevertheless [place] is not *just* (or, for many, *even*) a space in which to work for a wage. It is a place . . . where they are socialized as human beings rather than just reproduced as bearers of the commodity labour power. (p. 182)

Local labor markets can be seen as institutional sites at which place and space intersect: they are social arenas in which the domain of capital comes into conflict with that of labor. The nature of this intersection is a matter not for theoretical predetermination, but for theorized concrete research. Moreover, it is very much a political issue in the prevailing neoliberal climate where labor standards are being deliberately eroded and competition between places deliberately encouraged. The fact that the commoditized labor relations imposed on the California harvest workers are no longer so geographically exceptional as they were when Fisher studied them in the 1940s represents both a theoretical and a political challenge. Far from vindicating orthodox theory, these geopolitical realities are a manifestation of exploitation, not efficiency. They underline the need for an ever more insistent search for the political bases of labor markets, as much to change as to understand them.

TOWARD A SPATIALIZED POLITICAL ECONOMY

In this book, Part 1 focuses on the social and institutional processes underlying the "making" of labor markets while Part 2 teases out some of the ways in which these processes contribute to their "placing." Beginning with an analysis of labor's pseudocommodity form (Chapter 2) and with a critical review of segmentation theories (Chapter 3), Part 1 lays the foundations for a political economy approach to the labor market. Following a kind of Polanyian method (see Block, 1990, pp. 38–42), those social and institutional considerations which orthodox economics shunts into the background (and regards as the source of "imperfections") are instead bought to the foreground. Such considerations are germane to the question how labor markets are regulated. Because the self-regulating market of orthodox economics is a myth, this question is very much an open one, and one that defeats state legislators and policymakers as often as academics (Boyer, 1992; Picchio, 1992).

This is one reason why the theoretical project on labor market segmentation remains incomplete. Chapter 3 traces three generations of conceptual development: from an early emphasis on technology and skill formation in the dualist model of Doeringer and Piore (1971); through the embedding, in the radical approach of Gordon, Edwards and Reich (1982), of labor market structures within the historical evolution of capitalist control strategies; to the contemporary emphasis on the institutional specificities of labor markets and their path-dependent nature (see Rubery, 1994). In this most recent, third generation of segmentation theory, labor markets are viewed as complex, contradictory, and institutionally mediated social systems. Yet the issue how these contradictory and imperfectly regulated social systems are reproduced—how they "keep going, 'reproducing' themselves, by means of the processes that define and determine them, laying the foundations for their own continuation" (Himmelweit, 1991, p. 197)—remains unresolved. Even less is known about the different ways that labor markets keep going in different places, where both their contradictions and their socio-institutional supports take different forms. Responding to this challenge, Chapter 4 lays the foundations for a fourth generation of segmentation theory. Arguing that labor markets are both institutionally *and* locally embedded, this chapter proposes a theoretical overhaul of the local labor market. The resulting framework, which focuses attention on the locally distinctive ways in which labor markets are socially regulated, is put to work in Part 2.

Labor markets are shot through with intractable dilemmas of social regulation. The invisible hand of market regulation cannot simply be supplanted by the visible hand of state regulation in accounts of the operation of labor markets. The term preferred here, *social regulation,* is unashamedly more ambiguous, encompassing the disciplining effects of market regulation, purposive regulatory action on the part of the state, and the diverse effects of social institutions, practices and conventions. There is no guarantee that their combined effects will be functional. Rather, the result is a complex and dialectical interplay between labor market structures and dynamics on the one hand and regulatory institutions and processes on the other. It is this complex dialectic which should lie at the heart of labor market analysis, and unpacking it is an essential prerequisite for understanding how real-world labor markets work and their variability over time and space.

Such an analysis requires opening the black box of social regulation. "Social regulation encompasses all of the diverse ways in which individual economic behavior is embedded in a broader social framework" (Block, 1990, p. 42). Perhaps not surprisingly, the notion of social regulation has acquired a certain elasticity despite its centrality to regulation, segmentation, and convention theory.[12] The following two chapters attempt to refine concepts of social regulation, culminating in Chapter 4 in an attempt to reconceptualize the local labor market. What is proposed is an *integrative* analysis of the local labor market, which begins not by abstracting labor from its social context but by concentrating on the ways in which it is embedded in and shaped by that context.[13]

Part 1 of the book addresses these questions on a largely theoretical level, and Part 2 develops and applies this approach in a series of case studies. The underlying contention—that labor markets are not wage-regulated but socially regulated, that this produces systemic spatial variability in labor market structures and dynamics, and that because labor markets are socially regulated, they operate in locally specific ways—is interrogated in different empirical contexts, challenging conventional assumptions of universal labor market processes with universal effects. There is a consideration of the locally variable forms of labor market flexibility (Chapter 5) and the role of local labor markets in shaping the course of industry restructuring (Chapter 6). Chapter 5 takes as its point of departure Scott's (1988b, 1988c) analysis of urbanization, flexibility, and the labor market, examining the contradictory nature of labor flexibilization and its diverse local forms. Chapter 6 begins by revisiting Massey's (1984) conception of the spatial division of labor before moving on to consider, by way of a case study of industrial homework, aspects of the relationship between industrial and local labor market restructuring.

Then, labor regulation and space are considered from a more institutional perspective. Chapter 7 examines the processes of state formation and restructuring with respect to labor regulation, critiquing and elaborating Jessop's (1993) theorization of the transition from Keynesian-welfare to Schumpeterian-workfare regimes. Chapter 8 concentrates on the effects of neoliberalism on the geographical reconstitution of both labor relations and labor regulation, beginning with Burawoy's (1985) notion of global despotism in labor relations and moving on to consider the remaking of labor regulatory structures at the local, national, and global scales. These two chapters attempt to unpack the contemporary geopolitics of labor market restructuring, drawing attention to some of the ways in which simultaneously globalizing and localizing tendencies are working themselves out in different situations.

Finally, Chapter 9 takes stock of some of the book's central claims. It suggests that a dialectical understanding of the labor market—as a site of non-necessary interactions between different causal processes and as an arena of indeterminate social struggles and institutional mediations—requires that space in general, and the local labor market in particular, be taken seriously. In other words, explaining the labor market necessitates closer attention to the causes and consequences of its locally variable form.

Perhaps this book's most ambitious objective is to contribute to the process of explanation and theory-building in a way which is sensitive to the inherent spatiality of the labor market. Work in this area is only just beginning, and what follows is pursued in the spirit of an exploration. It represents some first steps in the process of mapping out, both conceptually and materially, the geographies of the labor market and the spatiality of its governance structures.

NOTES

1. As Hall (1975) puts it, "The central argument of good economics . . . [is] that economic forces determine institutions and not the other way around" (p. 444).

2. Among many important texts, see Marsden (1986); Hodgson (1988); Purdy (1988); and Solow (1990).

3. See Piore (1983) and Taubman and Wachter (1986).

4. As Harrison (1971) put it, the division between the primary and secondary labor market is "functional and not simply semantic; workers, employers, and even the underlying technologies in the two segments behave very differently in important qualitative ways" (p. 123).

5. "The contrast between the internal labor market and competitive, neoclassical economic theory . . . should not be over-emphasized. Many of the rigidities which impede market forces in the short run are eventually overcome, and there is probably a tendency for the economy to adjust, in time, in a direction consistent with the predictions of competitive theory" (Doeringer and Piore, 1971, p. 7).

6. Significantly, the commuting behavior of this average worker serves as the basis for the conventional definition of the local labor market (see Chapter 4).

7. According to Fisher (1949), the market for harvest labor in California, "though not a perfect market, possesses more of the characteristics of such markets than most labor markets. The individual laborer is anonymous to his [sic] employer and there are, therefore, none of the customary ties and informal obligations which restrict the mobility of labor in other employments. Labor is unorganized and collective bargaining is absent. Employment is seasonal, and even the most skilful and reliable of workers has little opportunity to gain preferment or tenure. The tasks which harvest workers are called on to perform are largely unskilled, and most harvests require very little capital equipment, so that there is little division of labor or gradation of skill to limit the substitutability of one worker for another. Finally, and most important is that payment is by the unit of product rather than by unit of time. . . . Notwithstanding the economic and ethical objections to viewing labor as a commodity to be bought and sold in the market place, the harvest labor market closely resembles a commodity market in important respects" (p. 1). Compare Doeringer and Piore (1971, p. 41n).

8. "Racist folklores" among the California growers dictated that Filipinos were presumed to be skilled agricultural workers, Mexicans were viewed

as suspiciously "independent," and "the Negro [was] least favorably regarded" (Fisher, 1949, p. 8).

9. For example, see Eberts and Stone (1992) for an attempt to explain the geographic variability of U.S. labor markets from a "starting point [in] the basic supply and demand model of the labor market" (p. 1). It is their initial premise—that profound geographical variability in general and local labor market shocks in particular, represent abnormal situations in which the "equilibrium state is disturbed"—that serves to undermine much of their subsequent analysis. For a U.K. example, see MacKay, Boddy, Brack, Diack, and Jones (1971).

10. See Urry (1985); Walker (1988); Lovering (1989); and Storper and Walker (1989).

11. However, see Clark's (1981) analysis of the spatial division of labor, which is more sensitive to labor market process.

12. For a range of different but largely complementary positions on social regulation, see Marsden (1986); Maurice, Sellier, and Silvestre (1986); Boyer (1988a); Castro, Méhaut, and Rubery (1992a); Salais and Storper (1992); and Théret (1994).

13. The perspective favored here is strongly influenced by that of the International Working Party on Labour Market Segmentation: "to develop a theoretical and empirical framework for an integrated approach to labour market analysis in which institutional and social factors are treated as both central and endogenous" (Castro, Méhaut, and Rubery, 1992b, p. 16).

PART 1
Making Labor Markets

Chapter 2

MAKING WORKERS

Control, Reproduction, Regulation

According to Block (1990), labor is at the same time "the most fundamental and the most inherently problematic of all economic categories" (p. 75). The initial premise of neoclassical economics— that labor is a commodity—denies the social nature of both labor and its reproduction. One consequence of this deliberate and fundamental misreading of the nature of labor is that orthodox conceptions of the labor market qua commodity market are critically flawed.

> [In] treating the major inputs into production—labor, capital, and raw materials—in a parallel fashion, economists tend to analyze labor in isolation from the social relations in which individuals are embedded. It is not actual human beings who are an input into the production process, but one of their characteristics—their capacity to do work. But this is an inherently paradoxical strategy since the individual's capacity to do work is not innate; it is socially created and sustained. (Block, 1990, p. 75)

Making workers is a complex and contradictory process. Unlike slave owners, capitalists do not buy workers per se but the capacity to work (labor-power). Once hired, workers must be prepared to cooperate in the workplace by being willing participants in production. They must be prepared not only to work today, but to return to work tomorrow. As a result, social relations in the workplace (the labor process) involve negotiating a fragile balance between control and consent: managerial despotism is rarely the best way to secure *and reproduce* a productive work force (Burawoy, 1979). The need to maintain this balance conditions the hiring and firing behavior of firms. Consequently, the social relations of the labor process are connected to those of the labor market. Establishing, for analytical purposes, these links between the hidden abode of production and the hidden hand of the labor market means raising fundamental questions about the nature of labor, employment, and work.

The purpose of this chapter is to make some of these links and, in so doing, to problematize the social nature of labor. In drawing attention to the ways in which labor is socially embedded, it provides a basis for investigating the labor market as an instituted process (after Polanyi, 1957). "Labour markets are institutional phenomena," Marsden (1986) has observed, "in that they depend on an institutional underpinning" (p. 231). The character, purpose, and dynamics of this institutional underpinning are linked to the problems of regulating labor, which in turn are linked to the social character of labor itself. In a nutshell, because labor is imperfectly and only partially regulated by market forces, the incorporation of labor into the labor market presents dilemmas of regulation.

The chapter begins by sketching the nature of labor as a "fictive commodity" before taking up a series of themes intended to illuminate the social character of labor and its reproduction. Four social processes are examined: the problem of incorporating labor into the labor market, the issue of labor allocation, the imperative of labor control, and the fundamental question of labor reproduction. The tensions and contradictions associated with each of these social processes are manifest in a series of regulatory dilemmas. The final section draws together these regulatory dilemmas, elaborating on some of their implications for the institutionalization and regulation of the labor market.

LABOR AS A "FICTIVE COMMODITY"

Marx, Marshall, and Polanyi all recognized that labor differed in crucial ways from true commodities and that this difference shaped labor market relations. Marx (1976, p. 279) characteristically emphasized *power relationships,* arguing that the asymmetrical social relations of the "hidden abode" of production had a distorting effect on the labor market. Marshall (1890, p. 572) conceded that the "peculiarities" of labor rendered the labor market distinct in many ways from conventional commodity markets. Polanyi (1944, pp. 72–73) explored the *social and cultural foundations* of labor's "fictive commodity" form. Storper and Walker (1983) have summarized the distinctions neatly.

> To confuse labor with true commodities means adopting the fol-
> lowing incorrect assumptions: the worker is the same as the objects
> of work; production is a purely technical exercise, a system of
> machinery that workers do not in any sense direct or contribute to.
> . . . The production process is devoid of social relations and social
> life that affect worker behaviour; wage-work equals slavery, i.e. the
> purchase of labour gives the capitalist complete ownership of the
> worker, rather than merely the right to employ the worker for a
> limited period of time; children are raised solely for the purpose of
> becoming workers for hire; labour has a fixed, objective cost of
> reproduction; the ownership of the means of production is the same
> as the "ownership" of one's own person; and the former confers no
> special power or benefits to the capitalist. (p. 4)

Though labor is forced to take on the *form* of a commodity, it is not a true commodity but a *pseudocommodity* (Storper and Walker, 1983). Despite this distinction, a central feature of capitalist labor markets is the subordination of labor to the discipline of market regulation. The clash between market discipline and the social foundations of labor renders the capitalist labor market a "satanic mill" (Polanyi, 1944). The ever-present danger in capitalist labor markets— which usually manifests itself during times *or in places* in which labor's bargaining position is weakened—is that labor will be reduced to the status of a mere commodity (see Chapter 8). As theorized by Offe (1985), the problematic relationship between labor and labor markets produces a number of contradictions.

From the perspective of neoclassical economics these contradictions tend to be interpreted as failures of the labor market. Orthodox notions of labor market failure convey the impression that such problems (for example, ruptures in skill formation or the persistence of mass unemployment) are in a sense periodic breakdowns within a broadly functional economic system. They are analyzed in terms of disrupted equilibrium, i.e., as a temporary departure from business as usual where supply and demand are in harmony (see Ebert and Stone, 1992).

Here, and in contrast, the failure of labor markets is viewed as systemic. The contradictions of capitalist labor markets are deep-seated and ultimately "resolvable" only in terms of temporary institutional containment. The institutional fabric of the labor market, while essential to its continued functioning, does not fully resolve its underlying con-tradictions,[1] which are logically (though not historically) *prior to* institutional responses. Institutional responses are just that: responses. Rarely if ever do they provide absolute solutions to regulatory dilemmas. Rather, the process of labor regulation is continuous and imperfect.

Historically, "regulation and markets grew up together" (Polanyi, 1944, p. 68). Thus, the "free" labor market was not an historical predecessor to the regulated labor market: instead labor market problems and their putative regulatory solutions evolved together through a process of iterative and dynamic development. While this may be historically accurate, it also presents analytical problems; in concrete research, it is difficult to distinguish the *object* of regulation (a labor market problem of some kind or other, here termed a regulatory dilemma) from the *means* of regulation (particular institutional responses). However, it is possible to tease out regulatory dilemmas through abstraction (see Jessop, 1990a), establishing at an abstract level the links between the "real," social nature of labor and the regulatory dilemmas of the labor market. Emphatically, this does not mean that the institutional underpinning of the labor market is functionally determined (Rubery, 1992). There are a host of potential institutional responses to the same regulatory dilemma. Some may involve state action, others may not; some may be the result of purposive action on the part of labor market actors, others may not.

But this is to anticipate arguments laid out in more detail at the end of the chapter. The point of departure is the contradictory nature of labor's incorporation, control, allocation, and reproduction within the labor market. These represent four "slices" through the question of the social nature of labor as well as four facets of labor's fictive commodity status.

Incorporating Labor

The first set of contradictions follows from the problems of incorporating labor into the labor market, where, the fictive commodity status of labor presents particular problems. The rate of production of true commodities (say, vegetables or automobiles) is conditioned by expectations concerning their saleability on the market. This does not hold for labor, the supply of which is significantly, though not entirely, autonomous from demand conditions on the labor market. For example, the supply of workers leaving school is not simply a function of the number of available jobs, but instead results from intersecting social, demographic, educational, and economic decisions. That is, the supply of labor is determined by "non-strategic demographic processes and the institutional rules of human reproductive activity [and also by] socio-economic processes which 'set free' labour power from the conditions under which it could maintain itself other than through sale in the market" (Offe and Hinrichs, 1985, p. 16). This lack of effective control over the conditions and volume of its own supply means that labor finds itself at a strategic disadvantage in the labor market vis-à-vis capital. Because labor is dependent on waged employment as a means of subsistence, it is unable to wait outside the labor market until conditions are more favorable (see Granovetter and Tilly, 1988; Purdy, 1988). In effect, it is thrown onto the labor market and must adjust its expectations to the prevailing (local) conditions.

The fact that labor is not produced for the market means that its supply is relatively autonomous from the level and composition of labor demand as expressed in the market. Contrary to the canons of neoclassical economics, the labor supply is not simply regulated by the market, but instead is shaped by relatively autonomous social forces such as state policies, ideological norms, and family structures (Humphries and Rubery, 1984). Because the task cannot be left to the market, the problem of governing the flow of workers onto the market presents itself as an intractable regulatory dilemma. According to Offe and Lenhardt (1984), there are three aspects to this regulatory dilemma, which also can be seen as stimuli for some form of extramarket regulation:

- The preparedness of those outside the labor market to offer their labor-power on the market must be ensured.
- The circumstances under which nonparticipation on the labor market is permitted must be defined.
- A sustainable aggregate balance between the waged and unwaged segments of the population must be maintained.

These institutional means set, and continually adjust, the parameters of the labor supply.

In capitalist societies, the preparedness of workers to offer their labor on the labor market is largely secured by the systematic erosion of possibilities of subsistence outside the wage system. Thus, the scope for independent means of subsistence (for example, in household production, welfare, or small-scale agriculture) tends progressively to be reduced with the spread of capitalist industrialization. However, it is not sufficient simply to "throw" workers onto the labor market (cf. Polanyi, 1944). To a certain degree, they must want to "jump." Complex processes of work socialization (operating within the family, the education system, and the wider community) serve to underpin *both* the economic necessity of waged employment *and* its social desirability. These processes shape not only the generalized desire to work, but social aspirations concerning different types of realistically attainable work; for example, they shape the process by which "working class kids get working class jobs" (Willis, 1977).[2] Although these subtle and complex processes cannot be explored here, it is important to note that access to waged work plays a key role in the acquisition of adult status and social validation. To be without work continues to be associated with social stigmatization and political marginalization. In other words, getting a job is socially as well as materially significant.

This said, it should not be surprising that it is necessary to regulate carefully the conditions under which nonparticipation in the labor market is permitted. The decision as to whether or not to engage in wage-labor cannot be left to the discretion of the individual worker, but must be closely regulated so as to ensure the effective minimization (given prevailing demand conditions) of nonparticipation (Piven and Cloward, 1971; Offe and Hinrichs, 1985). This is achieved, first, by delimiting social groups with a *legitimate* alternative role (usually those involved in "reproduction work" and those who, due to age or incapacity, are unable to make a significant contribution to production); and second, through the pernicious conditions under which nonparticipation is permitted (necessary to ensure that it is not perceived as an attractive alternative to wage-labor).

Finally, a sustainable balance must be struck between the waged and unwaged segments of the population. This balance has both cyclical and structural components. Cyclical movements in economic activity result in temporary fluctuations in the level of employment. The increases in unemployment which follow tend to place strains on both the welfare system and the family, both of which must find ways of absorbing and maintaining unemployed workers. Consequently, the relative size of social catchment areas outside the waged sector fluctuates along with aggregate demand conditions, as state policies and household strategies are constantly adjusted (Wilkinson, 1988). However, these adjustments are not unproblematic. Structural changes in the labor market are producing particular stresses on this system, which in many parts of Europe and North America have been such as to call into question long-established welfare structures and entitlements as some social groups find themselves excluded from waged employment on a more or less permanent basis (Hinrichs, Offe, and Weisenthal, 1988; Esping-Andersen, 1990; see Chapter 7). In many such areas, the old, the young, and certain disadvantaged groups have become in effect structurally excluded from the labor market.

Thus, profound regulatory dilemmas are associated with the incorporation of labor into waged employment. The supply of labor is not and cannot be regulated solely by competitive forces in the labor market. While it is influenced by market factors, it remains largely a product of extramarket forces such as demographic conditions (changes which, needless to say, take several decades to work their way through to shifts in the labor supply, and which operate independently of short-term fluctuations in labor demand) and social and institutional rules governing labor market participation for different groups. To expose the labor supply to the naked discipline of the market would be to precipitate the "demolition of society" (Polanyi, 1944, p. 76), to unleash a kind of economic Malthusianism in which minimal levels of subsistence would be undercut.[3] The only genuinely viable alternative is some form of social regulation of the labor supply. State regulation is a central and, some would maintain, necessary component (de Brunhoff, 1978; Offe, 1985; Block, 1994; Théret, 1994). Thus, it has been argued that the process of transforming "*dispossessed* labor-power into active wage-labor was not and is not possible without state policies" (Offe and Lenhardt, 1984, p. 93).

State policies certainly have a crucial role to play in the incorporation of labor. The parameters of labor supply are substantially set and periodically modified by the state (see Chapter 3). One need only consider the labor supply implications, for example, of changing levels of state provision in full-time education or childcare, variable state commitments to vocational education and training or labor market programs, and shifting state definitions of welfare levels and entitlements. However, these are not the only ways in which the parameters of labor supply are adjusted in accordance with fluctuations in labor demand. The family, too, has important roles to play in absorbing surplus labor during downturns in labor demand, socializing the rising generation, and underwriting the costs of wage-labor through the provision of unpaid domestic work.

Responses to the regulatory dilemmas associated with the incorporation of labor need not be sought only in the realm of state action, nor are they automatically secured. Broader questions of nonstate social regulation also are raised, and the institutional forces operating on the supply side of the labor market have complex and often unpredictable effects upon the supply of labor. Little wonder that despite its paragon significance for orthodox theory, equilibrium—the judicious balancing of supply and demand—is a comparatively rare event.

Allocating Labor

The social nature of labor also is reflected in patterns of allocation in the labor market. Examination of labor market variables (such as the

social distribution of unemployment and socially undesirable or physically hazardous jobs) reveals two important facts. First, whatever the
measure chosen, the *same* social groups tend to suffer the brunt of
labor market disadvantage. Second, labor market disadvantage tends
to be distributed in accordance with the ascribed rather than achieved
characteristics of workers, varying more closely with ethnicity, gender,
and age, for example, than with education, training, and skill. The
risks of poverty and unemployment are related more strongly to social
characteristics than to human capital. The existence of such persistent,
socially ascribed differences in labor market attainment provides a
basis on which to challenge orthodox theories in which inequalities
can be traced only to variations in supply-side, human capital attrib-
utes (Ryan, 1981).[4]

The allocation of labor cannot be accounted for adequately in
terms of the market validation of acquired human capital. The matching of workers and jobs "almost never occurs in the impersonal auction
markets of stylized neoclassical economics," but instead is the outcome
of the complex intermeshing of employers' recruitment networks and
workers' supply networks (Granovetter and Tilly, 1988, p. 191).[5] Both
these networks are socially structured and each is driven by a distinctive set of imperatives (such that the term "matching," as Purdy (1988)
suggests, understates the frictions involved). Institutional forces also
are at work.

> The key to explaining the differential access of ascriptively defined
> groups [to labour market rewards] is not to be found in any
> [difference in the] quality of labour power or its use-value for the
> production process. . . . The emergence of "problem groups" in the
> labour market cannot be explained by some physical "inferiority"
> of their labour market bid, but only by the fact that their chances
> of "marketing" their otherwise "equal" bid have been worsened by
> political and normative factors. The role-specific impairment of
> opportunities to adapt [strategically] in the labour market must
> therefore be explained in relation to institutional mechanisms, not
> by the "natural" qualities of those who hold these roles. (Offe and
> Hinrichs, 1985, p. 36)

As Offe and Hinrichs observe, those social groups placed at a
disadvantage in the labor market—young people, women, older workers, the disabled, migrant workers—also tend to be bearers of characteristics which, in the political and cultural spheres, are used in the
granting of access to forms of unwaged subsistence. It is seen as both
normal and legitimate for such groups to participate in the labor
market on a discontinuous basis. The fact that the members of such

groups have access to a socially sanctioned alternative role outside the labor market (for example, as welfare recipients or unpaid domestic workers) tends to undermine their strategic position in the waged sphere. Irrespective of whether it is appropriate for their individual situation, members of these groups are treated by employers, unions, and state agencies alike *as if* they have a weak attachment to the labor market. Access to stable, primary sector jobs is effectively denied. For example, employers tend to use ascriptive criteria to calculate turnover risks (Blackburn and Mann, 1979; Boddy, Lovering, and Bassett, 1986). Expectations of irregular work behavior among supposedly marginal groups, which affect hiring decisions and welfare entitlements, reinforce those selfsame behavior patterns, with the result that certain groups are socially constructed as contingent workers.[6]

While social divisions within the work force are not *created* by capital or by the state, they are nevertheless exploited in the allocation of labor and regulation of the labor supply.[7] For Offe and Hinrichs, the processes shaping access to alternative roles bear directly upon the way in which capitalist labor markets are regulated.

- The criteria for exemption from wage-labor cannot be chosen freely by individuals, as the option of voluntary withdrawal from the labor market would erode the social relations of wage dependency on which the labor market is constructed.
- The exempted groups must be defined in such a way as to minimize the possibility of effective political opposition or claims-making.

Therefore, contingent workers tend to be defined by ascribed status and by their relationship to "institutions located on the outer limits of the labor market" dominated by "relations of force and control which deprive people of the resources for collective action and thus prevent them from realizing their economic interests: family systems, schools, prisons, social security programmes, armies, hospitals and so on" (Offe and Hinrichs, 1985, p. 37).

The functioning of these institutions, underscored by state action and cultural norms, has an important influence on the structure and dynamics of the labor market, despite being located on its "outer limits" (see Chapter 3). In fact, they play an important part in defining the social limits of wage-labor: not only do they define and regulate the contingent work force, but they also help to maintain a social balance between the crosscutting processes of inclusion and exclusion in the labor market. Labor markets could not function if the entire population sought actively to participate in waged work or to withdraw their labor from the market. The institutional formation of a contingent work force helps to resolve the questions how to distribute primary and secondary jobs socially as well as how to adjust the labor supply to fluctuations in aggregate employment levels. Institutions like the family or educational system have a profound effect on stratifying the labor supply and structuring the labor market, and this plays a significant part in regulating the labor market as a whole (Rodgers and Rodgers, 1989). These institutions, too, are sites of regulatory dilemmas.

Controlling Labor

Much of the discussion thus far has concerned regulatory dilemmas surrounding the point of entry to the labor market. Once workers enter the hidden abode of production, the social nature of labor is revealed in different ways. For Marx, of course, this is the point at which buyer and seller of labor-power become capitalist and worker. While their class relation was seen by Marx (1976) as permeating the labor market, "preconditioning their relationship as buyer and seller" (p. 1015), the labor process remained the anchor of his analysis. Having completed their transaction on the labor market (by comparison, "a very Eden of the innate rights of man") a change takes place "in the physiognomy of our *dramatis personae*. He who was previously the money-owner now strides out in front as a capitalist; the possessor of labor-power follows as his worker. The one smirks self importantly and is intent on business; the other is timid and holds back, like someone who has brought his own hide to market and now has nothing else to expect but—a tanning" (p. 280).

Rhetorical flourishes notwithstanding, Marx was all too aware that the hiring of workers was only the beginning of the story. He distinguished between the activity of work (labor) and the capacity to work (labor-power) in order to underline the fact that a labor market transaction—the sale and purchase of labor-*power*—did not imply transfer of ownership of the worker per se, but of her or his capacity to work. In order to realize this capacity, it was necessary for the capitalist to enlist the *consent* of the worker in a way consistent with the maintenance of control over the labor process. It was not the worker's hide but the opportunity to use it that was being bought and sold.

The distinction between labor and labor-power goes to the heart of the social nature of the labor market. Achieving and maintaining a balance between consent and control in the workplace is not simply a matter of setting appropriate wage rates, but involves continuous negotiation within both the labor process (for example, around the introduction of new technologies) and the labor market (for example, around hiring and promotion decisions). In short, it is a *political process.*

A key issue here is the nature of employment contracts (see Cartier, 1994). These differ from contracts in conventional commodity markets because, from a legal point of view, employment contracts are indeterminate. They permit the employer to utilize a worker's capacity for a specified period of time (and typically also in a specified place), but the precise content and pace of work cannot be predetermined contractually. They are intrinsically variable and, to a certain extent, subject to continuous renegotiation on the job. When signing an employment contract, neither the worker nor the employer knows exactly what they are letting themselves in for. After signing on the dotted line, the worker may discover that her job is dangerous or stressful, that management practices are Draconian, or that her work mates are unfriendly, while the employer may be dismayed to find her new employee lazy, unpunctual, or disruptive (see Miller, 1988).[8]

Thus the process of matching a worker to a job is infinitely more complex than determining that she possesses the technical skills to carry out the required tasks. Blackburn and Mann (1979) revealed that most working-class people use more technical skill driving to work than they do once there, and that employers were more interested in assessing the potential reliability of job applicants than their technical skills. On the basis of an exhaustive empirical study, they concluded that "responsibility, stability, trustworthiness—such are the qualities by which [employers] wish to select and promote . . . [As a result] little support [can] be given to the human capital, neoclassical view of 'worker quality' in the labour market" (p. 280). While employers may be skeptical about the value of educational qualifications, for example, as predictors of workplace competence (Williams, 1981), these may nevertheless offer useful surrogate measures of employability in the sense that those willing to conform to educational authority may also be amenable to workplace authority (see Willis, 1977; Collins, 1979). In this sense, human capital may shape the distribution of jobs (cf. Becker, 1975), but as a political surrogate rather than as a direct measure of technical ability.

The labor contract is a *social contract,* endowed with tacit expectations and embedded in relations of trust. In his analysis of the multiplicity of institutional forms taken by the employment relationship, Fox (1974) contrasted "low trust dynamics," in which mutual suspicion between management and workers leads to periodic conflict and low productivity, with "high trust dynamics," in which mutual trust and cooperation coexist with more efficient production (see also Burawoy, 1979; Akerlof, 1984). Consequently, the process of assessing a person for a job goes beyond whether they are capable of operating the technology in the required way, but also involves consideration of inherently unpredictable factors such as reliability, creativity, sociability, initiative, deference to authority, and adaptability.[9] These traits, and their unpredictability, follow from the fact that labor is not a commodity but a set of capacities borne by *people*.

Labor market theory, it hardly needs to be said, must take account of the social relationships through which labor market processes are mediated. While segmentation theories take this as axiomatic, it remains alien territory for orthodox economists, whose *Homo economicus* comes "close to being a social moron" (Sen, 1982, p. 99). Yet, in hiring workers, employers must make difficult and often expensive decisions based on imperfect information. With any one hiring decision, they may be recruiting either a future employee of the year or a future shop-floor agitator. How can they be sure they are making the right decision? Of course, they never can be sure, but they do have strategies to minimize risk that have a significant impact on who gets which jobs and, therefore, on how the labor market works. Employers seeking to fill stable, well-paid primary sector jobs (in which training, induction, and socialization costs are typically high)[10] are at pains to ensure that turnover risks are minimized (Blackburn and Mann, 1979). Although it is effectively impossible to determine the actual likelihood of an employee quitting prematurely (i.e., before she begins to turn a profit for the employer), employers resort to ascriptive criteria in calculating turnover risks. This process of social structuring in recruitment systems tends to reproduce and concretize existing patterns of inequality (Granovetter and Tilly, 1988).[11] Migrant workers, women, young people, and the disabled tend to be the victims, in part because they are viewed as having alternative roles outside the labor market and therefore as having weak attachments to work. When such groups are excluded from primary employment, it strengthens their "subjective orientation to their respective 'alternative role.' . . . [In this way, the pattern of disadvantage] is reinforced by the hiring practices it gives rise to" (Offe and Hinrichs, 1985, p. 40).

In order to understand labor control, then, it is necessary to look over the factory gates, to consider the social production and reproduction of work forces and the values which unite and divide them.[12] Because labor control cannot be secured simply through despotic management strategies, it comes to depend in important ways on the social context in which employment relations are embedded. Labor process studies have progressively broadened their earlier narrow focus on managerial control, exercised at the point of production (Braverman, 1974), to take account of workers' struggles and the wider politics of production in which labor process struggles are situated.[13] A notable strand in post-Braverman studies has been the distinctive emphasis placed on labor markets, and the recursive relationship between labor markets and labor process control.[14] The answer to the question of *how* labor control is secured is partly dependent on *who* is being controlled. Labor control regimes tend not only to vary with production technology, industry, and plant size, but as studies which have sought to control for these factors have revealed, with the nature of the labor supply and the system of labor regulation (Maurice, Sellier, and Silvestre, 1986; Michon, 1992).[15]

Maintenance of labor control represents perhaps the most intractable regulatory dilemma of the labor market. Contracts and markets alone cannot be relied upon to perform this complex and fundamentally social task, and there can be no stable solution when the interests of labor and capital are fundamentally at odds. Workers' interests in "defending their autonomy, the physical integrity of their labor power and their skills" conflict with their employers' interests in "maximum economic utilization of the 'purchased' labour power, whose productive use-value is by no means assured by the worker merely showing up at the work-place and remaining there for the duration of working hours" (Offe and Hinrichs, 1985, p. 24). Neither legal regulation nor market despotism can resolve this regulatory dilemma, which contributes to the irreducibly *politicized* nature of labor market structures and strategies.

The labor process literature contains vivid accounts of different institutional and political responses to the dilemma of labor control, often represented in the form of historical periodizations. Braverman (1974) interpreted late capitalism in terms of a transition from craft to Taylorist control, while Edwards (1979) identified three, successive labor control regimes (simple, technical, and bureaucratic). Similarly, Friedman's (1977) analysis of the historical development of the labor process focused on a posited shift from direct control to "responsible autonomy."

While Burawoy (1985) acknowledges the importance of these contributions, he notes that they tend to conflate the *labor process* ("a particular organization of tasks") with the *politics of production* ("the political apparatuses of production conceived as its mode of regulation") (p. 125). For Burawoy, these two social structures are both analytically distinct and causally independent. He argues that state regulation plays a structuring role in the politics of production; first, social welfare provision guarantees minimal conditions for the reproduction of labor which are independent of the immediate process of production, and second, labor legislation curbs managerial domination by granting workers the rights of collective representation and employment protection. Together, these developments have underwritten a shift from market despotism in wage relations to a postwar, hegemonic regime.

> Now management can no longer rely entirely on the economic whip of the market. Nor can it impose an arbitrary despotism. Workers must be *persuaded* to cooperate with management. Their interests must be coordinated with those of capital. The *despotic regimes* of early capitalism, in which coercion prevails over consent, must be replaced with *hegemonic regimes,* in which consent prevails (although never to the exclusion of coercion). Not only is the application of coercion circumscribed and regularized, but the infliction of discipline and punishment itself becomes the object of consent. (p. 126)

Although he notes the existence of significant geographic variations in both despotic and hegemonic labor regimes, Burawoy concludes that it is the relationship between labor reproduction and capitalist production (unified under despotism, separated under hegemonism) that is decisive in his proposed periodization.[16]

Reproducing Labor

Burawoy's distinction between the despotic regimes of early capitalism (in which labor depended for its reproduction on the emergent class of capitalists) and contemporary hegemonic regimes (in which the responsibility for labor production is increasingly shouldered by the state) draws attention to the social character of labor and its reproduction. One reason for the proneness to crisis of despotic capitalism was its tendency to undercut labor's ability to reproduce itself to the point of destruction. Wages were driven below subsistence levels while capital, having undermined the market demand on which it depended, found itself facing crises of overproduction. The exposure of labor to such pressures clearly was not in the long-term interests of either labor or capital. At the systemic level, unrestrained market despotism would have resulted in the demolition of society (Polanyi, 1944, p. 76).

"A man must always live by his work," Adam Smith (1976) observed, "and his wages must at least be sufficient to maintain him" (p. 85). Yet, the capitalist employer need not carry the full costs of the reproduction of labor, a point of distinction between the slave (whose *labor* is bought and sold) and the wage-laborer (whose *labor-power* is bought and sold). "The wear and tear of a slave, it has been said, is at the expense of his master; but that of a free servant [or wage-laborer] is at his own expense. . . . I believe that the work done by freemen comes cheaper in the end than that performed by slaves. It is found to do so even at Boston, New York, and Philadelphia, where the wages of common labour are so very high" (Smith, 1976, pp. 183–184).

Behind this urban "subsidization" of wage-labor, there is another kind of labor: unpaid domestic labor.

> Housework is the *production* of labour as a commodity, while waged work is the *exchange* of labour. To be exchanged, labour must be produced; and to be used in the production of other commodities, labour must be produced and exchanged. This is not a question merely of time sequences, but one of functional relationships between processes. While wages are a cost of production, housework as unpaid labour is a deduction from costs. Needless to say, housework itself has its costs (the subsistence of the houseworker), but the relationship is such as to guarantee a high surplus. This is not directly obvious because labour is not sold by capitalists: the surplus is realized by capitalists not in selling labour but in buying it. (Picchio, 1992, pp. 96–97)

This is by no means a matter of theoretical sophistry, for what is "paradoxical for the theory of value becomes tragic for women as the system's contradictions and conflicts materialize in their personal lives" (p. 97).

The overwhelming majority of domestic tasks continues to be performed by women, whose increased participation in wage-labor has altered the ways in which their domestic work is organized rather than bringing about a significant "re-gendering" of household responsibilities.[17] The organization of domestic labor both conditions and is conditioned by the organization of wage-labor. In this sense, the gendered constitution of domestic labor is reflected in *men's* waged work as well as women's, hence in the way that the labor market as a whole operates.[18] Thus, analyses of work done by men should always pose the question, "who does the laundry?" (Massey, 1993b, p. 4); the way in which these jobs are constructed "requires that the people who fill them have someone *else* to look after them" (p. 13).

The sphere of social reproduction should not be seen as a mere appendage to the labor market. The "processes of reproducing people" and the process of capital accumulation are not only analytically distinct but also contradictory, involving "continual and often lacerating conflicts arising from the separation between the times and the places of the two processes" (Picchio, 1992, p. 108).[19] Reproducing people involves an enormous variety of processes—from biological procreation to media consumption, from education and training to clothing and caring—which tend to be anchored not only in the labor market but in the household, community, and state.[20] These sites of social reproduction are neither organized exclusively in the interests of the labor market nor are they insulated from it. Although the family, for example, plays a crucial role in the reproduction of wage-laborers, it is not organized solely for this purpose (cf. Becker, 1981). Rather, the family is a site (and in some analyses the preeminent site) of patriarchal oppression, regulated by customs and historically embedded practices which often predate capitalism itself (Barrett, 1980; Walby, 1990). This said, it is also the case that the structures of the family in particular and patriarchy in general have been reorganized continually through their historical interpenetration with the capitalist system of wage-labor (Ferguson, 1989).

Thus, the boundary between the spheres of production and reproduction is porous. For example, skills are produced in each of the two spheres, and they shape the ways in which domestic and waged work are organized and distributed. It is commonly observed that women's skills are undervalued in the labor market because they are associated with their domestic roles (Phillips and Taylor, 1980; see Chapter 6). Women tend to be clustered in occupations which both reflect and reinforce their perceived domestic roles: sewing machinists and personnel officers, cooks and care assistants, secretaries and health workers are all profoundly gendered occupations presuming and perpetuating "women's skills" in providing services for men, dealing with people, and meeting basic human needs (McDowell and Court, 1994).[21] The fact that these skills are often formed (or assumed to be formed) outside the workplace means that they are invariably cheap (Beechey, 1977). In turn, women's marginalization in the labor market tends to exacerbate patriarchal oppression in the domestic sphere. Their subordinate position within the family and the sphere of reproduction is then both cause and effect of their constitution as a cheap, contingent labor supply. Gender roles are made at work as well as at home.

While the formation of a cheap labor supply is functional for capital, that alone does not provide an adequate explanation of why or how this labor supply came into being (Offe, 1985). Capital did not create the patriarchal structures that constitute women and the young as propertyless dependents, but it is well placed to exploit the consequences. Capitalist and patriarchal power become mutually conditioning although not necessarily coincident in structures or effects. Thus, explanations of labor market phenomena (whether wage-setting or employers' selection procedures, occupational choice or the operation of internal labor markets) cannot be blind to forces rooted "outside" the labor market in the sphere of social reproduction. Extramarket processes, such as the division of domestic labor or the structure of educational systems, both structure *and are structured by* the wage-labor sphere. Recognition of this relationship implies the abandonment of neoclassical formulations in which the market is abstracted from its social context (Picchio del Mercato, 1981; Ryan, 1981; Mingione, 1991).

The inescapable conclusion is that the spheres of production and social reproduction are both separate and connected. They are separate in the sense that they each have their own structures of dominance, along with their own distinctive rhythms and tendencies, but they are also related in the sense that each conditions and interacts with the other. More formally, production and social reproduction must be seen as relatively autonomous. "Social reproduction provides a prime example of the ways in which the organisation of the working class can provide a basis of protection against the harshness of competitive wage labour markets through the use of family and community systems of income sharing, and yet at the same time set up divisions between workers based on their position within these income-sharing units which provide a basis for relative exploitation within the wage labour market" (Humphries and Rubery, 1984, p. 344). In calling for a dialectical treatment of production and reproduction, Humphries and Rubery underline the need for "historically-specific analyses in which the supply-side structure of the economy shapes and limits the scope for capital to mould the labor market to fit its current requirements" (p. 343).[22]

Recognition of the relative autonomy of the sphere of social reproduction explodes the neoclassical myth of the wage-coordinated labor market: equilibrium cannot be guaranteed because the supply of labor is not regulated solely by the wage mechanism. Because, as a fictive commodity, labor is socially rather than capitalistically produced, it is manifestly untrue to say as Adam Smith (1976) did that "the demand for men, like that for any other commodity, necessarily regulates the production of men" (p. 98). The production of men as wage-laborers depends on the unpaid domestic labor of women and the wider systems of social reproduction through family, community, and state. While shaped by the market, these systems do not simply dance to its tune.[23] Consequently, the relationship between social reproduction and production (or, as the economist would have it, between the supply and demand sides of the labor market) is not one of smooth and mutually effective coordination but in fact, one of jarring adjustment, contradiction, and conflict. It is a site of mutual and dynamic conditioning. In the "interactions between the spheres of production and reproduction . . . [c]ausal connections are not unidirectional: what was once *effect* can become a *cause* and *vice versa*" (Humphries and Rubery, 1984, p. 339).

The regulatory dilemma concerns how to coordinate social reproduction effectively, given that the hidden hand of the market is manifestly not up to the task. This is not simply a problem of ensuring that the right *number* of workers is offered up to the labor market; it also raises the wider questions of why and at what laborers should want to work, or the "social bases of obedience" (Purdy, 1988, pp. 63–69). Social reproduction is an area of concerted and (for Burawoy, 1985, among others) tendentially expanding state intervention.[24] The domain of state policy is prefigured by tacit assumptions concerning women's domestic work; state interventions in health provision, childcare, social services, and education are predicated on and effectively supplement substantial domestic toil (Wilson, 1977; Picchio, 1992). Thus, where neoliberal states have been active in rolling back the welfare state, they are not so much exposing the process of reproduction to market forces as often forcing it back into the domestic sphere by enlarging the scope of women's domestic "responsibilities" (Phillips, 1983; Esping-Andersen, 1990).

DILEMMAS OF LABOR REGULATION

The nature of labor, or more precisely of labor-power, is such that the market for labor is riven with contradictions, conflicts and dilemmas of regulation. Because labor is not a true commodity, the self-regulating mechanisms associated with conventional commodity markets cannot be expected to regulate the labor market. The idea of a self-regulating labor market is a fiction. In essence, this is because labor itself is a fictitious commodity: it is not produced for sale, it cannot be stored, it cannot be separated from its owner, it is "only another name for human activity which goes with life itself" (Polanyi, 1944, p. 72). To treat labor as a commodity and the labor market as a commodity market is to *desocialize labor*. It is to ignore the fact that both its production and reproduction are intrinsically social. It follows that the labor market cannot be self-regulating in the sense of an abstract commodity market, but must be *socially regulated*. As Polanyi argued, a labor market left to its own devices would destroy the social basis through which human labor is reproduced.

It is for this reason that in capitalist societies, labor regulation and labor markets have tended historically to grow up together (Polanyi, 1944; Wilkinson, 1981a). The history of state labor regulation reveals, however, that although "the labor market cannot rely on any automatic or endogenous mechanisms of adjustment . . . the role of the state as an adjustment mechanism is [also] a very difficult one: plans to control the reproduction of labour like the production of other commodities have never succeeded. The whole process of social reproduction of labour involves forces and agents whose power has never really been understood" (Picchio, 1992, p. 72).

Pressures for regulation do not necessarily result in effective regulation. The plethora of ways in which the state alone exerts an influence on labor regulation—through the framework of employment legislation, structure of the welfare and education systems, policy interventions in industrial training and labor market programs, regulation of marital and family life—are likely to be associated with a myriad of intended and unintended consequences. It would be a mistake to reduce state labor regulation solely to purposive government intervention through the deployment of labor market programs or changes in legislation. These represent just one aspect, albeit an important one, of the ways in which the actions, structures, and capabilities of the state influence labor regulation.

The assertion that the labor market's internal and systematic capacity for self-destruction necessitates state regulation[25] should be confused with neither the crude functionalist position that appropriate state responses will somehow be called into being nor with the institutionalist position that dilemmas of labor regulation are somehow soluble in an absolute sense once the institutional framework and policy mix are right. The necessity for extramarket regulation of labor does not imply a certain institutional response (see Boyer, 1992). Nor can the effects of institutional interventions be guaranteed. For example, referring to growing state regulation in the restriction of managerial discretion and constitution of the social wage, Burawoy (1985) argues:

> The *necessity* of such state intervention is given by the logic of capitalism's development. But the *mechanisms* through which the state comes to do what is "necessary" vary over time and from country to country. . . . There is, of course, nothing inevitable or inexorable about these state interventions; nothing guarantees the success or even the activation of the appropriate mechanisms. Thus, although we have theories of the conditions for the reproduction of capitalism in its various phases, and therefore of the corresponding *necessary* state interventions, we have only ad hoc accounts of the *actual*, specific and concrete interventions. (p. 128)

Acknowledging that recent changes in the global economy have meant that "[nation] state intervention is less relevant for the determination of changes and variations in the form of production politics," Burawoy suggests that the very success of the hegemonic labor regimes of the welfare-Fordist era itself played a part in triggering a crisis of profitability and the globalization of accumulation (cf. Notermans, 1993; Peck and Tickell, 1994). Although current strategies of deregulation may represent a historic reversal of the trend toward increasing socialization of labor reproduction (perhaps prefiguring a new but unstable era of *global despotism*), they do not undermine the case for the necessity of extramarket regulation. Regulatory tasks still need somehow to be performed, which unfortunately does not preclude reckless experimentation with deregulation and the commodification of labor. Abdication of regulatory responsibility does not mean that regulatory dilemmas have gone away.

This is not the place to discuss particular historical conjunctures or national and local regulatory strategies. The ramifications of the current tendency toward deregulation are discussed in detail in Chapter 8. The argument here is that while the systematic failure of labor markets implies the necessity for social regulation, the condition of necessity does not call forth a particular institutional response. This standpoint—which might be summarized as *regulatory necessity but institutional indeterminacy*—is not rooted in naive faith in the efficacy and rationality of government action, but rather in the strength of the case for *systemic* labor market failure. Regulatory dilemmas arising from the incorporation, allocation, control, and reproduction of labor cannot be solved by the market or the state. It is beyond even the most sophisticated state policies to iron out the contradictions of capitalist labor markets (see Boyer, 1992; Sayer and Walker, 1992). Moreover, state actions invariably produce unanticipated consequences as the behavior of labor market actors is adjusted in complex and dynamic ways to the changing regulatory environment. The condition of institutional indeterminacy extends beyond the chosen means of intervention to their unpredictable effects.

If the competitive, abstract labor market is internally crisis-prone, the regulated labor markets of the real world also are problematic. Regulatory dilemmas of the labor market are, in this sense, intractable. Although the state cannot afford to be "outside" the labor market, being "inside" itself creates problems (Théret, 1994); that is, because there is no policy solution to the regulatory dilemmas of the labor market, state intervention should be seen not only as problem-solving but also problem-creating. Consequently, state intervention in the labor market is perhaps best characterized as a continuous process of regulatory experimentation and learning. These state experiments (be they in legislative or institutional reform, welfare or training policy) variously assume, exploit, or seek to modify conditions in the labor market and the wider civil society. For example, the structure of the welfare state is predicated on a set of patriarchal beliefs concerning women's domestic roles[26] while training policies have been constructed around the interests of dominant capital fractions in accordance with prevailing industrial relations norms.[27] Once established, such institutions acquire their own bureaucratic and political momentum, which only fortuitously will happen to coincide with the shifting regulatory requirements of the labor market.

Consequently, regulatory dilemmas in the labor market, rooted in the social character of labor, trigger a complex institutional dialectic. The labor market cannot survive without regulation, but neither, apparently, does it unproblematically thrive with it. Perhaps there is a parallel with the higher-order question of the relationship between capitalism and the welfare state. As Offe (1984) has memorably remarked, "Capitalism cannot coexist with, neither can it exist without, the welfare state" (p. 153). Just as capitalism requires *some kind* of welfare state for its reproduction (Jessop, 1994), so the labor market requires *some kind* of social regulation for its reproduction.

NOTES

1. Similar claims are made by regulation theorists with respect to the macroinstitutional framework through which the accumulation process is reproduced (Boyer, 1990b; Jessop, 1990a; Théret, 1994). See Chapters 4 and 7.

2. Cf. Bowles and Gintis (1976); Bourdieu and Passeron (1977); and Hollands (1990).

3. As Chapter 8 argues, however, in the current climate of neoliberalism, accelerated place-competition is generating a *geographic* form of social undercutting in the labor market.

4. For the classic treatment of this issue, see Thurow (1975). Useful discussions can be found in Blackburn and Mann (1979) and Fevre (1992).

5. As Hanson and Pratt (1995) have demonstrated, these networks also tend to be strongly localized, contributing to the unevenness of local labor markets.

6. This contingent status is reflected in worker identities. Ascriptively defined groups who are granted access to nonwaged subsistence are "characterized by a 'broken' social identity [because their] conduct always appears to themselves (and to their labor market partners) in the light of their

alternative role to which they can always switch for rationally justifiable reasons" (Offe and Hinrichs, 1985, p. 38).

7. See Hartman (1979); Gordon, Edwards, and Reich (1982); and Rueschemeyer (1986).

8. Offe and Hinrichs (1985) underline the political nature of this process: "for the appropriation of 'work' from 'labour power,' conditions that have been secured initially and abstractly only through the labour contract, the employer is always dependent on the medium of *organization* which cannot, of course, fully guarantee that the labour process will function without conflict" (p. 24).

9. See Blackburn and Mann (1979); Granovetter and Tilly (1988); Miller (1988); and Ashton, Maguire, and Spilsbury (1990).

10. The concepts of primary and secondary sectors of the labor market are derived from segmentation theory. For a full discussion, see Chapter 3.

11. See Manwaring (1984); Jenkins (1986); and Fevre (1992).

12. See Burawoy (1979) and Peck and Lloyd (1989).

13. In the wake of the classic study by Braverman (1974), Elger (1979), among others, stressed the importance of workers' struggles in labor process dynamics. Burawoy's (1985) account remains the most persuasive treatment of social reproduction and the wider politics of production.

14. For contributions on this theme see Friedman (1977); Rubery (1978); Edwards (1979); Lee (1982); and Kelly (1985).

15. It follows that labor control regimes vary across space, as Jonas (1996) has argued. See Chapters 5 and 6.

16. In Burawoy's study, exceptions to the hegemonic regime tend to be *local:* migrant farmworkers in California and urban enterprise zones. The geographic implications of his analysis are drawn out more fully in Chapter 8.

17. See Gershuny (1983); Meissner, Humphreys, Meis, and Scheu (1988); and Horrell, Rubery, and Burchell (1990).

18. See Picchio del Mercato (1981); Purdy (1988); Mingione (1991); and Hanson and Pratt (1995).

19. Mingione (1991) relates the meaning of the term "social reproduction" to four sources: "the social conditions connected with procreation and the early years and education of children . . . education and cultural transfer from schools, families and societies to children and young people . . . the conditions through which a wider social order is preserved, or reproduced, and adapted without losing its main typical features as a result of social change [and] . . . the diverse conditions and organizational relations which allow human beings to survive various social contexts and groups" (pp. 123–124; quoted in Lee, 1995). Cf. Kearney (1991).

20. See Murgatroyd (1983); Humphries and Rubery (1984); and Purdy (1988).

21. Jobs are not simply a set of "empty slots to be filled . . . jobs are not gender-neutral; rather, they are created as appropriate for either men or women. Jobs and occupations themselves, and the set of social practices that

constitute them, are constructed so as to embody socially sanctioned but *variable* characteristics of masculinity and femininity" (McDowell and Court, 1994, p. 233). See also Hartman (1979) and Massey (1993b).

22. As will be argued in Chapter 4, these analyses also need to be geographically specific. See McDowell and Massey (1984) and Massey (1993b).

23. The domestic order is a *social space* structured by specific social relations irreducible to either an economic or a political logic. It is "a separate entity [which] can be described as a socio-demographic or anthroponomic regime" (Théret, 1994, p. 10).

24. See de Brunhoff (1978); Lerner (1986); Hollands (1990); Piven and Cloward (1993); and Mizen (1994).

25. For arguments in this vein, see de Brunhoff (1978); Burawoy (1985); Offe (1985); Purdy (1988); and Block (1994).

26. See Pateman (1989); Esping-Andersen (1990); and Walby (1990).

27. See Anderson and Fairley (1983); Ashton, Green, and Hoskins (1989); and Lee (1989).

Chapter 3

STRUCTURING
THE LABOR
MARKET
A Segmentation Approach

The conception of the labor market as a complex, not to say contradictory institutional structure could hardly be further from the neoclassical image of a self-equilibrating labor market in which individual actors pursue rational self-interest within a framework of free competition. In that neoclassical world, the labor market is a social space in which the actions of all actors are governed by a particular set of rules: those of competitive and optimizing behavior (Marsden, 1986, p. 142). With its diverse origins in institutionalist labor economics, Marxian, and post-Keynesian approaches, segmentation theory has developed in recent decades into the leading alternative to the prevailing neoclassical orthodoxy.[1] While disputes between segmentation theorists and orthodox economists often focus on empirical questions (such as the extent of occupational segregation or patterns of wage dispersal), they also reflect fundamental theoretical disagreements. In particular, these disagreements concern the *rules* governing labor market behavior or how the labor market is regulated.

Crucially, segmentation theory holds that the social space of the labor market is not only divided into submarkets (a contention many orthodox economists are able to accept), but also that the rules governing the behavior of labor market actors differ from one segment of the labor market to the other. "What distinguishes segmentation from mere division is that each segment functions according to different rules" (Michon, 1987, p. 25). This does not deny the existence of competitive rules, which segmentation theorists concede play an important role in some segments of the market. Rather, it represents a rejection of the bundle of claims made by orthodox theorists concerning this competitive state, namely, that

1. It represents the *prevalent* system of rules;
2. It is historically and logically *prior* to other (more regulated or institutionalized) rule systems;
3. It represents the *natural* underlying state to which labor markets are tending.

Segmentation theorists take issue with all these claims, arguing that labor markets are "social constructs, incorporating within them *various rules and forms of organisation* which both condition their mode of operation and also structure to some extent the actors themselves and determine their behaviour" (Castro, Méhaut, and Rubery, 1992b, p. 7, emphasis added). The competitive form is only one mode of labor market organization, coexisting alongside other modes of organization. The ideal-typical internal labor market, in which bureaucratic rules and organizational norms govern the allocation of labor, is one (albeit generic) example of a noncompetitive segment of the labor market (Osterman, 1984).

Despite the distinctiveness of its position, the segmentation approach has always struggled to establish and maintain its theoretical integrity.[2] Much of this difficulty stems from the diverse origins of segmentation theory, its sometimes eclectic embrace of a wide range of causal explanations, and its commitment to theorization rooted in the material, institutional, and historical realities of labor markets. However, it is also related to the position of segmentation theories vis-à-vis the neoclassical mainstream, which refuses doggedly to engage with critics on anything other than its own territory, usually in econometric terms (Piore, 1983; Reder, 1989).[3] Significantly, as segmentation theorists have begun to experiment with econometric testing, orthodox theorists previously unmoved by sophisticated historical accounts have started to take more seriously the challenge of segmentation theory (Dickens and Lang, 1985, 1988).

It is debatable whether this emerging econometric rapprochement marks a tactical victory for segmentation theorists. Equally, it might be seen as absorption of the empirical phenomenon of segmentation by positivist orthodoxy in such a way as to maintain the underlying integrity of the competitive model. Perhaps reflecting this trend, the institutionalist labor economists of the 1940s and 1950s, who laid down many of the foundations of contemporary segmentation theory, are increasingly cast as neoclassical revisionists rather than as theoretical opponents (see Kaufman, 1988). For example, Reder (1985) finds many of the claims made by institutionalists such as Reynolds and Kerr to be "quite compatible with acceptance of neo-classical theory."

> Many of the ad hoc regularities [which the revisionist institutionalists] described could be readily accommodated within the neo-classical framework as short-run phenomena. But these regularities . . . are specific to time and place, and difficult to distinguish from the possible realizations of one or another stochastic process on the disturbances. Thus, they are not proper "laws of economics."
>
> Nevertheless, the Revisionist type of research can continue to make a very real contribution by providing insightful descriptions of the process by which wages, labor qualities, and characteristics of particular labor market institutions are generated in particular times and places. These descriptions are of analytical value because they identify the characteristics of situations in which particular processes operate; such identification is rarely, if ever, provided by a formal model. (p. 458)

By implication, the formal models of neoclassical theory remain impervious to the "insightful descriptions" of the revisionists, who are denied the right to question the iron "laws of economics." Reder's confidence in the long-run efficacy of competitive forces is such that he is willing even to cede issues of process—the way in which labor market phenomena are "generated in particular times and places"—to the revisionists. Apparently, the level of abstraction at which the competitive model of the labor market is formulated is such as to render such considerations negligible (Jacoby, 1990; Iacobacci, 1992).

A rather different view of labor market process is adopted by segmentation theorists, notably those associated with the International Working Party on Labour Market Segmentation,[4] who continue vigorously to defend and develop a nonorthodox position. In contrast to the a priori reasoning of neoclassical economics, these theorists begin with the proposition that

> economic, social and political forces *combine* in determining how economies develop. . . . [T]he result is a dynamic non-equilibrium process which can only be revealed by empirical investigation. This is not to suggest that abstract reasoning has no role to play but rather to argue that *there are and can be no universal, pre-determined, "true" systems to which underlying economic forces are*

tending. . . . It is necessary at the outset to recognise that the abandonment of conventional economic theorising requires sacrificing the formality of its modelling and the surety of its conclusions. (Wilkinson, 1983, p. 413, emphasis added)

Defining features of this approach include its root-and-branch rejection of orthodox equilibrium theory, its advocacy of theoretically informed empirical research and multicausal explanation, and its openness to the role of contingency.[5] Contrary to the orthodox preoccupation with unilogical explanation, based on the empirically unassailable competitive model, this branch of segmentation theory has been concerned to examine the combined effects of technological, social, institutional, and economic forces in the generation of labor market structures. As Villa (1986) has observed, "the crucial problem [for segmentation theory] is neither a problem of categorization nor a question of competing explanations, but *a problem of explaining labor markets in terms of their different structures*" (p. 24, emphasis added).[6]

Emphasis on the nature and bases of labor market *structures* represents a considerable advance on the revisionist rendering of dualism in the labor market from which it drew initial inspiration (see Rubery, 1978). Emphasis in segmentation theory is placed on the roles of class struggle, institutional forms and processes, and the sphere of reproduction in labor market structuration, representing an increasingly credible and nuanced alternative to the orthodox paradigm. This chapter examines the origins and contributions of this body of work, tracing it through three generations of conceptual development (summarized in Table 3.1).[7]

Beginning with the first generation of dual labor market models, segmentation theory developed an insistent critique of economic orthodoxy. The second generation of radical models and the more heterogeneous third generation of multicausal approaches established an adversarial stance vis-à-vis neoclassical orthodoxy, proposing an increasingly sophisticated and multilayered explanation of the forms and processes of segmentation. Through this rather uneven evolution, explanation within segmentation theories has shifted from an initial preoccupation with technology and market structure (for example, in the first-generation work of Doeringer and Piore), through an appreciation of labor process–centered control imperatives (for example, in the second-generation work of Reich, Gordon, and Edwards), to multifaceted and institutionally sensitive accounts (for example, in the third-generation work of the Labour Studies Group).

ORIGINS OF SEGMENTATION THEORY:
APPROACHES TO DUALISM[8]

First-Generation Approaches

Segmentation theories have their foundations in the notion of the dual labor market, developed by Doeringer and Piore (1971) to explain low pay and unemployment in ghetto labor markets and, more broadly, by institutionalist approaches to labor economics as exemplified by Kerr's (1954) path-breaking analysis of the internal labor market. Doeringer and Piore extended Kerr's approach by considering groups *excluded* from internal labor markets.

Table 3.1. Three Generations of Segmentation Theories

	Dominant model or approach	Key authors	Intellectual origins	Innovations
First generation	Dual market labor	Doeringer and Piore	Institutionalist economics	Concepts of primary and secondary labor markets Identification of basic causes of labor market internalization
Second generation	Radical labor market theory	Edwards, Gordon, Harrison, Reich	Marxism	Segmentation as an historical tendency Links labor market structure to labor process (control) imperatives
Third generation		Michon, Picchio, Rosenberg, Rubery, Wilkinson	Post-Keynesianism, neo-Marxism	Multicausal explanation Contingency approach Emphasis on regulation, governance, and institutional variability

Their work, which represents the first generation of segmentation theories, developed the concepts of primary and secondary sectors of the labor market. For Doeringer and Piore, the primary sector contains the better jobs in the labor market, those offering relatively high wages and secure employment to workers who can expect to enjoy some form of career progression through an internal labor market. Formal skill levels in this sector are high and production processes technologically advanced. By contrast, the secondary sector contains the labor market's least desirable jobs, those with poor wages and working conditions in which the threat of unemployment is constant. Secondary employment is associated with small firms in the most backward sectors of the economy. The two sectors of the labor market are held to exhibit significant differences in social composition: the low-status jobs in the secondary sector are filled by ethnic minority workers, women, the disabled, and young people, while the primary sector is the domain of white, prime-aged males. These discontinuities in job and social characteristics between the two segments of the labor market are summarized in Table 3.2.

In the Doeringer–Piore model, the causes of dualism are traced to technical imperatives and the industrial structure. In some sectors of the economy, technical change requires increasing specificity in workers' skills so that employers seek to induce stability in their expensively trained labor force. In other words, labor is treated as a quasi-fixed factor of production (Oi, 1962; Piore, 1978). Parallel changes in industrial structure permit the development of internal labor markets; oligopolistic market conditions create an environment in which job stability can be induced and its benefits captured. Stability is secured by restricting the number of ports of entry to a firm and by attaching them to career ladders (the means by which senior posts are filled). For Doeringer and Piore, then, it is the coincidence of technological developments and a particular industrial structure that provides the preconditions for growth of the primary sector (Rubery, 1978). In particular, these conditions ensure the stability necessary for the establishment of internal labor markets, the defining feature of primary sector employment.

The secondary sector is defined almost as a residual of the primary sector, consisting of that area of the labor market that remains technologically backward and prone to strong competitive pressures. The secondary sector provides a great deal of the flexibility required by the economic system, as increases in output required in the primary sector at the peak of the trade cycle can be achieved by recruiting secondary workers on a temporary basis or by subcontracting from the primary to the secondary sector (cf. Atkinson, 1987). While it is true that dualist theory endows the primary sector with most of the positive features of the labor market, regarding the secondary sector as backward and anachronistic,[9] it also postulates a dynamic between the two sectors.

In spite of the apparent theoretical significance of the concept of a dual labor market, Doeringer and Piore (1971) were at pains to retain close links with economic orthodoxy, reducing the explanatory status of the institutional forces they had identified to "short-term phenomena [which] could perhaps be incorporated into a suitably modified neoclassical model" (p. 7). While they may have been satisfied with a

Table 3.2. The Dual Labor Market: Job and Social Characteristics[*]

	Primary Sector	Secondary Sector
Employment patterns	Stable	Unstable, irregular
Wages	Higher	Lower
Training and skills	On-the-job training; firm-specific skills	No on-the-job training; appropriation of skills
Working conditions	Better, with good fringe benefits	Poorer, including health and safety problems
Worker organization	Higher: highly unionized	Lower: disorganized
Technology	Sophisticated	Crude
Labor process control	High degrees of autonomy, discretion, and responsibility	Rigid work rules
Internal promotion	Much	Little
External recruitment	Limited to low- and entry-level jobs	Principle recruitment method
Typical social groups	White, prime-aged males	Women, immigrants, ethnic minorities, younger, older, and disabled workers
Typical industries	Oil, chemicals, gas and electricity, defense engineering	Textiles, clothing and footwear, food, glassware
Typical occupations	Civil service, skilled engineering, clerical	Laborers, machinists, catering hands

[*]Adapted from Loveridge and Mok (1979), pp. 126–128. © 1979 by Kluwer Publications. Adapted by permission.

revised version of orthodox theory, the same could not be said of the so-called radical proponents of the dualist thesis (Gordon, 1972; Reich, Gordon, and Edwards, 1973; Vietorisz and Harrison, 1973). Constituting a second generation of segmentation theory, this group of writers interpreted dualism quite differently.

Second-Generation Approaches

Although the radical view of the labor market shared a great deal with the Doeringer–Piore model empirically it sought to situate itself theoretically within a broader ideological and historical framework. In contrast with Doeringer and Piore's preoccupation with technical requirements, the radical school emphasized the role of labor market segmentation as a capitalist control strategy. For the radical theorists, segmentation strategies became necessary with the advent of routinized production techniques in which the work force was increasingly deskilled and homogenized.[10] Labor segmentation provided a means by which capital could overcome the contradictions inherent in deskilling: through a strategy of divide and rule, it sought to maintain control over the production process. The subdivision of clusters of work tasks and their integration with internal labor markets enabled capital to undermine the bases of class consciousness and solidarity in the work force while inducing worker motivation within an increasingly inhumane work system (Gordon, 1972).

The radical theorists argued that monopoly capitalist firms sought to segment their labor forces in the face of declining skill levels (and, therefore, formal skill differentials) through the development of extended hierarchies and exploitation of racial and gender differences. Hierarchies were formed within the primary sector itself; more routine jobs constituted a subordinate primary sector while those requiring a greater degree of discretion and initiative were assigned to an independent primary sector (Reich, Gordon, and Edwards, 1973). Where possible, such divides were deepened by the exploitation of racial and gender cleavages within the work force. Through these practices, employers counteracted tendencies toward solidarism. Contradictory class relations consequently lay at the heart of the radical reading of labor market dualism.

The Contribution of the Dualist Models

The dualist models represented a significant shift in labor market theory: first, they focused on characteristics of jobs rather than those of workers; and second, they sought to bring to labor market theories an understanding of institutional processes. The dualist model focuses on jobs as opposed to workers in the sense that jobs and job structures are seen to differ qualitatively, contrary to the assumptions of homogeneity in orthodox theory (Sorensen and Kalleberg, 1981). Because the number of primary jobs is limited by demand-side factors, some form of rationing must occur. The mechanisms of job creation in the dualist model are treated as largely independent of the quality of the work force as measured in terms of education and skills.[11] Certainly, the process of job creation is aided by the existence of a well-trained work force, but the degree of interdependence between the two is held by dualists to be grossly overstated by human capital theory.[12]

In the dualist model, the process of job creation is treated as analytically prior to the mechanisms of job filling: the economy generates a certain set of jobs, a proportion of which are primary sector jobs, and these are then rationed out among the available work force. This rationing process could, of course, be responsive to human capital considerations, as individuals could be assigned places in a job queue according to their potential productivity. The dualist model, however, describes a different set of selection criteria. Access to the primary sector is conditioned by employer discrimination, the effects of union-imposed constraints on labor supply, information shortages, and the operation of feedback mechanisms. It suggests, too, that secondary sector workers develop behavioral traits deemed to make them unsuitable for primary sector employment.

For dualists, the distribution of labor market opportunities is highly sensitive to the ascribed rather than achieved characteristics of the work force. Access to labor market opportunity is systematically restricted for such groups as women, ethnic minority and migrant workers, the disabled, and young people,[13] who bear the brunt of a bundle of labor market risks (Offe and Hinrichs, 1985). While such groups are subjected to discrimination in the education and training systems, the scale and scope of their disadvantage in the labor market is greater than can be attributed to variations in human capital (Thurow, 1975). In other words, there are forces at work *within the labor market itself* which are contributing to social inequality. The labor market does not simply mirror extramarket inequalities (as orthodox theorists would have it), but plays a part in the generation of inequality (Ryan, 1981).

However, the dual model treats processes of job allocation rather crudely. While Bluestone (1972) argued that secondary workers were barred from primary jobs "because of racism, sexism, economic depression and uneven development of industries and regions," Doeringer and Piore (1971) and Gordon (1972) highlighted feedback processes, the development of unstable working habits among workers in the secondary sector. These differing explanations are a product of the difficulties in (1) making dualism a theory of workers as well as jobs (Sorensen and Kalleberg, 1981) and (2) conceptualizing the process by which individuals are matched with their socioeconomic roles (Granovetter, 1981; Purdy, 1988). The conceptual problem is to separate the characteristics of jobs from those of the people who fill them. For example, women are not innately suited to secondary sector employment by virtue of low attachment to the labor force. Although their dual role as domestic laborers and as wage-laborers is reflected in the tendency for women, as a group, to exhibit high turnover rates, it is also true that the inherent instability of secondary sector *jobs* is a determinant of high labor turnover.[14] Within the secondary sector, women often exhibit longer job tenures than men.

The dualist models are rather more successful in their exploration of institutional forces in the labor market. Their most important contribution has been to introduce into mainstream debates the notion of the internal labor market. This was defined as an "administrative unit, such as a manufacturing plant, within which the pricing and allocation of labor is governed by a set of administrative rules and procedures," in contrast to the orthodox model of the labor market in which "pricing, allocation and training decisions are controlled directly by economic variables" (Doeringer and Piore, 1971, pp. 1–2). While orthodox theory can accept that labor markets are divided into submarkets, it is seriously challenged if any of these submarkets appears to operate under different sets of rules (Hall, 1975; Marsden, 1986; Michon, 1987).

As Osterman (1984) has observed, the concept of the internal labor market represents a challenge to the orthodox model of the labor market on several grounds.

- If it is accepted that internal labor markets have even a medium-term impact on wage determination, this will influence patterns of factor payments and levels of employment and impinge upon the wage-equilibrating process in the external labor market.
- While considerations of economic efficiency are not entirely absent from the internal labor market, these structures are governed primarily by bureaucratic rules and procedures in which sociological and political factors, rather than purely economic ones, come into play.
- The importance of seniority rules in job allocation within internal labor markets implies that human capital considerations are likely to be diluted and, eventually, perhaps overridden.
- The long periods of time spent by individual workers within

internal labor markets tend to break down any clear relationship between earnings and productivity.

- The notion of the internal labor market highlights alternatives to the wage-clearing mechanism. Adjustment mechanisms such as production subcontracting, changing hiring standards, and job redesign might also be used. By their very existence, these alternatives undermine the orthodox view that the wage mechanism constitutes the primary source of adjustment.

Together, these features of internal labor markets represent a fundamental challenge to the orthodox view that competitive rules are somehow preeminent in the operation of labor markets.

Although the dualist model significantly altered the terms of the debate over labor market theory, it has been rightly criticized for its descriptive and taxonomic character, and for its consequent lack of explanatory penetration (Wachter, 1974; Cain, 1976). The dualist model clearly aspires to more than a taxonomic classification of job types (for which it is so often dismissed by orthodox economists), but it must be conceded that the causal foundations of the original model were underspecified. Nevertheless, particularly in the hands of radical theorists, the dualist model helped to open up a series of fundamental questions around the operation of labor markets.

CONTEMPORARY SEGMENTATION THEORIES: THIRD-GENERATION APPROACHES

Taking dualism as its inspiration, segmentation theory has begun to claim the status of a mature, alternative paradigm to economic orthodoxy (though this remains strongly contested). In so doing, it has shifted increasingly away from crude dualism. The segmentation approach "has moved far beyond the specific models associated with either the American institutionalists . . . or the American radicals . . . [and having] escaped from the shackles of Anglo-American intellectual hegemony . . . has been taken up and developed within a variety of rich cultural and intellectual traditions in Europe and elsewhere" (Rubery, 1992, pp. 245–246). This diverse body of work is characterized here as third-generation segmentation theory.

From Dualism to Segmentation

Segmentation theories are being developed on a number of fronts. Perhaps their most important contribution has been to specify some of the causal factors and mechanisms underpinning segmentation, seeking to embed them in their relevant institutional and social contexts. In contrast to the effectively monocausal explanations of Doeringer and Piore (where dualism is seen essentially as a product of the skill and stability requirements of different production processes) and of Reich, Gordon, and Edwards (where dualism arises principally from managerial control strategies), multicausal explanations have increasingly been sought by third-generation theorists. Although tendencies for segmentation continue to be traced to labor market uncertainty, product market conditions, technological requirements, and labor process–control strategies (as in the first- and second-generation approaches), they also have been identified in processes of social reproduction, actions of the state, and collective struggles of labor unions.[15] Table 3.3 outlines the different explanatory bases of the three generations of segmentation theory. Illustrative rather than exhaustive, it reveals the multilayered quality of explanation that has developed under the broad umbrella of segmentation theory. Third-generation approaches therefore represent a significant advance over the early dualist models.

In the dualist models, the supply side of the labor market was inadequately conceptualized (Craig, Garnsey, and Rubery, 1985), with the result that connections between labor supply and demand often constituted no more than reading off labor supply characteristics from labor demand conditions.[16] For example, young people were characterized as typical secondary sector workers when not only are there discontinuities in the labor market experiences of this heterogeneous group, but the position of young people within the overall labor market hierarchy tends to fluctuate with the business cycle.[17] The casual sociology of the dualist models, employed to explain the channeling of social groups into different segments of the labor market in terms of feedback mechanisms, reflected a less than adequate conception of either job filling or the influence of the sphere of reproduction on labor market structure.[18] Serious treatment of the processes of social reproduction (such as occupational socialization within the family and education system or factors stemming from the domestic division of labor) was absent from the dualist models.

The dualist models also failed to consider the role of the state. As the previous chapter argued, the state is induced to intervene not only in cases of explicit market failure (such as persistent unemployment or skill shortages) but also in such fundamental and continuous processes as work-force reproduction, management of wage-labor mobilization, and legislative enforcement of the employment contract. Through these multifaceted interventions, the state performs a crucial regulatory role in the labor market.[19] The immanence of state action

Table 3.3. Explanation in Segmentation Theories

	Causal bases of labor market segmentation		
	Labor demand and the labor process	Labor supply and social reproduction	The state and social regulation
First generation	Dualism caused by increasing demands for skill specificity deriving from technical change Dualism conditioned by industry structure: primary employment associated with core firms in oligopolistic markets, secondary employment with peripheral firms in competitive markets	Feedback mechanisms: behavioral traits develop or are reinforced by labor market experience	
Second generation	Dualism a product of labor process–control strategies: divide-and-rule approach deployed by management in order to maintain control over deskilled labor processes Segmentation as a historical tendency linked to the strategies of monopoly capitalist firms in the context of long-run changes in the pattern of accumulation	Exploitation of racial and gender divides and uneven economic development to counteract work-force solidarism	

(cont.)

Table 3.3. *(cont.)*

	Causal bases of labor market segmentation		
	Labor demand and the labor process	Labor supply and social reproduction	The state and social regulation
Third generation	Diverse demand-side causes of segmentation (factionalized industry structures, imperatives of labor control, workplace struggles, variable product market conditions, divergent technological development, etc.) are afforded explanatory primacy, but take institutionally and socially variable forms	Structure and dynamics if the sphere of social reproduction exert relatively autonomous influence on forms of segmentation Social restructuring of labor supply not reducible to demand-side causes, but related to a range of relatively autonomous factors (e.g., structure of household division of labor, gendering of work, union structures and conventions, occupational socialization)	State actions and institutional forces are afforded central explanatory role Social regulation of labor market seen as a necessary but contradictory process Sources of segmentation traced to structure of education and training system, industrial relations and labor contracting regimes, welfare systems, etc.

in the labor market is underlined by the fact that nation-state forms are typically cited as causal factors in accounts of the uneven international development of labor market structures and dynamics (see Ashton, 1986).[20] It is surely significant that those neoliberal nation-states that are ideologically committed to stripping away institutional rigidities in the labor market in the interests of anticipated improvements in labor market efficiency have not completely withdrawn from labor market policymaking. On the contrary, in most cases the boundaries of the state have been not so much rolled back as repositioned, while it has become common for nation-states to engage in *active* programs of labor market deregulation and flexibilization with a view to the *inducement* of marketlike conditions (see Chapter 7).

According to Rubery, (1992) "there is now no single 'model' of segmentation but more a cluster of models or theoretical approaches which have arisen out of labour market research in the 1970s and 1980s" (p. 246). However, this is not merely an eclectic bundle of labor market literature, but one sharing both common misgivings about orthodox theory and methods, and a common set of analytical precepts. Contemporary segmentation theories share a concern with the following three phenomena:

(1) Primacy is accorded to the demand-side of the labour market, as the area where job structures are shaped and the level and form of demand is determined. This contrasts with neoclassical approaches where individualised labour supply behaviour in terms of acquisition of human capital or in terms of job search and wage demands affects the form and level of demand.

(2) Institutions and social forces are taken to be central determinants of the structure and organisation of employment. There is no division between the economic and the institutional as 'markets' are formed through institutions. Although primacy is accorded to labour demand, this demand necessarily has an institutional and social form.

(3) There are no inherent tendencies towards convergence in employment organisation, either within or between societies. Segmentation, in the sense of inequalities in form and access to employment, is likely to be found both within and between societies; and this segmentation is as much created by market or economic conditions as by social organisation. (Rubery, 1992, pp. 246–247)

This mixture of substantive empirical interests and analytical priorities is of course not exclusive to segmentation theories. As Rubery (1992) and Michon (1992) point out, there are increasingly porous boundaries between segmentation theories and the complementary work conducted by the LEST school (Maurice, Sellier, and Silvestre, 1986), French regulationists (Boyer, 1990b), and convention theorists (Salais, 1992). In the priority placed on demand-side forces, there also are continuing echoes of the American radical school, though contemporary segmentation theories tend to emphasize the *relative* priority of the demand side of the labor market (and its mutual conditioning by the supply side).

The following overview of this diverse segmentation literature is organized in terms of a simple threefold breakdown, reflecting the different causal emphases of contemporary theories:

1. *Segmentation of labor demand*, for example, the technical requirements of different labor processes, stability of different

product markets, labor control strategies used by employers, and effects of industrial structure

2. *Segmentation of labor supply,* for example, the role of the household division of labor in shaping labor market participation, stigmatization of certain social groups as secondary workers, processes of occupational socialization, and the influence of labor unions in restricting the labor supply to certain occupations

3. *Segmentation and the state,* for example, the structure of welfare provision and its eligibility rules, industrial relations and labor contract regimes, the structure and emphases of the education and training system

This is not to say that it is possible to isolate the tendencies for segmentation arising from the demand side of the labor market, the supply side, or the state. Concrete manifestations of segmentation processes are multiply determined, resulting from the *combined effects* of these three sets of causal tendencies. This threefold classification is therefore a heuristic framework, not intended to prioritize one set of factors over another.

The Segmentation of Labor Demand

The processes surrounding the derivation of labor demand and segmentation are complex. The Labour Studies Group (1985) offers a succinct explanation: the overall level of market demand for labor is an outcome of the aggregate level of market product, while the structure of labor demand is determined by the combined effects of the technological requirements of the production process and power relationships. It is, of course, impossible to assign analytical priority to these determinants. The processes of technological innovation and diffusion are themselves conditioned by political structures and struggles, forces which are particularly accentuated at the point of the adoption of technologies (Lazonick, 1981; Coombs, 1985; Zuscovitch, Heraud, and Cohendet, 1988). Technology is socially structured as well as socially structuring.

The two main determinants of the structure of labor demand—technology and power relationships—were fundamental in the development of the early dualist theories. Doeringer and Piore traced the causes of dualism to the structure of technology and especially to the particular labor requirements of different production systems, an approach Piore extended in later work (Berger and Piore, 1980). By contrast, Reich, Gordon, and Edwards (1973) rooted the differentiation of labor demand in the power relations between capital and labor in the context of struggles to maintain control over the labor process.

In their more recent *Segmented Work, Divided Workers,* patterns of labor segmentation are integrated more closely with the structure and evolution of the American economy (Gordon, Edwards, and Reich, 1982), relating forms of segmentation to long swings in the development of U.S. capitalism. Stable, primary labor markets are associated with the large, core corporations of monopoly capitalism. Stable employment in the core sector allows employers to "organize job tasks more systematically in order to permit more control, greater differentiation among workers' tasks and greater fragmentation of internal work groups" (p. 173). Large corporations at the core of the economy are able to pursue such strategies because of the considerable power and comparative stability following from their dominance of product markets. By contrast, peripheral firms exist in the shadow of the core firms, exploiting less stable and less profitable markets and absorbing many of the business risks of the core sector. Radical labor market theory continues to take the issue of control within the workplace as the underlying cause of segmentation and as a source of the labor market's fundamental dynamic. As Edwards (1979) has argued, "to understand why segmentation occurs, we must look to how labor power is consumed in the labor process" (p. 165).

Segmented Work, Divided Workers has been criticized for its structural-functionalist approach and for its sometimes spurious interpretations of historical evidence.[21] In particular, the argument that the current period of increasing segmentation in the United States was preceded by a period of labor homogenization (1893–1940) is difficult to sustain in the face of the often deeply segmented labor markets described by labor historians of the period.[22] The book is also susceptible to criticism on the grounds of the direct connections it asserts between industrial structure and labor market segmentation; while it is important to make these connections, it is equally important that they not be made too straightforwardly.[23] Labor market structure (including segmentation) is more than simply a derivative of industrial structure (and segmentation). There is a complex and iterative relationship between the two.

While accepting the contention that stable patterns of labor utilization are more likely to be sustained in core sectors where the degree of control over product markets is high, Jones (1983) suggests that the industrial structure and labor segmentation nexus needs to be rethought on two fronts. First, labor market segmentation is both an *intraindustry* and an *intrafirm* phenomenon; instances of secondary employment conditions are found in some core firms while primary jobs are found in some peripheral firms.[24] Jones (1983) maintains that such phenomena are not occasional aberrations, but rather "are an integral and pervasive element of the capitalist labor process" (p. 28). Moreover, as core firms shift toward the utilization of core-periphery models and contingent labor strategies, distinctions between the primary and secondary sectors are becoming increasingly blurred (Harrison, 1994). Second, it is necessary to recognize that the character of labor segmentation differs *qualitatively* between industrial sectors. Capital intensity and industry scale are particularly important sources of variation.

More recently, an essentially dualist conception of labor demand segmentation has informed the much-popularized "flexible firm" model (see Atkinson, 1987). Here, it is argued that pressures for flexibility and market responsiveness are inducing firms to segment their work forces into a core element for which employment is relatively secure (approximating the primary sector of the dualist formulation). In the core sector, flexibility tends to take a functional form; deployment of workers within an organization and the content of their jobs are adjusted in accordance with external demands. (Multiskilling is an example of such functional flexibility.) In a less secure position are those peripheral workers who may or may not be employees of the flexible firm, but who are engaged in various kinds of contingent relationship (ranging from part-time or temporary employment, for those on the company payroll, to different forms of arm's-length employment via the engagement of self-employed workers or the use of subcontractors and employment agencies). In this segment of the labor market, flexibility is of the numerical type, representing a strategy for ensuring that the amount of labor input is finely tuned to (fluctuating) demand requirements. The case of the flexible firm, summarized diagrammatically in Figure 3.1, illustrates one of the ways in which tendencies toward segmentation of labor demand, clearly emanating in this instance from firms' responses to (what is seen as) market uncertainty and fragmentation, might be reflected in the wider structure of the labor market.

Needless to say, core-periphery models grossly understate real-world complexities. It is perhaps more appropriate to regard capital as factionalized (Wilkinson, 1983) and its fragmentation as the product of a host of causal processes, including industry scale and capital intensity. Wide variations in individual capital units also occur with regard to access to finance and other factor markets, which combine to produce a hierarchy of market power (Labour Studies Group, 1985). Within this overall hierarchy, a complex web of interfirm relations develops, many of which act to reinforce the subordinate position of those firms in a weak market position. For example, production subcontracting is commonly portrayed in terms of the exploitation of small firms by large, market-dominant firms.[25]

Although labor market structure is not a direct product of industrial structure, it remains less likely that stable employment patterns will be found under conditions of product market instability, for the simple reason that firms find it difficult to insulate themselves from the effects of declining product demand (Craig, Rubery, Tarling, and Wilkinson, 1982). Nonetheless, the association between industrial and labor market structures is not causally direct. The complex relationships between the two are perhaps best understood as *tendential*, being associated with tendencies that may or may not be realized in the concrete circumstances of different industrial sectors (see Elbaum and Wilkinson, 1979; Villa, 1986). Demand-side factors remain the primary but not exclusive determinant of segmentation in third-generation theories. In effect, they define a differentiated structure of jobs

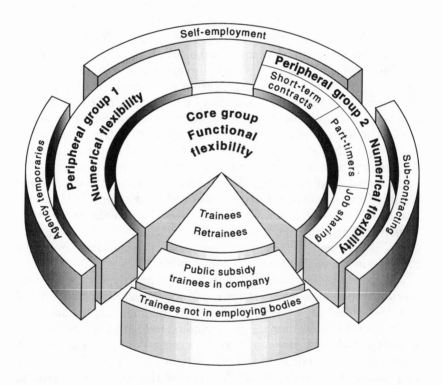

FIGURE 3.1. The Flexible Firm. From Atkinson (1987), p. 94. © 1987 ILO Registry, Geneva. Reprinted by permission.

which itself acts as an essential precondition for segmentation. However, concrete forms of segmentation are seen as forged by the *interaction* of demand-side factors and the structures of the supply side along with the wider sphere of social reproduction.

The Segmentation of Labor Supply

Examining patterns of wage-labor mobilization on the supply side allows a much fuller view of the dynamics of the labor market. Labor and capital are mutually dependent (Wilkinson, 1983). Even if capital did operate as a fully coherent class, it could not control completely the labor market or the means by which labor-power is reproduced. The supply of labor, as Chapter 2 emphasized, is *socially* produced and reproduced. Capital did not create the particular constellation of social groups in the secondary work force, although it can and does exploit those cleavages. To accord capital absolute control over the labor market is to sidestep a rigorous examination of the complexity of labor market structures and their derivation.

> Social phenomena can never be explained by the argument that their existence and preservation is "in the interest" of a social power group. . . . That something is "in the interest" of the corporations (for example) does not mean that it becomes a permanent part of social reality; many things would be in the interest of corporations which have been successfully prevented from becoming social reality because of the formation of opposing social power. Therefore social phenomena actually occurring in reality must be methodically screened not only for those interests which are orientated towards their *preservation,* they must also be examined as to why their preservation was not met by *resistance,* especially successful resistance. (Offe and Hinrichs, 1977; quoted in Kreckel, 1980, p. 538)

The gendered division of labor is a case in point. Though capital did not create the patriarchal social structures that underpin the marginalized role of women in the labor market, it exploits and thereby perpetuates gender divisions (Hartman, 1979). Moreover, Marshall (1994) argues that there is now "a recognition that men and women *supply* their labour on different terms" (p. 44), reflecting role specialization within the family and the complex of social expectations attached to roles. A notable feature of recent segmentation research, representing a considerable advance on the dualist models, has been the specification of the role of labor supply factors in structuring the labor market. Three areas merit detailed consideration: social reproduction and the role of the family, labor union structures and strategies, and the position of marginal groups in the labor market.

Social Reproduction and the Family

The institution of the family—"the basic unit for the reproduction of labour" (Villa, 1986, p. 259)—exerts a profound influence on patterns of wage-labor mobilization, being focal in the dynamic between the spheres of production and reproduction.[26] The labor market is structured, third-generation theories insist, in ways reflecting the structures of the sphere of social reproduction and its attendant divisions of waged and unwaged work. Acknowledging that the domestic sphere and wage-labor each have their own logics of organization and change, segmentation theorists nevertheless argue that the two spheres interpenetrate, each conditioning the other.[27] The family exerts an important influence on labor market activity in three ways: first, it plays a key role in the social conditioning and education of the young; second, it provides support for workers in the labor market as well as for other dependents (such as the sick and the old); and third, the sharing of income within the family unit impinges on both male and female roles in the labor market, as well as the distinctive functions fulfilled by younger and older workers (Garnsey, Rubery, and Wilkinson, 1985).

The first is particularly significant. In tandem with the formal education system and wider community structures (in ways considered explicitly in Bourdieu's concept of habitus),[28] families play a crucial role in socialization for work. As expectations about the world of work evolve, they affect the terms under which individuals will make their labor available.[29] The pertinent process involves occupational socialization, not occupational choice per se. As Willis (1977) has argued, the important questions concern how working-class youth come to want and how they are socialized into accepting working-class jobs. This process of occupational socialization is related to "other social affiliations, with the effect being that career paths are highly compartmentalized and dependent upon the social milieu that originally moulded the individual participant" (Seccareccia, 1991, p. 48).[30] Through socialization there is an "occupational structuring" of the supply side of the labor market (Offe and Hinrichs, 1985), which reflects not only labor market opportunities but also the domestic and labor market expectations of different social groups. These occupational orientations tend to be regarded in orthodox theory as preferences, a completely inappropriate term given their origin.

A second way in which the institution of the family serves to structure the supply side of the labor market is in the allocation of domestic responsibilities. Socially encoded divisions of labor are constructed around received notions of male "breadwinner" and wage-earning roles and female domestic labor and child-rearing roles (see Marshall, 1994). This division is reinforced by labor market structures in which career interruptions and part-time work are penalized (Dex, 1984). Even for those women who do not conform to the stereotypical work pattern, the very expectation among employers that they will, or may, serves to restrict their access to primary jobs.

The family's income-sharing is a third way in which this institution impinges on the labor market. Socially, there is a continued ideological association between the male and the family wage, and between women's income and pin money. There is historical evidence that the family wage has exerted upward pressure on real wage rates as the household division of labor has effectively restricted the supply of labor (Humphries, 1977), although this view has been disputed by those stressing the role of the family in enforcing women's oppression and dividing the working class (Barrett and McIntosh, 1980).

Women are likely to remain trapped in the most unstable segments of the labor market until there is a change in their (real and perceived) position within the household division of labor, or until these household "responsibilities" become more compatible with primary sector employment (Rubery, 1988; Picchio, 1992). The role of female labor within the secondary sector is crucial because segmentation theory holds that this sector acts as a structural safety valve for the labor market as a whole, facilitating the mobilization or demobilization of this group of workers in line with fluctuating demand requirements (Humphries, 1976; Rubery and Tarling, 1982). The secondary sector clearly does not disappear in its entirety during periods of recession. Similarly, female workers as a group cannot be regarded as constituting a completely disposable segment of the labor market.[31] Nevertheless, flexibility in the secondary sector (which is not nearly so readily available in the primary sector) acts as an important determinant of the aggregate size and composition of demand for labor over the business cycle. Secondary workers do not have access to the shelters constructed by primary sector employers and workers as a defense against the vagaries of the labor market (Freedman, 1976). Thus, the actions of both employers and organized sectors of the working class act to heap the burden of economic downturn upon those workers consigned to the secondary sector (Sengenberger, 1981; Wilkinson, 1988).

Labor Union Structures and Strategies

In the process of workplace struggle, organized factions of the working class have performed a powerful function in defending, maintaining, and extending their employment opportunities in the primary sector.

In so doing, labor unions exert an important influence on the structure of labor markets, processes of rule-setting, and patterns of labor mobility. Rubery (1978) has argued that it is necessary to "include more fully the effect of worker organization in the development of structured markets. However, trade union development is not to be regarded as an exogenous influence on labour market structure. Rather worker organization attempts to control the competition in the labour market that the capitalist system generates, and, further, adapts and restructures itself in response to developments in the economic structure" (p. 33).

Discontinuities in the distribution of power within the working class should be seen as a product of both the actions of workers *within* the labor market and uneven distribution of power *prior to* entry into the labor market. In other words, labor union power has both demand- and supply-side determinants. Collective exclusionary action on the part of suppliers of labor-power is, of course, a logical strategy in the face of labor market competition (Offe and Weisenthal, 1980; Offe and Hinrichs, 1985). Trade unions and professional associations derive much of their power in the labor process from the restrictions they are able to place on the supply of labor to their particular niche of the labor market.[32]

Such restrictive strategies are pursued through a variety of means, such as apprenticeship and other training systems, licensing, accreditation, and credential requirements. Through these and other means, groups of workers exert their collective power in an exclusionary way to bring about some degree of insulation from the external labor market, this being one of the principal means by which asymmetries of power in the labor force are formed and maintained (Freedman, 1976). Of course, because the basis of these strategies is exclusion, labor's strategic disadvantage in the market is not reduced in an absolute sense but redistributed within the working class. Typically, excluded workers are concentrated in the secondary sector and drawn from a familiar cluster of social groups: women, ethnic minorities, the young, and the disabled. One of the defining features of disadvantaged groups in the labor market is, therefore, their lack of collective organization (Craig, Rubery, Tarling, and Wilkinson, 1982). They are in a sense victims of the successful collective organization of other (more powerful) groups of workers, their own organizational weakness being both cause and consequence of their marginal position in the labor market.

The ability to exercise control over the labor supply does not reflect the innate attitudes and abilities of collectively organized workers. Other factors are at work, creating an uneven terrain of possibilities for collective organization. First, and on the demand side of the labor market, there is a longstanding debate over the extent to which labor union power can be explained by the uneven distribution of genuinely scarce production skills (Turner, 1962; Dunlop, 1964). Those with scarce production skills, it is suggested, are in a stronger position to organize and bargain collectively and to win concessions from management. Ultimately, this becomes a chicken-and-egg argument as skill does not refer just to physical and mental capabilities, but also has an important ideological component reflecting the distribution of power in the labor market and in the sphere of social reproduction (Allen, 1977; Cockburn, 1983; Miller, 1988). Second, it has been argued that certain industrial sectors are particularly vulnerable to disruption and thus have spawned powerful labor unions (Parkin, 1974; Zeitlin, 1979). For example, this may have been one of the factors behind unionization of the newspaper industry, a sector especially vulnerable to strikes. It is possible (although, in practice, apparently not common) for workers from disadvantaged social groups to be located within one of these strategically vulnerable industries. Third, and on the supply side of the labor market, Offe and Hinrichs (1985) have argued that marginal and unorganized groups tend also to be those which "enjoy the licence to conduct a lifestyle outside the labour market" (p. 37). These groups are denied access to primary jobs, and opportunities for collective organization, because they are perceived to have an alternative role (or means of support) outside the waged sector.

Marginal Groups in the Labor Market

While concurring with Craig and her colleagues (1982) that "the number of good jobs in the economy is mainly determined by the development of the industrial and technological structure, largely independent of labour supply" (p. 77; cf. Bluestone, 1970), there also is a need to consider the cluster of related processes acting to generate the supply of labor considered appropriate for secondary work. One reason secondary work exists is the *prior* existence of a group of workers who can be exploited in this way.[33] The processes of job allocation in the secondary sector are governed, not by direct measures of productive potential as orthodox theory would have it, but by ascriptive criteria connected to the distribution of economic, social and political power.

> Firms can claim labour from segments where pay is low relative to labour productivity in order to compete more effectively and can

possibly retain otherwise obsolete techniques. The existence of segments of the labour force with different labour market status may also create the situation where jobs are classified not by their content but according to the labour market position of the workers normally undertaking the work. Thus jobs are secondary because they are performed by workers generally considered secondary: jobs are regarded as unskilled because they are feminized and not feminized because they are unskilled. . . . [The] existence of non-competing groups may be of considerable social and political importance for the maintenance of labour force segmentation. (Craig, Rubery, Tarling, and Wilkinson, 1982, p. 77)

Offe and Hinrichs (1985) take up this issue, arguing that the utilization of contingent workers plays an important part in the wider process of labor regulation. The exploitation of social divides is one way in which fluctuating labor demands are reconciled with a comparatively inelastic supply of labor (the size and needs of which, in the short to medium term at least, are constant).

[R]ecourse to constituting ascriptive categories is the means by which industrial capitalist societies try to institutionally overcome a dilemma, namely, that they cannot possibly force the *entire* population into direct participation in the labour market, while, at the same time, they cannot make generally available the option of non-participation in the labour market (and thus dependence of means of subsistence external to it). If the latter option were available, a "mass exodus" from market relations—which are also power relations—would have to be reckoned with. To overcome this dilemma . . . these societies are dependent upon criteria of exclusion or exemption from the labour market that must have two qualities: (i) they may not be freely chosen individually and thus potentially usable as a means of strategic withdrawal from the labour market; and (ii) they must be selected in such a way that the "exempted" portion of the population . . . is not in a position to place "excessive" demands and politically effective expectations about its need for the means of subsistence on the production and occupational system. (pp. 36–37)

This approach is useful in that it locates domestic labor within the overall rationale of capitalist labor markets and their regulation.[34] The existence of groups of workers with alternative roles provides a regulatory safety valve for the labor market. In fact, this is a mechanism of *social* regulation.

While alternative roles can account for much of the unevenness in the social distribution of labor market risks, it is just one among a range of factors structuring the labor supply. Not all marginalized workers have an alternative role on which to fall back. In the case of migrant workers, for example, the alternative role hypothesis is less appropriate in the British context than it is for the German guest-worker system (Kreckel, 1980). The alternative role hypothesis alone is not sufficient to explain patterns of disadvantage in the labor market. The social structures of patriarchy and racism, though clearly mediated by labor market attachments, exert autonomous influences on labor market disadvantage. These factors, alongside the alternative role hypothesis and the few possibilities or low propensities of some social groups to organize collectively, form a constellation of causes of labor market disadvantage.

If there is a single, definitive characteristic of secondary sector workers, it is that they are stigmatized in some way (Kreckel, 1980). The roots of this stigma need to be traced carefully in specific contexts. The alternative role hypothesis, which shares a great deal with Piore's notions of weak labor-force attachment (Berger and Piore, 1980), has been criticized for the way in which it separates the determinants of social and political power from labor market power relations (Humphries and Rubery, 1984). Offe and Hinrichs (1985) were certainly thinking of these problems when they maintained that the limited access afforded disadvantaged groups to primary employment would lead, "in a circular fashion, to a decline in their subjective hopes and expectations of strategically asserting themselves in the labour market, and to a strengthening of their subjective orientation to their 'alternative role' " (p. 40). However, this is little more than a reworking of the dualist conception of feedback processes. While the subjective orientations and material labor market positions of workers are clearly related, one cannot be reduced to the status of by-product of the other (see Miller, 1988). The link is more dynamic: material experiences of work and the formation of labor market expectations are dialectically related and mutually constitutive (see Craig, Rubery, Tarling, and Wilkinson, 1982; McDowell and Court, 1994).

Certainly, the participation of stigmatized social groups in the labor market often serves only to reinforce their lack of economic and political power. Although work in the secondary sector typically requires skill and discretion and though the secondary work force may exhibit stability and loyalty to an employer,[35] it is by virtue of the very presence of low-status groups in such jobs that their skill and social status become devalued.[36] Consequently, the subordinate position of stigmatized workers is both perpetuated and legitimated, illustrating one way in which segmentation on the demand and supply sides of the labor market become mutually conditioning. Labor segmentation does not result *only* from organization of the labor process and related demand-side factors; it is also conditioned by the social actions of those who find their way into different kinds of jobs. Segmentation is partly a product of who does the jobs, social conventions concerning appropriate forms of waged and unwaged work undertaken by different social groups, and the relationship between the labor market and the sphere of social reproduction.

Segmentation and the State

Given their quite different structures, dynamics, and logics, the interface between the demand and supply sides of the labor market involves contradiction and mutual adjustment, not seamless coordination. Much of the responsibility for managing this jarring relationship (or, perhaps more precisely, dealing with its contradictions) falls to the state. State action in the labor market tends to be as continual as it is imperfect. The actions of states are bedeviled by inadequate analysis and prescription, the lagged nature of interventions, and the multiplicity of unintended consequences with which they are inevitably associated. It is this flawed and sometimes haphazard process which is charted in analyses of the state's regulatory role in the labor market.[37] This regulatory role tends to be particularly intense and problematic around the sphere of social reproduction and supply of labor, which is not regulated by mechanisms indigenous to the labor market (such as expectations about potential saleability) as could be argued with other commodities. In the previous chapter, the broad parameters of the state's regulatory functions in the labor market were seen to be connected to enduring regulatory dilemmas. The focus here is on aspects of the regulatory role which impinge more directly on the processes of segmentation.

De Brunhoff (1978) maintains that the state is "immanent in the process of capitalist accumulation at the same time as it is fundamentally external to it" (p. 11).[38] Thus, the state's role in the labor market stems from a requirement to secure the necessary conditions for the reproduction of labor-power and, more broadly, of market relations. De Brunhoff argues that although the state's role in the labor market is necessary, the form of its intervention is not determined directly in a functionalist manner.[39] Its role is revealed in efforts to counteract, or at least to minimize, the negative effects of imbalances in the supply and demand of labor. Thus, in periods of labor market buoyancy, state initiatives tend toward mobilization of segments of the labor supply from the margins of the labor market. For example, the British government's commitment to childcare provision peaked during the Second World War and quickly dissolved following the demobilization of men after the war (Labour Studies Group, 1985). More recently in the U.K., policies for the incorporation of "women returners" and disadvantaged groups entered into ascendancy in the late 1980s, as concerns grew over a looming demographic dip in the supply of young workers (Haughton, 1990).[40] Conversely, during periods of high unemployment, the state is likely to pursue policies aimed at temporarily restricting the supply of labor. Measures promoting early retirement, job sharing, and make-work often figure in such periods. It is also true, however, that states often take steps to reinforce the disciplining effect of the market during periods when labor is strategically weakened by high unemployment (Piven and Cloward, 1993).

One of the principal means of state regulation of the labor market is institutionalization of nonparticipation in wage-labor. The requirement that this sheltered area of the labor market stop short of being attractive to wage-laborers is met by the degrading and punitive way in which these groups are treated (Piven and Cloward, 1971; Block, Cloward, Ehrenreich, and Piven, 1987). Wilkinson (1988) has described the process by which disadvantaged social groups are progressively excluded from the labor market during periods of recession; the demobilization of segments of the labor supply is by no means a straightforward process. Moreover, structural change in the economy, and in particular long-run shifts in the job-generating capacities of some national economies, has meant that the state must construct institutional means by which elements of the marginal work force can be excluded from the labor market on a more or less permanent basis (Hinrichs, Offe, and Wiesenthal, 1988). The result is that "social 'catchment areas' outside the process of production are required to ensure the reproduction of labour power even when no actual employment within the production process results" (Böhle and Sauer, 1975; quoted in Offe and Lenhardt, 1984, p. 99).

A key way in which labor supply is regulated is the imposition of controls on the initial entry of young people to the labor market. Child labor laws, compulsory education, the raising of school-leaving ages, and training programs restrict the supply of youth. Thus, the state exerts a profound influence on both patterns of supply side segmentation (its policies tending to focus on particular social groups) and the dynamic of the labor market as a whole (as it takes steps to combat or control imbalances between supply and demand). The state is drawn into the regulation of labor markets not only in terms of the maintenance of aggregate demand and the construction of welfare safety nets, but also in validating and repeatedly adjusting the social distribution of work.

This regulatory function has been thrown into particularly sharp focus under the current period of state-induced flexibilization in the labor market. Couched in the rhetoric of deregulation and the liber-alization of market forces, these strategies in fact have served to underline the simultaneously central and problematic nature of the state's role in the labor market.

> Government policies to free-up the labor market have not resulted in the creation of a competitive labor market with the neoclassical hallmarks of competitive equalization of prices, increased flexibility and mobility and real wages levels responsive to overall conditions of demand and supply. . . . *Deregulated* labor markets are . . . not synonymous with *competitive* labor markets; they increase the scope for inequality primarily by removing protection from the weak and not by exposing all groups to competition. Moreover, deregulated labor markets have in practice required a more frequent recourse to the law in order to regulate the system of industrial relations. (Rubery, Wilkinson, and Tarling, 1989)

Flexibilization strategies need to be understood for what they are. They are not so much concerned with the restoration of labor market efficiency as with the *political re-regulation of the labor market* during a period of excess labor supply and weakened labor unions. Thus, the opportunity is seized by the state (and by neoliberal nation-states in particular) to discipline the unemployed with the economic whip of market forces while further weakening labor unions and breaking up institutional structures used by labor (and employers) in defense against the market. In the process, contours of labor segmentation are profoundly reworked in the interests of capital.[41] Contrary to the rhetoric of labor market flexibility, segmentation does not disappear under a supposedly free and fair, flexible labor market, but instead social inequalities widen, power relations are reinforced and wage polarization occurs. The labor market is just as unequal and it is still structured; the difference is that it is structured less on labor's terms. Ideologically, of course, the state must be represented as reestablishing market forces, not as disciplining labor on the part of capital. Hence the prevailing rhetoric of flexibility and competitiveness.

EXPLANATION IN SEGMENTATION THEORIES

Segmentation theories are no longer concerned solely with patterns and processes of labor market inequality, but are increasingly moving to explore the fundamental dynamics and social foundations of the labor market. The conception of the labor market developed by third-genera-tion segmentation theorists stands in sharp contrast to the orthodox model in which labor demand and supply mesh with one another in response to wage signals. The supply of labor is not governed simply by market forces, but also by demographic factors, social norms concerning the participation of different groups in wage-labor (mediated through the institution of the family), and state functions in such areas as employment contracts, welfare provision, and training. While undeniably influenced by labor supply factors, labor demand is driven principally by a quite different set of forces—in particular, struggles over labor processes, technical change, patterns of competition in product markets, and state policies in areas such as taxation, monetary strategy, and public expenditure. The state's role in the labor market is also vital. Indeed, the ongoing regulatory activity of the state (which itself is mediated through political struggles and therefore not determined in a direct, functional way by the requirements of the labor market) constitutes one of the key means by which the inevitable discordance between labor supply and demand (which has quantitative and qualitative dimensions) is minimized, adjusted, and accommodated.

Thus, labor market structures and dynamics do not derive from a fully coherent inner logic, as the orthodox model would suggest. There is not one set of (competitive) labor market rules, embedded within an overarching (market) rationality. Rather, the labor market is a complex, composite structure bearing the imprints of a diverse range of influences. Some of these influences, identified in this chapter, have been grouped together in the spheres of labor supply, labor demand, and the state. Each sphere has its own characteristic structure and dynamic, and each brings with it *different tendencies toward segmentation.*

Consequently, one would not necessarily expect a close fit between primary and secondary jobs, primary and secondary workers, and core and periphery firms (see Lever-Tracy, 1984). Segmentation refers to *tendencies,* not a taxonomy of labor market positions (Gordon, Edwards and Reich, 1982). For example, the allocation of social groups to different segments of the labor market is sensitive to the contingencies of time and space (Peck, 1989; Hiebert, 1994). Segmentation is the outcome of the contingent and dialectical interaction of several causal tendencies; the state, the sphere of social reproduction, and demand-side factors exert *relatively autonomous* influences on patterns and processes of labor market segmentation (see Table 3.3). The task of disentangling the forces at work in particular labor markets is, of course, largely empirical. Concrete labor market structures represent the product of a synthesis of causal powers; their precise form cannot be determined purely by a priori reasoning (see Wilkinson, 1983).

Segmentation and Causality

Segmentation theory seems destined never to exhibit the analytical purity of the orthodox model of perfect competition. In stressing the complexity of labor market processes and outcomes, however, it has a strong purchase on the concrete realities of the labor market. However, if segmentation theory is to rise above criticisms that it is no more than a descriptive, mid-level approach, more attention must be given to clarifying and refining its conceptual foundations. This task is not without difficulties, as Lever-Tracy's (1984) review of third-generation segmentation theories illustrates.

> It is not necessary for Marxists, or indeed for any school of sociology, to allow its problematic to be defined . . . by an adversary role vis-à-vis orthodox economics. Since we have never taken very seriously the view that inequality, wage levels, class structures, and so forth, were due to the laws of supply and demand, it is not necessary to group together labour market deviations from these laws as a single phenomenon. (p. 81)

On the contrary, although it should not be their entire rationale, segmentation theorists must engage in the struggle over labor market theory and attempt to break the hegemony of neoclassical orthodoxy. While segmentation theory must be more than reactive (in the sense that its scope is bounded by the flaws and questions of the orthodox approach), one of its fundamental goals must be establishment of a credible and internally consistent alternative paradigm. Almost by definition, this requires the establishment of an analytical position which is both distinct from *and critical of* orthodox theory. The basis for such an alternative paradigm is already in evidence.

The segmentation approach represents an "inclusive" treatment of the labor market, emphasizing both the *necessarily social* nature of labor-power and the *necessarily institutional* form of labor market processes. This can be contrasted with the "exclusive" treatment in orthodox accounts where the competitive bases of labor market transactions are both exaggerated and abstracted from the social and institutional context in which they are embedded. It is this focus on social embeddedness[42] which has led segmentation theorists to investigate the differentiated form of labor market structures.

> Thus, if we define segmentation as the separation of the market into different segments within which workers are treated differently, independently of their own characteristics, then we have to explain

the different structures of the labour market as a complex phenomenon within which different structuring relations interact. What is needed is a comprehensive conceptual framework, capable of including different levels of analysis, from the social reproduction of labour power to the transformation of labour power, and their interrelations. (Villa, 1986, p. 257)

The conceptual framework proposed by Villa concentrates on the interactions between four relatively autonomous social processes: the social reproduction of labor, determination of employment opportunities, allocation of workers to jobs, and transformation of labor-power into labor (pp. 258–272). Labor market structures are viewed as multiply or conjuncturally determined, hence the emphasis on empirical investigation and the variability and unpredictability of outcomes (cf. Wilkinson, 1983; Tarling, 1987).

Regulation, Institutionalization, and Contingency

Processes of institutionalization are of particular importance in third-generation segmentation theories. Institutions and social factors—captured here under a broad conception of social regulation—represent a central analytical focus, being conceived as endogenous to the labor market and deeply implicated in its structures and dynamics (Castro, Méhaut, and Rubery, 1992b). This is not merely to say that labor market processes are institutionalized (as in the original dualist conception of internal labor markets). Rather, it is to stress the ways in which the labor market is *itself* an institution, governed by a complex set of rules and evolving in a continuous and reciprocal way alongside other social institutions. Thus, labor markets bear the imprints of (and reciprocally condition) the institutional structures and dynamics of, for example, the education and training systems, the welfare and social insurance systems, and the industrial relations system.[43] In this sense, the labor market does not have a single institutional dynamic, but is a composite of several institutional dynamics.

As institutionalized, codetermined, conjunctural phenomena, labor market structures vary over both time and space. Economists tend to privilege the former over the latter, reflecting perhaps their longstanding preoccupation with questions of history, evolution, and equilibrium (see Robinson, 1979).

In the orthodox view, economic theory was synchronic: an abstraction from reality that isolated its transhistorical and universal aspects. [The] institutionalists asserted that the abstractions of economic theory were neither timeless nor placeless but instead were an ideal-type—an enhancement of features unique to modern Western capitalism. . . . [Their] empirical research led them to view [the] distance [between abstraction and reality] as substantial, at least for some parts of orthodox theory, as historically variable. . . . Hence, they insisted that diachronic analysis—*how the economy acquired its features and the conditions that cause those features to vary over time and place*—had to be part of economics, alongside synchronic abstraction. (Jacoby, 1990, pp. 319–320, emphasis added)

Synchronic analysis—abstracting to that placeless, timeless world in which equilibrium rules—raises the danger of misspecifying labor market processes. Rejection of the synchronic abstraction of economic orthodoxy opens the door to both historical and geographic contingency, a defining feature of a realist approach.

The strongest and most developed realist feature of institutional SLM [segmented labor market] research is its use of historical analysis to understand the nature of any given labour market phenomenon by identifying the conditions of its emergence and subsequent mutation. In contrast, neoclassical theory relies . . . on a synchronic form of analysis, in which abstraction is used to isolate factors independently of time and locality. Institutional SLM researchers do not object to the use of abstraction per se, but rather to the specific way in which abstraction is used to isolate only time- and place-independent aspects of observed economic phenomena. They argue that *labour market outcomes are historically contingent* and that this cannot be ignored without possibly biasing the explanations—i.e., identifying incorrect causal mechanisms. (Iacobacci, 1992, p. 28, emphasis added)

Thus, sensitivity to historical and geographic contingency raises fundamental explanatory issues in labor market analysis.

However, segmentation theorists have proved more comfortable with historical than geographic contingency. Their conceptual frameworks, conditioned by "empirical and historical investigation" (Wilkinson, 1983, p. 414), have been described as "historically specific and non-functionalist" (Humphries and Rubery, 1984, pp. 337). Although geographic specificity is occasionally acknowledged, it is typically only at the level of variations between national labor systems or what Rubery (1994) terms "societal-specific production regimes."[44] Similarly, uneven development in labor markets is often recognized between the productive sectors of national economies,[45] but rarely between different regions. Even when their philosophical critique of economic orthodoxy suggests the need to take account of temporal *and spatial* contingency, segmentation theorists remain largely space-blind. As Hiebert (1994) puts it, "segmented labour-market theory is aspatial, implying the same processes operate at all places simultaneously" (p. 9) and, one might add, with more or less the same effects.

Beginning with the next chapter, the remainder of this book is dedicated to bringing space into segmentation theory. This requires a substantial clarification, recodification, and development of its conceptual foundations, representing a fourth-generation approach that emphasizes the spatiality of the labor market and its underlying regulatory forms. A first step must be to reclaim the concept of the local labor market.

NOTES

1. See Fine (1987); Dickens and Lang (1988); Seccareccia (1991); and Rubery (1992).
2. For different positions, see Wilkinson (1981a); Lever-Tracy (1984); Fine (1987); Jacoby (1990); and Iacobacci (1992).
3. The most thorough orthodox responses to segmentation theory are found in Wachter (1974) and Cain (1976).
4. The lineage of the Working Party's development can be traced through Wilkinson (1981b); Tarling (1987); Rosenberg (1989c); Castro, Méhaut, and Rubery (1992a); and more recently, in contributions to the journal *International Contributions to Labour Studies*.
5. For methodological statements, see Labour Studies Group (1985); Woodbury (1987); Lawson (1989); and Iacobacci (1992).
6. It is partly with respect to this goal that segmentation theorists are beginning to make common cause with regulation theorists (see Michon, 1992; Théret, 1994).
7. In emphasizing these different generations of segmentation theory, the intention is not to periodize the relevant literature, but instead to point to significant steps in its evolution. Despite important continuities, each generation marks an important development in the conceptual architecture of this approach.
8. The central section of this chapter is a substantially revised version of an article published in *Labour and Industry* 2(1989): 119–144. I wish to thank the editor of *Labour and Industry* for permission to adapt and reprint the article here.
9. On this issue, see Rubery (1978); Rubery and Wilkinson (1981); and Wilkinson (1983).

10. See Braverman (1974) and Bray and Littler (1988).

11. For evidence and arguments, see Wootton (1955); Thurow (1975); Ryan (1981); Craig, Rubery, and Wilkinson (1982); and Curtain (1987).

12. Compare the leading human capital theorist, Becker (1975), with the first-generation dualist position of Doeringer, Feldman, Gordon, Piore, and Reich (1969) and the more radical analysis of Harrison (1971, 1972).

13. There is substantial evidence of labor market exclusion affecting different social groups. On women, see Barron and Norris (1976); Haig (1982); and Rubery (1988). On ethnic minority and migrant workers, see Smith (1981); Collins (1988); and Lever-Tracy and Quinlan (1988). On the disabled, see Walker (1982) and Berthoud, Lakey, and McKay (1993). On young people, see Kalachek (1969) and Osterman (1980).

14. See Pettman (1975); Barron and Norris (1976); Kenrick (1981); O'Donnell (1984); and Rubery (1988).

15. Key contributions in each of these areas include labor market uncertainty, product market conditions, and technological requirements (Berger and Piore, 1980); labor process–control strategies (Gordon, Edwards, and Reich, 1982); the sphere of reproduction (Humphries and Rubery, 1984; Picchio, 1992); state action (Offe and Berger, 1985; Rosenberg, 1989d); and labor union struggles (Kahn, 1975; Rubery, 1978; Marsden, 1992b).

16. See Sayer (1985); Rubery (1989); and Marshall (1994).

17. See Kalachek (1969); Osterman (1980); and Junankar (1987).

18. See Fine (1987); Miller (1988); Purdy (1988); and Picchio (1992).

19. See de Brunhoff (1978); Wilkinson (1983); Offe (1985); Purdy (1988); Fevre (1992); Block (1994); and Théret (1994).

20. For context, see Stein (1976); Elbaum and Wilkinson (1979); and King (1995).

21. Lever-Tracy (1983); Tomlins (1984); Littler and Salaman (1984); and Fine (1987).

22. Among many contributions, see Shergold (1982); Jackson (1984); and Burawoy (1985).

23. See Althauser and Kalleberg (1981); Lawson (1981); Wallace and Kalleberg (1981); and Jones (1983).

24. Cf. Lever-Tracy (1983, 1984).

25. In particular, see Friedman (1977). Cf. Rainnie (1984); Holmes (1986); and Shutt and Whittington (1987).

26. This argument has been made most persuasively by Humphries (1977); Meillassoux (1981); Picchio del Mercato (1981); Humphries and Rubery (1984); Picchio (1992); and Marshall (1994).

27. As Rubery (1994) puts it, "Instead of seeing social reproduction systems as either determined by the economic production system or, as in more cultural arguments, entirely independently determined, [segmentation theorists argue that] each sphere should be considered to be 'relatively autonomous.' For example, developments in the production sphere influence the path of development of social reproduction, but the adap-

tations these bring are not determined by the economic system but arise out of the dynamic of development within the social reproduction sphere" (pp. 352–353).

28. Bourdieu (1973); cf. Bourdieu and Passeron (1977) and Mingione (1991).

29. See Bowles and Gintis (1976); Willis (1977); and CCCS (1981).

30. These social milieux are structured in accordance with not only ethnicity, gender, and class but also *location,* contributing to the geographically distinctive process by which segmented labor supplies mesh with segmented job structures (Peck, 1989; Hanson and Pratt, 1995). This represents one of the ways in which labor markets are locally embedded, as job-filling mechanisms and conventions vary from place to place.

31. See Milkman (1976); Beechey (1977); Bruegel (1979); O'Donnell (1984); and Rubery (1988).

32. See Friedman (1977); Rubery (1978); Edwards (1979); Cockburn (1983); Jackson (1984); Lorenz (1984); and Marsden (1992b).

33. This is one of the ways in which processes of job-generation and labor process change (and more broadly the course of industry restructuring) are shaped by the contours of the labor supply, including its geographies (see Chapter 6).

34. For complementary arguments, see Beneria (1979); Mingione (1991); and Picchio (1992).

35. See Lawson (1981); Craig, Rubery, Tarling, and Wilkinson (1982); Craig, Garnsey, and Rubery (1984); and Manwaring and Wood (1985).

36. See Barrett (1980); Phillips and Taylor (1980); Coyle (1982); and Finnegan (1985).

37. See Piven and Cloward (1971); de Brunhoff (1978); Offe and Lenhardt (1984); Block, Cloward, Ehrenreich, and Piven (1987); Moulaert (1987); Rosenberg (1989d); Boyer (1992); Cortés and Marshall (1993); and Théret (1994).

38. For a slightly different perspective, emphasizing the mutual constitution of the state and market, see Block (1994).

39. In Chapter 2, this regulatory function was conceptualized as a series of imperfectly coordinated institutional responses to enduring regulatory dilemmas in the labor market, neither the form nor the consequences of any such regulatory incursions being in any sense guaranteed. This conception is compatible with the regulationist perspective outlined by Boyer (1990b); Jessop (1990a); and Théret (1994).

40. Regrettably, though perhaps predictably, this concern for those at a disadvantage in the labor market did not survive the early 1990s recession in the United Kingdom. They were quickly to slide off the policy agenda as unemployment rose again to over three million. Policy emphasis duly shifted from a concern with the incorporation of marginal workers to their effective exclusion.

41. See Deakin and Mückenberger (1992); Standing (1992); and Streeck (1992).

42. See, particularly, Granovetter and Swedberg (1992) and Amin and Thrift (1994).

43. For education and training, see Harrison (1972); Lee (1991); and Méhaut (1992). For welfare and social insurance, see Deakin and Wilkinson (1991); Rubery (1989); and Toft (1992). For industrial relations, see Friedman (1977); Cockburn (1983); and Marsden (1992b).

44. For example, see Elbaum and Wilkinson (1979); Michon (1992); and Rubery (1992).

45. For example, see Craig, Rubery, Tarling, and Wilkinson (1982) and Villa (1986).

Chapter 4

LOCATING THE LOCAL LABOR MARKET
Segmentation, Regulation, Space

T he term "local labor market" is as ambiguous as it is ubiquitous. Extensively deployed in studies of urban and regional restructuring,[1] the local labor market remains "puzzling to many economists" (Rees and Schultz, 1970, p. 3). For others, it is "theoretically unprincipled" (Warde, 1982, p. 1) or "perplexing and underresearched" (Scott, 1988b, p. 120). Apparently, it has been possible to use the term without having worked out what it really means. Moreover, problems of theoretical underspecification are compounded by seemingly intractable dilemmas of empirical definition and where to draw the edges of commuting zones.[2] In short, the term "local labor market" is used in the absence of both theoretical and empirical specification. As a result, we are poorly placed to ask, let alone answer the question: what is *local* about the local labor market?

So far as established labor market theories are concerned, the answer to this question is an unsatisfactory "not very much." In orthodox theory, the local labor market fulfills a (largely implicit) role as one scale at which equilibration occurs. *Within* local labor markets, labor is viewed as freely interchangeable in line with the dictates of competitive theory and the classical tradition.

The whole of the advantages and disadvantages of the different employment of labour . . . must, in the same neighbourhood, be either perfectly equal or continually tending to equality. If in the same neighbourhood, there was any employment evidently either more or less advantageous than the rest, so many people would crowd into it in the one case, and so many would desert it in the other, that its advantages would soon return to the level of other employments. (Smith, 1976, p. 99)

In the orthodox conception, the atomistic labor market of competitive theory is projected directly onto space, defining localities as social spaces in which rational optimization and free and fair competition constitute the dominant modes of interaction (see Agnew, 1979; Peck, 1989). Just as the same set of labor market rules is thought to predominate across all occupations in a labor market, so each local labor market operates in accordance with a supposedly universal logic.[3] Space is reduced to a passive and merely contextual economic backdrop: the local labor market is portrayed as a container for universal processes (see Clark, 1983).

In orthodox theory, then, the local labor market is no more than a pale geographic reflection of the abstract competitive model. The synchronic reasoning on which this theorization is based lends itself to both aspatial and ahistorical analysis. While orthodox labor economists may write about "modern American labor markets," few are in a position to identify what is specifically modern or American about them (Wright, 1987). In the timeless, placeless world of neoclassical theory, such considerations are irrelevant; "laws of the labor market" exist on a higher plane than the historically and geographically contingent (Reder, 1989). Labor markets operate, as it were, in the heavens, unsullied by events occurring on the ground. The rules of the local labor market also are fixed at this divine scale, operating in the same way, with the same effects, in every place.

Although segmentation theories provide an alternative, they give analytical precedence to historical rather than geographic contingency.[4] Further, though differences in national labor systems and development paths are acknowledged,[5] references to subnational variation tend to be as oblique as they are sporadic (see Wilkinson, 1983, p. 422). The notion of the local labor market has no significant place within segmentation theory, whose modus operandi is based on the historical development of national labor market structures.

However, there is no theoretical justification for conceding geographic contingency *only* at the level of the nation-state. Unevenness in labor market phenomena and forms of regulation may be just as marked *within* nation-states as between them. If labor market structures and processes vary between national spaces, then so also might they vary within these spaces. Similarly, if labor market processes are shaped by their institutional context, then geographic variability in contextual factors (such as labor union conventions or structures of domestic work) is likely to be associated with spatial unevenness in labor markets. Given that in third-generation segmentation theory nontrivial theoretical claims are made on these selfsame grounds of social-institutional contextualization (see Rubery, 1994), then it follows that space needs to be made for the local labor market in the explanatory architecture of fourth-generation segmentation theory.

In rejecting the synchronism and universalism of orthodox theory, segmentation theories also must confront more explicitly the questions of geographic contingency. Working within the Cambridge tradition, Wilkinson (1983) recognized some time ago that systems of labor organization are not all tending towards some optimally efficient form, but that "each system is the unique outcome of its own history," which raises questions about "the conditions leading to the emergence of different productive systems and the terms on which systems coexist" (p. 421). In her recent review of segmentation theories, Rubery (1992) takes issue with the privileged analytical role afforded the nation-state; moving beyond it need not "presume a return to the desocialized universalist approach [but instead requires a recognition that] systems of economic, social and institutional coherence can establish themselves at levels other than those of the nation state, including regions, industries and even organisations" (p. 248). Emphasis on the variability of labor systems over time and between industries and places should be one of the defining principles of segmentation theory.

> The centrality accorded to institutions and social organisation in the segmentation framework necessarily leads to a rejection of the "universalist" approach to economic organisation. Given the diversity of institutional and social organisation, and the historical and embedded nature of these institutions there can be no presumption, as in neoclassical orthodoxy, that there is one best method for organising production. Heterogeneity of economic organisation is not evidence of market imperfection but of the different ways in which societies, industries and regions have developed their integrated systems of social and economic organisation. (p. 247)

Beneath these claims—that labor markets are institutionally embedded and unevenness and diversity are systemic—lurks a set of issues that segmentation theories have yet to confront adequately. If labor market structures, norms, and practices are conditioned by the (uneven) social contexts in which they are embedded, then the functioning of labor market processes will vary across space.[6] Similarly, given that production systems have developed through a variety of evolutionary and path-dependent means,[7] and given that coherence and discontinuity in the labor market occur at a variety of levels within as well as between nation-states,[8] space is likely to matter to the operation of labor markets. The explanatory significance attached to regulatory milieux suggests that the functioning of labor markets is contingent on institutional geographies or the shape of the regulatory terrain.[9] Labor markets *operate* in different ways in different places (though, as Salais and Storper, 1992, observe, conventional economic theory is not well equipped to deal analytically with such variation in economic processes).

While the observation that labor markets function in place-specific ways is consistent with the methodological precepts of segmentation theory, it has not been subjected to serious theoretical or empirical scrutiny.[10] To deal with the spatial dimension—to come to terms with geography—represents an important stage in the development of segmentation theory, representing the basis for a fourth generation (see Table 3.3).

Engagement with geographic contingency marks a step closer to the objective of explaining the workings of *real-world* labor markets. This is important not least because labor markets are *lived* locally (see Hanson and Pratt, 1995); playing a significant role in workers' lives. This matters theoretically because it concerns both how labor markets are experienced and how they work. What is at stake here is the status of the local labor market as a conceptual category. Local labor markets are not containers for universal processes, and the local labor market is much more than an empirical category akin to a data-collection unit or case study area. In fact, the local labor market has a real claim to theoretical status.

This chapter considers the problematic issue of empirical specification, surveying received notions of the local labor market and arguing for moving beyond cartography to focus on processes. It makes two cuts through the question of the theoretical integrity of the local labor market. The first concerns its conjunctural nature as the complex outcome of not one but many intersecting social processes. Given that these processes intersect in different ways in different places, it follows that labor market structures also vary geographically. The second cut is institutional, concerning the different ways in which labor markets are socially embedded and institutionally regulated.

BEYOND LABOR MARKET CARTOGRAPHY

Conventional approaches to the study of the local labor market do not provide a particularly useful starting point for the kind of theoretical treatment proposed here. The problem is that they are weighted down with implicitly orthodox views of labor market processes. However, because they exert such a powerful influence on received notions of the local labor market, they must be considered.

From the Edges . . .

Conventionally, the local labor market has no theoretical status. It has been reduced essentially to a spatially delimited commuting field.

> A local labor market is the geographical area containing those actual or potential members of a labour force that a firm might induce to enter its employ under certain conditions, and other employers with which the firm is in competition for labour. . . . In reality, it is often extremely difficult to specify the boundaries of the local labour market as fringe members come and go, and the boundaries can be extended. . . . A concession to practicality is to decide that a certain area, say a town, is a local labour market, and that firms in the area will be compared with each other while those outside will not . . . Applied research had very often to take such information and statistics as are available and make the best of them. Despite their limitations, it is often possible to undertake an analysis and draw conclusions which appear reliable. (Robinson, 1970, pp. 29–30)

Defined in terms of "average" commuting patterns, the local labor market represents a spatial unit for the collection, analysis, and presentation of labor market data (see Champion, Green, Owen, Ellin, and Combes, 1987). Scare quotes are used deliberately because the process of delimiting local labor markets is dogged with problems. Not only do travel-to-work patterns vary enormously within and between social and occupational groups, they are also highly fluid and substantially overlapping. Those of women, for example, are quite different from those of men, which is not merely an evidentiary quibble but concerns the social construction of home and work (Hanson and Pratt, 1995).[11] Commuting behavior also varies significantly with age, social class, income, ethnicity, and numerous other variables such that the "average commuter"—like the "average worker" of orthodox theory—is in fact a statistical myth, not a social reality.

Such problems make quite intractable the process of delimiting local labor markets empirically. In the final analysis, largely arbitrary judgments must be made about where to draw the line and about the acceptable proportion of workers allowed to cross it.[12] For some, these definitional problems invalidate the local labor market as a unit of analysis. "Far from offering a well-founded proxy for a broad mix of socioeconomic subsystems, the LLMA [Local Labor Market Area] appears to break down under close scrutiny and so may seem to be severely 'reductionist' in its impression of a single set of boundaries onto a multilevel mosaic of differing commuting patterns" (Coombes, Green, and Owen, 1988, p. 314).

No matter how accurate the commuting data or how powerful the computer system into which it is fed, the problems of delimiting the boundaries of local labor markets are insoluble. The task is futile because it amounts to trying to draw a line around complex and dynamic social processes.

. . . to the Center

Social processes rarely rate a mention in what tends to be an arid and technicist debate over the empirical determination of local labor markets. A perverse preoccupation with boundaries has distracted attention from the processes at work *within* local labor markets. As a result, only a handful of studies hold together the concerns of labor market delimitation with those of labor market process.[13]

What matters analytically in the local labor market is not the pattern of commuting per se, but the social context in which such patterns are situated. As Hanson (1992) has observed, "the center of the local labor market is not the CBD [Central Business District], but the relationship between home and work. . . . The home/work relationship is at once deeply gendered and intimately geographic" (p. 576). Home and work are much more than points on an isotropic plane, and the relationship between them amounts to much more than a question of how far people commute and in what direction. This relationship, which as Hanson has stressed lies at the heart of the local labor market, is intricately connected with processes such as the gendering of work, suburbanization, and the social reproduction of labor.

It is from this starting point that Harvey (1989b) conceives the urban process under capitalism.

> The working day, Marx long ago emphasized, is an important unit of analysis. It defines a normal time frame within which employers

can seek to substitute one laborer for another and laborers can likewise seek to substitute one job opportunity for another. I therefore propose to view the "urban" in the first instance as a geographically contiguous labor market within which daily exchanges and substitutions of labor power are possible. Plainly, the geographical extent of that urban labor market depends upon the commuting range, itself determined by social and technological conditions. (pp. 127–128)

From these foundations, Harvey goes on to examine the ways in which the mutual adaptation of labor demand and supply, and the strategies of capital and labor, are conditioned by the urban context (cf. Castells, 1977, p. 445). Under the concept of "structured coherence," he analyzes links between a particular technological mix and a particular set of local social relations in the regulation of urban(izing) accumulation (Harvey, 1989b, pp. 139–140).[14] For Harvey, the urban labor market is both a site of class struggle and a space in which the contradictory imperatives of production and social reproduction collide. Consequently, "a prima facie argument of considerable plausibility can be advanced which sees the urban-regional labor market as a unit of primary importance in the analysis of the accumulation of capital in space" (p. 128).

Quite rightly, Harvey's concern is not with the edges of the labor market, which tend in any case to "fade out over space rather than end at some discrete boundary" (p. 128), but with the processes operating *within* the labor market. His concern, moreover, is not with the local labor market as a *space* in which universal labor market processes operate, but as a *place* in which these processes may be channeled and modified to produce unique local outcomes. Following Storper and Walker's (1983) characterization of labor as "idiosyncratic and place-bound," he concludes that "each urban labor market . . . is unique" (Harvey, 1989b, p. 128).[15] Uniqueness stems from the geographically variable nature of labor qualities, spatial patterns of labor mobilization and utilization and, more broadly, the ways in which structures and practices are institutionalized in different places.

Such work produces a quite different agenda for local labor market research, concerned less with cartography, and more with the geographic foundations of structures, practices, and conventions. For Hanson and Pratt (1992), this means discovering

the role of place in labor market formation. . . . [S]pace is not a *container of* different labor market segments but the *medium through which* different segments are forged. Local labor markets are . . . heterogeneous because of gender, race and class-based segmentation . . . but they are also spatially segmented through the fine-scaled processes defining labor supply and demand. . . . [T]he geography of labor markets is far richer than simply a measure of distance. . . . Individuals' knowledge of the universe of jobs available to them, their expectations about wages and benefits, and the gendering and racialization of jobs all are shaped locally. . . . Job opportunities are more than just dots on a map; they are to a considerable extent socially constructed through the interactions embodying everyday life. (p. 404)

There is a need, then, to put *place* into the local labor market. It is with a view to responding to this challenge that the remainder of this chapter outlines some of the preconditions for a theoretically informed analysis of the local labor market.

THE LOCAL LABOR MARKET AS A CONJUNCTURAL STRUCTURE

Labor markets are immensely complex social structures and, in seeking to explain them, segmentation theories should produce complex, multilayered accounts. They cannot fall back on primitive analogies with the market for cabbages.

One reason for their failure to break the hegemony of orthodox economics is that their stories always seem more convoluted than the pure, competitive model. For example, the labor market cannot be explained solely in terms of a production logic (or the requirements of capitalist production) for this cannot account adequately for the ways in which work is divided along race and gender lines or for the role of state and nonstate institutions in shaping labor market structures and trajectories. Thus, segmentation theories cannot posit a single logic of the labor market to rival the simple elegance of demand-and-supply schedules. Jettisoning the conception of the labor market as a self-regulating commodity market also means abandoning simple descriptions of how labor "markets" operate.

In contrast to the monocausal explanations favored by orthodox economics, third-generation segmentation theories propose a multicausal explanation of labor market structures and dynamics. By implication, the labor market is a product of not one but a variety of generative structures. In Chapter 3, the roots of these generative structures were traced to three families of social processes: production imperatives and the associated design of jobs and structuring of labor demand which follow from them; processes of social reproduction and the structuring of the labor supply; and forces of regulation, with particular emphasis on the role of the state.[16] Each of these generative structures exerts a particular and relatively autonomous influence on the ways in which labor markets are structured. In this sense, labor markets are conjunctural, the combined result of intersecting social processes (Villa, 1986).

Thus, the labor market is a product of the dialectical interplay among generative processes. As with any dialectical process, a priori reasoning—defining relationships and setting the parameters for causal interactions—can go only so far in determining the concrete form of labor markets, as it is impossible theoretically to predetermine the outcome of social articulation. Nonetheless, a place for space needs to be identified in the causal architecture of segmentation theory.

A Method of Articulation

How should this complex process of articulation be dealt with epistemologically? For regulation theorists such as Jessop (1990b), the answer lies in a *method of articulation,* a critical realist framework which recognizes the role played by the "non-necessary interaction of different causal chains [in producing an] outcome whose own necessity originates only in and through the contingent coming together of these causal chains in a definite [*time-space*] context" (p. 11).[17] Underpinning this method, Jessop (1990a) observes, is a critical realist epistemology that has been influential in recent studies of economic restructuring and is consistent with the architecture of segmentation theories.[18] As Iacobacci (1992) has argued, "the institutional SLM [segmented labor market] approach and its nonorthodox practices are . . . based on a critical realist methodology, which is predicated on a search for, and understanding of, the causal mechanisms responsible for generating the observed phenomena of interest" (p. 9).

The goal of critical realist methodology is to understand the "real" causal structures, mechanisms, and processes shaping concrete outcomes. In short, critical realism attempts to understand the "total process" by reference to generative structures and their associated causal properties (Lawson, 1994). Causal properties are embedded in the nature of social structures themselves and are perhaps best understood as tendencies.

> Thus once we understand the natures of copper, trade unions and private enterprise, for example, we can deduce their respective powers to conduct electricity well, defend conditions of workers, or seek profits, etc. Now central to this realist view is the notion that powers may be exercised without being (precisely) manifest in

> actual states of, or happenings in, the world. . . . [This] notion of a
> power that may be exercised and yet unrealised in manifest phe-
> nomena . . . is designated a tendency [or law]. . . . Laws, for the
> realist . . . are ascriptions of tendencies to certain kinds of things—
> they describe how generative structures behave. Now such tenden-
> cies do not lead to regularities at the level of events because they
> will typically be juxtaposed with tendencies of other structures.
> Thus a break-away leaf does not fall to the ground in strict
> conformity with an empirical regularity, for its actual path is
> influenced by aerodynamic, thermal and other tendencies. Yet its
> path is still recognised as being subject to the law of fall understood
> as a tendency, and this explains why the leaf eventually ends up on
> the ground (when it does). (Lawson, 1989, pp. 62–63)

Consequently, the means by which a particular causal process is
realized as an empirical event is conditioned by the *contingent* interaction of this process with other, *simultaneously operating* processes.
For example, whether (and if so, how) the general tendency toward
deskilling is manifest in a specific concrete situation will depend on
the interaction between this process and simultaneous processes, such
as those related to factory regimes, the gender division of labor, and
the regulatory framework (see Burawoy, 1985). This methodology
echoes the Marxian conception of the concrete as the "synthesis of
many determinations, the unity of diverse aspects" (Marx, 1973, p.
101), and underlines the link between realism and dialectical reasoning
(Bhaskar, 1993).[19]

Realism, then, is not predictive. On the contrary, it rejects the
notion of a one-to-one correspondence between cause and effect,
which can be simulated only in experimental, closed systems. Because
human societies are open systems in which a multitude of interacting
causal processes are simultaneously at work, it is impossible to predetermine the empirical effects of a single causal process. In contrast to
the *ceteris paribus* world of the closed system (which does not exist in
social reality), there is a one-to-many correspondence between cause
and effect where a single causal process may generate many possible
outcomes (Lawson, 1989; Lawson and Staeheli, 1990). By definition,
the "laws" of critical realism are tendential, contrary to those Humean
laws which claim universal applicability on the grounds of empirical
regularity and one-to-one correspondence between cause and effect
(Chouinard, Fincher, and Webber, 1984). For realists, laws are statements of necessity rather than universality, essential causal relationships rather than general empirical associations.

Realists seek to relate abstract social structures to the complexity
of concrete situations through the process of abstraction. An attempt

is made to understand the operation of a single causal process by examining it in a one-sided manner, i.e., abstracting from the concrete context (Sayer, 1981; Jessop, 1990b). This is one side of the dual movement required in Jessop's method of articulation: moving from the abstract to the concrete along a single plane of analysis.[20] Complex phenomena (such as the labor market) which are multiply or conjuncturally determined must be "resolved into their causal components; that is resolved into the different effects of various causal mechanisms" (Lawson, 1989, p. 68), which means going beneath the surface of empirical phenomena to uncover the deeper mechanisms and structures at work. Through this process, the realist excavates what Bhaskar (1979) terms "multitiered reality." This often involves the deployment of Kaldorian "stylized facts" or the development of mid-level theoretical devices in order to link the different tiers. An example of such a device is Massey's (1984) conception of the spatial division of labor, a conceptual framework for understanding the relationship between abstract processes of industrial restructuring and the concrete forms of restructuring experienced in different localities. Massey reveals how the *same* general process can produce *different* effects in different places, depending on contingent interactions with preexisting concrete structures and coexisting abstract processes.

While abstraction can provide an effective means of isolating the causal properties and liabilities of particular social processes, it must be remembered that these processes do not operate in the heavens. Rather, they are reconciled on the ground in concrete situations. This is the other side of Jessop's double movement: moving from the simple to the complex through consideration of the articulation of different abstract processes (or planes of analysis). Realist analysis is particularly conscious of the temporal and spatial contexts within which all social processes operate. Where phenomena represent the synthesis of several simultaneous processes—i.e., for a particular empirical outcome to be achieved—a particular conjuncture of causal processes must occur *in time and space.* As Sayer remarks, gunpowder has the causal capacity to explode, but it will only do so in the presence of a spark; for causal powers to be realized, an appropriate set of contingent conditions must exist. "In social systems we have a continually changing jumble of spatial relations, not all of them involving objects which are causally indifferent to one another. So even though concrete studies may not be interested in spatial form *per se,* it must be taken into account if the contingencies of the concrete and the differences they make to outcomes are to be understood" (Sayer, 1984, p. 135).

In labor markets, then, whether (and *how*) the propensities of labor unionists to strike or of employers to discriminate against women are activated (realized as empirical events) depends on the contingencies of time and space. As Lawson (1989) observes, "The employer-worker relationship . . . may be identified as a transhistorical, pancultural feature of human society. But this observation, in itself, abstracts from the numerous variations in the nature of this relationship across time and space, and it is certainly insufficient, for example, to any understanding or explanation of work practices and activities that exist at a specific stage of human evolution *in any particular region or place*" (p. 72, emphasis added).

Segmentation theories can claim no more than a partial understanding of labor market processes and their underlying generative structures if they are not attuned to the essentially contingent manner in which these processes/causal properties are realized as concrete *local* labor market outcomes. For example, it is argued that labor markets are not self-regulated but socially regulated. The means through which this social regulation is achieved are not functionally preordained, but may be realized, or partially realized, through a plethora of institutional forms and regulatory mediations. Like Lawson's falling leaves, the processes of social regulation are tendencies that may be realized in a variety of ways in different concrete situations, adding another layer of indeterminacy to the process by which labor markets are constructed as "syntheses of many determinations."

The Local Construction of Labor Markets

In many ways, the labor market is a classic example of a conjunctural causal structure. It is the product of not just one, convenient and overarching causal logic, but of the indeterminate intersection of several generative structures. In the previous chapter these were grouped into three families of causal processes: production, reproduction, and social regulation. Though intricately and dialectically interrelated, each has unique "laws of motion" in the sense of possessing independent propensities and causal liabilities.

It is in this context that the importance of space needs to be reasserted. It is axiomatic for realists that spatial and temporal context affect the ways in which causal powers are realized in concrete circumstances. This is especially true of conjunctural structures like the labor market. There can be no pregiven rules dictating how diverse causal forces will be reconciled in a particular empirical context, as the triad of causal processes associated with production, reproduction, and social regulation interact in different ways at different times *and in different places*.

For example, the social constitution of the secondary work force varies from place to place depending on how the different tendencies toward segmentation interact. Thus, geographical unevenness in child-care provision, social mores regarding gendered distributions of waged work, labor processes and workplace politics, welfare entitlements, male and female participation rates, and levels of single parenting affect the *local* constitution of the secondary work force. What is often termed the contingent work force is in fact just that: contingent. Its size and composition are contingent on a host of local influences. In fact, there is wide geographic variation in the social composition of the secondary work force. Hiebert's (1994) study of Canadian labor markets reveals the extent to which the ethnic and gender composition of labor market segments is spatially variable, with the same ethnic and gender groups occupying different positions in the secondary labor markets of different cities.[21] This suggests that job filling and labor allocation operate in rather different ways, and certainly with different effects, in different places.[22]

Going a step further, it can be argued that *all labor markets are "locally constituted"* (Peck, 1989). Although a broadly similar set of causal processes underpins the operation of every local labor market, each local labor market is unique in that it reflects a unique intersection of those processes. While all local labor markets are shaped by, say, gendered domestic labor or ethnic stratification and marginalization, "generic" tendencies do not have universally even outcomes. Instead (and as Hiebert's 1994 study, among others, shows) they have variable local outcomes because of the different ways in which they intersect with one another and with other "generic" tendencies, such as those linked to industry restructuring or labor legislation. Further, local labor market differences are magnified by the fact that these processes are not operating on a tabula rasa, but in their realization are affected by the inherited social, economic, and institutional geographies of the labor market. Prior forms of geographically uneven development shape emergent geographies of work and employment (Massey, 1984). For example, Chapter 6 argues that the historically evolved and geographically embedded structures of garment industry labor markets are exerting a significant influence on restructuring strategies in the industry.

Space certainly matters, but how much? Among realists, there are different answers to this question. For Sayer (1984), the difference that space makes is largely restricted to the realm of the concrete; the spatial configuration of social entities affects the way in which causal powers are realized. Others, however, have a stronger argument, insisting that all social structures are spatially constituted and therefore that the "difference that space makes" matters for abstract as well as concrete research (Massey, 1985; Urry, 1985). The nature of social processes may itself be shaped by the way these processes operate through time-space (Urry, 1981) and particular combinations of causal liabilities may generate *local* causal processes (see Duncan, 1989; Cox, 1991). Again, the garment industry can provide an example. The revival of hyperexploitative employment (reminiscent of nineteenth-century sweatshops) in cities like Sydney, New York, and London has been predicated on a particular constellation of circumstances at the urban scale, including pressure on production costs emanating from developing-country competition; the formation of disenfranchised migrant labor pools, resulting from racism in housing and labor markets, and labor and immigration policies; and the presence of the kind of social networks in some inner-city communities on which exploitative labor market relations can be constructed.[23]

Falling between these strong and weak understandings of the relationship between social processes and spatial structures, it may be necessary to consider the role of space at intermediate levels of abstraction. In underspatialized segmentation theory, the notion of the local labor market can be deployed as a mid-level theoretical device in order to specify and understand the ways in which different segmentation processes intersect and are differentially reconciled at the local scale (Peck, 1989). This standpoint is in sympathy with Massey's (1994) conception of the spatial and the social, where the spatial is "constituted by *the interlocking of* 'stretched out' social relations" (pp. 21–22, emphasis added). Local labor markets are different, in part, by virtue of the ways in which their underlying generative structures (for example, relating to class and gender) interact in time-space. This recognition is especially important for interactions at the heart of the labor market, relating to the intersection of labor demand and supply (or, more broadly, between the social structures of production and reproduction). The interrelation between these relatively autonomous social structures—which might be termed the *production-reproduction dialectic*—occurs in different ways in different places, shaping the workings of labor markets in different ways in different places. As the product of complex causal articulations, labor markets are made locally.

INSTITUTIONS AND LOCAL LABOR MARKET REGULATION

An alternative but complementary way of approaching the theoretical status of the local labor market is through the processes of institutionalization and regulation. Contrary to the flawed method of orthodox economics (where the analytical point of departure is an idealized set of pure (labor) market processes, abstracted from context), a substantial body of recent work seeks not only to embed the economy in its social and institutional context, but to take as a starting point the functioning of economic institutions and processes of social regulation.[24] This body of work, which has been labeled socioeconomics,[25] draws inspiration from influences spanning economic sociology, international political economy, institutionalist economics, and regulation theory. Its approach, consisting of tackling institutions head-on rather than as an afterthought, might be characterized as Polanyian (Block, 1990). A unifying characteristic of this wide body of work is its concern to demonstrate ways in which institutions matter to the operation of the economy, while avoiding the pitfalls of functionalism.

Regulation and Space

One of the most influential institutionalist approaches, regulation theory, has not always been successful in negotiating this knife-edged path. Working mostly at the macroeconomic scale, regulation theory posits a strong relationship between the employment relationship, or *rapport salarial,* and the overall pattern of regulation. Boyer (1988b) argues that the regulation approach "is sufficiently broad for us to be able to anticipate *a priori* close linkages between the form of wage/labour relations and the method of regulation. . . . [To a considerable extent] economic crisis and change and change in wage/labour relations determine one another" (p. 10).

Some argue that the cluster of social norms, political practices, and state forms constituting the mode of social regulation (MSR) seems to be ushered in (or established by the state) to meet the needs of the regime of accumulation and, therefore, that these institutions are functionally determined (Teague, 1990; Clark, 1992). This charge is denied by regulationists,[26] who insist that modes of social regulation are formed through indeterminate political and social struggles. The establishment of a harmonious relationship between accumulation and regulation should be understood as a "chance discovery" (Lipietz, 1987; Jessop, 1990a). This process of struggle and happenstance is conditioned by the vagaries of national politics: "struggle and institutionalised compromises tend to arise within the framework of individual nations; hence the methodological priority [in regulation theory] given to . . . *primacy of internal causes*" (Lipietz, 1987, pp. 21–22).

Although regulation theory is best known for wide-ranging historical analysis of generic or archetypal patterns of regulation (such as Fordism-Keynesianism), in principle it is sensitive to institutional variability at a more fine-grained level. As Boyer (1986) has argued, "Whereas members of the regulation school initially thought in terms of homogeneous institutional forms, they refer nowadays to the articulation of *a wide variety of forms existing within the shadow cast by a archetype.* Similarly, research has clearly revealed . . . the diversity of modes of regulation and thus of the exact form of crises" (p. 32). Nevertheless, in ways not dissimilar to segmentation theorists, regulation theorists continue to reduce institutional variability to the historical dimension and to differences between national social formations (Michon, 1992; Peck and Tickell, 1995). There is no reason the regulationist method should be truncated in this way. The complex dialectic between accumulation and regulation can be played out in a variety of ways and, not least, at all spatial scales.

Moreover, because the social structures of accumulation and regulation are relatively autonomous yet bound together dialectically in a necessary relation, the causal liabilities with which they are endowed will be realized in different ways at different times and places, depending on contingent circumstances. What matters is not simply that institutions have effects, but *what* effects they have, *when,* and *where.* Boyer (1990b), Théret (1994), and others call for moving beyond the listing of institutions to considering the precise nature of their interactions and outcomes. For Théret, this means unpacking the mode of regulation so as to understand the causal interrelationships and "regulatory articulations" that link its constituent institutions and social orders (see Figure 4.1). The mode of regulation may be seen as a complex social structure spanning partially independent social orders (such as those related to the family, labor market, and political regime). Discontinuities and tensions among them represent an everpresent threat to social cohesion and are associated with unpredictable and variable outcomes.

> The concept of a mode of regulation can thus be specified topologically: it is in theory a structured set of regimes reproducing social invariables—essentially, capital, State and family—and mediations which simultaneously guarantee their separation and their compatibility; empirically, it is a set of economic and political regimes linked by regimes of mediations. . . . By providing a *map of the social* which helps us locate the various structures of social interests, topology enriches our analysis of class relations, which are no longer reducible to relations of production. (Théret, 1994, pp. 12, 19–20)

Although Théret (1994) and others theorize a complex dialectical terrain, the mode of regulation is typically reduced to "various *na-*

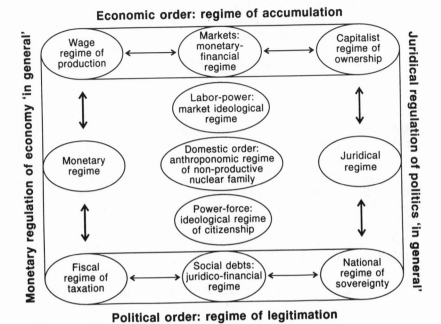

Economic order: regime of accumulation

Monetary regulation of economy 'in general'

Juridical regulation of politics 'in general'

- Wage regime of production
- Markets: monetary-financial regime
- Capitalist regime of ownership
- Labor-power: market ideological regime
- Monetary regime
- Domestic order: anthroponomic regime of non-productive nuclear family
- Juridical regime
- Power-force: ideological regime of citizenship
- Fiscal regime of taxation
- Social debts: juridico-financial regime
- National regime of sovereignty

Political order: regime of legitimation

FIGURE 4.1. The Mode of Regulation as a Social Topology. From Théret (1994), p. 14. © 1994 Routledge. Reprinted by permission.

tional configurations of the mode of regulation" (p. 1, emphasis added). This is true despite the programmatic insight that "the variability of economic and social dynamics within national spaces is a question as central to regulation theory as that of historical variability" (Michon, 1992, p. 226). Regulation theory tends to reduce intranational variability to contingent variability around dominant historical-national "models."[27] In the broad sweep of regulationist analysis, socioeconomic dynamics and forms of regulation associated with particular industries or regions tend to be confined, in Boyer's (1986) telling phrase, to the "shadow cast by an archetype." There is a need to bring subnational regulation out of the shadows, not in ritual celebration of diversity and difference but in order to understand *of what* national systems are constituted.

> The social variability of the forms taken by the wage-employment relationship . . . play[s] a significant role in structuring the [national] system and . . . reflect[s] the heterogeneity of the economic and social space. It is true that institutional forms can be observed

at the national level, but they also exist at regional, sectoral and even firm level. In some countries, the regional level is critical in organisational and institutional terms. . . . Collective agreements, one of the main institutional forms of the wage-employment relationship, are negotiated at sector or firm level, depending on the country in question. (Michon, 1992, p. 227)

In order to strike a balance between mesoinstitutional analysis and regulationists' macroeconomic focus, labor regulation (at, say, the regional and industrial levels) should be understood not only on its own terms, but also in terms of its "mode of insertion" into national and international regulatory structures (Boyer, 1992; Peck and Tickell, 1992). This theme is taken up in Part 2, where Chapter 8 in particular explores the tension between localizing and globalizing forces in labor regulation.

For the time being, there remains scope for progress in the regulationist conception that "economic adjustments cannot be disentangled from social relationships and values, political and economic rules of the game, and more generally the web of interrelated institutions" (Boyer, 1992, pp. 11–12). Although it is undeniable that institutions have economic consequences, connecting *particular* institutions to *particular* economic consequences is immensely problematic, both analytically and politically. Their indeterminacy makes their effects almost as difficult to assign retrospectively as to predict. While analytically perplexing, this is only to be expected. If labor institutions are indeed part of the fabric of the labor market and not an addition to, or corruption of it, it follows that they must be understood as integral to the labor market itself. Labor institutions and the labor market are bound together in a necessary but dialectical fashion, rendering analysis of labor institutions as difficult as it is vital.

Putting Labor Institutions in Their Place

It is perhaps a legacy of orthodox economics that labor institutions should be considered both separate and dispensable aspects of labor market analysis. However, removing them from consideration requires both departing from reality (after all, which labor markets actually do operate indpendently of such "institutional supports" as the family, labor legislation, or work norms?) and willfully misspecifying labor market processes. As an exercise in abstract thinking, it might be compared to attempting to deduce how the human body would function in the absence of its vital organs. On the other hand, it is patently not enough for regulationists or others to rest their case after arguing that institutions matter. *How* they matter is the important question.

> Labour institutions do not represent mere frictions or approxima-
> tions with respect to canonical and unique pure labour markets, but
> they shape individual behaviours and consequently their macro-
> economic outcomes. This does not mean that any labour law will
> succeed in altering the functioning of labour markets, and improv-
> ing the welfare of wage earners: French history is rich with such
> misplaced hopes! Nevertheless, via a trial and error process, the
> institutional building of the wage labour nexus is clear enough:
> compare for example the American and the Japanese configura-
> tions, or alternatively the German and the French ones. In the very
> long run labour institutions matter as regards mobility, wage for-
> mation, technical change and ultimately standards of living. . . .
> [However] the time scale needed for such an adjustment of institu-
> tions and economic dynamics is far longer than economists imagine
> and politicians hope: at least a decade and rather [more] likely a
> quarter of a century . . . but this has been observed for old European
> countries and will not necessarily apply to . . . fast growing Asian
> NICs. (Boyer, 1992, p. 23)

Boyer clearly recognizes not only institutional indeterminacy, but systematic geographic variability. Other regulationists are prepared to go further, recognizing that labor systems can and indeed should be defined at the regional as well as national levels (for example, see Leborgne and Lipietz, 1988). Regional systems, it must be underlined, are more than mere derivations from a (dominant) national model: after all, national models are themselves constituted of a series of regional systems. Several models raised to the status of regulatory trajectories by Leborgne and Lipietz (1988) are in fact *distinctive regional systems* located within the United States. Elsewhere, when Leborgne and Lipietz (1992) describe the U.S. model as a case of flexible neo-Taylorism, it is clear that they are drawing attention only to certain features of a heterogeneous national model. Similarly, while general observations may be made about flexible labor regulation in the United Kingdom, in reality it means quite different things in the deindustrializing North East and postindustrializing South East.[28]

Yet, it is important not to dismiss the national as a level of analysis. What is needed is an approach that takes into account the ways in which local and regional institutional forms are both geographically distinctive *and* embedded in their national and international con-texts.[29] Institutional variability should neither be dismissed as noise around a basic national model (from a top-down perspective) nor used as evidence of the redundancy of national models (from a bottom-up perspective). Rather, it should be understood as part and parcel of a wider process of *spatially uneven development*. The question is not simply which scales are becoming more or less significant, but instead concerns the changing *relations* within and between scales.[30] Here, however, existing theoretical formulations are somewhat lacking. From a top-down viewpoint, many regulationists remain to be convinced of the importance of subnational scales of analysis, being rather defensive about the integrity of their archetypal models and national variants.[31] From a bottom-up perspective, both convention theory and socio-institutionalist theories are comfortable with plant-, industry- and (sometimes) regional-level analysis, but remain rather sceptical about what they see as overgeneralized national models.[32]

This impasse cannot be overcome eclectically. While there are complementarities, there also are significant tensions and conflicts between these approaches (Michon, 1992). The approach favored here is to build down from regulation theory, combining its sophisticated analysis of macroeconomic and macroinstitutional forces with a methodological openness, in principle, to issues of uneven development (Peck and Tickell, 1995). From this standpoint, it is possible to conceive the relationship between labor regulation and uneven development at three levels of articulation.

• The uneven development of the labor market must itself be regulated, in the sense that the national regulatory framework must be capable of containing the tensions and contradictions following from uneven subnational distribution of employment, income, welfare, and access to labor market resources.
• National labor regulation produces uneven geographic results. Legislation and state policies and programs have a wide range of local outcomes, both intentionally and incidentally.
• Processes of labor regulation result contingently in uneven spatial effects due to the way in which they interact with, modify, and are modified by historically prior uses of space (for example, through their interaction with preexisting local institutional legacies and local labor market structures).

Regulating Uneven Development

Uneven development must itself be regulated in that a regulatory system must be capable of containing the *geographic* contradictions of the mode of growth. Each mode of growth tends to be associated with a particular form of uneven spatial development: regimes of accumulation typically exhibit a distinctive spatial core and a distinctive spatial periphery, geographies evident at both the subnational and international scales (Webber, 1982; Lipietz, 1986). For example, during the Fordist era patterns of accumulation and regulation took on a particular *and regionalized* form such that each national variant of Fordism displayed a specific form of uneven spatial development.[33]

Similarly, in the period of political and economic experimentation that has characterized *"after* Fordism," new growth models have emerged, each with its own forms and contradictions of uneven development, though none yet has demonstrated the durability necessary to stabilize under a new regime (Dunford and Perrons, 1994; Peck and Tickell, 1994). For example, Thatcherism proved incapable of sustaining the growth pattern of the late 1980s in the United Kingdom. Though some saw in Thatcherism the seeds of a sustainable mode of regulation (see Jessop, Bonnett, Bromley, and Ling, 1988; Jacques and Hall, 1989), this political-economic project has been unable to contain its internal contradictions. Significant among them are the geographic contradictions popularized in the "North-South divide" debates of the late 1980s, but materially manifest in the collapse of the South East economy in the early 1990s recession (Peck and Tickell, 1992). These geographic contradictions are linked to systemic failures of neoliberal labor regulation in the United Kingdom (see Chapters 7 and 8).

Spatially Uneven Effects

A second aspect of the relationship between social regulation and uneven development concerns the generation of spatially uneven effects, notably by state policies. Policy initiatives produce uneven spatial effects for one of two reasons. First, some are designed explicitly as spatially targeted interventions (for example, regional policies, enterprise zones, and urban and community development initiatives). Second, although other policies may appear to be aspatial, they inevitably produce uneven spatial effects because of the uneven geographic distribution of the affected phenomena (e.g., an industrial sector or social group). For example, uneven geographic effects tend to follow from the operation of such nominally aspatial policies as industry support measures, regulation of competition, welfare systems, taxation structures and incentives, and enterprise policies.

The implicit and explicit spatial tendencies are nontrivial: they produce not only quantitatively but qualitatively different effects in different places. Thus, they raise questions beyond geographic distribution (for example, when region A receives a larger share of national defense expenditure than region B) to what might be termed the social multiplier effects of state policies. For example, because of the role played by defense spending in region A, it evolves a particular labor market structure—with a high but specialized skill base and stable job tenures, which is robust during cyclical recessions but vulnerable to structural decline—along with particular forms of production politics.

Because state policies produce uneven spatial effects, their functions also may be geographically differentiated. For example, in the 1980s, British youth-training programs performed quite different functions in the buoyant economies of the south of England and in the depressed regions of the north (Lee, 1989, 1991). In expanding labor markets with a high rate of vacancy generation, these programs performed the primary function of subsidizing employment by underwriting the costs of recruitment, induction, and initial wages; in depressed areas, their primary function was to contain unemployment in a comparatively cost-effective manner through the provision of alternatives to employment (Peck, 1990c). In Offe and Berger's (1985) terms, the predominant function of these ostensibly aspatial policies was to support labor market inclusion in the buoyant labor markets of the south (where the principal effects concerned redefinition of recruitment and work norms) and labor market exclusion in the depressed north (where the programs were used to redefine the welfare system). Thus, geographies of state policy are important not as deviations from a hypothetical national average, but as an integral aspect of the architecture, functions, and effects of policy. They have material, geographically uneven effects on labor markets.

Similarly though perhaps less evidently, spatially uneven functions and effects characterize nonstate social regulation. The much-vaunted enterprise culture in the United Kingdom has had material and ideological resonances in the South East of England which it never could have had in the deindustrializing north, with its quite different economic structure and political norms (see Keat and Abercrombie, 1991; Shields, 1991). The imposition of an ideology of southern growth— with its emphases on individualism, minimalist and privatized social welfare, entrepreneurship, and self-help—was one of the ways in which the north was subordinated and its problems redefined in the Thatcher era. "Soft" geographies of labor market norms not only reflect but condition the "hard" geographies of labor market structures.

Local Contingencies

The third and final set of relationships between social regulation and uneven development concerns "interaction effects" resulting from the interplay between regulatory processes and historically prior uses of space. These interaction effects result from the essentially contingent ways in which regulatory processes are realized as concrete events in particular local contexts. For example, while a particular policy program may carry immanent tendencies, whether and how those tendencies are realized as empirical outcomes will vary from place to place depending on their interaction with preexisting institutional and economic structures. Again, training policy illustrates the point.

The local consequences of national training policies depend on both the overall architecture of the package and the particular configuration of institutional structures and interests at the local level. For example, the local effects of the British youth-training program (YT) vary partly as a result of the ways in which the institutional machinery of the program interacts with preestablished and uneven institutional structures (such as those developed under earlier policy regimes) and with the particular configuration of labor-capital-state relationships at the local level (Peck and Haughton, 1991). Similarly, the character and policy priorities of the recently established Training and Enterprise Councils (TECs), the business-led agencies charged with labor market governance functions at the local level, are geographically variable. The sources of this variation have been traced to locally distinctive factors such as the institutionalization of business politics, the role of individual business leaders and key companies, the history of relationships between the public and private sectors, the structure of the local economy, and the prior nature of the local training infrastructure (Peck, 1992c). Despite powerful centralizing tendencies in the TEC system (deriving from the national contractual and financial framework within which local TECs operate), these other factors have significant material effects on TEC structures, policy styles, and modes of program development (Emmerich and Peck, 1992; see Chapter 7) and therefore on local systems of skill formation.

To sum up, there is a complex and multifaceted relationship between labor regulation and uneven development, such that it is ill-advised to speak of ubiquitous functions and effects of labor regulation. Rather, these functions and effects vary inevitably from place to place. The geographical anatomy of labor regulatory systems results not only from their internal tendencies and causal liabilities, but also from the complex and indeterminate ways in which these are reconciled with other, simultaneously unfolding social processes and in contingent interactions with prior institutional uses and space. Though general statements can be made about national models of labor regulation, it is important to emphasize that national systems are internally differentiated sectorally, socially, and regionally.

Geographies of Labor Market Governance

Taken together, the above three sources of uneven spatial development in labor regulation provide a basis for *systematically* conceptualizing geographies of labor market governance. The argument thus far can be summed up in four interrelated claims.

1. Labor markets are not regulated by the wage mechanism, but are socially regulated through complex and interrelated socio-institutional processes.
2. The outcome of these processes—a kind of socio-regulatory architecture that performs a vital function in the reproduction of labor markets—is geographically varied.
3. Labor regulation is spatially differentiated not only in terms of institutional form, but also in terms of socioeconomic effects.
4. By implication, the nature of local labor market regulation cannot be determined a priori, but instead is a matter for theoretically informed concrete research.

A logical conclusion is that *labor markets are socially regulated in geographically distinctive ways,* i.e., labor regulation has a significant territorial component. This is not to say that all regulatory institutions are locally based. Rather, it highlights the need to investigate the ways in which processes and institutions of labor regulation are locally articulated. This also is not to say that control of labor regulation resides at the local scale. While there is undeniably some scope for local agency, it occurs within a set of structural parameters relating, for example, to nation-state policies and the imperatives of global accumulation.

What most certainly is being claimed is that there is a theoretically nontrivial *territorial dimension to the process of labor regulation.*[34] This marks an important point of departure from conventional treatments of the local labor market, for it opens up the distinct possibility that labor market *processes* are spatially varied, not necessarily in their causal origins but certainly in the manner of their operation. It also suggests that discussions of national models of labor regulation may be somewhat overgeneralized and that greater attention needs to be paid to their internal, subregional constitution. It has become increasingly clear that universalist labor market theories are insufficiently sensitive to the "geoinstitutional distinctiveness" of local labor market processes.

At the concrete level, a range of *localized institutional forms* underpins the distinctive ways in which local labor markets are regulated. Lash and Urry (1994) have drawn attention to the ways in which the local political environment (pre)conditions patterns of restructuring in the labor market.

> Those preconditions amount to a local configuration of constraints: the economic, such as factory regimes, occupational structure and labour market characteristics (including forms of segmentation); the political, such as the embodied material consequences of previous political action (for example, council housing and the built environment), the vitality of local political associations (measured by party strength and activity), local political ritual and political socialization (including distinctive political histories); and the social/cultural, such as the symbolic boundaries between different "imagined communities." (p. 218)

Focusing on the local institutional configuration of regulatory functions, and merely as an indicative starting point, the following factors are likely to be involved:

- The particular local forms exhibited by national and international regulatory processes with respect to, say, international labor conventions, labor legislation, training and job creation programs, the structure and dynamics of welfare systems, taxation structures, industry policies and competition frameworks.
- Those more locally based processes of labor regulation related, say, to local state policies and programs (for example, in childcare, local economic development, immigration laws, and the delivery of education, training, and social services); local inter-enterprise agreements (such as no-poaching agreements, wage-fixing deals, and industrial relations conventions); local social and industrial mores (relating, for example, to the locally reconciled occupational aspirations and expectations of different social groups, locally acculturated work patterns and rhythms, patterns of labor turnover and work-force attachment, and traditions of solidarism or individualism); and local household structures (with particular reference to gender divisions in domestic and waged labor and the organization of care for the young, sick, and old).

Together, these and other regulatory processes combine to form what can be seen as *distinctive regulatory milieux* at the local level, exerting a significant influence on the structure and dynamics of local labor markets, the social distribution of waged and unwaged work, patterns of recruitment and retention, and therefore, on the ways that local labor markets work.

To take a brief example, while segmentation theories often make much of the fact that the structure and development of labor markets are conditioned strongly by national forms of unionism (see Elbaum and Wilkinson, 1979; Marsden, 1992b), this tacit acceptance of the role played by distinctive, geographically defined systems of labor regulation should be extended to the subnational scale. Labor union structures, traditions and politics (and the labor market effects with which they are associated) not only vary between different national systems, but also exhibit distinctive regional forms.[35] Moreover, the geography of labor unions is not a simple by-product of regional industrial structures, but may be understood as a durable and institutionally embedded phenomenon.

> In the past few years a number of studies of industrial relations in Britain and elsewhere have highlighted the existence of significant regional and sub-regional differences in union recognition, union membership, density, collective bargaining coverage and industrial relations practices. Such geographical variations are evident even in those nations in which industrial relations are ostensibly described as "centralized," that is, dominated by national-level agreements and forms of concertation. Furthermore, these differences remain after geographical variations in industrial structure, firm size, firm ownership, and so on have been taken into account. . . . [W]orkplace industrial relations and labour organization are . . . influenced, both directly and indirectly, by locally-specific factors and circumstances. (Martin, Sunley, and Wills, 1994, pp. 457–458)

This insight throws new light on the role of unionization in local labor market regulation. In a comparatively aspatial way, Marsden's (1992b) reasoning is that, first, union strategies are conditioned by the different structures of (national) labor markets; second, unions' and workers' struggles are central to the construction of institutional and regulatory frameworks; and third, these frameworks are both variable between nation-states and of key explanatory significance in accounting for the operation of labor markets. It follows that regionally distinctive union structures and regionally socialized patterns of collective behavior are performing a comparable function in the institutionalization of local labor markets.[36]

This understanding of the local constitution of social regulatory systems has clear echoes in work on "local labor regimes," emphasizing as it does the variability and significance of local political struggles;[37] distinctive "worlds of production," a convention-theoretic account of systemic geoinstitutional diversity in the organization of production;[38] and "local modes of regulation," attempting to develop regulationist tools of analysis for the local scale.[39] Whatever the term, local regulatory systems are not viewed as locally autonomous or in the exclusive domain of local agency. In a profound sense, they are both embedded in and part of wider regulatory systems (see Massey, 1991; Peck and Tickell, 1995). Analytically, parallel emphasis needs to be placed on *both* the "place-distinctiveness" of systems of labor regulation and on their "place" within national and international networks.

To underscore this point, the distinctive regulatory milieux of the local labor market should be conceived not so much as a locally organized regime or system, but more as a set of local regulatory dialectics. Just as there is a non-necessary interaction between production and reproduction (the production-reproduction dialectic), there are equally important and equally unpredictable regulatory/institutional dialectics articulated at the local scale. Relevant here is the distinction drawn in French political economy between the *rapport salarial,* a term of regulationist origin referring to the configuration of the wage-employment relationship with respect to the exchange, utilization, and reproduction of the labor force, and the *fait salarial,* the specific institutional form exhibited by the wage-employment relationship in particular industries, production complexes, and countries.[40] Due emphasis needs to be placed on the importance of localized *faits salarial,* or the specific local institutional forms exhibited by the wage-employment relationship and the wider organization of the labor market. Concrete research on local labor market restructuring consider the intersection of localized *faits salarial* with the broader processes of uneven development in the *rapport salarial.* It is at this interface that the geographies of the labor market are made, or more appropriately, as Polanyi would have it, instituted.

REINSTATING THE LOCAL LABOR MARKET

This chapter has attempted to lay the foundations for a fourth-generation segmentation approach (see Table 4.1) concerned to underline the spatiality of labor market processes and the variable institutional terrain in and through which they operate. The theoretical status of the local labor market has been rethought in an attempt to establish a rationale and framework for local labor market studies. This task has been tackled by way of two theoretically derived cuts through the local labor market. The first explored, at an epistemological level, the relationship between labor market processes and space, drawing on critical realism for a conception of the local labor market as a causally conjunctural social structure. The spatiality of the *production-reproduction dialectic* was emphasized. The second cut took regulation theory as its point of departure to argue for a focus on the distinctive ways in which labor markets and their regulatory infrastructures interrelate, and are institutionalized, at the local level. The spatiality of *regulatory dialectics* was underlined. Together, these arguments suggest that local labor markets are both constructed (in terms of the concrete working out of generative forces underpinning them) and socially regulated (in terms of the distinctive regulatory milieux formed in and around them) in locally specific ways. If each local labor market represents a unique geographic conjuncture of labor market processes,[41] it follows that the institutional form of the wage-employment relationship—the *fait salarial*—also will take on a locally distinctive character. The kind of dialectical analysis called for here *requires* sensitivity to the inherent spatiality of labor market relationships.

These largely theoretical arguments have been marshaled with a view to carving out territory for local labor market research. For too long, local labor market studies have been preoccupied with sterile questions of delimitation to the effective exclusion of issues of process. In effect, these studies have occupied a theoretical vacuum. An underlying theme of this chapter has been to construct a case for shifting analytical focus away from the "edges" of the local labor market and toward its "center," where the concern should be less with commuting patterns or where local labor markets "stop," and more with social regulatory processes and how local labor markets "work." This opens up an alternative and theoretically relevant agenda for local labor market research.

This alternative agenda should be both theoretically informed and theoretically informing. Local labor market studies should elucidate the geographically varied forms and consequences of supposedly universal labor market processes, which is not to undermine the status of general labor market processes (such as employment segregation or wage regulation), but rather, to press the case for their analysis at a somewhat lower level of abstraction. A strength of local research is its capacity to throw light on the functioning of labor market processes

Table 4.1. Toward a Fourth-Generation Segmentation Approach

	Causal bases of labor market segmentation		
	Labor demand and the labor process	Labor supply and social reproduction	The state and social regulation
First generation	Dualism caused by increasing demand for skill specificity deriving from technical change but conditioned by industry structure	Feedback mechanisms: behavioral traits develop or are reinforced by labor market experience	
Second generation	Dualism a product of labor process–control strategies Segmentation as a historical tendency linked to the strategies of monopoly capitalist firms in the context of long-run changes in the pattern of accumulation	Exploitation of racial and gender divides and uneven economic development to counteract work-force solidarism	
Third generation	Diverse demand-side causes of segmentation (factionalized industry structures, imperatives of labor control, workplace struggles, variable product market conditions, divergent technological development, etc.) are afforded explanatory primacy, but take an institutional and social form	Structure and dynamics of the sphere of social reproduction exert relatively autonomous influence on forms of segmentation Social structuring of labor supply not reducible to demand-side causes, but related to a range of relatively autonomous factors	State actions and institutional forces are afforded central explanatory role Social regulation of labor market seen as a necessary but contradictory process

(cont.)

Table 4.1. *(cont.)*

	Causal bases of labor market segmentation		
	Labor demand and the labor process	Labor supply and social reproduction	The state and social regulation
Fourth generation	Emphasis on the non-necessary and geographically variable interaction between the structures and dynamics of labor demand (and the labor process) and the structures and dynamics of labor supply (and the sphere of social reproduction) Labor segmentation as a locally constituted process deriving from unique intersections of labor demand structures and labor supply structures *The production-reproduction dialectic*		Investigation of the spatially varied institutional forms, functions, and effects of social regulation, tracing connections to uneven (but specifically local) labor market structures and dynamics *The regulatory dialectic*

in different local institutional contexts, and to generate explanations rooted in the scale at which labor markets are lived—the local. These arguments amount to a plea for a mid-level theorization of the local labor market, deployed to explain discrepancies between general labor market processes and their (variety of) local outcomes. In this locally sensitive approach lies the prospect for a more nuanced theory of labor segmentation and regulation. In both these bodies of theory, space has been reserved for geographic contingency at the level of the nation-state, but no such role is acknowledged for regional and local contingency. At the theoretical level, this myopic view is not defensible; at the concrete level, it sits uneasily with what is known about the pronounced subnational variability in labor market structures, dynamics, and institutions.

If the local labor market is to be raised from the lowly status of a case study area to that of mid-level theory, the pressing need is for theoretically informed, concrete research at the local level. While there are numerous suggestive studies (for example, concerning the operation of rural labor markets, the link between labor markets and local politics, the construction of gender divisions in local labor markets, and urbanization and the labor market),[42] theoretically informed, local labor market research remains for the most part in its infancy. Part 2 attempts to move toward this goal through more empirically grounded investigations. Each chapter takes up a different question pertinent to local labor market structuration, building in each instance from a major piece of related work in the field and exploring the local constitution and regulation of local labor markets.

NOTES

1. For example, see Clark (1986); Cooke (1986); Lovering (1989); Moore and Townroe (1990); and Heinelt (1992).

2. For discussion of the technical and conceptual issues, see Clark, Gertler, and Whiteman (1986); Coombes, Green, and Owen (1988); and Peck (1989).

3. For attempts to deal with the complexity of local labor markets within the neoclassical paradigm, see Eberts and Stone (1992) and MacKay, Boddy, Brack, Diack, and Jones (1971).

4. The case for a contingency approach is developed by the Labour Studies Group (1985). For advocacy of historical analysis, see Gordon, Edwards, and Reich (1982).

5. For example, see Maurice, Sellier, and Silvestre (1986); Rosenberg (1989d); Castro, Méhaut, and Rubery (1992b); and Rubery (1994).

6. See Maurice, Sellier, and Silvestre (1986); Salais and Storper (1992); and Martin, Sunley, and Wills (1994).

7. See Wilkinson (1983); Castro, Méhaut, and Rubery (1992b); and Storper (1995).

8. See Purdy (1988); Boyer (1992); and Rubery (1992).

9. See Marsden (1986) and Michon (1992).

10. In practice, segmentation theory remains preoccupied with explorations of the national and national sectoral diversity of labor market forms. Thus far, it replaces methodological universalism with methodological nationalism.

11. Cf. Bowlby, Foord, and McDowell (1986); Hanson (1992); and Hanson and Pratt (1992).

12. For discussion, see Goodman (1970) and Ball (1980).

13. Among the best examples are Lever (1979) and Scott (1984, 1988b). For the most comprehensive and sensitive treatment, see Hanson and Pratt (1995).

14. Cf. Rubery (1992, p. 248).

15. This claim is all the more significant given Harvey's (1987) well-known skepticism toward assertions of geographic uniqueness.

16. In the genealogy of segmentation theories, work on each of these three families of processes has followed in more or less chronological sequence, beginning with the dualist theories' emphasis on production imperatives and the demand side of labor market (see Table 3.3). Dualist theories placed the burden of explanation on technological requirements and divergent development in industry structure; the radical school went a step further, situating dualism within a broader historical context and drawing attention to the role of labor segmen-

tation as a control strategy. The response to this demand-side orientation in early segmentation theory came in the form of assertions of the importance of collective action and of the wider sphere of social reproduction in the determination of labor market structures. These supply-side structures, while strongly conditioned by the demand side, are relatively autonomous from the specific nature and requirements of the job structure. Due to this relative autonomy, the labor market *cannot* be self-governing; thus, the incorporation of labor becomes an intractable regulatory problem.

17. Epistemologically, Jessop's (1990b) method requires a form of theory construction based on a dual movement: from the abstract to the concrete (along a single plane of analysis) and from simple to complex (focusing on the articulation of different planes of analysis in concrete situations) (p. 11).

18. For realist work on industrial restructuring, see Morgan and Sayer (1988); Sayer and Walker (1992); Massey (1994); and Pratt (1995). On labor segmentation, see Storper and Walker (1983, 1984) and Iacobacci (1992).

19. Edgley (1990) defines Marxian dialectics as a method that regards "concrete reality [as] a unity, but a differentiated unity in which the elements are all essentially interrelated and integrated but not reducible to one another. . . . Reality is a unity that is specifically contradictory, and it is the conflict of opposites within unity that drives reality onwards in a historical process or progressive change" (p. 117; cf. Stedman Jones, 1990). Similarly, Wilde (1991) says that it is "when considering the *moving world* that Marx uses dialectical contradictions to denote opposing tendencies in the system" (p. 290, emphasis added).

20. See note 17.

21. For a parallel analysis of Australian cities, see Morrison (1990).

22. Hiebert (1994) concludes that "there are important geographical variations in labour-market segmentation that are ignored by economists" (p. 20).

23. For evidence on this, see Massey (1984) and, in particular, Sassen (1991). Further discussion can be found in Chapter 6.

24. In particular, see Granovetter (1985); Boyer (1990b); Zukin and DiMaggio (1990); Mendell and Salee (1991); Granovetter and Swedberg (1992); Sayer and Walker (1992); Amin and Thrift (1994); and Lash and Urry (1994).

25. See Grabher (1993) and Amin and Thrift (1995).

26. Specifically, see Lipietz (1988) and Théret (1994). For the wider debate, see Peet (1989); Jessop (1990a); Brenner and Glick (1991); and Hirst and Zeitlin (1991).

27. For a discussion of these issues with respect to the problematic case of Japan, see Nohara and Silvestre (1987) and Peck and Miyamachi (1994).

28. See Hudson (1989); Peck and Tickell (1992); and Massey (1993b).

29. See Peck and Tickell (1995).

30. See Gertler (1992); Jessop (1993); and Dicken (1994). See also Chapter 8.

31. See Boyer (1990b).

32. See the socio-institutionalist approaches of Marsden (1986) and Maurice, Sellier, and Silvestre (1986), and the convention theory arguments of Salais (1992) and Salais and Storper (1992).

33. See Martin (1988); Florida and Jonas (1991); and Dunford (1993).

34. This is certainly evident in the significant body of empirical evidence for spatial variability in labor market structures and institutions. See Clark and Gertler (1983); Moulaert (1987); Nohara and Silvestre (1987); Leborgne and Lipietz (1988); Scott (1988b, 1988c); Fincher (1989); Storper and Walker (1989); Storper and Scott (1990); Streeck (1992); Haughton, Johnson, Murphy, and Thomas (1993); Perulli (1993); and Martin, Sunley, and Wills (1994, 1996). For a theoretical argument, see Jonas (1996).

35. See Peet (1983); Massey and Painter (1989); Perulli (1993); and Martin, Sunley, and Wills (1994, 1996).

36. A parallel example of localized forms of labor market institutionalization is provided by policy responses to unemployment and labor market exclusion, which need to be sensitive to the particular *local* ways in which barriers to employment are constructed and maintained (Haughton, Johnson, Murphy, and Thomas, 1993).

37. See Herod (1991b); Jonas (1992, 1996); and Martin, Sunley, and Wills (1994).

38. See Salais and Storper (1992).

39. See Peck and Tickell (1992, 1995) and Goodwin, Duncan, and Halford (1993).

40. See Maurice, Sellier, and Silvestre (1986); Boyer (1990b); and Michon (1992).

41. See Harvey (1989b); Peck (1989); and Storper and Walker (1989).

42. Examples of theoretically informed research on local labor markets include work on rural economies (Bradley, 1984; Day and Murdoch, 1993); local politics (Warde, 1989; Jonas, 1992; Beynon, Hudson, and Sadler, 1994); gender divisions (McDowell and Massey, 1984; Nelson, 1986; Bagguley, Mark Lawson, Shapiro, et al., 1990; Hanson and Pratt, 1995); and urbanization (Broadbent, 1977; Scott, 1988b).

PART 2
Placing Labor Markets

Chapter 5

FLEXIBILIZING LABOR

Insecure Work
in Unstable Places

Recent controversies around post-Fordism, flexible specialization, and flexible accumulation have been at their most acrimonious around the issue of labor (see Amin, 1994). The underlying analyses in these much-popularized transition models hinge on assertions about changing uses of labor: reorganized (and flexible) labor processes, restructured (and flexible) labor markets, new (and flexible) applications of shop-floor technology, and so on. Invariably, too, alternative models of economic organization are differentiated by their implications for labor: offensive and defensive labor regulation, individualized and collectivized labor relations, qualitatively and quantitatively flexibilized labor processes, and so on.[1]

Although these alternatives are often cast as historical branching points (e.g., between neo-Taylorism and flexible specialization or between the "high" and the "low roads" to flexibility), increasingly they are represented as geographic alternatives. Not only are there Brazilian, Japanese, and German ways, but there also are numerous local and regional variants such as the Emilian, Californian, and Naples models. Leborgne and Lipietz (1988) have underscored the important methodological point.

> Types of professional or interfirm relations may differ across sectors, even in the same region. . . . But, according to our experience, a hegemonic model—a combination of these types of relations—is

more likely to appear at the national or regional level. A model of development is *territorial*: social relations of the same kind spread across sectors in the same territory. This is because a model is based on cultural, social, ideological habits and behaviours, which crystallize in national or regional political settlements. (p. 275)

By implication, it is necessary to conceptualize economic restructuring not only in terms of successive phases or regimes of development, but also in terms of historically *coexistent and competing* local alternatives.

This chapter examines the relationship between labor, flexibility, and place. Concentrating on the territorial organization of labor markets, it suggests a rather different take on flexibility. Its labor market focus requires careful consideration of the wider social and institutional contexts in which flexibility strategies are pursued, resisting attempts to read off societal-level conclusions from changes in the organization of the labor process.

The point of departure is Scott's (1988c) seminal work on labor and spatial agglomeration,[2] where labor market processes are afforded an important role in generating the renewed tendencies toward industrial agglomeration believed to underpin the formation of modern flexible production systems, or "new industrial spaces." As the social division of labor deepens under flexible accumulation, Scott argues, labor market forces and the logic of intensified interfirm transactions combine to unleash powerful centripetal tendencies (p. 31). Although persuasive, his thesis remains by his own admission partial, based on a narrow and somewhat economistic conception of labor market processes. However, it has opened up issues of production and labor market restructuring in ways which are sensitive to their territorial constitution.

Emphasis here is placed on labor reproduction and control, hence on the fundamentally contradictory relationship between labor and agglomeration. Agglomeration may play a part in reducing costs, in a ceteris paribus world, but the social and political ramifications must also be taken into account. These in fact are indicative of nascent regulatory crises in many of the new industrial spaces of rapid growth and flexibilized labor relations. The new industrial spaces may be at the leading edge of capitalist expansion at the present time, but their labor markets are also exposing the contradictions of this fragile mode of growth. Celebration of the growth potential and flex-efficiency of the new industrial spaces may be premature, given the shaky institutional foundations on which some of them are built.

Three implications of Scott's analysis are evaluated, namely, the definition of labor market flexibility, role of labor segmentation, and constitution of new industrial spaces. This is followed by an examination of the contradictions of labor market flexibility, focusing on those associated with the imperatives of labor control and skill formation. The next section of the chapter explores several different forms of local labor market flexibility and their associated regimes of labor regulation, again with reference to skill formation. On the basis of this analysis, the chapter is concluded with some observations on the role of institutions in local labor markets and regional growth.

LABOR, FLEXIBILITY, AND AGGLOMERATION[3]

In *Metropolis* (1988b) and *New Industrial Spaces* (1988c), Scott seeks to specify the linkages between industrialization, urban structure, and the formation of territorial production complexes. He assigns a "strong analytical privilege to the functioning of the production apparatus and its expressive effects in the division of labor" (1988b, p. 2). Although much of his analysis is pitched at mesoscale (i.e., at the level of the production complex), his argument is rooted in the institutionalist theory of the firm (pp. 29–33). Following Coase (1937) and Williamson (1975, 1985), he pursues a transaction costs approach in which the boundaries of the firm and configuration of the production system are understood as an outcome of the relative costs of internal (intrafirm) and external (market) transactions. For Scott (1988c), the virtue of this approach is that

> it allows us to seize production in general (a confusing assemblage of labor processes, technologies, physical stocks, and so on) as a coordinated system of internal hierarchies and external markets. . . . [Moreover] since there is not in reality a sharp break between internal (hierarchical) and external (market) relations, but an irregular continuum extending over a variety of intermediate forms (joint ventures, partnerships, quasi-vertical integration, and so on), we can see production as a complex but rationally comprehensible organizational structure rooted in the polarities of the firm and the market. (p. 24)

Scott deploys transaction costs economics to establish the incipient agglomeration tendencies seen as inherent in contemporary capitalist industrialization. An important outcome of restructuring, he asserts, is the revitalization of spatial agglomeration economies, resulting in the creation of new industrial spaces. The case is made as follows:

- Forces in contemporary capitalism, which he captures under the rubric of the transition from Fordism to flexible accumulation, are engendering a need for enhanced flexibility in production systems (Scott and Cooke, 1988, pp. 241–242). Fragmentation of consumer markets and heightened levels of business uncertainty are two key factors behind this shift (Scott, 1988b, pp. 35–37).

- The imperative of flexibility is stimulating a process of dynamic vertical disintegration in the production system, as companies seek to enhance their flexibility and responsiveness by externalizing many of the functions previously performed within the firm. This amounts to more than breaking up established production chains. Because flexible production systems are expansionist and innovation-rich, new and independent forms of specialist production emerge as the system expands (Scott, 1988c, pp. 27–28).

- In this deepened social division of labor, individual producers become locked into "networks of extremely malleable external linkages and labor market relations" (Scott, 1988a, pp. 174). The redrawing of the boundaries of individual production units, and the concomitant downsizing and narrowing of organizational specialities, brings about heightened interdependence in the production system as firms become deeply embedded in complex webs of interorganizational transactions.

- The twin requirements of minimizing external (interfirm) transaction costs and establishing appropriate labor market relations bring about a marked agglomeration of economic activity. New industrial spaces, then, coalesce around "dense networks of transactional interrelations" (Scott, 1988c, p. 31) and are associated with the establishment of new local labor market norms, based on numerical and functional flexibility (Scott, 1988a, p. 177; 1992, p. 266).

Scott conceives new industrial spaces as highly integrated, territorial production complexes the logic of which is *collective,* representing more than the simple outcome of aggregated individual behaviors (Scott, 1988b, p. 42; 1988c, p. 29). Of particular concern is the collective logic associated with the functioning of labor markets, as the search for flexibility in production is paralleled by that for flexibility in the labor market. Three strategies for labor market flexibility are identified (Storper and Scott, 1990, p. 575).

- There is an attempt to individualize the employment relation, moving away from (institutionalized and therefore comparatively rigid) collective bargaining and negotiation systems in key areas such as wage-setting.

- Firms are seeking to achieve enhanced internal flexibility through labor process changes such as multiskilling and reduced job demarcation.
- External flexibility is being sought through strategies (such as the deployment of part-time and temporary workers) that enable rapid quantitative adjustments of the labor intake in accordance with fluctuating production needs.

These strategies generate increased polarization and segmentation. More often than not, they are associated with the diminution of labor market security and establishment of regressive work norms (Scott, 1988a; Storper and Scott, 1990). Exceptionally high levels of labor turnover (even among upper-tier workers), low rates of union density, deinstitutionalization of worker protection, and the presence of a large, contingent labor pool of politically marginalized workers (such as immigrants, women, and agricultural laborers) are characteristic of flexible labor markets in the new industrial spaces.[4] Thus, these labor markets combine high levels of flexibility with deep segmentation.

In the labor market, too, significant agglomeration economies can be obtained. "All such labor market fluidity is enhanced as the size of the local pool of jobs and workers increases" (Scott, 1988a, p. 177). This echoes Marshall's (1890) classic account of industrial districts, emphasizing the benefits of a "constant market for skill" and the advantages

> which people following the same skilled trade get from near neigh-bourhood to one another. The mysteries of the trade become no mysteries; but are as it were in the air, and children learn many of them unconsciously. . . . And subsidiary trades grow up in the neighbourhood, supplying it with implements and materials, organ-izing its traffic, and in many ways conducing to the economy of its material. . . . [These] industries, devoting themselves each to one small branch of the process of production, and working it for a great many of their neighbours, are able to keep in constant use machin-ery of the most highly specialized character; and to make it pay its expenses. (p. 332)

For Scott, the search for flexibility places a premium on economies of agglomeration, and the need for flexible labor is seen as engendering spatial agglomeration. Agglomeration economies follow from five interrelated labor market conditions.[5]

- Labor turnover rates tend to correlate positively with the overall size of the local labor market. Given the strong random component in job separations and accessions, these flows are more likely to converge toward equilibrium in large labor markets than in smaller ones. The enhanced predictability of labor market flows allows firms to fine-tune their labor utilization to changing production needs: large, volatile labor markets provide a ready supply of workers who can be hired as and when they are needed.

- Workers are better able to adjust to unstable job tenures (hence, less likely to out-migrate) in large, turbulent labor markets where the supply of alternative jobs is plentiful, enabling workers to move from job to job with relative ease and rapidity.
- Information and search costs tend to fall as the size of the local labor market increases. High rates of job changing and filling place a premium on efficient job search mechanisms. The greater the size of the labor market, the lower the marginal cost of search activities (such as newspaper advertising for firms or visits to a labor exchange for workers).
- Workers accustomed to secondary labor markets tend to be drawn into large, volatile labor markets, where their chances of finding (and refinding) work are highest. In turn, employers of such labor gravitate toward the spatial core of their preferred labor supply. Consequently, there is recursive relationship between the tendencies for firms to cluster around appropriate labor supplies and for workers' residences to cluster around major centers of employment opportunities.
- As workers become acclimatized to particular work rhythms and develop appropriate labor market strategies, processes of local socialization tend to reinforce agglomeration tendencies. Over time, patterns and processes of labor market behavior become socially embedded and, to a certain extent, self-perpetuating.

In these ways, labor market agglomeration tendencies become mutually reinforcing and self-sustaining. Labor market forces interact with those associated with the restructuring of production systems. Economic change and agglomeration are mutually conditioning.

Thus, on the one side, the social division of labor provokes spatial agglomeration as a way of lowering external transaction costs; on the other side, agglomeration encourages further social division of labor and in-migration of new producers precisely because it lowers these costs; and so the cycle of action and reaction continues until its inner energy is exhausted. . . . With the rise of any industrial agglomeration, local labor markets are set in motion, and they too help boost processes of spatial concentration and growth. (Scott, 1988c, p. 33)

For Scott (1988c), the most theoretically significant conjuncture at which the inner energy of cumulative causation breaks down is the transition between regimes of accumulation. Each regime of accumulation is held to have a distinctive geographical logic: the shift to flexible accumulation is associated with the emergence of a new form of uneven development. Accordingly, the locational logic of flexible accumulation consists of twin tendencies toward, first, the active *evasion of Fordist labor pools* (with their politicized working class, institutionalized labor processes, and high cost structures), and second, the selective *re-agglomeration of production* in locations insulated (either socially or, more often, geographically) from the core regions of Fordist industrialization (pp. 11–15). Thus, empirical examples of new industrial spaces range from enclaves within the old manufacturing regions, through suburban extensions of major metropolitan areas, to craft communities, and from established central business districts to rural communities with an agricultural heritage.[6] Significantly, through a kind of backwash effect, innovative production and labor market norms established in new industrial spaces are imported back into the devalorized old industrial regions as the new regime of accumulation becomes established (p. 108). Through this process, flexibility becomes the tendentially dominant mode of organization in both production systems and labor markets.

New Flexibility?

A central tenet of Scott's argument is that increasing flexibility in the production system is related to increasing flexibility in labor markets. Trends such as the rise in relative and absolute size of contingent work forces (comprising those employed on a temporary, part-time, or contract basis) and the shift toward decentralized bargaining over pay and working conditions are indeed indicative of increased labor market flexibility *of some kind*.[7] However, the question how to *interpret* such changes, theoretically or politically, is intensely problematic.[8] Several interpretive difficulties are readily apparent.

- Cyclical, temporary, and ephemeral phenomena must be distinguished from structural change over the long term. Flexibility strategies may be only a short-term reaction by firms to the loosening of labor markets, permissive labor legislation, and high unemployment.

- The search for flexibility must be understood in terms of the historical and geographic evolution of particular labor market and production systems. There is a need to clarify what is new about labor market flexibility and how its forms and causes might vary over space.
- It is necessary to establish the extent to which such changes relate to (and further modify) the balance of power in the labor market. The capital-labor relation is likely to be restructured in complex ways by flexibility strategies.
- Instances of and strategies for labor market flexibility must be interpreted in light of the restructuring of the state's regulatory systems and with regard to contemporary political discourses. To seek to understand or portray flexibility strategies as purely economic is to overlook the diverse ways in which they interpenetrate with parallel developments such as welfare reform, labor market deregulation, and the neoliberalization of political rhetoric.

In a study of labor market restructuring in old industrial regions, Hudson (1989) argues that many phenomena interpreted as evidence of rising flexibility are in fact manifestations of quite different processes. The causes of increasing labor market flexibility here do not lie with production efficiency in a narrow sense, but instead may be traced to the erosion of the power of organized labor, the imposition of neoliberal, anti-labor regulatory systems, the presence of a permanent pool of the long-term unemployed, and the need to restructure established (Fordist and pre-Fordist) industries. Hudson concludes that labor market flexibility reflects not so much the emergence of a new regime of flexible accumulation as a "reworking of existing accumulation strategies as capital takes advantage of its greatly enhanced strength vis-à-vis labour on the market" (p. 25). Labor market flexibility may thus be traced to a variety of causes and it has different meanings in different places.

To be sure, there is no straightforward connection between industrial structure and labor market structure, let alone between flexibility in production and flexibility in labor markets. Indeed, surface manifestations of flexibility and fragmentation—as such vertical disintegration or the breaking up of collective labor market structures—are often associated with powerful tendencies toward the further concentration of social capital and the extension of oligopolistic control.[9] Disintegration and fragmentation on the surface often reflect underlying processes of integration and centralization. This is certainly true of labor markets, where many of the "new" flexibility strategies (individualized employment relations, plant-level pay bargaining, incentives-based contracts) are in fact long-established means of deepening control over the labor process and commodifying labor market relations. As a result, they look more like (a roll-back of) old forms of exploitation than new forms of flexibility. Self-evidently, it is more appropriate to analyze exploitation as a social relation than a transaction.

Far from being a recent phenomenon associated with the rise of flexible accumulation, flexible labor markets have a long history (see Chapter 6). Indeed, different forms of flexibility have been associated with different phases of capitalist development (see Gordon, Edwards, and Reich, 1982). There is a need to clarify, first, which aspects of contemporary flexible labor markets are *residuals* of earlier phases of accumulation; second, which are the product of *contingent conditions,* including those suggested by Hudson (1989); and third and most important, which are *necessary* features of the posited emerging regime of flexible accumulation. Inevitably, these three processes overlap and interact: part of the seesawing logic of the historical geography of capitalist industrialization involves exploitation of economically disenfranchised labor pools created in earlier periods.[10] Firms also opportunistically seize upon changing external conditions (such as the tendency for cyclical recession to reduce the power of labor unions) in their efforts to restructure the labor process.[11] The point at issue is not the manner in which flexible accumulation can take hold initially in a particular labor market (for example, the form in which it engages with the disorganized immigrant labor pools of inner Los Angeles), but rather how it is sustained and, most important, reproduced.

Given that a plausible argument can be advanced that flexible labor markets are no more than manifestations of relatively short-term phenomena (such as high levels of unemployment, the imposition of regressive employment policies, and capitalist plundering) the question of their reproducibility as political-economic structures is particularly important. There may indeed be significant obstacles to sustainable labor market flexibility; drawing on the French experience, Michon (1987) has demonstrated structural limits to external flexibility (as pursued through strategies such as subcontracting and homework).

[Once] personnel management and/or the supply of labour and/or the training and supervision of the workforce are involved, the externalisation of activities runs up against some particular difficulties . . . linked to the control of the labour force. . . . [The] need to control the workforce seriously restricts the use of externally supplied manpower. More generally, the desire to retain control over all manufacturing processes, and to avoid any sort of dependence on other individual capitals considerably restricts the scope for implementing an extreme division of labour. In other words, the processes in the division of labour seem to be doubly dependent, first, on the processes of capitalist competition, and second on the need to control the workforce, and thus on the processes that determine the "rapport salarial." (pp. 42–43)

While external flexibility favors some forms of labor control (for example, breaking up collective labor structures), it simultaneously undermines others (for example, direct supervision and firm-specific skill formation). Whether these fragile labor market relations can be reproduced in the medium term is debatable.

The contradictions of flexibility strategies are not confined to external flexibility: internal flexibility also is problematic. Through strategies such as multiskilling, broadening of job categories, and formation of flexible work teams, firms are seeking to enhance the qualitative or functional flexibility of their core work forces (Atkinson, 1987). However, restructuring firms' internal labor markets may have undesired effects.[12] First, the formation of multiskilled core work forces, with bundles of specialist skills crucial to continuing production, can afford this group of workers substantial bargaining power vis-à-vis management. Second, multiskilling may also increase the tradability of core workers' skills on the external labor market, with the result that labor turnover increases and firms become reluctant to reinvest in training. Ensuing wage inflation in the local labor market may stimulate even higher rates of mobility among skilled workers.

If appropriate mechanisms of labor control and reproduction are not set in place, flexible labor markets will begin to break down. The technopoles of southern California have already displayed signs of "market failure" in their training systems (Scott and Paul, 1990), while wage inflation became a serious problem in British growth centers such as Cambridge (Crang and Martin, 1991). Internal economies of scale, associated with training and the long-term and risk-laden nature of skill investments, suggest that the process of skill formation will always be problematic in labor markets composed of networks of small interdependent firms, particularly if the degree of interfirm competition is high (Peck and Haughton, 1991). Critical to the effective operation of any system of skill formation is the establishment of an appropriate system of social regulation. Indeed, the existence of such an institutional system is a measure of "maturity" in a local labor market (Scott, 1988b, p. 182), but few coherent systems are currently in place in the growth centers of either Europe or North America.[13]

Structural flaws are evident in the process of labor reproduction within flexible labor markets. Certainly, the model of the flexible labor market which is based on institutional deregulation and high levels of external flexibility seems particularly crisis-prone. Unless workable political and economic mechanisms for the reproduction of flexible labor markets can be established, these economic structures may prove to be no more than transitory economic phenomena, the combined product of short-term plundering strategies on the part of capital and political opportunism on the part of neoliberal nation-states. In the flexibility debate, greater care needs to be taken in distinguishing between reproducible social structures and (possibly unsustainable) experimental strategies.[14]

New Segmentation?

New industrial spaces tend to be characterized by deepening labor market segmentation and income polarization (Storper and Scott, 1990). The search for enhanced flexibility induces firms to restructure primary sector labor markets and to export certain labor functions to the expanding secondary sector. Thus, in accounts of new industrial spaces, labor market flexibility and labor market segmentation are seen as evolving side by side.

In fact, there is a great deal of conceptual slippage between these two sets of processes despite their quite different intellectual origins. While segmentation theories are critical of economic orthodoxy, much of the discourse of labor market flexibility has roots in supply-side economics, with its emphasis on the logical priority (and real-world desirability) of competitive labor markets freed of "imperfections" and operating in accordance with the laws of supply and demand (Pollert, 1988; Standing, 1989). For the supply-side economist, segmentation—with its discontinuities in labor mobility and internalized shelters from labor market competition—is anathema to flexibility. The response is to deregulate *and flexibilize* the labor market to remove barriers to labor mobility and the adjustability of wage rates.

Contrary to the canons of supply-side economics, deregulated labor markets tend to be associated not with convergence upon equilibrium but with a disturbing trend toward job and wage polarization.[15] Deregulation also tends to shift the balance of power in the labor market in favor of employers (Deakin and Mückenberger, 1992). Are labor markets becoming more flexible or are they being resegmented or both? Present evidence is inconclusive and, again, the central issue is one of interpretation. In Atkinson's (1987) core-periphery model, different types of flexibility strategies are associated with different segments of the labor market: qualitative flexibility for the primary sector and quantitative flexibility for the secondary sector. Observing that in the era of flexibility "the institution of segmented labor markets has actually been elaborated," Harrison (1994) draws attention to the "dark side" of the process.

> According to a central tenet of best-practice flexible production, managers must first divide permanent ("core") from contingent ("peripheral") jobs. The size of the core is then cut to the bone—which along with the minimization of inventory holding, is why "flexible" firms are often described as practicing "lean" production. These activities, and the employees who perform them, are then located as much as possible in different parts of the company or network, even in different geographic locations. . . . I call this the dark side of flexible production. (pp. 11–12)

For Wilkinson (1988), segmented labor markets also can be flexible labor markets; indeed, given dynamic interdependence between the primary and secondary sectors, flexibility is part of the very rationale of segmentation. Developing this view, Rosenberg (1989a) regards the search for flexibility, quite rightly, as part of an *ongoing process of labor market restructuring:* "As the search for flexibility proceeds and labor markets become restructured, the boundaries of labor market segmentation change. The labor markets do not necessarily become less segmented. And even if they become less segmented, that does not necessarily mean that they are more flexible" (p. 392).

In analyzing labor market restructuring, it is important to distinguish between different forms of flexibility. Michon (1992) draws a critical distinction between defensive flexibility, associated with deregulation, individualized employment relations, job insecurity, and sharpened competition, and offensive flexibility, associated with regulated and collectivized labor markets.[16] Defensive and offensive flexibility have different rationales, causes, and impacts. Flexible labor markets, then, do not have a single, universal logic but a variety of logics. Their character tends to vary from one place to another, along with the local regulatory and social context and along with the balance of power in the labor market. These differences and their causes must be unraveled with care. It is far from certain that they are rooted in a "common causal dynamic," the theoretically definitive feature of new industrial spaces (Scott, 1988b; Storper, 1990; cf. Henry, 1992).

One way of overcoming this impasse is again to focus less on the short-term mechanisms of restructuring than on the more long-term processes of labor market reproduction, i.e., less on strategies than structures. Two points are worthy of mention. First, the means by which highly polarized labor markets are politically reproducible in the medium to long term have yet to be specified.[17] Widening socio-economic inequalities and political tensions are predictable consequences of the more extreme forms of labor market flexibility. As Saxenian (1983) demonstrated in her analysis of the urban contradictions of industrialization in Silicon Valley, these problems may be of sufficient magnitude to put a brake on local economic growth and even to trigger restructuring of production.

> [It] became increasingly difficult to accommodate and reproduce both segments of [the semiconductor industry's] dichotomized workforce within the same metropolitan area. Inflation of housing prices, transportation congestion, labour shortages and the no-growth movement are all manifestations of the limitations of the local spatial structure for accommodating the industry's bifurcated workforce. These urban contradictions eventually caused the industry itself to restructure, thus preserving Silicon Valley as a site for headquarters, high level research and prototype production activities. (p. 256)

Second, the intrinsic problems of skill formation in flexibly externalized labor markets imply that enlargement of the secondary sector may not be a sustainable option. As Doeringer and Piore (1971) emphasized, one of the main causes of segmentation is the differentiated nature of skills and training: primary sector employers create internal labor markets in order to reduce employee turnover following costly investments in training, while lower and more irregular skill needs in the secondary sector enable employers to forgo training investments and recruit directly from the external labor market. Thus, the generalized enskilling of the work force anticipated in some visions of post-Fordism[18] may be incompatible with deepening segmentation, structural growth of the secondary sector, and the emergence of a small firms–oriented economy. Under such conditions, the supply of skills may soon dry up.

Although there are some early signs of modes of skill formation that may be compatible with small firms–based economies (Perulli, 1990) and with the higher echelons of the secondary labor market (Peck and Haughton, 1991), all such systems are invariably fragile. Regulatory responses to the problem of skill formation are proving to be one of the decisive factors in determining whether economies take the high or the low road from Fordism.[19] Low-road approaches, based on defensive flexibility, already seem to be faltering; unregulated competition breeds short-termism and a reluctance to invest in either skills or technology, "resulting in a vicious, downward-spiralling cycle" (Sengenberger and Pyke, 1990, p. 10). High-road approaches, based on offensive flexibility, seem to be more sustainable (with their high standards of social protection for workers and collectivized economic systems), but in practice remain comparatively rare (Leborgne and Lipietz, 1988; Brusco, 1990). Crucially, they also may be susceptible to competition and regulatory undercutting from regions of defensive flexibility, particularly in the current climate of global deregulation and neoliberal hegemony (see Chapter 8).

One of the most testing issues facing new industrial spaces is the establishment of effective forms of local economic governance (Storper and Harrison, 1991) or local modes of social regulation (Peck and Tickell, 1992). These relate to wide-ranging issues of local social reproduction (such as the socialization of the rising generation or the establishment of sustainable household divisions of labor) as well as to more specific concerns of social regulation in labor markets and interfirm relations (such as measures to ensure the continuation of skill investments or to contain the rate of exploitation to socially acceptable levels). One of the most basic requirements for such a regulatory system is that it should be capable of sustaining risk-laden, long-term investments in innovation, technologies, and skills. Nowhere is this more important than in skill formation, where unregulated competition leads to underinvestment. If institutions and networks appropriate for the reproduction of labor skills—specifically, to socialize the process of skill formation—are not set in place, then economic growth is likely to be short-lived. Thus, industrial disintegration and labor market segmentation (on which the logic of flexible production systems is predicated in Scott's analysis) ultimately may undermine the (supposedly) nascent growth model of flexible accumulation itself.

New Industrial Spaces?

For Scott (1988c), one characteristic of flexible production is that it is "always some distance—socially or geographically—from the major foci of Fordist industrialization" (p. 14). In some instances, flexible production is found outside the old manufacturing regions, in others within it: "new" industrial spaces are sometimes located within old industrial regions. Thus, in some cases capital seeks a tabula rasa, where flexible employment relations can be created "with a minimum of local obstruction" (Scott, 1988a, p. 178), whereas in others it is apparently possible to reconstruct employment relations in situ. Capital's periodic need to reconstruct the employment relation induces the abandonment of regions inculcated with socialized labor processes deemed inappropriate for continued accumulation.[20] This imparts an important dynamic to the process of uneven development. Webber (1982) has suggested that this process of spatial switching is necessary: each regime of accumulation generates new core-periphery relations, including in the geographical sphere. From this perspective, spatial restructuring for the new regime of flexible accumulation seems partial, almost hesitant, in that colonization of new regions coexists with a great deal of staying put. Does this mean that accumulation can be revived in situ?

Certainly, there are possibilities for restructuring employment relations *within* as well as *between* local labor markets, for example, by recruiting from different segments of the labor market or the rising generation (Morgan and Sayer, 1985; Barnes, Hayter, and Grass, 1990). It is just as important to understand why capital does not move and local labor markets do not decline as it is to understand relocation and restructuring through space. Indeed, they are part of the same question. Presumably, firms do not consider relocation until the possibilities for in situ adjustment have been exhausted. Geographers are sometimes guilty of focusing primarily or exclusively on spatial restructuring processes and relocation strategies and ignoring those in situ. Scott implies as much when he remarks that we know little about the processes of local labor market adjustment.[21] In calling for more work on in situ employment restructuring, Barnes, Hayter, and Grass (1990) note that because geographers have tended to emphasize "the geographical solution, they have not always unpacked the internal dynamics of particular segments of local labour markets in a given place and time" (p. 146).

The existence of in situ strategies, by which capital is able to reconstruct local labor market relations, poses some problems for conventional conceptions of industrial restructuring. There is a need to explore the conditions under which restructuring capital opts for either in situ or spatial strategies. Harvey (1989a) maintains that the existence "side by side within the same space" of alternative labor strategies enables capitalists "to choose at will between them" (p. 187). Clearly, however, in situ restructuring has limits, such as those imposed by the continued existence of inappropriate local regulatory frameworks.[22]

One of the key tasks for theorists of flexible accumulation (and indeed of capitalist restructuring in general) must be to determine the conditions under which "choices" between restructuring strategies are being made and to specify likely outcomes in different situations.

Given the body of knowledge that already exists on spatial restructuring,[23] priority should be given now to mechanisms of local labor market adjustment and their relationships with the process of industrial restructuring. What is important in theorizing flexible production systems is not so much the pure effects of geographic proximity per se (in the Marshallian sense), but the distinctive local institutional contexts in which economic and social relations are embedded.[24] This implies a more long-term focus on the reproduction of labor market structures. Will those labor markets which are flexible and successful today *still* be flexible and successful in a decade or two? The answer need not be entirely speculative, for the incipient contradictions of labor market flexibility are already in evidence.

CONTRADICTIONS OF LABOR MARKET FLEXIBILITY

Imperatives of Labor Control

Several issues remain problematic or unresolved in Scott's approach to labor and agglomeration. Some difficulties (such as the problem of skill formation in flexible labor markets or the role of in situ versus spatial restructuring strategies) derive from his somewhat mechanistic approach to labor market analysis. Transaction costs analysis shares with mainstream neoclassical economics a vulnerability to criticisms of methodological individualism (see Marsden, 1986). Labor markets are viewed as populated by utility maximizers and configured in accordance with cost considerations. As Henry (1992) points out, Scott sees the firm as an exchange mechanism rather than a production organization. Segmentation, power relations, and imperatives of labor control are afforded no more than a subsidiary role in an approach that places logical priority on the market-related phenomena of transaction costs.

Although Scott (1988c) maintains that his approach is "complementary to, and not in opposition with" those which emphasize the "tense force-field of capitalist-worker relations" (p. 24), such considerations play no more than a minor role in his analysis. Scott's approach is less unbendingly orthodox (cf. Lovering, 1990) than selectively eclectic: a combination of institutionalist economics, a particular reading of regulation theory, and post-Weberian economic geography.[25] Aside from the epistemological problems of such an eclectic approach (see Fincher, 1983), Scott's emphasis on transaction costs represents an implicit subordination of both forces rooted in the capital-labor relation and institutional influences in general. This has serious implications for his argument, for the transaction costs market (on which the burden of explanation is ultimately placed) is itself socially constituted. Correspondingly, transaction costs are *socially constructed;* they are the malleable outcome of social struggles and institutional mediations rather than the mathematical derivative of some set of ostensibly apolitical economic processes.

The role of social relations needs to be integrated into analyses of labor and agglomeration, rather than added on post hoc. Asymmetries of power within the labor market—rooted in the labor process, the sphere of social reproduction, and the regulatory regime—are principal determinants of the structure and segmentation of labor markets (Kreckel, 1980; Rueschemeyer, 1986). In addition to the primary asymmetry between capital and labor, secondary asymmetries reflect an uneven distribution of power. These secondary asymmetries are evident both among employers (for example, between monopoly and competitive firms or between those in stable and unstable product markets) and within the work force (for example, between unionized and nonunionized sectors or between different age, gender, and ethnic groups). The distribution of primary and secondary sector jobs is shaped by these secondary asymmetries within the work force; politically marginalized groups must bear the brunt of low pay, poor working conditions, and unemployment.

Profound discontinuities in the labor market are legitimized through the attribution of skilled status. In this sense, skill should not be seen simply as a resource that is rewarded in accordance with the precepts of human capital theory, but as an ideological construct reflecting the distribution of power in the labor market. A common characteristic of secondary workers is that they are denied access to skilled *status* even though the technical requirements of their job may warrant it (Craig, Rubery, Tarling, and Wilkinson, 1982). Accordingly, skill formation represents considerably more than the simple activity of training workers for jobs: it is one of the principal mechanisms by which inequalities in pay and power are produced, reproduced, and legitimated. Not surprisingly, struggles over skill have been among the most bitter in the history of industrial relations (More, 1980), and many recent struggles have been triggered by attempts to redefine skills in some way (Mahon, 1987). The process of reconstituting skills as *flexible* skills is not just an issue of workplace organization or efficiency, but has wider ramifications for the distribution of power in the labor market. Indeed, employers' desire to redistribute labor market power may be the motivation for many flexibility strategies. Reorganizing skills means reorganizing power relationships.

Gender and ethnicity are particularly important dimensions of the social construction of skill. The continued segregation of the labor market along the lines of gender and ethnicity feeds, and is fed by, the social processes through which the value of skills is determined (see Horrell, Rubery, and Burchell, 1990). It is no coincidence that flexibility for white, male workers tends to be about multiskilling, responsible autonomy, and task redefinition, whereas for many women and black workers it means lower pay, irregular employment, and harder work (see Pollert, 1988; McDowell, 1991). Moreover, flexibility for men in the waged sphere is typically predicated on the flexible (and unpaid) labor of women in the domestic sphere (Massey, 1993b). Labor market flexibility is both a racialized and gendered concept.

New forms of labor flexibility are associated with new forms of labor control, new forms of labor exploitation and, by implication, new forms of gender and racial exploitation. Again, because these processes are socially constructed, they tend to vary in character and intensity from one place to another.[26] Local forms of labor segmentation, local norms of labor control, local patterns of informal work, and so on represent a geographically variable, prior set of possibilities for the establishment of new labor market relations. Even within Scott's (1988c) sample of new industrial spaces (Silicon Valley, the Third Italy, and Scientific City, Île de France south), the social relations of the labor market vary considerably, reflecting the diverse economic histories, regulatory structures, and social conditions of these areas. It is far from clear that these areas share *common* labor market dynamics. The social and institutional fabric of the labor market is quite different in each case, even if patterns of employment share some superficial similarities. The three areas, it might be said, exhibit *different* flexibilities.

Contemporary flexibility strategies seem to be widening both primary and secondary asymmetries in the labor market. Increased work flexibility is often associated with the reassertion of managerial dominance (Pollert, 1988) while within the work force, "the burden of adjustment [is being placed] on the shoulders of the weakest" (Meulders and Wilkin, 1987, p. 4). Flexibility in the labor market is as much political as economic: there will be losers as well as winners under a new flexible regime (Kern and Schumann, 1987), a point that seems sometimes to be lost on academic advocates (for this is the role they are increasingly fulfilling) of the new flexibility. There is a need, then, to challenge aspects of the emergent politics of post-Fordism (Graham, 1992). Viewing the labor market as a system of power relations brings into question interpretations of flexibility as a "new deal" for labor (see Piore and Sabel, 1984); instead, Pollert (1988) may be closer to the truth in asserting that the search for labor market flexibility represents an "ideological offensive which celebrates pliability and casualization, *and makes them seem inevitable*" (p. 72).

Power relations in the labor market profoundly affect the course of economic development. They cannot be held in suspension while transaction costs are calculated, but should be afforded a central role at the very outset. Power introduces a new dimension to Scott's valuable but one-sided analysis of labor and agglomeration, and by placing labor control at the center of analysis, some of the contradictions of agglomeration become apparent. For example, the massing of workers in urban locations is known to facilitate the process of union organization (Clark, 1983; Lane, 1988; Harvey, 1989b); thus, agglomeration may undermine labor control unless appropriate countermeasures are taken (such as developing internal labor markets or monopolizing a segment of the labor supply).

Labor control strategies vary both historically and geographically. In *Contested Terrain,* Edwards (1979) developed a periodization of labor control strategies (from simple to technical to bureaucratic), which Gordon, Edwards, and Reich (1982) later integrated with a more wide-ranging treatment of historical shifts in the social structures of accumulation in the United States. Their approach is useful in that it links, albeit in a rather schematic way, different forms of labor control with different segments of the labor supply, establishing relationships between the labor process and the labor market (although the former was viewed as shaping the latter). Burawoy (1985) deepened the approach to labor control by taking into consideration the role of the state and of the related conditions surrounding the reproduction of labor. His explicitly politicized treatment centers on the notion of "factory regimes" or a form of production that brings together the labor process and those "*political apparatuses* which reproduce [the] relations of the labour process through the regulation of struggles" (p. 122).

Burawoy (1989) demonstrates how political apparatuses are shaped by and subsequently shape the labor process under different historical and geographic conditions, but he stops short of considering the theoretical implications of spatially uneven development in the politics of production. Warde has taken up this point, arguing that "the nature of the *local* labour market and the impact of the *local* political system often have immediate consequences for factory discipline" (p. 51). As his case study of Lancaster reveals, conditions of labor market dependency (following from the area's domination by a handful of large employers and the paucity of alternative employment opportunities) help to explain both the exceptional quiescence of the local working class and the choice of labor control strategies by local firms. Even so, labor control strategies were not set in accordance with the free will of management, but were formed within the parameters given by the local political and social milieu. In this sense, the contested terrain of labor control has a significant territorial as well as historical dimension (see Jonas, 1996).

Thus, firms' labor strategies are defined within a complex political and institutional arena. Among the factors shaping them are the role of the state in the reproduction of labor, the relationship between internal and external labor markets, the dynamics of local political movements, and the structure of household divisions of labor. Reducing these complex and locally articulated processes to a set of ostensibly universal rules based on transaction costs denies the both social nature of labor and the institutional character of the labor market. It also represents an unbalanced, monocausal explanation for what is in reality a conjuncturally determined, and therefore historically and geographically contingent set of empirical outcomes. Labor strategies are not calculated; they are struggled over. It is these struggles—mobilizing particular political resources and capacities, constrained by different sets of political and economic parameters, regulated in contrasting ways—that hold the key to explaining what is local about the local labor market. Further, though Scott's rather economistic account does not consider how labor markets are regulated in locally specific ways, this must surely play a part in shaping new geographies of labor, as is evident in the problem of skill formation. Taking skill formation and its associated regulatory dilemmas as an alternative point of departure raises a quite different set of questions to those privileged in the transaction cost analysis. Most tellingly, it brings to the fore issues of space, power, and social reproduction.

Problems of Skill Formation

Investments in skill formation are expensive, risky, and realized only in the medium term. Predictably, firms making such investments take steps to ensure that it is they, and not their competitors (for labor), who realize the benefits. Dual labor market theorists see this as a principal motivation for constructing internal labor markets, which impede labor turnover and capture the benefits of skill formation within the enterprise. Yet, internal labor markets are costly: premium wages must be paid in order to retain workers, while the stable employment conditions that are created may become vulnerable to institutionalization, inertia, and collective labor organization.

Comparatively speaking, firms with internalized labor markets are "insulated" from external labor market conditions, hence free(r) to locate in a variety of spatial contexts (see Clark, 1981). Some employers may seek further guarantees of immunity from interfirm labor competition by opting for relatively isolated locations. Primary sector firms can locate in such environments because in effect, they can reproduce their own labor supply: the process of skill formation is *internalized.*

By contrast, firms utilizing labor from the secondary sector of the labor market—where formal skill levels are generally lower and skill demands tend not to be enterprise-specific—must rely upon the haphazard process of external skill formation ("buying in" skills from the external labor market). Often such firms "poach" labor skills formed in either the primary sector (for example, when they recruit redundant workers), or in the domestic sphere (when, for example, they hire workers for their physical strength, basic mental capabilities, or the ability to drive a car or operate a sewing machine). Inevitably, this process of *externalized* skill formation is unreliable and results in a low degree of control over the labor supply. One example of such a precarious strategy is the garment industry's exploitation of immigrant labor pools (see Chapter 6).

Firms dependent on externalized skill formation are subject to powerful agglomeration tendencies, as clustering in large, urban labor markets permits the socialization of the costs of skill formation. In effect, these firms seek to become free riders on the social infrastructure of the city. Skills formed in other spheres (such as homes, schools, and other workplaces) and possessed by marginal workers (such as women, immigrants, young people, and redundant workers) are plundered by secondary firms able to survive only on the margins of the labor market. Such parasitic strategies are tenable, of course, only when the host organism is sufficiently large.

That agglomeration tendencies are inherent in the process of skill formation supports Scott's general conclusions, albeit by way of a different analysis. However, this is only a partial account because labor market agglomeration is a contradictory process. While users of flexible labor tend to agglomerate in order to socialize the costs of labor reproduction, in so doing they inadvertently initiate a set of countervailing forces. Agglomeration raises the level of interfirm competition for labor, which may trigger local wage inflation and almost certainly will lead to labor recruitment and retention difficulties for firms with a weak purchase on their labor supply; their hold on secondary labor is inevitably tenuous and, with heightened labor competition, even that tenuous grip may be lost. In this way, the agglomeration of secondary sector employers in urban labor markets begins to undermine the utility of such locations. Through overexploitation (to return to the metaphor), the parasites may eventually destroy the host organism.

Although ultimately self-destructive, resort to plundering is commonplace where capitalists are unable to regulate interfirm competition for labor (Harvey, 1989b). How do secondary sector firms respond to this contradictory situation? Suburbanization is rarely an option as they depend on urban location in many ways (such as for externalized skill formation or, because these typically are small firms, for subcontracting). In Cox and Mair's (1988) terms, such firms are "locally dependent" and, as a result, they must evolve in situ coping strategies by reorganizing the labor process or tapping into different labor supplies in the urban labor market.[27] These strategies, which effectively entail adjustments in firms' *local labor market relations,* often involve yet further plundering of secondary labor supplies. Strategies such as homework and casualization allow such firms, perhaps only temporarily, to establish a "new" coupling between the (restructured) labor process and a segment of the urban labor supply. (Significantly, this reactive coping strategy may be mistaken by advocates of post-Fordism as evidence of rising flexibility!) The most favored strategies will be those allowing firms to establish some degree of monopoly control over their labor supply. Their preference will be for labor supplies in which the degree of interfirm labor competition is low (such as women bound to the home by domestic responsibilities or immigrant workers with poor language skills). In these ways, secondary sector employers are induced to embark on a destructive, spiraling descent into ever more regressive labor practices. The collective urban problem of skill reproduction is intensified, not solved.

Thus, urban labor markets are profoundly contradictory places. Although they offer possibilities for socializing the costs of skill formation (along with other scale economies Scott identifies), agglomeration also triggers contradictory and ultimately self-destructive plundering. Because the basic requirements for the reproduction of the labor supply are not met, urban labor markets are systemically crisis-prone. The challenge for the flexible labor markets of the new industrial spaces is therefore to overcome these self-destructive tendencies by establishing effective mechanisms for labor reproduction.[28] In essence, this is a problem of social regulation. In the absence of appropriate regulatory structures, flexible labor markets may turn out to be no more than temporary phenomena: a manifestation of decline rather than a symbol of growth. Analytical work on the restructuring of urban labor markets must recognize that they are complex social as well as economic structures; that they are sites of competition and conflict among firms and among other potential users of labor; that they are the product of interacting geographies of paid and unpaid work and of production and service work; and that their tensions and contradictions pose intractable dilemmas of social regulation. Critical attention should therefore be shifted from the supposedly universal inner logic of flexible labor markets to the complex and variable ways in which they are regulated.

REGULATING LOCAL FLEXIBILITIES

It is becoming clear already that flexible labor strategies are not only contradictory but diverse. There is no single, universal form of flexible labor market, but a variety of local forms, each associated with rather different political and economic effects (see Boyer, 1987; Albo, 1994). At the crudest level, these can be arranged between the three poles of defensive, offensive, and classic flexibilities (after Boyer, 1992; Michon, 1992).

- *Defensive flexibilities* have been associated with labor market restructuring in the United Kingdom and United States. They involve the selective deregulation of the labor market (specifically, the erosion of social protection for the unemployed and low-paid), establishment of more individualized employment relations (as collective representation and bargaining structures break down), insecure job tenures, rising inequality, and the exposure of the work force to sharpened competitive pressures.
- *Offensive flexibilities* tend to be associated with more "organized" labor markets, such as those of Germany and the Scandinavian countries, combining high wages with well-developed forms of social protection, secure job tenures, collectivized political structures, and a high degree of qualitative (i.e., cross-skill) flexibility in the workplace.
- *Classic flexibilities* characterize the development path of many southern European labor markets. They combine flexible forms of wage labor (notably part-time and seasonal work) with farm and family work systems, employment conditions typically being highly exploitative in each sphere.

In far more subtle ways than this, a host of commentators have pointed to a range of distinctive forms of labor market flexibility.[29]

What needs to be underlined is the importance of social structures and regulatory mechanisms in not just setting the context, but also in shaping the character of local labor markets. Though Storper and Scott

(1989) note the coincidence of the posited shift toward flexible accumulation and the presence of governments "committed to varying degrees to attempts to dismantle the apparatus of Keynesian welfare-statism" (p. 25), they stop short of explaining how flexible labor markets can be regulated or reproduced. This is a significant omission because flexible labor markets are shot through with internal tensions and contradictions which, if they are not contained in some way, can put a brake on the development process. In particular, they are vulnerable to crises of labor control and reproduction.

This points to the fragility of growth in flexible labor markets, underscoring the importance of developing appropriate systems of social regulation. The nature of labor market flexibility is a product of the local social and regulatory milieu in which it is embedded. The contradictions of flexible labor markets pose a host of regulatory dilemmas,[30] medium-term solutions for which must be found or happened upon if growth is to be sustained. What is important is the response to these dilemmas in different temporal and spatial contexts. The contrasting ways in which the social regulation of skill formation has been tackled (under conditions of defensive, offensive, and classic flexibility) are illustrative.

Skill Formation

The British case illustrates the limits of defensive flexibility strategies. The breakdown of growth in southern England during the recession of the early 1990s was in part a consequence of the problems of regulating skill formation under defensive flexibility. Under the clarion call of deregulation, the British training system was restructured substantially during the 1980s; state support was effectively withdrawn for all but the most basic, transferable skills for the unemployed.[31] Launched in 1988 to develop locally tuned training responses, employer-led Training and Enterprise Councils (TECs) lack the financial or organizational resources to respond to anything but the most basic skill needs, they still cater to a predominantly unemployed group. Ironically, because they inherited from the government responsibility for unemployment programs, the TECs are weakest in buoyant areas of the country where unemployment levels have been low historically (Peck, 1992c).

In the absence of any legislative or organizational framework for training in intermediate and high skills, British firms have become dependent on internal structures of skill formation (where feasible) and the haphazard process of labor poaching (see Lee, 1989). The dismantlement of the statutory training framework, and its replacement by a market-oriented and voluntarist system, has destabilized interfirm relations in the labor market. Powerless to regulate private skill formation, the TECs find themselves caught between the government's conflicting objectives to drive down public expenditure, contain mass unemployment, and reform the system of industrial training. As a result, they seem locked on a course that will result, on the one hand, in the further degradation of labor-power as the unemployed are subjected increasingly to market discipline and, on the other hand, in the paralysis of private skill formation as unregulated plundering of labor undermines the basis on which firms' training investments are made.

In this sense, deregulation has meant the "law of the jungle": the self-destructive dynamic of the market has been released. Accelerating turnover of skilled labor, deepening skill shortages, and spiraling wage inflation have been the predictable consequences, particularly in sectors unable to sustain internal labor markets (such as the construction industry and parts of the financial services). By the late 1980s, these difficulties had become endemic in the booming local economies along the M4 and M11 corridors (Murray, 1989). Symptomatic of the wider problem of overexploitation of the region's social, economic, and physical infrastructures during this period, the skills and training crisis was part and parcel of the wider crisis of regulation, which eventually contributed to the suffocation of the south's neoliberal growth strategy (Leadbetter, 1991; Peck and Tickell, 1992).

Certainly insofar as skill formation was concerned, the deregulationist approach of the British government was destined for failure. As Streeck (1989) has argued, such strategies fail to recognize the character of skills as collective goods: firms pursuing their individual, "rational" self-interest tend to underinvest in skills when they cannot be assured of realizing the full value of training investments (particularly when they are surrounded by other firms that have made the same calculation and concluded that poaching is the solution). According to Streeck (1989), the answer to this dilemma is not to return wholeheartedly to state provision of training (which is often insufficiently relevant to workplace needs), but to instigate a state-regulated, neocorporatist approach along the lines of the German dual system.

> While market motives and processes play a significant and recognized part in [this] system, they are controlled by, and embedded in, what are essentially collective agreements between monopolistic employers associations and trade unions exercising, under a state licence, delegated public responsibility which enables them to impose effectively binding obligations upon their memberships. . . . [The growing needs of] firms for collective, non-appropriable production factors, like a rich supply of high and broad functional and extrafunctional skills,

opens up political arenas where corporatist self-government of social groups may be a superior mode of regulation compared to both state intervention and the free market. (p. 103)

The dual system, which is highly formalized and combines elements of workplace-based training with off-site provision in training schools, is widely recognized to have made a significant positive contribution to the productivity of German industry.[32] This system, based on extended apprenticeships (usually of three and a half years), was reformed substantially in the 1980s so as to deliver more broad-based skills and greater capacities for skilled workers' autonomy. For Lash and Urry (1994, pp. 86–89), the training system is one of the corner-stones of the distinctive *Beruf* (craft) model of economic governance in Germany.

The German training system has a strong regional component. Although the overall framework for workplace training is national, training schools are under the control of individual *Lander,* which have also tended to develop distinctive systems of complementary institutions and programs. For example, Baden-Württemburg enhances its basic training infrastructure with regional programs for the support of innovation and technology transfer.[33] Regional differences are widening as strains on the dual system lead to "increasing disparities between experiences at the level of the firm, the region and the individual" (Rees, 1990, p. 72). Tensions within the German training system can be traced to two sources. First, acceleration in the rate of technological change and the concomitant shortening of product cycles (particularly in dynamic regional economies such as Baden-Württemburg) has reduced the effective shelf life of technical skills (Cooke and Morgan, 1990a). In turn, there is increased demand for continuing training which, because it is overwhelmingly workplace-based and beyond the scope of direct state regulation, varies both qualitatively and quantitatively and between regions, sectors, and firms (Rees, 1990; Mahnkopf, 1992). Second, though accommodated by most large corporations, the need for continuing training poses organizational problems for the small-firm and craft sectors. These sectors have begun to explore new institutional means of satisfying their continuing skill needs, including training consortia, partnerships, and subcontracting to specialist training agencies (Hoch, 1988). Consequently, further unevenness is emerging in the training system.

While Germany retains one of the most robust systems for initial and basic training, there is increasing evidence that the cumbersome process of institutional reform is lagging—perhaps even disrupting—technical and labor process change, particularly in the more dynamic sectors of the economy (Rees, 1990; Lash and Urry, 1994). For example, the process of redesigning and implementing regulations for training in the metal trades took virtually ten years to complete. Thus, some firms and some sectors are becoming partially disenfranchised in the dual training system, which remains oriented primarily to the needs of large employers. Under conditions of offensive flexibility, formal, institutional approaches to skill formation are by no means universal panaceas, but create their own tensions and contradictions.

The situation is different under the classic flexibility characteristic of such areas as Emilia-Romagna. In accounts of the development of small-firm networks in this region, much is made of the role of local institutions and the virtues of spatial clustering in the development and exploitation of a rich skills base (see Amin and Robins, 1990). However, as these and other writers have pointed out the initial, Marshallian-style growth of flexible production in Emilia-Romagna was very much predicated upon the prior existence of traditional agrarian social structures.[34] Many of the skills deployed in these paradigmatic flexible production systems were appropriated initially from the domestic and agricultural spheres. This "dependent" mode of skill formation was later superseded in part by collaborative training institutions, where small firms cooperated with one another (and often with local state and business associations) in establishing more formal network structures (Perulli, 1990), but such responses to the collective good problem of skill formation were only partially successful. The difficulties in Italy arose because most responses were local, partial, and uncoordinated at the regional scale. As Trigilia (1991) argues,

> the role assumed by forms of flexible productive organization poses a *regulative problem of a regional nature*. These forms require, in fact, innovations of an organizational and technological character, managerial and entrepreneurial training, the training, reskilling and mobility of the labour force. . . . [This requires] more so than in the past, an "intermediate government" of economic development; a regional dimension which is certainly not capable of managing directly, but rather of stimulating and coordinating relations between different public and private actors, and also between areas with different characteristics. . . . Technological innovation, training and labour mobility . . . are supplied with difficulty through bureaucratic structures which lack the consent, information and collaboration of the interested parties. Only authoritative representative organizations, at a level wider than the local, could "internalize" the benefits derived from efficient regional intervention and would therefore have a greater incentive to contribute to the realization of such interventions. (pp. 313–315)

Because the regional tier in Italy is comparatively weak, no such formal institutionalization has occurred. Though for completely different reasons than the British case, the mode of growth exhibited by Emilia-Romagna also is fragile. It is predicated upon a unique but changing social structure in which the institutions for socioeconomic reproduction are only partially formed.

As Hadjimichalis and Papamichos (1990) have demonstrated, the social structures that initially fostered flexible production in Emilia-Romagna are beginning to break down. There is growing reluctance to accept irregular and semilegal employment; the cultural values of agrarian society are being eclipsed by the lures of modern consumerism; traditional family structures are decaying as women begin to challenge their subordinate roles in both the domestic and wage-labor economies; and the old systems of political patronage are being eroded by economic modernization and political reform. Ironically, the very successes of the regional economy—in particular, its progressive integration into the global economy and its inculcation with global competitive imperatives—have begun to undermine the bases of its competitiveness. Emilia-Romagna now faces the challenge of overcoming these "social blockages" and recreating new forms of local social solidarity and cooperation in the context of international competition (Cooke and Morgan, 1991). This exceptionally delicate operation may prove impossible to realize with the comparatively blunt instruments of policy.

In these three regional cases, different responses to the regulatory dilemma of skill formation underscore differences in labor market flexibility. The point is not just that *regulation matters* (i.e., that it has important, material effects on accumulation), but that *regional regulation matters*. Systems of social regulation are unevenly developed across space, not only in situations where regulatory norms seem clearly to have emerged from the bottom-up (as in Emilia-Romagna) but also in the top-down, state-articulated regulatory regimes of Britain and, to a lesser extent, Germany. Even centrally designed and nationally imposed policy programs, such as the labor market interventions of Conservative governments in Britain, have very different effects in different places and play a part in the formation of distinctive regional regulatory milieux. These, in turn, influence the form of local labor markets and shape the course of regional economic development.

For example, while the re-regulation of the British training system may have played a role in polarizing the skill and wage structure in the expanding economies of the south of England (by underwriting secondary sector recruitment, induction, and employment and by exposing the higher echelons of the primary sector to external labor market forces, poaching, and wage inflation), a different set of forces was unleashed in the high-unemployment areas of the north (where the principal impacts occurred in the containment of unemployment and the unpicking of the welfare safety net). Similar arguments about the regionally specific character of regulatory systems and regulatory effects can be developed for Italy, where the unique, regional social structures of Emilia-Romagna conditioned the nature of the flexible production and labor market structures that emerged there. In Germany, regionally articulated policy synergies, plus spatially variable interaction between technical and labor process imperatives with the rigidities of the dual training system, contributed to distinctive regional economic trajectories.

Social Regulation As Local Regulation

Local variation in flexible regulation raises the question of the extent to which regulatory structures can be portable from place to place. Superficially, forms of state regulation (including state institutions and policy systems) may seem more portable than nonstate forms, such as the particular function of the family and agrarian traditions in Emilian labor markets, which seem so self-evidently rooted in place. But state forms, too, are less mobile than they seem. While it may be possible to clone particular institutional structures or imitate particular programs, it is quite a different matter to reproduce the *effects* of state regulation because of the indeterminate way in which they are realized in different spatial contexts. For example, if the German dual training system were to be transplanted into Britain, its institutional form and economic effects would vary greatly from one area of the country to another, depending upon interactions with such spatially variable phenomena as the nature of the local class bargain between labor and capital, the prior nature of local training infrastructures and cultures, the character of public-private relations, and the structure of local economies.

While in broad terms some regulatory institutions may be duplicable, their effects most certainly are not. This is because the process by which such effects are generated depends on contingent local conditions, which might be theorized as *rooted regulation*. Even though most regions face similar regulatory dilemmas, their institutional response tends to be regionally idiosyncratic. Different regions may attempt different regulatory experiments while national (and, for that matter, international) regulatory strategies will take different forms in different places. Geographic diversity is a nontrivial issue. Indeed, an appreciation of spatial unevenness is a precondition for understanding the meaning and significance of regulatory experiments. As Salais and Storper (1992) observe,

> [N]ew forms of "strategic alliance" in a variety of producer and
> consumer goods industries . . . the "corporatist" industrial systems
> found in metal working and machinery building in Bavaria and
> Baden-Württemburg . . . and the "contractual" production net-
> works typical of American high technology industry . . . [are all]
> means of trying to resolve tensions introduced by rapid changes in
> products, the increasing complexity of the division of labour, and
> existing worlds of production and their [regulatory] conventions.
> In the process, new conventions are being developed and with them,
> perhaps, new worlds of production. A significant implication . . . is
> that there are important local and national (and not only sectoral)
> variations in such experiments. This adds yet another dimension to
> the industrial diversity which we expect from the existence of
> different kinds of products: the locally- and regionally-specific
> development of conventions (which may not be easily diffusable to
> other places). (p. 189)

Experimentation with regulatory systems and projects is likely, then,
to be an ongoing process, intensified during periods of economic
restructuring. However, regulatory "solutions" discovered in particular local situations may not be generalizable to other local contexts,
even within the same nation-state.

Moreover, *labor regulation* will be especially locally embedded.
Due to the social nature of its production and reproduction, labor is
the most placebound of the "factors of production." The production
and reproduction of labor-power depend on the supportive effects of
certain key social institutions (such as family structures, schools, and
recreational organizations) and consequently, require a substantial
degree of stability (Storper and Walker, 1983). The social institutions
underpinning the regulation of labor markets tend themselves to take
on distinctively local forms. The labor market is indeed one of the most
socially—and, in this sense, *locally*—embedded of economic systems.

LOCAL INSTITUTIONALIZATION
AND THE LABOR MARKET

In labor market research greater attention needs to be paid to processes
of labor control, reproduction, and regulation at the local level.
Although Scott has offered a stimulating analysis of labor market
flexibility, his approach remains partial. The richness and complexity
of the social relations of employment cannot be reduced to calculations
of transaction costs. The labor process and labor market are much
more than cost structures; they are arenas of political power and

conflicting class, gender, and ethnic forces. For firms, the question of the "cost" of labor is inextricably tied to the problem of labor control, understood in its widest sense (see Chapter 6).

Decisions concerning where to locate the boundaries of the firm and how far to internalize or externalize labor are influenced by labor control factors as well as cost calculations.[35] This is particularly important in flexible production complexes where the tendency toward externalization of labor is likely to be associated with increasing problems of labor control and reproduction. The questions of if and how these problems will become manifest are essentially regulatory questions; they also refer to the *local* social regulatory context, local institutions, and the political dynamic of the local labor market. Strategies for labor flexibility that are feasible in one local context may be untenable in others, while the shift to flexible labor may or may not prove to be sustainable in the medium term. This question of sustainability warrants further consideration in local labor market research. As Warde (1989) observes, "different modes of institutionalisation [of labour reproduction have] differing effects on industrial discipline. . . . The way in which the reproduction of labour power is organised locally is an important determinant of workplace discipline, a key element in the means used to regulate struggles around the relations of domination in any workplace" (p. 61).

One implication of local institutionalization is that regulatory systems are unlikely to be portable from place to place, achieving similar results wherever they are deployed, but instead are deeply rooted in local social structures. This holds just as much for top-down state institutions and policies (the effects of which vary from place to place) as for what are often perceived as the bottom-up elements of modes of social regulation (custom, habits, norms, and the like).

The geographies of regulation exert nontrivial influences on the course of accumulation in general and the nature of labor markets in particular. One of the root causes of the variable nature of labor market flexibility is the differential process by which labor markets are embedded within national, regional, and local regulatory milieux. Although one can deduce a priori that flexible labor markets will be vulnerable to generic regulatory dilemmas, institutional responses and effects will vary from one place to another. In short, the social and spatial context in general and the regulatory milieu in particular will have a major influence on the form of labor market flexibility that emerges in a region, and its durability. This is one reason flexible labor markets are associated with poverty in one place and prosperity in another, conflict in one place and cooperation in another, development in one place and decline in another. To bundle all forms of contemporary labor market restructuring together under the generic and increasingly elastic term "flexibility" is manifestly inadequate.

Analytically, the key issue concerns reproducibility. It is not enough to accomplish local economic growth; it has to be sustained, and the long-run viability of flexible labor markets has yet to be demonstrated. Though it is an evidently straightforward matter to identify sustainable and unsustainable forms of growth and labor markets retrospectively, it is inevitably much more difficult in current research. However, by focusing on reproduction, regulation, and how different regulatory dilemmas are tackled institutionally, it may be possible to differentiate some of the more durable from some of the more fragile forms of local growth, thereby distinguishing flash-in-the-pan new industrial spaces from those capable of sustaining medium-term growth (see Dunford, 1990; Harrison, 1992).

From the perspective of the politics of regional economic development, there may yet be some way to go before a new generic mode of social regulation becomes hegemonic. There are unlikely to be any easy solutions. While local success stories continue to provide hope for local economic policymakers,[36] the evidence suggests that regulatory solutions must be homegrown, not imported. For regions leached by years of neoliberal deregulation, the concern has to be that the social subsoil may now prove barren.

> The productivity of labor . . . like that of the soil . . . can build up over time, provided proper care is taken. The effect is to make each [local] labor market even more unique, because the long processes of sociopolitical development within an urban region can build up unique mixes of [labor] qualities. The plundering of those qualities through de-skilling, overworking, bad labor relations, unemployment, and so forth can, however, lead . . . to the rapid depletion of a prime productive force. . . . The problem, of course, is that the coercive laws of competition force individual capitalists into strategies of plundering, even when that undermines their own class interest. Whether or not such a result comes to pass depends upon the internal conditions of labor demand and supply, the possibilities of replenishing labor reserves through migration either of labor power or capital, and the capacity of capitalists to put a floor under their own competition by agreeing to some kind of regulation of the labor market. (Harvey, 1989b, pp. 133–134)

There is a need, then, to focus on the ways in which local labor markets (and forms of flexibility) are regulated, and how they are institutionally and territorially constituted. This requires a closer look at the flip side of spatial restructuring: in situ labor adjustment.

NOTES

1. See Leborgne and Lipietz (1988); Sengenberger and Pyke (1990); Standing (1992); and Harrison (1994).

2. In particular, see Scott (1986, 1988b, 1988c).

3. The remainder of this chapter is a substantially revised version of an article published in *Economic Geography* 68(1992): 325–347. I wish to thank the editors of *Economic Geography* for permission to adapt and reprint the article here.

4. Scott (1988c); Storper and Scott (1989, 1990).

5. Scott (1988b, pp. 120–138; 1988c, pp. 33–38).

6. See Scott and Cooke (1988) and Storper and Scott (1990).

7. See OECD (1986a, 1989); Williams (1986); Hakim (1987); Boyer (1988a); and Laflamme, Murray, Belanger, and Ferland (1989).

8. See OECD (1986b); Standing (1986); Boyer (1987); Harrison and Bluestone (1987); Tarling (1987); Hyman (1988); Pollert (1988); Hudson (1989); Rodgers and Rodgers (1989); Rosenberg (1989b); Howell (1992); and ILO (1995).

9. See Michon (1987); Sayer (1989); and Amin and Robins (1990).

10. See Webber (1982); Massey (1984); and Smith (1984).

11. See Braverman (1974); and Wood (1982, 1989).

12. See Saxenian (1983); Gertler (1988); and Sayer (1989).

13. See Harrison and Bluestone (1988); Boyer (1988a); Rosenberg (1989d); and Storper and Scott (1990). Cf. Chapters 7 and 8.

14. See Jessop (1992a); Leborgne and Lipietz (1992); and Peck and Tickell (1995).

15. See Standing (1986); Harrison and Bluestone (1988); Rosenberg (1989d); Howell (1992); Sengenberger (1992); and Harrison (1994). Recently, there are signs in policymaking circles that recognition of these problems may be turning the tide against the new orthodoxy of deregulation (see ILO, 1995).

16. These relate to Leborgne and Lipietz's (1988) Californian and Saturnian models of labor regulation, respectively.

17. See Mahon (1987); Rubery, Tarling, and Wilkinson (1987); Brunhes (1989); Storper and Scott (1990); Teague (1990); and Tickell and Peck (1992). Cf. Davis (1986) and Jessop, Bonnett, Bromley, and Ling (1988).

18. See Piore and Sabel (1984); and Applebaum and Shettkat (1990); cf. Graham (1992).

19. Among the many contributions of this kind, see Mahon (1987); Leborgne and Lipietz (1988, 1990); Brunhes (1989); Rojot (1989); Boyer (1990a); Michon (1990); Sengenberger and Pyke (1990); Green (1992); and Albert (1993).

20. See Webber (1982); Storper and Walker (1983); and Smith (1984).

21. Scott (1988b, p. 120); cf. Clark, Gertler, and Whiteman (1986).

22. See Moulaert (1987); and Heckscher (1988); compare Chapter 6.

23. In particular, see Bluestone and Harrison (1982); Massey (1984);

Clark, Gertler, and Whiteman (1986); Scott and Storper (1986); and Storper and Walker (1989).

24. For useful discussions with reference to the Marshallian case, see Lorenz (1992); and You and Wilkinson (1994).

25. On the methodological bases of Scott's approach, see Scott and Storper (1990, pp. 5–6). See also Lovering (1990, 1991) and Scott (1991a, 1991b).

26. For example, see Harrison and Bluestone (1987); Capecchi (1989); Hadjimichalis and Papamichos (1990); Crang and Martin (1991); and Massey (1994).

27. As Cox and Mair have argued, conditions of local dependence may have implications for the politics of local economic development. Such conditions constitute one of the specifically local influences on social regulation in the labor market.

28. See Mahon (1987); Perulli (1990); and Sengenberger and Pyke (1990).

29. See Lash and Urry (1987); Mahon (1987); Leborgne and Lipietz (1988, 1990); Amin (1989); Brunhes (1989); Rojot (1989); Rosenberg (1989b); Amin and Robins (1990); Boyer (1990a, 1992); Hadjimichalis and Papamichos (1990); Michon (1990, 1992); Sengenberger and Pyke (1990); and Standing (1992). Albo (1994) provides a compelling analysis of the wider politcal-economic context of the current flexibility offensive.

30. See Chapter 2; see also Selznick (1985) and Marden (1992).

31. See Finegold and Soskice (1988); Lee (1989); and King (1995).

32. For evidence, see Steedman and Wagner (1987) and Prais and Wagner (1988).

33. See Cooke and Morgan (1990a, 1990b).

34. See Amin (1989); Camagni and Capello (1988); and Hadjimichalis and Papamichos (1990).

35. This point has been made in a series of contributions by Clark (1981, 1983) and Clark, Gertler, and Whiteman (1986).

36. See Cooke and Imrie (1989); Luria (1990); and Murray (1991).

Chapter 6

DOMESTICATING WORK

Restructuring at Work, Restructuring at Home

Restructuring takes place at home as well as at work. Yet, the prevailing view that home and work constitute separate spheres—materially, analytically, and politically—undermines attempts to explain restructuring holistically (Picchio, 1992; Sayer and Walker, 1992), and makes it difficult to understand "women's work" or the roles of women in waged and unwaged employment. Spanning home and work, women's work raises fundamental questions about the boundaries implicit in mainstream conceptions of the labor process, labor market, spheres of production and reproduction, and industrial restructuring. More specifically, industrial homework provides a lens through which to view the complexity of the relationship between industrial restructuring and the local labor market.

As Hanson and Pratt (1995) have argued, the relationship between home and work should be at the heart of an adequate conception of the local labor market. At the same time, they stress that the boundary between home and work is blurred; the social organization of domestic work conditions is conditioned by the social organization of wage-work. Moreover, the blurred boundary between home and work is not coterminous with either the equally blurred boundaries between waged and unwaged work or between production and reproduction.

As waged work performed in the home, industrial homework straddles these boundaries. Indeed, it is a highly problematic analytic category. It tends to be socially constructed as either marginal or invisible by virtue of its association with women's domestic labor; because it is often organized in an informal or even illegal way; and due to its presumed anachronism and/or peripherality to the mainstream economy.

> The dominant conceptualisation of social activities in industrial societies, which is reinforced by the legal system, persistently distinguishes home and work as separate spheres, the one being labelled "private" and the other "public" or "social." These are assumed to be divided spatially, to entail different types of social relationships, and to require separate investigation. . . . [Mainstream social theories] assume that with industrialisation the locus of work moved outside the home; that work came to encompass only activities remunerated through the wage relation; and that the link between the family and the economy [was] confined to the work of only some household members, notably the husband/father, unmarried sons, and, on some occasions, unmarried daughters. . . . [This] perception of the centrality of the wage relation has been accompanied by an ideological construction of the division of labor which domesticates women. (Allen and Wolkowitz, 1987, pp. 14–15)

An examination of homework can shed fresh light on interrelations between the labor process and the labor market, and their respective roles in industrial restructuring. Moreover, it illustrates one of the ways in which labor markets are socialized in different ways in different places, and consequently, how distinctive local labor market structures shape the course of industrial restructuring.

In order to theorize the contribution of local labor markets to processes of industrial restructuring, this chapter begins by revisiting Massey's (1984) account of the spatial division of labor. Although it unpacked the relationship between changes in the labor process, industrial restructuring, and the geography of employment change, it largely overlooked the role of local labor markets. The remainder of the chapter explores industrial homework as an example of ways in which local labor market structures are related to the dynamics of industrial restructuring. The growth of homework in the Australian garment industry reflects not only the pressures placed on firms to reduce costs and enhance production flexibility (the conventional wisdom of labor process–oriented explanations), but also represents an attempt by these firms to reconstruct their urban labor market relations. The case of homework reveals that processes specific to labor markets (such as the gendered labor supply, ethnic segmentation, and interindustry competition for labor) exert a powerful influence on the direction and form of industrial restructuring.

SPATIAL DIVISIONS OF LABOR

Initiated by Marx and reinvigorated by Braverman, a rich vein of work on industrial restructuring has taken as its focus the labor process, or the capital-labor relation at the point of production.[1] In *Spatial Divisions of Labour,* Doreen Massey produced an influential, geographic extension of this tradition, arguing that labor process dynamics have shaped not only the general course of industrial restructuring, but its specific geographic form. As execution has been separated from conception, different functions in the technical division of labor have been stretched out over space and sited in different locations, creating a pattern of uneven development which itself is amenable to further exploitation; "the very existence of such differences between locations may be a stimulus for the development of a technical division of labour which enables advantage to be taken of them" (Massey, 1984, p. 74). Although some of her empirical claims have been challenged (Lovering, 1989), the book's enduring value lies in the way in which it exposes the essentially reciprocal relationship between social relations and spatial structure.[2] It is not a "theory" built in the positivist sense on unimpeachable empirical generalizations, but rather, codifies an analytical framework in which geography matters in social relations.[3]

The spatial divisions of labor framework permits analysis along two dimensions. The first situates restructuring in companies, sectors, and industrial branches in relation to unfolding rounds of accumulation, as "a product of the interaction between, on the one hand, the existing characteristics of spatial differentiation and, on the other hand, the requirements at that time of the particular process of production" (Massey, 1979, p. 234). Viewing uneven development from a sectoral perspective foregrounds the strategic calculations of profit-seeking capital confronted with constantly shifting labor pools. Along the second dimension, the changing position of individual localities can be understood, both internally and regionally, as the "complex result of the combination of [their] succession of roles within the series of wider, national and international, spatial divisions of labour" (p. 235). Local economic and social structures derive in large part from the distinctive roles played by localities in different spatial divisions of labor, described as the "layering" of successive rounds of accumulation and the "combination effects" associated with this.

Massey argued that spatial differentiation was increasingly important to capital in the competitive search for profit; changes in production created new demands for labor and therefore new locational imperatives, and the constantly shifting map of labor qualities (together with their underlying economic and social relations) spurred new restructuring strategies. At the risk of oversimplification, her account can be summarized in six steps (see Lovering, 1989).

1. Imperatives of global competition are driving processes of industrial restructuring;
2. As control and conception are increasingly separated from execution, restructuring entails the reorganization and breaking up of established labor process and production functions;
3. The separation of control from execution has a geographic manifestation as different functions are located in accordance with the geography of their preferred labor supply (typically, for example, deskilled execution functions move to peripheral areas and control and R&D functions concentrate in dominant cities);
4. This process is conceptualized as one in which rounds of accumulation unfold across the economic landscape, producing in their wake new geographies of production and new relationships between places (which may be gaining or losing functions in the new round of accumulation);
5. New spatial divisions of labor are forged through the complex process by which new rounds of accumulation interact with, and remake, preexisting geographies of production and social relations, resulting in locally contingent "combination effects";
6. The concept of the spatial division of labor encompasses a reciprocal relationship between locality-level conditions and unfolding rounds of accumulation.

Central to Massey's approach was a particular kind of explanation tackling the "impossible dichotomy" of the social and the spatial: "It is not . . . just a question of mapping social relations *on to* space. The fact that those social relations *occur over* space matters . . . social processes are constructed over space" (1984, p. 53). From a critical realist perspective, she criticized the regional studies tradition which, in a positivist fashion, had sought to explain one spatial pattern by reference to another and to account for industrial location patterns by

listing "location factors." Instead, she focused on the mutual constitution of social process and spatial structure, or the way in which social
relations are made and remade as they are stretched out over space (cf.
Giddens, 1984).

> The first task was to blow apart the notion of a spatial world
> which was internally self-explanatory—where spatial change was
> explained by spatial factors (the movement of industry explained
> by regional policy), where the fortunes of areas were explained
> by their characteristics (blaming the cities). . . Spatial form . . . is
> to be explained not by "spatial" factors but by, for instance, what
> is going on in the economy. The spatial is, in that very material
> sense, socially constructed; and an understanding of the spatial
> must entail an understanding of the economy and society more
> generally. . . [Moreover] class relations too [can] be understood
> as having a spatial form. The geography of social structure is a
> geography of class *relations,* not just a map of social classes; just
> as a geography of the economy should be a map of *economic
> relations stretched over space,* and not just, for instance, a map
> of different types of jobs. Most generally, "the spatial" is consti-
> tuted by the interlocking of "stretched out" social relations.
> (Massey, 1994, pp. 21–22)

If social and spatial structures provided the conceptual architecture of Massey's work, its bricks and mortar included the familiar
themes of technical change, deskilling, class restructuring, and regional
industrial change, albeit with a unique analytical spin.

The spatial division of labor framework is based on seven underlying principles (Massey and Meegan, 1989):

1. Production is organized not randomly but systematically over
   space, the dynamic of the system deriving from the competitive
   search for profit;
2. Local and regional economic development are linked to national and international processes of restructuring;
3. Analysis of the changing geography of production is embedded
   in a broad framework in which the interactions of economic,
   social, cultural, and political factors are taken into account;
4. The approach embraces the implications of labor's uniqueness
   as a location factor—its social character—in its explanations
   of industrial restructuring;
5. The active role of geography is emphasized, as it both provides
   an uneven opportunity surface to be exploited by capital and
   shapes restructuring strategies;

6. Perhaps the definitive feature of this approach is the attempt to hold together analytically the general processes of industrial restructuring and unique local effects;

7. The layering of successive rounds of accumulation engenders changes in the pattern and form of regional inequality, the structure of places, and the structure of the relationships between them.

Massey's central concerns were industrial restructuring and the concomitant reorganization of the labor process on the one hand and, on the other, spatial structures of production and the recomposition of regional class structures. The organization and restructuring of labor markets had no explicit part in her account (Warde, 1985), being reduced to the status of a passive context against (or over) which the above processes operated (cf. Clark, 1981). In perhaps the most far-reaching critique of the spatial division of labor, Warde (1985) has suggested that it is essentially reducible to a geological metaphor.

> The metaphor is geological; successive rounds of accumulation deposit layers of industrial sediment in geographical space. That sediment comprises both plant and persons, the qualities of the latter, deposited in one round, being of primary importance at the beginning of the next round. . . . The chain of reasoning about the political effects of industrial change [is] a direct one, from industrial structure, through occupational structure, to regional class structure. This is not necessarily an objectionable initial procedure, but it renders all spatial effects as class effects. (pp. 196–197)

Although Warde amply exposes the limits of "simple geology," it should be pointed out that Massey (1993a) never used and has subsequently disowned the metaphor. "Geological stratification allows for little of the mutual interaction and influence of strata that I insisted on in whole chapters of the book" (p. 71). In retrospect, Warde's critique seems to have focused (not without validity) on the way her approach was put to work initially rather than on its conceptual architecture, which undoubtedly is more subtle and reflexive than the geological metaphor would suggest.

Nonetheless, in Massey's early work, the neglect of the complex and geographically variable ways in which labor markets are regulated and reproduced is a serious shortcoming.[4] Warde's critique remains telling on the issue of interactions among strata, which is central to Massey's dialectical conception of the generation of spatial divisions of labor.

The basic metaphor presents a very truncated view of what comprises a spatial division of labour. No contemporary account of the division of labour can afford to ignore the broad range of social relationships which derive from the process of the (re-)production of labour power. . . [T]here are considerable temporal and spatial variations in the conditions under which labour power is produced, and different sets of social arrangements appear to have pertinent political effects. These effects are germane to the formation of a local surface. (Warde, 1985, p. 199)

As Warde (1985) points out, a labor market perspective offers a more sophisticated understanding of, first, the make up of the "surface layer" (of variable labor qualities and practices); second, the roles of collective consumption and gender inequalities in structuring the distribution of waged work; and third, the relationship between firms' labor strategies and (re)location decisions, given the existence of segmented labor markets and the possibilities these present for the in situ remaking of labor relations.[5]

Although the local labor market represented a conceptual blind spot in Massey's original analysis, it may be seen as an important mediating influence on the link between "general" processes of industrial restructuring and "specific" local outcomes, the two levels of analysis which she quite rightly sought to "hold together" (1984, p. 8). The local labor market acts as a kind of intermediary transmission mechanism between the labor process (and associated labor demand) and concrete patterns of industrial restructuring (and regional employment change), contingently shaping the outcomes of the restructuring process. Labor market forces (which decide who gets which jobs and where) can thus be seen to intervene between the labor process (which generates demand for different kinds of work) and restructuring outcomes on the ground.

Massey's failure to specify this intermediating function exposes her to criticism on the grounds that (1) geographic shifts in employment are somehow being read off from labor process imperatives and (2) the interaction between labor process imperatives and locality-level conditions is underspecified. The first criticism may be inapposite; Massey's framework allows for a reciprocal relationship between the general process and the local effect. However, she is more vulnerable to the second criticism. Although she observes that the "actual geographical pattern adopted for a particular labour process in a particular country will depend on the interaction between the requirements of the labor process and the geographical surface inherited from the previous history of the country" (1984,

p. 23), much of this interaction occurs *through the local labor market,* which conditions the way in which abstract imperatives of labor demand are translated into actual employment outcomes. The labor market constitutes a kind of filter between tendencies within the labor process and their realization in particular (local) contexts (see Lee, 1982; Penn, 1985). Failure to consider its role opens up the possibility that restructuring outcomes will be wrongly inferred from changing labor process imperatives.

An elaborated conception of local labor markets provides a way to develop Massey's framework (understood in its broadest sense and not as a minimalist geological metaphor) and to throw new light on the links between labor and industrial restructuring and between changes in the labor process and regional employment. In fact, for some time the labor process literature has been exploring the interface between the labor market and the labor process, suggesting (and in many ways echoing the principles of Massey's approach) that the relationship should be understood as dialectical and mutually constitutive.[6] More recently, some of these insights, including work specifically on the labor market, have been built into more nuanced treatments of the processes of regional adjustment and restructuring.[7] This work may be seen as fulfilling some of the promise of Massey's original formulation, providing further means of unpacking the complex and contingent relationship between labor and industrial restructuring.

The remainder of this chapter pursues this goal by taking a close look at industrial homework in the Australian garment industry. Hitherto, work on restructuring has tended to privilege the labor process (and the social relations surrounding production) over the labor market (and the social relations surrounding the sale and purchase of labor-power). The subordination of labor markets to the labor process also has been typical of research on industrial homework (Rubery and Wilkinson, 1981; Peck, 1990b), where its functions in cost-cutting, deunionization, and enhanced production flexibility have been prioritized.[8] While specifying key aspects of the general logic of homework, these analyses have been insensitive to the local context in which homework strategies are formulated.

Again, a local labor market perspective sheds new light on this most ambiguous of employment forms, suggesting that local labor market is more than a passive backcloth against which labor process and industrial restructuring imperatives are played out. Rather, labor market processes play a role in shaping and setting the parameters for the wider course of industrial restructuring.

RESTRUCTURING AT HOME:
THE CASE OF INDUSTRIAL HOMEWORK

Recent years have seen spectacular growth in an employment form which for decades had been dismissed as an industrial anachronism. Typically associated with the darkest days of nineteenth-century industrialization, industrial homework has reemerged on a large scale. Significantly, the "new" homework often has little to do with the fanciful notions of electronic cottages and telecommuting popularized in the 1970s (see Toffler, 1981), but continues to be associated with arduous, poorly paid work and exploitation of the most disadvantaged groups in the labor market.[9] In the majority of contemporary accounts, industrial homework appears to be largely, although not exclusively, an urban phenomenon, one which is apparently no less common in the "advanced" metropolitan economies of North America and Europe than in the rapidly industrializing cities of the Third World.[10]

> Homeworking . . . is a global phenomenon. In highly industrialised countries such as Britain or the United States, women working at home produce everything from clothes, shoes and quilts to windscreen wipers and industrial transmission belts. They process insurance claims, peel vegetables, and do company accounts. In India and Bangladesh homeworkers assemble electrical components, roll cigarettes, and make cane furniture and many other goods. Homeworking takes place under most kinds of political systems, in vastly different economic circumstances, using traditional craft skills and highly sophisticated computer technologies. (Allen and Wolkowitz, 1987, p. 1)

Wherever it is found, homework tends to inhabit the margins of the formal economy. Its domestic location, coupled with the fact that there is usually something illegal about homework (such as evasion of taxes and employment legislation), mean that it represents an almost clandestine form of employment.[11] Consequently, research is hampered by the lack of official data, low "visibility" of the work, and the reluctance of those involved to disclose details of their activities. Nevertheless, some progress has been made in establishing links between homework and industrial restructuring.[12] However, less attention has been paid to the role of homework in restructuring urban labor markets, despite the fact that accounts of homework have become increasingly sensitive to its diversity of forms and effects (see Boris and Daniels, 1989).

In an exception to this general rule, Fernández-Kelly and García (1989) conducted a prescient comparative study of industrial homework, involving Hispanic women in the garment industries of Miami and Los Angeles, which served to highlight the importance of local sociopolitical and labor market factors. Their research revealed that quite different local outcomes were associated with the same general process (i.e., homework in the same industrial sector, exploiting an immigrant, Hispanic labor supply), and underlined the need for a "reassessment of industrial homework as a highly diversified phenomenon rather than a secondary outcome resulting from the interaction of abstract economic factors" (p. 178). Given its evident geographic variation, they argued for a more nuanced and grounded analysis.

In Los Angeles, homework took on a highly proletarianized form, associated with the hyperexploitation of successive waves of Mexican immigrants. For the women involved, many of whom were undocumented workers, homework was a strategy of last resort; that is, it was a strategy to raise households above the poverty line pursued by women in a particularly vulnerable position in the labor market. In contrast, homework in Miami had a rather different underlying logic. In a situation of generalized labor shortage, an enclave of Cuban refugees turned to homework not in desperation, but as a strategy for reconciling the cultural and economic demands facing their comparatively secure community. The presence of a Cuban entrepreneurial class, and the opportunity this afforded women to work within their (albeit patriarchally organized) ethnic community, afforded a degree of shelter from the market forces to which the Mexican homeworkers of Los Angeles were so completely exposed. Fernández-Kelly and García (1989) conclude that the key differences between the two groups of homeworkers stemmed from their

> distinctive patterns of labor market insertion. Historically, Mexicans have arrived in the U.S. labor market in a highly individuated and dispersed manner. As a result, they have been extremely dependent on labor demand and supply—forces beyond their control. Their working-class background and the stigma attached to their frequent undocumented status has accentuated even further their vulnerability vis-à-vis employers. By contrast, Cubans have been able to consolidate an economic enclave containing immigrant businesses which hire workers of a common culture and national background . . . [Here, these] commonalities of culture, national background, and language between immigrant employers and workers can become a mechanism for collective improvement of income levels and standards of living. (p. 171)

Consequently, the forms of homework strategies, including their underlying rationales and social contexts, vary over space. For Fernández-Kelly and García, "Class, ethnicity, and household composition intersect with regional economic structures to define the function of homework" (p. 166). Thus, it is the particular way in which the structures of class, ethnicity, and gender intersect in specific locations that contextualizes and configures strategies in the labor market (cf. Beneria and Roldan, 1987). Rather like labor market flexibility, homework strategies are profoundly shaped by the local socioinstitutional context in which they are formed. This is not to deny the importance of those supposedly universal—transhistorical and transgeographical—logics of homework, such as deunionization and cost control, but rather to point to their local variants and permutations. Moreover, labor market strategies such as homework are not simply *outcomes* of the restructuring process; they are part and parcel of the *calculus* of industrial restructuring.

The Reemergence of Homework in Australia[13]

The rapid contemporary growth of homework (or outwork as it is often termed) is not without precedent in the Australian garment industry. Historical accounts suggest that it flourished in the highly casualized Australian labor market of the late nineteenth century, being nowhere more prevalent than in the garment industry.[14] By the turn of the century, however, homework was on the decline. Concerted opposition by unions and reformers, innovative legislation, and the drift towards mass production combined to drive "the sweating evil" from the industry. By the First World War, homework was confidently dismissed as a relic of a bygone age. Although it was to reappear briefly following the Second World War, in response to the twin shortages of labor and factory space (Baker, Flood, Meekosha, and Jakubowicz, 1984), homework, it seemed, had entered a phase of terminal decline.

The 1950s and 1960s witnessed a mushrooming of factory production in the Australian garment industry, fueled by an enormous influx of immigrant workers, notably from southern Europe (Boyce, 1984; Collins, 1988). However, the long boom was disrupted in the mid-1970s, when rising competition from the Third World coincided with a number of domestic pressures, especially a reduction in tariff protection, currency revaluations, and wage increases. The industry was plunged into a period of profound rationalization, shedding almost one-quarter of the factory work force between 1974 and 1976 (Peck, 1990a). Although the restoration of tariff protection halted this precipitate decline, a profound wave of restructuring had been set in motion, and it was in its wake that homework was again to emerge in the late 1970s.

The reemergence of homework in the garment industry was noted by researchers in Melbourne in the late 1970s (Cusack and Dodd, 1978), and soon was corroborated elsewhere in Australia.[15] More recent work attests to the growing scale of homework in the industry.[16] Given its underground nature, enumeration is difficult, but a growth trend seems clear. Beginning at a level probably below 5,000 in the late 1970s, the size of the home-based work force in the garment industry, according to union estimates, rose rapidly to between 30,000 and 40,000 by 1983, then to over 60,000 by 1987; the figure for registered factory employment in the industry in 1987 was only 49,600 (ABS 1988). In the late 1980s, a survey of garment producers in Melbourne revealed that according to employers (who are hardly likely to exaggerate its incidence), the home-based work force was approximately 60 percent of the size of the factory work force. In small firms (employing fewer than twenty factory workers), the ratio of home-workers to factory workers was 2:1 (Peck, 1990b).

Since that time, there has been further expansion of homework. Following a recent high-profile campaign across the country, the Textile, Clothing and Footwear Union of Australia (TCFUA) has argued that the "most significant shift in the [garment] industry in the last five years has been a move from factory towards home-based production" (TCFUA, 1995, p. 4). The union maintains that there has been nothing less than an explosion in the number of homeworkers in the industry, which it estimates now to exceed 300,000. This would mean that homeworkers outnumber factory workers by a ratio of 14:1, and consequently, that the "bulk of the clothes currently made in Australia are being made in private homes" (p. 5). While the precise figures may be questioned, there can be no doubt that homework plays a significant and growing part in the Australian garment industry.

What is clear from these findings is that homework is by no means a marginal form of employment. In fact, the TCFUA claims that homework "is not only a *characteristic* of the [garment] industry in Australia, the industry is structured around it" (1995, p. 4). By implication, the process of industrial restructuring in the industry is intrinsically tied to and predicated on the increasing use of homework. Correspondingly, it must be acknowledged that the problems associated with homework—very low pay, long hours, inadequate health and safety provisions, and racial and sexual harassment—will doubtless be reaching epidemic proportions. The realities of homework are vividly conveyed in a report by Melbourne's Centre for Working Women Co-operative (CWWC, 1986):

Vicki has worked 15 years at home. She was told by her boss to pay tax herself although she is a registered outworker. She has not been receiving regular work, holiday pay or sick pay. She mainly works weekends. Her boss structures the work that way because he has so much extra work on weekends. (p. 23)

Pervin is a Turkish outworker who gets the work directly from the factory. She has to negotiate the rate of pay at the factory door and pick up and deliver it using a shopping trolley. She brings the work home to her Housing Commission flat which is on the 22nd floor. (p. 25)

Dimitra works very hard all day long with just little breaks to feed her son and prepare meals. Many times she works up to midnight because her son goes to sleep and her husband works afternoon shift. (p. 26)

Panagiota complains to her family about her sore arms and legs, back and neck pains. When the pain comes on she continues working. She sits on a wooden chair with padded cushions on it which she rigged up herself. Her husband has been retrenched from work for a year now, so she feels she must work. It is important for her family. (p. 32)

In Australia, as in many countries, it has proved difficult to address many of these problems of exploitation because of the exclusion of homeworkers from employment legislation. In the United States, the Reagan administration's attempts to deregulate homework in the 1980s, by lifting bans originally imposed by the 1938 Fair Labor Standards Act, had the effect of reopening issues of the economic rationale and legal status of homework (DuRivage and Jacobs, 1989). Debates in Europe have followed a rather different course, although in several countries the deregulation movement continues to hold sway (Tate, 1993). Reflecting in part the different institutional and political structures of the Australian labor market, legislative and social issues around homework have been tackled there in a distinctive way. As enshrined in the Clothing Trades Award, Australian employment law regards homeworkers as independent contractors, not as employees per se. Australian labor unions have long opposed this interpretation and, in 1987, successfully appealed to the Conciliation and Arbitration Commission for an amendment to the Clothing Trades Award (CATU, 1987). In arriving at its landmark decision, the Commission finally acknowledged that homeworkers are engaged in an employer-employee relationship. It described the homework system in the garment industry as closely integrated with factory production: homework is just one part of the overall manufacturing process, homeworkers usually being engaged to assemble and machine garments which have been designed and cut in the factory; further, homeworkers must work to rigid specifications, are permitted virtually no personal initiative, and are "certainly subject to control and direction" (ACAC, 1987, p. 37). These are undeniably relations of employment.

The designation of homeworkers as employees under the Clothing Trades Award places new requirements on employers. Homeworkers in Australia must now be provided with a written employment contract (including guaranteed hours), and employers must both pay Award-level wages (at the same rates as factory workers) and comply with Award requirements concerning sick pay, holiday entitlements, overtime bonuses, and maternity leave (*Ragmag*, 1988). Employers intending to use homeworkers also are required to register with the Industrial Registrar. The impact of the 1987 amendment on the material conditions of homework has been significant, but should not be overstated. The system is very difficult to police, so that many employers can and do continue to operate outside it (see TCFUA, 1995). A significant element is likely to remain beyond the scope of legal regulation because the viability of the system itself is predicated partly on "disorganization": employers often hire homeworkers as a means of evading Award wages and obligations; that is, homeworkers serve as a cheap (and flexible) alternative to factory workers. Remove the cost differential and homework loses its attractiveness for many employers to whom regulation is tantamount to prohibition (see *EIRR*, 1990; Herod, 1991a).

Explaining Homework:
The Labor Process and the Labor Market

Analysts of the economic rationale of homework have emphasized the following three factors.[17]

- Homework results in savings on both variable and fixed production costs. The fixed costs associated with operating a factory (for example, rent, light, heat, and building maintenance) are passed on to homeworkers. Savings on variable costs are achieved by holding down wage rates and evading payments for overtime, sick leave, and holidays.
- Homework allows employers to achieve heightened levels of production flexibility. Homeworkers are paid piece rates (i.e., only for actual output), and they can be dismissed and reengaged as required, enabling employers to adjust purchases of labor-power in accordance with their immediate production needs.
- Homework serves as a deunionization strategy. Homeworkers'

spatial dispersion and social isolation presents an obstacle to collective organization, and the existence of a pool of home-workers also confers a bargaining advantage upon employers in dealing with unions.

These explanations of the economic logic driving homework may be considered labor process–based. Homework is portrayed as a means of overcoming contradictions of the factory labor process, particularly its relative inflexibility and susceptibility to collective organization. Such factors figure prominently in accounts of the growth of homework in the Australian garment industry.[18]

Production Restructuring and Homework

In recent years, the Australian garment industry has come under intense pressure to reduce costs as import restrictions have again been relaxed (under the 1989–1996 federal government restructuring plan) and as import competition has intensified.[19] Compounding these pressures, the large apparel retailers—parlaying the bargaining strength derived from both their increased ability to source cheaply overseas and their expanding market shares (TCF Council, 1987)—have developed a heightened degree of control over prices and manufacturers. Retailers not only have been able to suppress wholesale price rises, but they also have used their power vis-à-vis manufacturers to insist upon design and quality improvements, shorter lead times, and smaller batch sizes.[20]

As a result, garment manufacturers face inexorable and unprecedented pressures both to reduce production costs and to enhance their organizational flexibility. As a cheap and flexible form of employment, homework has been crucial. Homeworkers are positioned at one extreme of the increasingly complex production chains which have evolved in the Australian garment industry in response to these pressures. As detailed by Cummings (1986, p. 30), these production chains, are headed by the major retailers (many of whom also possess import licenses). Beneath them are apparel agents, wholesalers, and importers; then manufacturers (some of which also are importers); next makers-up (small firms that assemble garments on contract to other firms); and finally, at the bottom of the production hierarchy, the homeworkers. As a recent union investigation put it, "The longer the contracting chain, the greater the number of outworkers" (TCFUA, 1995, p. 5).

In response to the imperatives of cost-cutting and flexibility, the configuration of the production hierarchy has changed markedly over recent years. Numerically, its upper echelons have narrowed, and the base has broadened.[21] Pressure to pare costs to the minimum has led to further concentration of bargaining power toward the top of the hierarchy. Critical here is the divisive, and ultimately destructive, role of competition: the asymmetrical relationship between the contractor and the larger number of potential subcontractors at each stage in the production chain engenders a climate of chronic undercutting. Retailers exploit wholesale agents, who in turn exploit manufacturers, who in turn exploit makers-up, who in turn exploit homeworkers. At each stage, the margins become tighter. Issues of profitability for retailers at the top of the production hierarchy become matters of subsistence for homeworkers at the bottom. Though clearly more flexible, the current state of the garment industry has little in common with the more optimistic visions of post-Fordism (Greig, 1990b; Peck, 1990a).[22]

Although there is strong evidence to suggest that the growth of homework is related to vertical disintegration, labor process-based explanations tell only part of the story. First, the cost-saving "benefits" of homework are not absolute; homework carries with it costs of its own, notably poor communications, problems in materials transfer, production-line imbalances, and uneven quality control. Second, insofar as they have either achieved a degree of regulation over homework or undermined its viability, the 1987 Clothing Trades Award amendments have eroded the cost-saving and flexibility-enhancing aspects of homework, as the costs of employing homeworkers have risen and employers have been required to establish binding employment contracts with them.

While important, labor process–based explanations of homework are incomplete. A fuller picture can be obtained by exploring the ways in which labor process imperatives have intersected with fundamental changes in the garment industry's labor market since the 1970s. Imperatives for restructuring are played out in and through the labor market; many firms have found themselves squeezed simultaneously by the ubiquitous threat of "cheap imports" and by the labor market strategies of unscrupulous Australian producers. As the TCFUA (1995) observes, "as well as the human cost of low wages and poor conditions, outwork constitutes unfair competition against employers who abide by the terms and conditions of awards. Many garment industry employers say that this is a bigger threat to them than cheap imports" (p. 6).

Labor Market Restructuring

Due to the highly urbanized nature of the Australian garment industry (Morrison, 1990), an analysis of the particular influence of *urban* labor market restructuring on industrial change is required. This gives a clearer view of the local context in which homework strategies are defined, and shows that industries and their associated labor processes both shape *and are shaped by* urban labor markets. Firms are attracted to urban labor markets in order to exploit agglomeration economies, but competition for labor among firms and industries also can be damaging. This is particularly true in the garment industry where interfirm relations tend to be dominated by cutthroat competition. Here, the labor market is competitively regulated, and high turnover, poaching, and skill shortages periodically lurch toward epidemic proportions. In this beggar-thy-neighbor environment, individual firms remain reluctant (or find it impossible) to raise wages, provide structured training, or develop internal labor markets.[23] Garment firms have been unable, in Harvey's (1989b) words, "to put a floor under their own competition" through some form of regulation of local labor market relations (p. 134).

The garment industry is a notorious plunderer of labor markets. Its dereliction in ensuring the reproduction of its own labor supply leaves it very much at the mercy of the vagaries of the urban labor market. Dependence on such an uncertain labor supply, the ebbs and flows of which are largely unpredictable, places the garment industry in a very insecure position, though for a considerable time its gamble paid off. Since the nineteenth century, the Australian garment industry has been able to rely on immigration to replenish its labor supply; more than any other, this industry depends on newly arrived immigrant workers, recruitment being restricted primarily to women.[24]

In the postwar period, immigrants from southern Europe (particularly Greece and Italy) formed the core of the garment industry's labor supply. Southern European immigrants entered Australia in large numbers between 1951 and 1966, but although male immigrants were quickly allocated jobs in the labor-hungry construction and manufacturing industries, no such arrangement was made for immigrant women (Collins, 1988). The patriarchal immigration policy of the time assumed that women's principal role would be reproductive rather than productive. Severe economic hardship, however, forced a great many working-class women into the labor market (Storer, 1976; Boyce, 1984). The majority of southern European women had only the most rudimentary knowledge of English and often had no previous industrial experience. They were ideal "factory fodder" for the expanding garment industry, which drew on skills they had developed (or were assumed to have developed) in the home and which required little in the way of English-language skills. Many factories recruited exclusively from a single ethnic community, permitting native languages to be spoken on the shopfloor.

Because immigrant women had virtually no alternative sources of employment, the garment industry acquired a captive work force. The ability to monopolize a segment of the labor supply was crucial for the industry which, with its low pay and poor working conditions, could not compete with other industries in more open segments of the labor market. By inhabiting the margins of the labor market and by utilizing skills which, because they were possessed by women, were systematically undervalued (Coyle, 1982), the garment industry secured almost exclusive access to this segment of the labor supply. In turn, privileged access to such a labor supply contributed to the backward nature of the industry; the pace of technical change was slow and Draconian work practices persisted.

Occupying a contingent position in the urban labor market, the garment industry was vulnerable. In the late 1960s and early 1970s, two changes in the Australian labor market undermined the garment industry's precarious position. First, the labor supply appropriated in the 1950s and 1960s began to dry up; immigration from southern Europe slowed markedly after 1966, causing a rupture in the immigrant labor supply which, within a few years, proved devastating to the industry. By the mid-1970s, the cohort of southern European immigrants who had entered the industry twenty years or so earlier began to shrink through natural attrition. Second-generation immigrants, it became clear, did not want to work in the garment factories where their mothers had toiled and, with their Australian education, they were able instead to enter the lower echelons of the white-collar labor market (Evans and Kelley, 1986; Hugo, 1986). A second key change in the labor market was the structural growth of the service industries, which opened up new employment opportunities for women and challenged the garment industry's hold on the female labor supply (Peck, 1990b). Low-paid, undervalued service work nonetheless compared favorably with the sweatshop conditions which prevailed in much of the garment industry.

In the late 1970s, a potential solution arrived in the form of a new wave of immigration, mostly from Vietnam (Collins, 1988). Following what was by then an established pattern, the majority of Vietnamese women found themselves consigned to the lowest echelons of the labor market.[25] However, although the garment industry was quick to exploit Vietnamese immigration, it had difficulty establishing monopolistic control over the new labor supply. In contrast to southern Europeans, Vietnamese immigration to Australia included the property-owning as well as working classes (Viviani, 1984) and, given the low barriers to entry in the garment industry, it was not surprising to find many new, Vietnamese-owned firms being established. These firms invariably employed working-class Vietnamese immigrants. Further, language barriers and a preference for working within their own ethnic community meant that Vietnamese women were rarely recruited successfully into the older factories (CATU, 1987). The more established firms, dominated by entrepreneurs born in Australia and southern Europe, were effectively denied access to the new labor supply of immigrants.

Since it remains common for first languages to be spoken on the shopfloor in immigrant-owned garment factories (Peck, 1990b), English-speaking entrepreneurs have a further inducement to resort to homework, as home-based women workers can be recruited through Vietnamese-speaking middlemen. These intermediaries allow established garment manufacturers to tap into pools of immigrant labor from Vietnam and elsewhere, overcoming some of the obstacles associated with ethnic resegmentation, while facilitating an arm's-length form of labor control, which exploits the social marginalization of immigrant homeworkers. Bilingual workers (employed on the TCFUA's help line for homeworkers) have described such control systems well.

> Our community [of Korean immigrants] is very close knit; people are reluctant to complain. They think they shouldn't complain because their boss is of the same ethnic background and they will never get a job in this community again.
> Many Laotian women stated that they were reluctant to reveal themselves. They are not sure if the union is independent of Social Security. Often the employer is a friend, or an acquaintance of the family, which complicates their ability to make any complaints about their work. (TCFUA, 1995, p. 14)

Thus, in the Australian garment industry, the expansion of homework is predicated on a complex set of urban social relations, which are simultaneously relations of class, ethnicity, gender and, in many cases, fear. The process of industrial restructuring is driven not simply by a production logic, but by the complex interaction of labor process imperatives and changing social relations in the local labor market. Local labor market relations more than passively reflect firms' restructuring and labor control strategies; they actively structure them.

By the early 1980s, much of the garment industry, particularly in the large urban centers of Melbourne and Sydney, had begun to experience chronic labor shortages.[26] Young workers proved particularly difficult to recruit, and the proportion of the industry's work force under age twenty-five fell by one-fifth between 1971 and 1986 (Peck,

1990b). In response, garment manufacturers tended to adopt one of two basic strategies. Some undertook a *spatial restructuring strategy*, relocating to the urban fringes and country towns, away from the areas of most intense labor market competition. Other firms adopted an *in situ restructuring strategy*, turning to homework to reestablish monopolistic control over their (urban) labor supply.[27]

In the first case, employment decentralization has been under way for some time. In the State of Victoria, for example, employment in the garment industry has been shifting away from its traditional inner-city base and expanding in the outer suburbs of Melbourne and country towns of rural Victoria. Between 1969 and 1988, employment fell by 56 percent (26,500) in the urban core and rose by 18 percent (3,000) in the suburban and rural periphery (Peck, 1992a). The attraction of nonmetropolitan areas lay in their abundant and stable supplies of female labor (Johnson, 1987; Peck, 1990a). Garment firms which relocated to the Queensland town of Maryborough, partly to escape the problems of urban labor markets, found their new work forces to be "generally stable and hard-working, receptive to change, easy to motivate, loyal and *aware of the importance of each company to the local economy*" (Sloan, Baker, McGavin, Ryan, and Wooden, 1985, p. 151, emphasis added).

The spatial restructuring strategy is not open to all firms. It has been the larger plants with comparatively long production runs which have relocated to the urban fringe and the country towns (Peck, 1990a; O'Neill, 1991); compared to the larger plants, the locational capability of small firms, particularly the makers-up who rely exclusively on small-batch subcontracting, is severely restricted. Smaller firms in the more volatile sectors of the industry, locked into dense networks of contracting and subcontracting,[28] could not contemplate such a relocation. Themselves effectively captive in the inner-city, such firms have sought an in situ strategy for coping with labor shortage: utilization of homeworkers.

Homework is more than a cheap and flexible alternative to the factory labor process; it is also a strategy for coping with labor markets. Faced with a chronic shortage of factory labor, garment firms have used homework to open up a new labor supply in a comparatively underutilized segment of the wage-labor market. Homework also enables the industry to reestablish the monopolistic labor market relations on which it has come to rely. As shown in numerous studies, the overwhelming majority of homeworkers are responsible for the care of children or aged relatives, and few have anything but the most rudimentary English-language skills.[29] With the inadequate scale and uneven geography of childcare provision,[30] these workers are largely excluded from factory work. Again, the garment industry is resorting to plundering strategies and exploiting a segment of the labor supply with few if any alternative employment opportunities.

Evidence from employers appears to support the proposition that the use of homeworkers is related to tight labor markets. Under the 1987 Award amendment, employers must register with the Industrial Registrar if they wish to employ homeworkers and must state their reasons for doing so. Those employers who continue to abuse the homework system are, of course, unlikely to register, and those who register will certainly name their reasons carefully. Bearing these caveats in mind, one still can gain insight into the factors underlying employers' use of homeworkers. An analysis of the registration records of garment firms who registered for the use of homeworkers in the state of Victoria in the late 1980s revealed that, for employers, the use of homeworking was in direct response to the (socially created) shortage of factory labor (see Peck, 1992a, and Table 6.1). The majority of employers cited labor market factors (such as shortages of skilled or suitable labor available for factory work, or employees' childcare responsibilities) in explaining their use of homeworkers, but only a small number referred to the cost-saving and flexibility-enhancing facets of homework (such as fluctuations in work load, efficiency considerations, etc).[31] Although it is to be expected that such factors might be understated in official documents, the argument that homework has labor market–based determinants must surely stand.

Table 6.1. Garment Firms Registered for the Use of Homeworkers, Victoria, Australia, 1988–1989

	Firms registered for employment of homeworkers		Estimated total population of firms		Registration rate
	Number	%	Number	%	%
Melbourne statistical division					
City center	14	5.5	48	6.3	29.2
Inner suburbs	125	49.0	248	32.6	50.4
Intermediate suburbs	32	12.5	125	16.4	26.6
Outer suburbs	74	29.0	271	35.6	27.3
Rest of Victoria	10	3.9	70	9.2	14.3
Total Victoria	255	100.0	762	100.0	33.5

Homework registration records.
From Peck (1992a), p. 681. © 1992 Pion Limited. Reprinted by permission.

Mapping Homework:
Exploring the Hidden Geographies of Work

Pursuing the above arguments, homework should be most common in areas of severe labor shortage (in the city centers and inner suburbs) and less developed where the garment industry is still able to recruit from the open labor market (in the outer suburbs and country districts). Registration records strongly confirm this proposition (see Table 6.1).

Overall, one-third of all garment firms in Victoria registered with the Industrial Registrar. Owing to the low propensity to register, this should be regarded as an underestimate of the extent of homework, but despite the limited data, geographic disaggregation proves revealing. Rates of registration for homework are lowest in rural Victoria (14 percent) and highest in the inner suburbs (50 percent). Relative to the industry as a whole (39 percent of all firms), a rather higher proportion (55 percent) of firms registered for the use of homeworkers is located in the urban core. Survey work in the inner Melbourne suburb of Collingwood suggests that actual levels of homework in such areas almost certainly exceed even this high rate (Peck, 1990b). The following comments from two employers, who clearly perceive themselves to be victims of a hostile local labor market (the dominant social relations of which are reproduced in no small part by their own employment strategies), exemplify widespread attitudes toward homework in the industry.

> The biggest problem is getting people to work in the factory. Even unskilled people are in short supply. That's why the country operations are so successful. Many of our ex-machinists are going into cleaning and catering jobs. They get better pay there. You see, they get sick of the clothing industry once they've been retrenched a couple of times. It's unscrupulous employers who cause these problems (Manager, large menswear company).

> There's a problem getting skilled labor. . . . This is why I started using outworkers. I wanted to get people in the factory, but I couldn't. . . . It's easier to have people in the factory, but the machinists want to work in big factories where the employment is more regular. . . . My outworkers can't work in the factory because they have children and can't do 8-to-4 hours (Manager, maker-up). (Peck, 1990b)

Not only is the overall level of homework related to local labor markets, but there also is systematic variation in the reasons given by employers for using homeworkers. Labor shortage tended to be cited by firms in tight, inner-city labor markets. In such areas, garment firms do indeed appear to be using homework to open previously untapped labor reserves in the context of highly competitive labor markets.

Beset with under- and misreporting, data derived from homework registration forms clearly have limitations. However, the Census of Population and Housing returns permit light to be shed on this phenomenon from a different direction: the supply side. From travel-to-work data, it is possible to distinguish those workers who work at home. Comparison with the factory-based work force reveals that homework is overwhelmingly urban. Although census data also grossly understate the level of homework and overstate that of factory employment (possibly as a result of deliberate miscoding by home-workers wishing to conceal their employment status), homeworkers' share of the total work force is almost twice as high in Australia's cities than in nonmetropolitan areas. Seventeen percent of the factory work force is located in rural areas as compared with only 10 percent of homeworkers (see Peck, 1992a).

Thus, although it is possible to obtain only a partial picture of the subterranean phenomenon of homework, the evidence suggests a distinctive geography. Moreover, its geography seems entirely consistent with the argument that homework is in part a product of *local* labor market pressures, not just a generic response to the internal contradictions of the labor process or the threat of overseas competition. Such labor market causes of homework, which may be dominant in some circumstances, need to be given analytical priority equal to that of the labor process, which seems to have attained the status of conventional wisdom. A critical reconsideration of the conventional wisdom is called for especially in Australia, where the 1987 Clothing Trades Award amendment appears to have been successful in regulating at least part of the homework sector, thereby undermining its cost-saving and flexibility-enhancing effects.

STRUCTURES AND STRATEGIES OF RESTRUCTURING IN URBAN LABOR MARKETS

The tendency for capital to create a collective worker is one of the central contradictions of the capitalist labor process. Capital combines labor in production (a physical expression of which is the factory) in order to capture the fruits of the social productivity of labor, but then must take steps to ensure that collective political consciousness does not develop in the work force (Lebowitz, 1987). Strategies of divide and rule (such as forging work-force hierarchies) are among those deployed by capital (Gordon, Edwards, and Reich, 1982).

There are parallel contradictions in capitalist labor markets. There is a tendency for firms and industries to cluster in space (a physical expression of which is the urban labor market) in order to exploit the substantial external economies associated with the reproduction of labor-power, but again, the exploitation of urban labor pools as a collective good has contradictory results (Castells, 1977). Capital gains from urban labor market locations through exploitation of the physical and social infrastructures of the city, collective shouldering of the costs of skill formation, and the enhanced opportunities for substitution which characterize diverse urban labor pools. However, cities also may become fertile breeding grounds for class consciousness while, within the capitalist class, competition tends to induce short-termism and plundering.[32]

Like the factory, the city is a contradictory site of capitalist accumulation. Marx's (1976) dictum that "the workers' power of resistance declines with their dispersal" (p. 591) while "concentration increases [the power] of the urban workers" (p. 638) applies at both scales of accumulation. Capital's ability to capture the benefits of socialized production turns upon its ability to divide and weaken the working classes. The fact that this endeavor has both labor process and labor market components means that labor market relations must be considered in industrial restructuring. As Lazonick found in his historical research on the British and U.S. cotton-spinning industries, the labor market imparts its own dynamic to industrial change.

> [Capital and labour] sought with varying degrees of success to supersede or at least counteract the operation of the [labour] market in order to be better able to control not only the terms of the wage bargain but also the intensity of labour effort and hence the level of labour productivity. The institutional character of the labour market in a given industry in a particular [location] will be one factor that, in the short run, is itself determined by [and reconstitutive of] the evolving nature of production relations. (1981, pp. 492–493)

The labor market is an important site of class struggle. It is a primary arena for capital's contradictory imperative to combine yet divide workers and, specifically, for its need to foster separation and segregation in order to assert authority over production. Strategies such as homework contribute to the fragmentation of labor's collective spaces (cf. Herod, 1991a).

Contingent Work, Contingent Strategies

In the Australian garment industry it is clear that labor market restructuring, and specifically *urban* labor market restructuring, has played an important role in industrial change. Historically, the industry has thrived on the free-rider benefits associated with its predominantly urban location, first, by evading the costs of skill formation through poaching and exploitation of women's skills developed in the domestic sphere; second, by exploiting labor market crowding through hiring and firing in line with fluctuating production requirements; and third, by tapping low-cost female labor reserves of the inner suburbs. In recent years, however, the foundations of its privileged urban location have begun to dissolve. The garment industry's labor market position has always been precarious; its reliance on a marginal labor supply, drawn from the periphery of the labor market, is paralleled by its own marginal labor market position vis-à-vis other urban industries. The industry was only able to develop anything approaching a firm purchase on its labor supply by using excess, secondary labor supplies in the absence of interindustry competition for labor. These labor market conditions persisted for two decades before beginning to break down in the early 1970s, triggered by the tightening of the immigrant labor supply, the ethnic resegmentation of the secondary labor market, and the rise of labor market competition from the service sector.

Labor market factors have been decisive in the rapid and substantial growth of homework in the garment industry since the late 1970s. Although the labor process plays a role, it cannot fully explain why homework has not been more enduring in an industry which has always placed a premium on cost-cutting and flexibility. After all, it was conditions in the labor market—not the labor process—which changed so dramatically in the 1970s. Homework seemed to provide a solution to the industry's labor market problems; it provided a means to tap into the vast domestic labor reserve present in Australia's inner-city areas which few, if any, other industries were able to achieve. In this sense homework constitutes an explicitly gendered employment form; its very existence is largely predicated on the existence of a pool of economically marginalized female workers.

Far from being contingent, the labor market mechanisms of job filling are integral to the process of job design. In other words, the nature of jobs is shaped by expectations about which social groups will fill them. More formally, the processes by which labor demand is constituted are partly dependent on the social structures of the (local) labor supply. Extending Massey (1984), this suggests one mechanism by which local labor qualities (and the nature of their mobilization in the labor market) impinge upon the evolution of the labor process and, through this, the unfolding round of accumulation.

As Harvey (1989b) has observed, capitalists prefer to be outside rather than merely ahead of the competition. Homework enables the garment industry to reposition itself within urban labor markets and to deepen its control over the labor process. The tendency for capital to seek out or create for itself sheltered areas of the labor market (in which the degree of interfirm competition for labor is low) is, of course, common in urban areas. Capitalists normally play an active role in securing a labor supply in the face of urban labor market competition. Two means of achieving this are (1) the payment of high wages, purposely exceeding the local or sectoral rate for the job, and (2) the construction of internal labor markets in which the majority of job filling occurs through internal bureaucratic procedures rather than external market mechanisms. The garment industry has never taken such active steps to secure its labor supply and indeed, an industry characterized by tight margins, short-term profits and extreme volatility is unlikely to take on such heavy and long-term investments in labor. Rather, the garment industry resorts to the destructive plundering of urban labor reserves in the hope that Providence and the Department of Immigration will look after the long-term reproduction of its labor supply.

Such instances of the spatial separation of labor reproduction and production often involve accelerated exploitation (see Kearney, 1991). As Villa (1986) has observed with respect to immigrant labor, the process of the "social reproduction of labour takes place outside the economic system that employs that labour power. As a result, the economic and social cost of reproduction of labour is not paid for by the economic system which consumes the labour power. We could say that, in the case of immigrants, it is the very low standard of living in their place of origin that induces them to emigrate, and to supply their labour power" (p. 259).

Alongside its (less than absolute) cost-saving and flexibility-enhancing advantages for employers, the reemergence of homework must be viewed in the context of attempts to overcome contradictions of urban locations. Homework provides a means to remake urban labor relations; in recent years it has provided a means of tapping into particularly vulnerable niches of the urban labor supply. However, it is ultimately a destructive strategy because it is typically deployed in order to evade—or, more precisely, *displace*—the costs associated with the reproduction of labor. In Australia as elsewhere, it is used by an industry apparently content to continue inhabiting the margins of the urban labor market, however precarious for the industry or pernicious for the work force.

LOCAL IMPERATIVES OF LABOR CONTROL

Labor markets play a decisive role in industrial restructuring, conditioning firms' choice of labor strategies and moulding the geography of industry and its social relations. The labor market plays a crucial mediating role in the process by which new rounds of investment, bearing new sets of labor process relations, are translated into locational imperatives. Such imperatives cannot be assumed to be born of the logic of new labor processes, but instead are the indeterminate product of the ways in which processes of restructuring in labor markets and the labor process interact. Thus, there is a need to deepen both conceptual and empirical understanding of the ways firms and industries position themselves in, accommodate to, and ultimately transform local labor markets. As Castro, Méhaut, and Rubery (1992b) argue, "Social organisation is not separable from economic organisation [and therefore there is an] interlocking dynamic between productive systems and the organisation of labour markets" (p. 3).

One way to bring together the labor process and labor market analytically is through an integrative concept of labor control. Understood broadly, labor control relates not only to the immediate concerns of the labor process ("getting the job done") but also to labor market relations ("getting the job done tomorrow and next month"). Consequently, labor control refers to reproduction of the social relations of both the labor process and the labor market. This conception of labor control embraces the interrelated processes of (1) securing an appropriate labor supply, (2) maintaining control within the labor process, and (3) reproducing this set of social relations. Imperatives of labor control (so defined) can exert a significant influence over the course and pattern of industrial restructuring, including integration or disintegration (see Friedman, 1977; Gordon, Edwards, and Reich, 1982). Here, the growth of industrial homework has been linked to the imperative of maintaining control over the garment industry's local labor supply. Similarly, employers pursue subcontracting strategies to extend control over the labor process; jobs are relocated from large, unionized factories to small, nonunion shops, thereby redefining the social relations of work (Holmes, 1986; Peck and Lloyd, 1989). Industrial structures and restructuring reflect the existing possibilities for establishing different forms of labor control within a given local labor market. Through an integrative concept of labor control, it is possible to theorize systematic links between industrial structure, labor process imperatives, and local labor market outcomes.

- A given production chain or industry comprises interrelated labor processes;
- Each of these labor processes tends to be associated with (a range of) qualitatively different labor supplies (although the chosen labor supply is not determined functionally by technical characteristics of the labor process);
- Each coupling between a particular labor process and a particular labor supply is associated with a different system of labor control;
- Industrial structure (including the degree of integration or disintegration) and the form of restructuring will be configured so as to secure, maintain, and develop appropriate forms of labor control;
- Industrial structure therefore reflects both the technical configuration of its constituent labor processes and the structure of the local labor market (representing a profile of different labor supplies, a set of institutionalized procedures for accessing them, and a particular system of social regulation).

Thus, there is a recursive relationship between industrial structure (with its set of labor processes) and the local labor market (with its segmented and compartmentalized labor supply and regulatory norms). These are configured so as to secure the most appropriate forms of labor control available within a local labor market.

Homework illustrates some of the ways in which geographies of labor control are changing. It also highlights the fact that the shifting map of labor control is both an outcome of and a stimulant to industrial restructuring. Following Massey (1984), industrial restructuring is conditioned by local conjunctures, or the differing ways in which labor process imperatives and labor market structures intersect at the local level. Strategies such as industrial homework are predicated on the prior existence of an appropriate set of labor process relations (such as a technically divisible labor process and/or relatively weak labor organization) *and* an appropriate set of labor market relations (such as the existence of a pool of home-based laborers whose ability to participate in the "external" wage-labor market is restricted and/or their close physical proximity to the employing organization). In the case of the garment industry it is also evident that restructuring strategies are conditioned by, perhaps even predicated on, specific local conjunctures of gender and ethnic relations. One of the functional features of homework is its capacity to tap deep into immigrant labor pools, reaching workers who are effectively excluded from the regular wage-labor market. Gender relations also profoundly structure the homework employment relationship, given that the class division between homeworker and contractor is typically also a gender division. For garment employers, homework strategies are really only feasible where local social arrangements permit the hyperexploitation of a captive labor pool.

The local confluence of labor markets and labor process also shapes the dynamics of restructuring. Massey's (1984) analysis revealed that multiplant firms stretched out production hierarchies over space in order to tap into appropriate labor supplies; in her work, restructuring of the social division of labor seemed to imply the formation of new spatial divisions of labor. However, firms and industries opt differentially for employment strategies involving spatial relocation or in situ change, and there is a need to investigate the link between their restructuring strategies and processes of adjustment within and between local labor markets. Clark (1981) has suggested closer attention needs to be paid to the circumstances under which firms opt to internalize or externalize their labor market relations, assuming that these strategies are conditioned by the balance of power in the labor process and the local labor market.

> [O]ne type of bargaining strategy open to the firm is to internalize the labor market, thereby reducing labor turnover and hoarding labor over the short-run. Another strategy is to externalize the labor market so that control and authority are maintained. Which strategy is chosen will depend on the balance of interdependence between labor and capital. . . . Differences in the extent of internal/external labor market relations are likely to be indicative of the advantages and disadvantages of different spatial arrangements of production. (pp. 423–424)

Following, say, technical change in the labor process or a shift in the local labor supply, the search for a new labor control "fix" can trigger either relocation (a spatial strategy for engaging with a new labor supply) or change in an industry's local labor market relations (an in situ strategy for engaging with a new labor supply). Thus, labor control affects the relative costs of restructuring in place or through space. Consequently, it is at the heart of the process by which new geographies of employment are formed.

NOTES

1. See Braverman (1974); Edwards (1979); and Wood (1982, 1989).
2. See Markusen (1993) and Martin (1993).
3. See Warde (1985); Lovering (1989); and Bagguley, Mark Lawson, Shapiro et al. (1990).
4. See Lovering (1989); cf. Massey (1993b, 1994).
5. On this latter issue, see Clark's (1981) early contribution.
6. See Friedman (1977); Edwards (1979); Lee (1982); Kelly (1985); and Penn (1985).
7. See Clark, Gertler, and Whiteman (1986); Harrison and Bluestone (1988); Scott (1988b); Walker (1988); Storper and Walker (1989); and Sayer and Walker (1992).
8. For example, see Albrecht (1982); Lipsig-Mumme (1983); and Dangler (1986). This, emphatically, is not to deny the importance of the labor process. Such a stance would be counterproductive. What is required is an approach which embeds the labor process within the wider circuits of capital (see Peck, 1990a). The labor process is but one moment in a circuit that begins with the purchase of labor-power in the labor market, moves through the extraction of surplus-value in the labor process, and continues to the realization of surplus-value in product markets and the subsequent reinvestment of profits.
9. For overviews, see Allen and Wolkowitz (1987); Singh and Kelles-Viitanen (1987); Boris and Daniels (1989); and Pennington and Westover (1989).
10. See Mitter and van Luijken (1983); Lipsig-Mumme (1983); Dangler (1986); Beneria and Roldan (1987); Sassen (1988); and Rowbotham (1993).
11. This point is made by de Grazia (1980); EIRR (1990); and Schneider de Villegas (1990).
12. See Cummings (1986); Mitter (1986); Beneria and Roldan (1987); Benton (1989); and van Luijken and Mitter (1989).
13. The remainder of this chapter is a substantially revised version of an article published in Environment and Planning D: Society and Space, 10 (1992):671–689 (London: Pion Limited). I wish to thank Pion for permission to adapt and reprint the article.
14. See Lee and Fahey (1986); Bennett (1986); and Frances (1986).
15. See TransNational Brief (1980); AAWL (1982); and Neumark and Eldestin (1982).
16. See IMRC (1984); TNC Workers Research (1985); Cummings (1986); CWWC (1986); CATU (1987); DIRE (1987); Scott (1987); Walker (1987, 1989); O'Donnell (1988); Alcorso (1989); Tassie (1989); and TCFUA (1995).
17. See Lipsig-Mumme (1983) and Allen and Wolkowitz (1987).
18. See IMRC (1984); TNC Workers Research (1985); and CATU (1987).
19. See CATU (1986a, 1986b); IAC (1986); and TCF Council (1991).

20. "By asserting control over the market, major retailers are effectively being supplied with local products—bearing the 'Made in Australia' tag—for wages as low as those in China, Indonesia or Vietnam" (TCFUA, 1995, p. 15). See also TNC Workers Research (1985); Greig (1990a); and Peck (1990a).

21. Official statistics reveal little about the changing configuration of the garment production chain beyond confirming that employment in factories has declined substantially since the early 1970s (ABS, 1986). Further job losses in this sector are predicted in the wake of trade liberalization (CATU, 1986a; IAC, 1986; McCreadie, 1990; DoL, 1991a, 1991b; TCF Council, 1991). Beyond this, only piecemeal evidence exists. At the head of the production chain, the concentration of the retail sector has vested enormous power in the hands of a very small number of corporate buyers (Rosewarne, 1983). Rationalization also has occurred at the next level down, the number of wholesale agents and importers having fallen considerably largely because of the increasing propensity of major retailers to deal directly with manufacturers (Cummings, 1986). At the bottom of the production hierarchy, the number of homeworkers has grown immensely since the late 1970s. However, little systematic evidence is available on the makers-up, that class of subcontractors believed to have grown substantially in recent years. It is known that the level of subcontracting among garment manufacturers increased in the 1980s (DEIR, 1985; Peck, 1990b); while telephone-book entries for Melbourne also suggest a strong rising trend. As a share of all garment industry entries, makers-up rose from just 1.6 percent in 1969 to 10.8 percent in 1990, representing the fastest growing element of the industry by a clear margin.

22. Similarly, Allen and Wolkowitz argue that "moves toward what is euphemistically called 'flexibility' are in fact often better analysed as ways of cutting costs or passing them on to other firms, state bodies, or, as in homework, workers themselves" (1987, p. 167).

23. See APS (1989); Greig (1990b); and Peck (1990a).

24. Storer (1976); Frances (1986); Tait and Gibson (1987); Alcorso (1989); and Peck (1990a).

25. A variety of factors affect the subordinate labor market allocation of Vietnamese immigrants, including their lack (or perceived lack) of English-language skills, their lack of work qualifications and skills recognized in Australia, and straightforward racism on the part of some employers (see Viviani, 1984; Collins, 1988; Loh, 1988; Burnley, 1989).

26. For evidence, see Lo Bianco and Boland (1980); DEIR (1985); Konstantinidis (1987); APS (1989); and TCFUA (1995). With its tight margins, the industry could not respond to labor shortages by increasing wages. In fact, as new service industries began to exploit the female labor pool and as intersectoral wage competition accelerated, the garment industry slipped yet further down the wages league table during the 1970s and 1980s (Peck, 1990a).

27. For a clear theoretical exposition, see Clark (1981).

28. This case has been made by Scott (1984) and Hiebert (1990).

29. See CWWC (1986); CATU (1987); and DIRE (1987).

30. See Brennan and O'Donnell (1986) and Fincher (1991).

31. Forty-three percent of the firms cited shortages of skilled or suitable labor available to work in the factory, 13 percent cited employees' childcare responsibilities, 9 percent used homeworkers for specialist tasks, 7 percent stated that their factory premises or facilities were inadequate, 5 percent said that homeworkers preferred to work at home, and 1 percent cited transport difficulties. By contrast, no more than a minority referred to the cost-saving or flexibility-enhancing features of the work system (10 percent said that homeworkers were used to cope with busy times, 5 percent used them to cope with the work load, and 2 percent cited efficiency and production costs).

32. See Gordon (1977); Webber (1986); Lane (1988); Harvey (1989b); and Peck (1992b); cf. Scott (1988b) and Storper and Scott (1990).

Chapter 7

BUILDING WORKFARE STATES

Institutions of Labor Regulation

Imperatives of labor regulation are deeply inscribed in the structures and strategies of contemporary capitalist states. Moreover, as Dehli (1993) argues, "the regulation, reproduction and qualification of labour power have gained renewed importance in state policy strategies in Western Europe and North America, as advanced industrial countries and regions compete to attract and hold the investment of corporations with 'no fixed address' " (p. 105).[1] Global competition, it would seem, is causing nation-states to scrutinize labor regulation and welfare policy not as sources of national social integration but as bargaining counters in global economic competition (see Barnet and Cavanagh, 1995). Thus, while President Clinton has talked of the need for a national training policy to equip Americans for the competitive global marketplace of the 1990s, he also threatens ominously to "end welfare as we know it."

Although these may seem to be quite separate policy domains, they are being melded together as nation-states (and particularly neoliberal nation-states) respond to globalization by hacking at the roots of the welfare state while framing economic policy solely in supply-side terms. In countries like the United States, Canada, and the United Kingdom, training policy and welfare policy are in danger of becoming one and the same. Arguments for welfare reform are couched in terms of global competition and what the treasury can afford while training policy is reduced to preparing the unemployed for an increasingly volatile labor market.[2]

In the United States, the attack on the welfare state is part and parcel of a wider "business offensive against labor": while "employers have been pressing for concessions from their workers, business interests have supported . . . administration[s which are] openly hostile to the welfare state" (Block, Cloward, Ehrenreich, and Piven, 1987, pp. xii–xiii). The fusion of business interests and neoliberal state strategies extends beyond general political commitments to be reflected in the structure and control of the state apparatus itself, where business leaders are drafted to steer, oversee, and remake the institutional machinery of the welfare state (see Peck, 1995). Significantly, private-sector involvement has been especially marked at the increasingly blurred interface between *privatizing* training policy and *marketizing* welfare policy. In the United States, local business leaders have been recruited to serve on Private Industry Councils (PICs), locally based, business-led agencies that oversee the contracting of training provision (mainly for those at a disadvantage in the labor market) under the Job Training Partnership Act,[3] which inspired the more far-reaching Training and Enterprise Councils (TECs) regime in the United Kingdom.[4]

In both the United States and the United Kingdom, the incorporation of business leaders at the sharp end of policy delivery (and sometimes in policy formulation) is predicated on the view that with them comes an appreciation of competition and the market. It is no coincidence that these are the selfsame principles guiding neoliberal welfare reform in both countries, where there has been a fundamental restructuring of what King (1995) calls the work-welfare regime (encompassing training programs for the unemployed, workfare, and job placement). Through these and other channels, the welfare state and its underlying principles are being remade. The strength of the political forces marshaled against the welfare state is nowhere more evident than in

> current discussions of "welfare reform" that center entirely on workfare—plans to drop individuals from the welfare rolls unless they agree to take available employment or sign up for training programs. There are differences between the various workfare plans with respect to the quality and quantity of the training opportunities offered, the level of coercion in requiring individuals to take particular jobs, and the determination of how quickly a mother must agree to place her small children in child care so that she can participate in work or training. Yet all of the workfare plans

reinforce the dominance of the market by pressuring participants to take whatever jobs happen to be available, at whatever wages employers see fit to offer. (Block, Coward, Ehrenreich, and Piven, 1987, p. xiii)

Workfare amounts to much more than a meanspirited goading of welfare recipients (although it is that, too). Fundamentally, it withdraws universal rights of access to welfare and asserts the primacy of the market as an allocative principle. Workfarism represents a thoroughgoing transformation of the institutional bases of labor market regulation. Recognizing its importance, theorists of the capitalist state have begun to talk in terms of the emergence of a *workfare state* (Jessop, 1993), which "marks a clear break with the Keynesian welfare state as domestic full employment is downplayed in favour of international competitiveness and redistributive welfare rights take second place to a productivist reordering of social policy" (Jessop, 1994, p. 263). In their own way, advocates of workfare also have drawn attention to the fact that it is much more than a strategy for reforming programs.

> Workfare should not be a short-term program to existing welfare clients, but a long-term program to destroy the culture of poverty . . . what's most important is not whether sweeping streets or cleaning buildings helps Betsy Smith, single teenage parent and high school dropout, learn skills that will help her find a private sector job. It is whether the prospect of sweeping streets and cleaning buildings for a welfare grant will deter Betsy Smith from having the illegitimate child that drops out of her school and onto welfare in the first place—or, failing that, whether the *sight* of Betsy Smith sweeping streets after having her illegitimate child will discourage her younger sisters and neighbors from doing as she did. (Kaus, 1986, p. 27)

Although "pure" workfare (requiring the unemployed to "earn" their welfare checks) remains comparatively rare even in the United States (Deacon, 1994), workfare is nevertheless emblematic of important shifts in labor regulation and work-welfare reform (see Block, Cloward, Ehrenreich, and Piven, 1987; Rank, 1994; King, 1995). Taking on diverse elements and institutional forms, workfarist shifts include:

- increasing market selectivity in access to welfare and labor market programs
- reductions in the levels of welfare support and scope of eligibility criteria

- the application of different forms of compulsion (or "incentives") to participate in education and training, make-work, or low wage employment
- ever tighter policing of benefits and surveillance of welfare recipients
- the imposition of increasingly stringent work requirements
- the privatization and deregulation of job training

Together, these developments represent a nascent *workfarist pattern* in labor regulation, the sense in which the term workfare will be used in this chapter rather than the strict (and narrow) program definition. This understanding of workfare as a political-economic *tendency* is supported by the emerging "workfare consensus" on the moral, political, and economic desirability of moving welfare recipients into the work force (Block and Noakes, 1988; Handler, 1995).[5]

More generally, if workfare experiments can be seen as part of a shift toward the marketization of work-welfare regimes, they are germane to the perspective argued in this book. First, market forces are not simply out there waiting to be released, but in fact are politically constructed and institutionally mediated. The process of marketizing work-welfare is intrinsically political, concerned with remaking institutional forms and forces which are immanent in the labor market (and therefore shape the way it works). Second, marketization is not inevitable, economically determined, or identical in all places. As Johnson, McBride, and Smith (1994) have argued on the neoliberalization of Canadian labor regulation, "nation-states are much less prisoners of circumstance than is implied in some rather deterministic interpretations of economic globalization. . . . Economic globalization obviously matters. However, ideologically conditioned policy responses to globalization also matter" (p. 9). Third, marketization— like the markets it seeks to "liberate"—is contradictory. As King (1995) has shown, U.S. and British work-welfare reforms are deepening rather than solving the low skills equilibrium in which the two countries languish.[6] It also has become clear that so-called deregulation requires large-scale (and often problematic) state intervention.[7]

This chapter explores these themes by looking closely at work-welfare reform in the United Kingdom, where attention is drawn to the political and institutional making of markets, institutionally and geographically specific forms of marketization, and its internally contradictory and crisis-prone nature. One way to tackle these subjects would have been comparative analysis, as exemplified by King's (1995) comprehensive and wide-ranging study (cf. Stein 1976). The approach taken here is rather different; beginning with Jessop's (1993) rendering of the transition from Keynesian welfarism to Schumpeterian work-farism, the chapter moves from the abstract to the increasingly concrete and complex, focusing on the specific form and functions of the British state, and then on a particular work-welfare policy initiative, the Training and Enterprise Councils. TECs both illustrate the problematic nature of neoliberal experiments in labor regulation and expose some of the contradictions of deregulationist responses to the regulatory dilemmas of skill formation and management of unemployment.

Methodologically, the objective of this chapter—to move from abstract claims concerning tendential state forms to the specificities of a policy area—is taxing. It raises the question of which sorts of analysis might complement or extend, at the level of concrete institutional conjunctures, the more abstract regulation approach. In its current state, this virtually demands abstract or macrolevel analysis. For Jessop (1995), while the regulation approach

> may provide a useful heuristic framework for contextualizing (integral) economic change, its emphasis on search processes, trial-and-error experimentation, structural coupling, costabilization, and so forth, implies that [it] should be applied over a relatively long time horizon rather than used to explain specific events in the immediacy of the here and now. . . . For the [regulation approach] is more concerned with the emergence over time of reproducible structural coherence in accumulation regimes in and through regulation than it is with the genesis of specific policy measures and their implementation in specific institutional or organizational sites. This is reflected, of course, in the relatively closed structural interpretations of Fordism (which lies behind us) and the more open speculations about what, if anything, comes *after* Fordism (with a stable post-Fordism still, at best, faintly discernible on the distant horizon). (p. 1617)

These are important qualifications and clarifications, not least because they serve to constrain post-Fordist speculation. Yet such speculation continues, and it is important to establish the criteria by which the durable wheat of reproducible political-economic structures can be separated from the ephemeral chaff of doomed experiments and short-term tactical shifts (see Peck and Tickell, 1994). Regulation theory provides generic concepts and propositions which can inform analysis of specific institutional conjunctures and, while this is not to say that it can explain every microscale event, it can help to formulate the questions that need to be asked.

The regulation approach also focuses attention on policy areas or institutional conjunctures that are critical to the sustainability of different growth models and regulatory strategies. Inevitably, some of them relate to those enduring dilemmas of labor regulation identified in Chapter 2 and, in this respect, the experience of TECs (and their U.S. counterparts, the PICs) is especially informative. They speak to some of the central contradictions of labor market reproduction and regulation, including skill formation, the incorporation of labor-power, and the management of structural adjustment, and they are central to the Anglo-American form of neoliberal labor regulation (see Albert, 1993; Hutton, 1995). There are strong institutional similarities between the British and U.S. systems which have been reinforced by deliberate emulation since the early 1980s.

> TECs are modeled on the U.S. system of Private Industry Councils. . . . The Thatcher administration "learned" from the United States: officials visited state programs and designed their long-term work-welfare scheme (ET) after these visits. Ideological sympathy between Reagan and Thatcher provided a rationale for the Conservative's decision to imitate U.S. practices. . . . The similarity between the content of the British and American work-welfare programs is most pronounced in measures for the long-term unemployed, welfare dependents, and in devolved administrative structure. (King, 1992, pp. 239–240)

Parallels between the British and U.S. work-welfare regimes should be borne in mind in the following analysis. Both underscore generic flaws in neoliberal labor regulation, and they also raise questions about the universality of Jessop's claims and their relevance to the current Anglo-American conjuncture. The succeeding section details his account of the tendential shift from the Keynesian welfare state (KWS) to the Schumpeterian workfare state (SWS), specifying its geographic dynamics and identifying three alternative SWS strategies (neoliberal, neocorporatist, and neostatist), followed by an unpacking of the political economy of the TEC initiative. Finally, the chapter concludes by considering Britain's flawed workfare state, focusing on the implications of the TEC experience for the formation, execution, and durability of neoliberal SWS strategies, which serves as the point of departure for Chapter 8.

TENDENCIES AND CONTRADICTIONS[8]

At the center of Jessop's analysis of state restructuring is a tendential shift from the Keynesian welfare state to the Schumpeterian workfare state, accompanied and partly driven by a fundamental spatial reordering as the nation-state is progressively "hollowed out." Together, these transformations are related structurally to the transition to post-Fordism, and rolling these claims together, Jessop (1993) issues an "audacious aphorism": the hollowed out SWS "provides the best possible political shell for post-Fordism" (p. 7). Characteristically, his claims are pitched "at high levels of theoretical abstraction, generality, and ideal-typicality" (p. 33), although they are largely consistent with more concrete work on state restructuring.[9] They also help to chart the terrain on which geographies of labor regulation are being remade, suggesting how links might be established between broad patterns of state restructuring and the changing institutional forms of labor regulation.

In Jessop's view, the transition to Schumpeterian workfare "helps resolve the principal crisis tendencies of Atlantic Fordism and/or its associated KWS regimes so that a new wave of accumulation becomes possible [and moreover that] the distinctive aspects of the evolving SWS correspond in crucial respects to the emerging growth dynamic of the new global economy" (1993, p. 11). Although there is variation in SWS regimes (just as there was in the KWS), he suggests that the SWS is gaining paradigmatic status as nation-states around the world seek to develop or emulate new accumulation strategies. Broadly speaking, these strategies promote innovation and structural competitiveness in economic policy (hence Schumpeter) and flexibility and competitiveness in social policy (hence workfare). While different nation-states may be moving towards SWS systems in different ways and at different rates, Jessop (1993) stresses that the SWS refers not simply to a bundle of restructured institutions but also to an "interpretative framework" through which the state deciphers and responds to changes in the global economy (p. 19). The mediation of SWS strategies through political-economic discourses and modes of calculation provides scope not only for political contingency, but also holds out the possibility of failure in the search for a post-KWS mode of social regulation.

Bold and far-reaching, Jessop's account also is nuanced and reflexive. He variously underlines the "somewhat speculative" character of his claims (1993, p. 7) and their "tendential" and unevenly developed nature (1994, pp. 251, 266–269), and on occasion presents them as little more than a "thought experiment [based on theories of regulation and state derivation, but] reinforced by a more casual awareness of the recent institutional restructuring and strategic reorientation of the state in the United States and elsewhere in Europe" (1992c, p. 14). Nevertheless, he clearly intends to provide organizing concepts and a theoretical template through which to interpret contemporary state restructuring. In the vast literature on post-Fordism and the Fordist-Keynesian crisis, Jessop's work provides a long-awaited counterbalance to the preoccupation with narrow concerns of production and the labor process. This productivism has rendered premature the claims that a post-Fordist or flexible regime of accumulation is in evidence. Crucial questions concerning the interpenetration and structural coupling of regimes of accumulation and modes of social regulation have remained unaddressed (Tickell and Peck, 1992). Without a parallel consideration of social regulation, it is impossible—at least from a regulationist standpoint—to sustain the argument that flexible production, for example, is reproducible.[10] This highlights the significance of Jessop's claim that KWS and SWS "are likely to correspond to different accumulation regimes . . . whereas the former was an 'integral' element in the expanded reproduction of Fordism, the latter could become just as 'integral' to its still emerging successor regime" (Jessop, 1993, pp. 8–9; cf. Jessop, 1992c). While implying the distinct possibility of a structural coupling between (some form of) the SWS and (some form of) flexible accumulation, he is nonetheless attentive to the "analytical asymmetry" between Fordism and post-Fordism and the need for more "cautious and critical" analysis of the latter (Jessop, 1992, p. 46). It is on the shifting terrain of social regulation—changing state and institutional structures, social and cultural mores, political-economic discourses, and interpretive frameworks—that post-Fordist claims are likely ultimately to stand or fall.

From Keynesian Welfare . . .

Jessop's analysis follows from his reading of the KWS, Fordism's "ideal-typical form of state" 1994, p. 252), and its place in the Fordist regime of accumulation. The KWS underwrote the social reproduction of Fordism in four main ways (pp. 254–257).

- Through labor market policies, the management of aggregate demand, and the regulation of the wage relation, the KWS normalized and moderated macroeconomic fluctuations in order that, at the microeconomic level, Fordist enterprises could anticipate market stability and growth (on the basis of which investments could be committed and economies of scale secured).
- Through infrastructure development and competition, transport, and housing policies, the KWS underwrote both the tendential monopolization of production and the massification of the consumer sphere, thereby securing Fordism's virtuous

circle of mutually reinforcing growth in investment, productivity, income, demand, and profit.

- There was an attempt to unify and normalize the collective interests of labor and capital around a program of full employment and universal welfare, underscored by ideological commitments to social partnership, collective bargaining, and big business.
- Particularly at the local level, the KWS helped to manage the social problems associated with Fordist growth, such as those deriving from accelerated commodification and urbanization, around which welfarist "solutions" could be formulated.

Thus, the KWS "helped secure the conditions for Fordist economic expansion, while the latter helped in turn to secure the conditions for the expansion of the Keynesian welfare state" (p. 256). However, the political-economic integrity of the Fordist-Keynesian relationship was by no means guaranteed. Beneath the consensual political vocabulary lay ambiguities and contradictions requiring continuous adjustment in both the state sphere and civil society. The faltering and haphazard evolution of the postwar settlement in Britain illustrates an only partially successful attempt to maintain a "simultaneous commitment to full employment and the welfare state, on the one hand, and, on the other, an international role for sterling and the City and costly global defence undertakings" (Jessop, 1992b, p. 16); just as Britain experienced a flawed Fordism, it also exhibited a weak KWS, the durability of which "was probably more due to its institutional entrenchment than to any real consensus" (p. 17). Britain's flawed Fordism may be explained partly by conflicts between the KWS and City-military commitments.

Just as the political-economic dynamics of Fordism and Keynesian welfare were intricately connected during their golden age, so also were their crises interrelated. The breakdown of the KWS should be seen in terms of both the internal contradictions of the state and the wider crisis of Atlantic Fordism. The crisis of Fordism exerted a scissors effect on welfare-state finances and attendant restructuring of taxation and credit; the fiscal crisis of the state was linked to a declining tax base, family fragmentation, and demographic change (Jessop, 1991b; cf. Gough, 1979). Rising costs of production and welfare triggered the internationalization of accumulation, which in turn exacerbated the mounting fiscal crisis of the state in the Atlantic Fordist countries. The globalization of finance also had a corrosive effect on the KWS; as private capital began to circulate globally on a deregulated basis, Keynesian nation-states lost control of one of the

most important macroeconomic levers—establishing interest rates—
and the loss of interest-rate sovereignty contributed to the breakdown
of the fragile international order established under Fordism (Glyn,
Hughes, Lipietz, and Singh, 1991). "Unregulated global credit was
[consequently] a factor of erosion of the (political institutional) regulation of the whole Fordist system" (Altvater, 1992, p. 37).

. . . to Schumpeterian Workfare

By definition, the SWS represents a response to (and perhaps resolution
of) tendencies toward crisis in the KWS. That is not to say that its
structures emerge automatically or even that the SWS depends on the
prior existence of a crisis-prone KWS. For example, Jessop (1993)
draws attention to nascent SWS systems in East Asia which were not
preceded by a KWS but "are often taken nowadays as models of crisis
resolution in the West" (p. 9; cf. Peck and Miyamachi, 1994). However, in the former KWS regions of Atlantic Fordism, emergent SWS
structures represent an in situ resolution to some of the crisis tendencies of the KWS. The SWS alone is unlikely to resolve these crisis
tendencies; change also is needed elsewhere in the mode of social
regulation: in the wage form, competition and innovation, and corporate organization (Jessop, 1993, p. 26). Unevenly, amid struggle and
experimentation, the SWS rises out of the ashes of Fordism-Keynesianism. Its capacity to "resolve the principal crisis tendencies of Atlantic
Fordism and/or its associated KWS regimes" (p. 11) is the basis of its
post-Fordist character. "[W]e can regard the SWS as post-Fordist to
the extent that: it directly or indirectly resolves (or is held to do so) the
crisis tendencies of Fordist accumulation and/or of the KWS as one of
its main regulatory forms; its emergence (for whatever reason) helps
to shape and consolidate the dynamics of the emerging global economy
and thereby encourages the renewal and re-regulation of capitalism
after its Fordist period" (pp. 25–26).

In the post-Fordist era, the strategic capacities of the state are
viewed as reorganized in accordance with the twin imperatives of
continuous innovation and competitive flexibility. Jessop (1993) implies that concerns with "innovation and structural competitiveness in
the field of economic policy [and with] flexibility and competitiveness
in the field of social policy," provide possibilities for virtuous interaction with the emerging growth dynamic of flexible accumulation (p.
18); "for any feasible reorganisation of the welfare state must resolve
not only the problems rooted in its own dynamic but also those rooted
in its regulatory role in relation to accumulation" (1991b, p. 101). He
maintains that contemporary processes of "restructuring in capital

accumulation . . . seem to *require* a break with the KWS" (1993, p. 17, emphasis added), and he anticipates a structural coupling between flexible accumulation and Schumpeterian regulation to parallel that previously established between Fordism and Keynesianism. Where the KWS failed, the SWS should be able to succeed.

In elaborating the distinctive features of the SWS, Jessop (1993) sets out deliberately to "make the contrast with the Keynesian welfare state as stark as possible" (p. 16). Some of his distinctions, which he seeks to justify critically as well as heuristically, are detailed in Table 7.1. The leading edge of SWS restructuring is indicated by changes in *state and corporate discourses,* where the emphasis on productivity and planning under the KWS has been displaced by a new discourse of flexibility and entrepreneurialism. One way in which the British state has been pioneering is its deployment of the "flexi-rhetoric" of popular capitalism and the enterprise culture (1991a, p. 143), providing an interpretive framework to guide, rationalize, and legitimate radical restructuring of the state.

In terms of the money form, the transition to the SWS is linked to the relative demise of national money and financial autonomy, and the attendant vulnerability of national economies to "increasing cross-border flows of financial capital" and "massive and volatile currency flows" (Jessop, 1993, p. 19). The SWS adjusts to these conditions by making a structural shift toward supply-side macroeconomic policy geared to the enhancement of global competitiveness, innovation, and economies of scope. Its new orientation is reflected in wage regulation which, in contrast to the Keynesian construction of the wage as a source of domestic consumer demand, is regarded as an international production cost (see Chapter 8). Emphasis on the wage as cost may be associated with either innovation and continuous reskilling where the wage is seen as a *fixed* cost (in high value-added economies such as Japan and Germany) or with short-termism and labor flexibility where it is regarded as a *variable* cost (in neoliberalized economies such as Britain and the United States).

Table 7.1 indicates changes in social and labor market policy that Jessop associates with the transition to the SWS. In terms of labor market policy, the fundamental change is toward rejection of the Keynesian commitment to full (male) employment in favor of a Schumpeterian emphasis on labor market organization as a source of competitive advantage. Innovation in labor market regulation assumes a central role in policy toward competition. In social policy, the emblematic shift from welfare to workfare is associated with movement away from meeting social needs and toward meeting business needs. There also is a shift away from the principles of universalism,

Table 7.1. The Transition from the Keynesian Welfare State to the Schumpeterian Workfare State

	KWS characteristics	Crisis	SWS characteristics
Money form	National money Nation-state control over monetary circulation Closed nation economies	Globalization of monetary flows Erosion of national financial sovereignty	Accelerating cross-border flows of finance capital
Wage relations	Collective bargaining Promotion of norms of mass consumption	Crisis of profitability triggered by international competition Pressure on wage rates	Flexi-wage systems Income polarization Heightened segmentation
State discourse	Productivity and planning	Monetarism	Flexibility and entrepreneuralism
Macroeconomic policy orientation	Countercyclical demand management Interventionist policies supporting economies of scale, big science, and productivity growth	Fiscal crisis of the state triggered by falling profitability, declining tax base, and growing welfare demands	Supply-side innovation through national and regional state Goals of structural competitiveness, economies of scope, and permanent, flexible innovation
Labor market regulation	Extensive state involvement in social reproduction of labor-power Goal of full (male) employment	Mass unemployment Stagflation	Labor market regulation subsumed within competition policy Deregulation and workfarism

(cont.)

Table 7.1. *(cont.)*

	KWS characteristics	Crisis	SWS characteristics
Social policy	Progressively redistributional Based on universalist welfare rights and social needs	Fiscal crisis of the state and welfare retrenchment	Productivist cost-saving concerns Subsumption to goals of labor flexibility and business needs
Spatial relations	Nationally constituted KWS supported by heavily regulated international relations under U.S. hegemony	Accelerated globalization of monetary and commodity flows Erosion of nation-state powers	Hollowing out of nation-state upward (to supranational states), outward (to cross-border networks), and downward (to local states)

Derived from Jessop (1991b, 1993).
From Peck and Jones (1995), p. 1368. © 1995 Pion Limited. Reprinted by permission.

progressive income redistribution, and social rights under the KWS toward a more selective, market-oriented, and workfarist approach under the SWS where "productivist and cost-saving concerns" are paramount.

Intricately related to the transition are fundamental shifts in spatial relations. Hollowing out is seen as an essential, not incidental characteristic of the SWS, although Jessop (1993) is careful not to imply the death of the nation-state. "By analogy, the 'hollow state' metaphor is intended to indicate two trends: first, that the nation state retains many of its headquarters functions—including the trappings of central executive authority and national sovereignty as well as the discourses that sustain them; and, second, that its capacities to translate this authority and sovereignty into effective control are becoming limited by a complex displacement of powers" (p. 22).

Displacement occurs in three directions (pp. 22–25). First, there is an upward movement as supranational states begin to assume functional responsibilities far beyond the Keynesian remit of monetary and trade regulation, including a "wide range of supply-side factors, both economic and extra-economic in nature." Jessop cites the European Commission's interventions in telecommunications, information technology, and biotechnology. Second and in a downward movement, local states are assuming a stronger and more proactive role encompassing "greater emphasis on economic regeneration and competitiveness," such as "new forms of local partnership" in labor market and training policies, venture capital, and technology transfer. Third, power is moving outward to circuit around new, typically international networks of local and regional states. Jessop observes that "cross-territorial coordination would seem necessary for the success of SWS policies" lest they succumb to "implementation failure" (the fate of blunt top-down policies) or "wasteful and ineffective 'municipal mercantilism'" (the fate of unregulated bottom-up policies). Jessop's examples include local-state networks in Europe and East Asia and on the U.S.-Mexico border. Together, these spatial transformations are so important that a "hollowed-out SWS could help to shape and consolidate key features of the new regime of accumulation on a world scale" (p. 28).

On Jessop's own admission, this reading of the SWS is pitched at a high level of abstraction. In seeking to come to terms with particular SWS regimes, Jessop moves down a level of abstraction to consider three ideal-typical variants. Paralleling Parisian regulationist accounts of production restructuring after Fordism (emphasizing the variety of politically mediated development paths),[11] he identifies three distinctive forms of state restructuring: the neoliberal, neostatist, and neocorporatist variants of the SWS (see Table 7.2).

The *neoliberal* SWS is fueled by the liberation of market forces achieved by the recommodification of labor-power, private-sector deregulation, privatization of state enterprises, and commercialization of welfare and other residual state activities. These measures promote a "mixed welfare economy" (Jessop, 1991b, p. 96) as the strategic capacities of the state are reorganized to encourage the growth of private profit–making (welfare) services and retrenchment of public provision.

> For the public sector [the neoliberal SWS strategy] involves privatization, liberalization, and imposition of commercial criteria in the residual state sector; for the private sector, it involves deregulation and a new legal and political framework to provide passive support for market solutions. This is reflected in government promotion of hire-and-fire, flexi-time, and flexi-wage labour markets; growth of tax expenditures steered by private initiatives based on fiscal subsidies for favoured economic activities; measures to transform the welfare state into a means of supporting and subsidizing low wages as well as to enhance the disciplinary force of social security measures and programs; and the more general reorientation of

Table 7.2. Alternative Schumpeterian Workfare-State Strategies

	Neoliberal SWS	Neocorporatist SWS	Neostatist SWS
Accumulation strategy	Flexibility through liberalization of market forces	Flexibility through virtuous balancing of competition and cooperation	Flexibility through active structural policy and market guidance
Internal structures of the state	Commercialization of welfare and privatization of state enterprises Mixed welfare economy with substitution of private for public provision	Delegation of governance functions to intermediary organizations Private-interest government Shift to selective corporatism	Highly interventionist Mixed welfare economy with emphasis on voluntary, not-for-profit, and self-help provision
Patterns of intervention	Recommodification of labor-power, re- and deregulation of markets, privatization and liberalization Stimulation of personal/community welfare provision	Economic intervention through corporatist negotiation Regulated self-regulation in social policy	Decommodification to compensate for market failures Active structural policies to channel and limit market forces with aim of medium-term dynamic efficiency
Social basis of the state	Polarization in income provision and service consumption Support for key workers Fragmentation and marginalization of working classes	Organized around functional interest groups and vested professional interests Pluralistic	Cohesive, solidaristic citizenry with organized labor at its core *or* selective (more fragmented, less inclusive) corporatism
Hegemonic project	Ideological support for enterprise, homeownership, profit sharing, and shareownership New voluntarism	Heterogeneous and selective incorporation Decentralized microcorporatism Attribution of public status to interest groups	Mobilization of new social movements Universal social citizenship and egalitarian social relationships

Derived from Jessop (1991b, 1993).

economic and social policy to the perceived needs of the private
sector. Coupled with such measures is a disavowal of social partnership in favour of managerial prerogatives, market forces and a
strong state. (Jessop, 1993, p. 29)

When these measures fail, a residuary role falls to the state as "last
resort" (1991b, p. 96), but wherever feasible the state will attempt to
displace the burden onto individuals, families, or the "community."
Innovation and competitiveness are achieved through the "liberation
of the animal spirits of entrepreneurs" (1993, p. 29) as the state acts
through ideological means to secure the conditions for a flourishing
enterprise culture.

In the *neocorporatist* SWS, governance functions are "delegated
to various intermediary organisations" (Jessop, 1991b, p. 97), relying
on neither the market nor the state, as the state seeks to establish a
favorable balance between competition and cooperation. The neocorporatist SWS differs from the corporatist KWS both in its emphasis
on innovation-driven growth and in its concern to meet the regulatory
requirements of an increasingly heterogeneous economy.

> [T]he scope of neocorporatist arrangements reflects the diversity of
> policy communities and networks relevant to an innovation-driven
> mode of growth as well as the increasing heterogeneity of labour
> forces and labour markets. Neocorporatist arrangements in an
> emerging SWS . . . will extend beyond business associations and
> labour unions to include policy communities representing distinct
> functional systems (e.g., science, health, education); and policy
> implementation will become more flexible through the extension of
> "regulated self-regulation" and private interest government. . . .
> Corporatist arrangements may also become more selective . . . and,
> reflecting the greater flexibility and decentralization of key features
> of the post-Fordist economy, the centres of neocorporatist gravity
> will move toward the micro-level of firms and localities at the
> expense of centralized macroeconomic concertation. (Jessop, 1993,
> pp. 30–31)

Crucial to the neocorporatist SWS is a pluralist mobilization of vested
political and professional interests, their endowment with public status
(cf. Offe, 1985), and arm's-length management of their "self-regula-
tion" (Jessop, 1991b, p. 98).

Finally, the *neostatist* SWS "involves a market-conforming but
state-sponsored approach to economic reorganization" (Jessop, 1993,
p. 31), combining market forces with market regulation in the pursuit
of "medium-term dynamic efficiency" (1991b, p. 98). The state engages in strategies of decommodification to compensate for structural

weaknesses in markets while developing active policies to channel and constrain market forces.

> It does so by deploying its own powers of imperative coordination, its own economic resources and activities, and its own knowledge bases and organizational intelligence . . . [involving] decommodification, state-sponsored flexibility, and other state activities aimed at securing the dynamic efficiency of a productive core. This is reflected in an active structural policy in which the state sets strategic targets relating to new technologies, technology transfer, innovation systems, infrastructure, and other factors affecting the overall structural competitiveness of the economy. (Jessop, 1993, pp. 31–32)

The neostatist SWS tends to favor active labor market policies geared toward qualitative flexibility; an active industry policy aimed at promoting sunrise sectors; and an active technology policy to develop the technological capacities of the productive base. In policy delivery, greater emphasis is placed on voluntary groups, self-help organizations, and not-for-profit bodies (Jessop, 1991b).

National Paths to Schumpeterian Workfare: The Case of Thatcherism

The identification of neoliberal, neocorporatist, and neostatist forms is based on ideal-typical regimes at a level of abstraction below that of the generic SWS. Because no ideal type is found in pure form, it is necessary to move down another level of abstraction in order to consider the specifics of a particular nation-state's development path. Empirically, strategies may be combined and the particularities of each case will reflect institutional legacies, conjunctural conditions, and the balance of political forces. For example, Thatcherism, "clearly involves the dominance of a neoliberal strategy . . . but has not totally rejected other strategies. Thus, central government programs (admittedly on a small scale) have been oriented to technology transfer and research into generic technologies; and notwithstanding blanket hostility to tripartite corporatism and national-level social partnership, it has promoted enterprise corporatism and a 'new realism' on the shop floor" (Jessop, 1993, p. 33).

In the 1980s, much of Jessop's work was devoted to Thatcherism (see Jessop, Bonnett, Bromley, and Ling, 1988), which provided the "empirical inspiration" for his later analysis of the SWS (1992c, p. 14). His work on Thatcherism was notable, not to say controversial, due to the emphasis he placed on the purposive and functional nature of the Thatcherite project: "Thatcherism does have an explicit economic strategy . . . [it] aims to restructure the British economy as part of a re-invigorated, post-Fordist international capitalism" (Jessop, Bonnett, Bromley, and Ling, 1985, p. 97).[12] Concerned to distance himself from those analyses reducing Thatcherism to either monetarism or an attack on unionism and the welfare state, Jessop (1991a) characterizes Thatcherism as a "strategy for securing flexibility" based on the following elements:

> (a) liberalization, promoting free market (as opposed to monopolistic or state monopolistic) forms of competition as the most efficient basis for market forces; (b) deregulation, giving economic agents greater freedom from state control; (c) privatization, reducing the public sector's share in the direct or indirect provision of goods and services to business and community alike; (d) (re-)commodification of the residual public sector, to promote the role of market forces, either directly or through market proxies; (e) internationalization, encouraging the mobility of capital and labor, stimulating global market forces, and importing more advanced processes and products into Britain; and (f) tax cuts to provide incentives and demand for the private sector. (pp. 146–147)

Working at this somewhat lower level of abstraction, Jessop (1989, 1991a, pp. 148–156) identifies six dimensions of the political system centered on the state, three of which are directly concerned with state structures and the remainder with the wider social relations of Thatcherism:[13]

- the representational regime
- the state's internal organization
- its patterns of intervention
- the social basis of the state
- the state project (through which the cohesion and political unity of the state are sought)
- the hegemonic project (defining the "illusory community" allegedly represented by the state)

His analytical claims are summarized in Table 7.3, along with institutional changes and contradictions to which he draws attention.

In the *representational regime,* Jessop identifies three significant shifts. First, tripartism (formal sharing of decision making by government, employers, and organized labor) has been displaced from core institutions such as the Industry Training Boards (ITBs) and the Department of Trade and Industry (DTI). As union representation has been terminated, privatized, bipartite relationships with business have

Table 7.3. A Thatcherite Road to Schumpeterian Workfare?

	Features	Institutional manifestations	Contradictions
Representational regime	Rejection of triparite corporatism Populist elitism in party politics and *raison d'état*	Downgrading of Neddy; disregard of review procedures; emergence of presidential politics; growth of business representation and local partnerships	Political alienation and disengagement; liability to implementation failure
Internal structures of the state	Centralization of power and supercession of elected local government by unelected, specialist agencies Emergence of integrated and social security state, underpinned by repressive state power	Growing importance of Whitehall and Cabinet Office; emergence of new local agencies such as UDCs; proliferation of quangos; shift in policy responsibilities toward economically oriented departments of state such as DTI and Employment Department; privatization of civil service delivery work	Exacerbation of regional divides and imbalances; return to stop-go as overheating in the South prompts measures which damage lagged recovery in the North
Patterns of intervention	Realignment of state boundaries and forms of intervention through privatization, recommodification, re- and deregulation, and liberalization	Reorganization of supply-side agencies such as TECs and UDCs; emergence of new regulatory bodies such as Ofgas and Oftel; key role for local government following incorporation of local business interests	Excessive vulnerability to international capital movements Chronic short-termism Inadequacy of market forces to compensate for past market and governmental failures

(cont.)

Table 7.3. *(cont.)*

Features		Institutional manifestations	Contradictions
Social basis of the state	Two-nations ethos	Remaking of "Establishment" institutions such as BBC, Church of England, and civil service Expansion of repressive workfare state	Political risks and social costs of polarization, including emergence of permanent underclass Tensions between rising social costs and political im- perative of tax cuts
State project	Conviction politics and the strong state	"Institutional Darwinism" Redistribution of powers at the local/ microsocial level	Inhibition of long- term innovation in subordinated (local) institutions; political resistance from policy communities
Hegemonic project	The entrepre- neurial society and popular capitalism	Rolling back of KWS, culminating in a reorganized "strong state"	Uneven geographic spread of enter- prise culture Reduced scope for middle-class tax concessions

Derived from Jessop (1991a) and Jessop, Bonnett, Bromley, and Ling (1988).
From Peck and Jones (1995), p. 1373. © 1995 Pion Limited. Reprinted by permission.

flourished. Active support has been given to business representation on national and local institutions and to "partnership" bodies, seen as building a bridge between community involvement (for legitimacy) and market organization (for efficiency). Second, there has been a movement away from the catchall electoral politics of the KWS period, in which political parties appealed to a comparatively stable set of social interests, toward a more elitist and populist party system of "quasi-presidential, plebiscitary politics" (Jessop, 1991a, p. 119). Third, the emergence of Thatcherite conviction politics has been associated with appeals directly to "the people" (bypassing repre- sentative and intermediary organizations) and with a radical *raison d'état,* as affected parties and due process are increasingly disregarded.

Equally far-reaching change is evident in the *internal structures of the state.* Jessop (1991a) draws attention to structural shifts the overall result of which is a move toward "undemocratic centralism." Particularly notable is the centralization of power in Whitehall and the Cabinet Office at the expense of Parliament and elected local government, and the progressive displacement of the latter by unelected, single-function agencies at the local level (echoed so strongly in the TEC initiative). "At stake here is the rolling back of the local Fordist welfare state and the rolling forward of local authorities as regulatory bodies which award contracts or franchises, set standards, monitor compliance, sanction poor performance and are overseen in these residual welfare activities by a centrist, executive power" (p. 150).

Linked to these changes have been the proliferation of unelected local-state bodies and increased reliance (in regulating these arm's-length agencies) on financial controls and "market proxies." More broadly, Jessop identifies a shift toward an "integrated social security state" (p. 151; a concept anticipating that of the SWS and underscoring the subordination of social to economic policy), organized on "two nations" principles and extending the canon of polarization beyond the distribution of incomes to the provision of welfare services. Further, this shift is related to activation of the state's repressive powers through policing, surveillance, and the mass media.

In terms of *patterns of intervention,* the direction of change—towards commodification, privatization, liberalization, and re- or de-regulation—has been "in line with the transition to post-Fordism" (Jessop, 1991a, p. 152). This shift is reflected, first, in industry policy, where support for declining industries has been withdrawn while indirect support has grown for sunrise industries (such as financial services, nuclear power, and some high-tech sectors), and second, in the reorientation of "supply-side agencies" where the promotion of economies of scale, productivity, and planning under the KWS has given way to new emphasis on flexibility, enterprise, and economies of scope. Jessop draws attention to the restructuring of DTI and the Manpower Services Commission (MSC), expansion of the regulatory state through institutions such as Oftel and Ofgas, and new ways in which *dirigiste* powers are being mobilized through bodies like the Urban Development Corporations and the Welsh Development Agency. Perhaps a little ambiguously, Jessop also identifies local authorities as the "key agencies for supply-side intervention [which due to their location] closer to the local economic action than the central state . . . can act more flexibly and effectively to encourage wealth and job creation" (p. 153).

The wider social relations of Thatcherism are an important dimension of transitional change. First, the *social basis of the state* has been transformed from the one-nation consensus of the postwar settlement to a radical two-nations project in which those gaining from the government's entrepreneurial turn are systematically subsidized while others are subjected to unyielding state and market discipline. Second, the Thatcherite *state project* is marked by the distinctive combination of a strong state and conviction politics; through vigorous policy experimentation, acute political pragmatism, and "institutional Darwinism" (in which interinstitutional competition is deliberately fostered),[14] the British state has acted to "penetrate local niches and macroeconomic sites [in order to] reinforce capital's ability to exploit even the smallest areas of surplus production and consumption and/or to influence the reorganisation of civil society at the micro-social level" (Jessop, 1991a, p. 155). Third, Thatcherism's *hegemonic project* has evolved gradually into a purposive, consolidated form based on the "entrepreneurial society" and "popular capitalism," the culmination of which Jessop enigmatically pronounces "would be the transition to a post-Fordist society—if only Thatcherism could get us there" (p. 156).

Even in this comparatively functionalist reading of Thatcherism, there is no guarantee that the British project can secure a post-Fordist transition. As a "high-risk strategy" (p. 156), Thatcherism is riven with economic, political, and geographic contradictions. Pointing to the deregulation of the City, "asset-stripping" of state enterprises, and influx of foreign direct investment, Jessop observes that many of the "benefits" of Thatcherism have taken the form of short-term or windfall gains. In the long term, these may prove to be fragile and short-lived, as they tend to undermine strategic investment in R&D, technology, and workers' skills, and to erode long-term industrial competitiveness. He observes that "[m]uch of the apparent success of the neo-liberal strategy actually depends on trends in the South-East" (p. 157), the subsequent overheating and dramatic economic collapse of which has raised questions about Thatcherism's durability (Peck and Tickell, 1995). In the recession of the early 1990s, then, Thatcherism may have crossed its Rubicon. Now, perhaps more than ever, its reproducibility as a political-economic project is open to question. This period, in which Thatcherism seems in so many ways to have overreached itself, includes the years when the TEC initiative was launched, only to flounder.

TRAINING AND ENTERPRISE COUNCILS: SCHUMPETERIAN WORKFARE AT THE LOCAL SCALE?

The structure, priorities, and discourse of TECs strongly echo Jessop's rendering of the neoliberal SWS. They are locally based, privatized, business-led bodies contracted by central government to provide market-relevant training and enterprise services, operate workfare-style programs for the unemployed, and restore the dynamism and competitiveness of local economies through supply-side measures. Although there is a gulf between the discourses and practices of TECs—between their rhetoric of innovation, competitiveness, market-relevance, and flexibility and their reality as cash-starved deliverers of low-level, market-subordinated training programs for the unemployed[15]—they exemplify many of the central strands in Jessop's analysis. These parallels are not lost on analysts of state restructuring in Britain, many of whom point to TECs as institutions emblematic of a post-Fordist or post-Keynesian turn.[16] In a country whose regulatory experiments have tended to acquire almost paradigmatic status (in that Thatcherism was a central plank of neoliberalism at the international scale), TECs are positioned at the leading edge of attempts to reconstitute welfare as workfare, to deregulate labor market relations, and to restructure relations between the central and local states along neoliberal lines.

In short, TECs epitomize a trend toward *local workfarism* (Peck, 1994). As one of the boldest regulatory innovations of recent years, they may be seen as an institutional metaphor for (late) Thatcherism. In their organizational structure, policy priorities, and economic discourse, TECs embody Thatcherite antipathies toward elected local government, unions, corporatism, planners, and the "welfare-dependent" unemployed, embracing a new agenda of deregulation in the labor market, marketization of welfare, and privatization of training and enterprise support (Peck, 1992c; King, 1995). Through TECs, the government has sought to "place 'ownership' of the training system where it belongs—with employers" (DE, 1988, p. 40). Almost one thousand private-sector employers heeded the call to become unsalaried TEC directors; they now exercise executive control over a national budget of almost £2 billion per annum, accounting for some 1.5 million training places spread across eighty-two TECs in England and Wales and twenty LECs (Local Enterprise Companies, similar organizations which also receive mainstream economic development funding) in Scotland.

The political and symbolic importance of TECs extends beyond their share of public expenditure or even levels of program participation. They represent many of the central strands of Britain's neoliberal project as well as many of its contradictions. The problems with which the TECs are bedeviled (skill shortages and poaching in deregulated labor markets; political accountability to local communities and financial accountability to central government; the management of an unemployment crisis under stringent public expenditure restraints) are also the problems of neoliberalism in general and late Thatcherism in particular. As exemplars of hollowed-out institutional forms of the SWS, TECs also illuminate contradictions of one of its neoliberal variants.

Radical Thatcherism and the TECs

The TEC initiative represented one of the most radical reforms of the "radical Thatcherite" period of the late 1980s, when a "neo-liberal strategy for reorganizing British society was gradually defined and attempts were made to implement it" (Jessop, 1991a). As if to underscore the degree to which short-term political expediency and medium-term state strategy were meshed together in Thatcherism, it took nine years of Conservative rule to do away with the classically corporatist Manpower Services Commission (MSC). Perhaps more than any other institution of Britain's flawed Fordist era, the MSC was identified with national strategic planning and the incorporation of social partners (Grant, 1989; King, 1993). Reflecting systemic and strategic weakness of the British state, the experience of the MSC represented another chapter in the country's "cycle of failed corporatist strategies" (Jessop, 1991a, p. 140); after all, it was not even established until 1973, a year which has acquired symbolic resonance as that in which the entire Fordist-Keynesian complex began its spin into terminal crisis (Harvey, 1989a).

Jessop (1991a) portrays the early phase of Thatcherism as one in which this institutional debris was being cleared. Through this "ground-clearing operation," state capacities were reorganized to remove institutional rigidities and "prepare a path to post-Fordism" in Britain (p. 142). Supposedly redundant institutional forms (such as the MSC) were "rolled back" and new forms of state intervention "rolled forward." The opportunity to roll forward the TECs, as part of a "sustained programme of deregulation in the labour market" (DE, 1988, p. 19), emerged in the post-1986 phase, when political expediency related to falling unemployment and high rates of economic growth (for the South East) combined with Thatcherism's most proactive period. Bolstered by an even larger electoral majority after the 1987 general election, the Conservatives "were far more strongly placed to impose their own ends on work-welfare and to undermine the MSC" (King, 1995, p. 169). This was their moment to tackle both the industrial training system (based on the interventionist, bureaucratic ITBs with their statutory rights to levy businesses in order to fund apprentice training) and the system of work preparation for the unemployed (based on the MSC's programs, which continued to be organized on the principles of universal access and noncompulsion in response to a social imperative to make work).

Sitting above these conspicuously corporatist systems was the MSC, with its labor and business nominees and its vestigial commitments to strategic planning and social provision. Things would have to change, radically. As King (1992) sees it, "the MSC in 1988 remained the final manifestation of corporatist tripartism . . . it was ripe for abolition" (p. 235). Replacing the centralized, tripartite MSC would be a network of locally based, business-led TECs, bringing private-sector expertise, innovation, and cash to the training system and ensuring that it met the needs of local employers (DE 1988, 1989; Training Agency 1989a). *Employment for the 1990s*, the white paper which launched the TECs, portrayed a training system liberated from the shackles of national and sectoral planning; the TECs would be locally based because "localities are more likely to find solutions that work" (DE, 1988, p. 39; cf. Jessop, 1991a, p. 153). Business organizations were quick to emphasize the new opportunities TECs provided for the implementation of locally focused, employer-led development agendas.

> TECs can be a powerful engine for change, mixing considerable government resources, with the drive and initiative of some of the country's best business leaders. They are not simply "yet another" scheme or initiative, but a potentially powerful delivery network. . . . Their leadership is vested in . . . the private sector. . . . [T]he TECs are unique in offering direct to employers, with government assistance, a fully professional and experienced back-up staff . . . and considerable funds to achieve industry's and the community's ends. Never before has government been willing to hand to employers the executive authority, executive responsibility, and most importantly, the resources for public programmes. And never before have employers responded so rapidly and with such enthusiasm to the vision and the opportunity. (Bennett and Business in the Cities, 1990, p. 8)

Notwithstanding this rousing call to arms, the TECs were born during the second major recession of the Thatcher era and, as a result, found themselves not steering growth but managing unemployment, being contractually obliged to provide training places for secondary-school graduates and unemployed adults.[17] Rather than moving away from labor market programs for the unemployed, they became implicated in the expansion and development of make-work. Despite its low level of skills content and poor reputation among both employers and trainees, the TECs' adult training remains based on the workfare-style program, Employment Training (ET), union opposition to which had been a key factor in the collapse of the MSC. Its unattractiveness is evident in that increasingly stringent welfare-benefit rules make participation effectively compulsory for the adult unemployed (Finn, 1988; King, 1995). The TECs must continually strive to achieve unemployment register effects in order to qualify for funding and performance bonuses,[18] so that they, too, are locked into a system with a strong workfare dynamic.

The Gordian knot tying the TECs to managing unemployment (drawing in both national political and local contractual imperatives) places them in the front line of the neoliberal attack on the welfare state. Through them, the welfare state is being selectively and unevenly restructured through the agency of the central state but in the name of local business. In Jessop's terms, the ground-clearing operation that abolished the MSC has been followed by more purposive and proactive intervention. So far as King (1993) is concerned, this heralds a radical reorientation in Britain's work-welfare regime. "The Conservatives have effected a shift from a national tripartite regime to a local, employer-dominated neoliberal training regime . . . [During the 1980s, the British government] ended the legacies of the postwar Keynesian framework, particularly tripartism, which had informed training policy, and substituted it with a neoliberal one, dominated by employers' interests and measures to counteract labour market disincentives" (pp. 214–215).

Although the institutional changes are real enough, care must be taken in interpreting their structural significance. Concrete institutional change certainly plays a role in Jessop's account of the transition from Keynesian welfare to Schumpeterian workfare (particularly in countries like Britain where there is a need to reorganize the structural capacities of the state machine), but strategic reorientations also need to be taken into account. These should not be confused; the same "institutional shell" can be endowed with different strategic orientations (see Hall, 1993). For example, the corporatist MSC was appropriated in the early 1980s as the central institutional agent in the Conservative program of active, neoliberal regulatory reform in the labor market (Robertson, 1986).

That said, the TECs (in both institutional form and strategic orientation) appear entirely consistent with Jessop's sketch of the generic SWS (Table 7.1) and more specific observations on the faltering British transition (Table 7.3). Strongly reminiscent of the TECs are Jessop's discussions of the "subordination of social policy to the demands of labour market flexibility" and the prioritization of "productivist cost-saving concerns in an open economy" (1993, pp. 9, 18). In the specifics of the British transition there also are powerful echoes of the TECs in the emergence of "essentially private, bipartite corporatist arrangements" along with a new "undemocratic centralism," and in the acceptance of growing "polarization [as] welfare policies are subordinated to economic objectives" (1991a, pp. 148–151). Indeed, Jessop periodically illustrates his argument by reference to the restructuring of the MSC and the British system of labor regulation.

What is important, however, is not these superficial similarities, but their underlying political-economic integrity. The question is not whether there is a match between *taxonomic* criteria used in Jessop's definition of the SWS and characteristics of the TEC system, but whether the TEC regime satisfies Jessop's *reproduction* criteria.[19] Although Jessop (1991a) is at pains to stress the contradictory nature of Thatcherism and the significant obstacles remaining on the "British road to post-Fordism" (pp. 159–160), he nevertheless continues to interpret the British neoliberal experiment in terms of the "white heat of a post-Fordist revolution" (p. 135) while conferring on the neoliberal SWS the capacity to promote a "market-guided transition towards the new economic regime" (1994, p. 266; cf. 1992b, p. 38). Implicit in his approach is the possibility that the seeds of a reproducible MSR-accumulation relationship may be germinating in neoliberal Britain. The extent to which these claims can be sustained in the case of the TECs will be questioned by way of three of Jessop's central themes: subordination to market forces, the new imperatives of productivist cost-saving and flexibility, and the hollowing out of the nation-state.

Market Subordination

The introduction of TECs marked a radical acceleration in the subordination of social welfare to market imperatives. While at one level this was not a new development, the extent and character of the marketization of welfare are without precedent. There have been efforts to create a "training market" around the TECs, for example, by differentiating program provisions to permit trainee "choice" (such as introduction of training credits for young people) and by fostering cost-based competition between TECs and their training providers (such as the introduction of TEC Challenge and competitive bidding for TEC contracts). Central to the philosophy of TECs is the desire to reconfigure the training and welfare system in line (supposedly) with the needs of local employers and requirements of different local labor markets (DE, 1988; cf. Bennett, Wicks, and McCoshan, 1994). Subordination to the market is thus conceived as geographically differentiated: marketization and localization go hand in hand (Peck, 1994).

Two forms of market regulation have emerged under the TEC regime. The first is the *passive* market regulation (cf. Jessop, 1993, p. 29) of the industrial training sphere (as the withdrawal of the ITBs has left a major regulatory vacuum around private skill formation), and the second is *active* market regulation of the welfare system (as TECs have restructured make-work schemes for the unemployed so as more closely to meet "local market needs"). Originally, the TEC initiative was conceived mainly in terms of passive market regulation; as unemployment fell, so would state funding for training and the TECs would inherit a minimalist enabling role, oiling the wheels of the private market for training. Since 1990, the unexpected rise in unemployment has drawn the TECs into more active market regulation; they remain preoccupied with unemployment, to which the bulk of their budgets is committed contractually, while industrial training lies in deregulated disarray.

A persistent theme in provision for the unemployed is that of subordination to the market. Work values are expounded as if the problem lay in attitudes of the unemployed rather than a shortage of jobs. Benefits or "training allowances" are set at a level significantly below market wage rates, attendance is effectively compulsory as other means of state support are removed, and the experience of "training" is typically degrading and penurious.[20] In a trend which began with the Holland Report in the late 1970s and accelerated during the 1980s and 1990s, provision for the unemployed has become increasingly market-led in rationale, structure, and form. By the end of the 1980s, MSC provision was not so much concerned with providing temporary shelters from the market as with subjecting the unemployed to the full force of market discipline. Programs such as the Youth Training Scheme (YT) were central to the Conservative labor market strategy in the 1980s. Based on the twin pillars of individualism and flexibility, this strategy placed crucial emphasis on training and redefinition of skill; training, it was asserted, had been appropriated by organized labor (CPRS, 1980), but the Conservatives would ensure that in the future it would be organized on employers' terms (Young, 1982).

YT was a key component of a barrage of labor market policies through which the Conservatives sought to weaken organized labor, lower reservation wages (those at which the unemployed are induced to enter employment), homogenize the labor supply, and reconstitute competitive relations among workers (Fairley and Grahl, 1983; Goldstein, 1984; Deaton, 1985). The scheme also performed a wider ideological function in reconstructing the young working class in the subordinate role of *trainee*.[21] According to MSC mandarin Geoffrey Holland, it was concerned not with "taking young people out of the labour market [but with putting] them in on terms which secure their entry" (quoted in Finn, 1987, p. 173). Through programs like YT, the unemployed were subjected *by the state* to market discipline (or institutional simulations of it). Thus, the market was mobilized to perform a crucial control function, applied collectively but experienced individually. Failure in the labor market implied personal rather than systemic failure, explained in terms of inadequate skill or poor attitude.

The process of subjection to the market has taken on a particularly hard edge in recent years. Under the TECs, a deliberate goal of policy has become the creation of a training market; the Conservatives' unbending faith in the market mechanism has led them to "introduce reforms designed to mimic the market in places . . . where full privatisation would either be difficult or politically unacceptable" (Felstead, 1993, p. 2). This marks a shift in the rhetoric and practice of the *training state* (Mizen, 1994) toward the use of training not for the production of skills per se, but as a means of lubricating labor market mobility—a development Standing (1992) terms "trainingitis" (p. 271).[22] While in the 1980s inadequate training was presented as a cause of unemployment, by the 1990s it apparently also had become a brake on Britain's newfound international competitiveness.

> Our economy leads the way in Europe in generating new jobs, and as a nation we are now in a better position than for decades to sustain a high level of employment growth. But our future success in generating new jobs is not guaranteed. It depends on our ability to update the skills and productivity of all those in the workforce, on our commitment to wealth creation and economic success and above all on an increased capacity to adjust to change and take advantage of the opportunities it offers. . . . There is now much ground to be made up if we are to have the skilled and flexible labour force we need for the 1990s. (DE, 1988, pp. 3, 28)

Yet, although the white paper which launched the TECs lambasted employers for their historic failure to invest in the skills of the work force (and coincided with a major report documenting Britain's desultory training record; Training Agency, 1989b), it could propose no other solution than dogmatic deregulation. More persuasive were those analyses linking Britain's skills problem with deep-seated institutional failures and regulatory deficits (see Finegold and Soskice, 1988).

Despite the well-documented liability of deregulated labor markets to failures of skill formation,[23] the solution proposed in the white paper was further deregulation. The statutory levying powers of the ITBs were abolished,[24] and TEC programs were to be funded by the state only insofar as they catered to the needs of the unemployed. In-company training would have to be funded by the private sector. According to the Employment Department's internal guidelines, the TECs' role was to "secure a greater level of private investment in education, training and enterprise" (quoted in *Financial Times*, 27 January 1989). With no mechanism for raising private-sector funds, with 80 to 90 percent of their funding linked to programs for the unemployed, themselves due for an "orderly rundown" (deputy director of TEED, quoted in *Working Brief*, May 1991), the TECs hardly seemed capable of defusing the "demographic time bomb" (the shortfall in the youth labor supply wrongly projected for the early 1990s; see Haughton, 1990). On the contrary, they seemed more likely themselves to be victims of the explosion.

In many ways, it was fortunate for the TECs that the demographic time bomb was never detonated. Contrary to forecasters' expectations, the rapid rise in unemployment to over three million began in the middle of 1990, before most TECs—with their corporate plans bulging with suddenly outdated policy objectives for tackling skills shortages and reintegrating women returners in an expanding labor market—had even achieved operational status. At the time, this was interpreted as a betrayal of the TECs' promise; the newly appointed TEC directors, it seemed, had been handed the poisoned chalice of mass unemployment (see Peck and Emmerich, 1991). The alternative, however, was an empty chalice. The unanticipated return of high unemployment and its spread to the south of the country at least had the effect of guaranteeing the TECs' funding base; in the absence of alternative funding, the fall in unemployment would have rendered TECs impotent in the face of spiraling skill and labor shortages.

In a deregulated training market, the basic problem facing TECs is that they lack the means either to stimulate company training on a generalized basis or to combat the free-rider problem that accompanies private skills formation. First, TECs can stimulate company training only insofar as it is possible to bend the program rules on centrally designed schemes such as ET and YT, or to the limited extent that it is feasible to develop customized training packages using local initiative monies or performance bonuses. Neither of these options is likely to yield more than a marginal effect on a local economy.[25] Second, TECs are powerless to deal with the problem of free riding, rooted in the tendency for some firms to poach labor skills produced in other firms by bidding up wage rates. The presence of poaching firms causes others to cease company training for fear that their investment will be wasted. The result is a classic case of market failure: a stalemate develops between poacher and trainer, training collapses, and a wage spiral is triggered as firms compete for labor within a dwindling pool of skilled workers. The levy-grant system used by the ITBs represented an attempt to respond to this problem (employers were taxed and the funds redistributed to those investing in training), but no such measures exist under the deregulated TEC regime.

With no real purchase on the private training sector other than TECs directors' occasional exhortations to the virtues of training, the TECs hardly represent a response to this fundamental regulatory dilemma (Coffield, 1990). Thus is exposed the inadequacy of the government's response, which effectively has meant giving the market its head and appointing business leaders to TECs to act as skills missionaries: "By increasing local employer responsibility for local training arrangements . . . TECs will generate more private investment in training. As employers recognise the economic necessity to train and the returns available, they will be encouraged to make a larger investment in training" (DE, 1988, p. 43). The result of deregulation is that training is liable to collapse both in booms (when poaching deters potential trainers) and in recessions (when long-term training investments tend to be forgone as a short-term cost-saving measure). Meanwhile, TECs remain financially dependent on the state and are locked into running low-grade programs for the unemployed. While this certainly was always envisaged as *part* of the TECs' mandate, it makes little sense for it to have become their main activity; disciplining the unemployed does not even address, let alone solve, the intractable collective-good problem of skill formation. As Finn (1988) observed some time ago, the effect of changes to the work-welfare system has been to "move Britain towards something like the American system of 'Workfare.' . . . However, the Government are likely to be more successful in creating anxiety among the unemployed than in satisfying Britain's training needs" (p. 521).

Cost-Saving and Flexibility

In Jessop's rendering of the neoliberal SWS, productivist cost-saving and flexible entrepreneurship are driving forces in the state's attempt to remake itself. These concerns have been central to the TEC regime and its emerging contradictions (see Table 7.4). When the TECs were launched, it was made clear that government funding would fall as unemployment fell (*Financial Times*, 27 January 1989); the unexpected rise in unemployment slowed the rate of financial retrenchment, but did not stop it. Between fiscal years 1988–89 and 1996–97,

Table 7.4. The Transition from the MSC to the TECs

	MSC	TECs	Contradictions
Ideological base	Corporatist centrism Labor market planning	Neoliberalism Labor market deregulation	Centrist localism Market failure
Institutional goals	Management of mass unemployment, with increasing orientation to employers' needs Regulation of industrial training through ITBs	Expansion in training activity through deregulation and liberation of market forces Reorientation of programs for unemployed to local market needs	Failure of voluntarism to stimulate training system Restricted scope for restructuring programs due to rise in unemployment
Policy objectives	Cost-effective management of unemployment Work preparation Regulation of industrial skill formation	Disciplining of unemployed by (local) market Local workfarism Privatized industrial skill formation	Growth of alienated underclass Inability to stimulate private skill formation through exhortation
Organizational structure	Quasi-autonomous status Staffed by civil servants and closely linked to ED	Constituted as private companies limited by guarantee, overseen by ED	Problems in financial management Lack of public accountability
Representational forms	Tripartite; TUC and CBI nominees with parity of representation on national commission and local area manpower boards	Business-dominated; prescribed two-thirds employer majority on TEC boards; less formalized national arrangements	Inability to pursue "business" objectives due to funding restrictions Marginalization of key interest groups

(cont.)

Table 7.4. (cont.)

	MSC	TECs	Contradictions
Policy mechanisms	National programs for youth and unemployed delivered through network of public, private, and voluntary providers Apprenticeship-based training system	Uneven restructuring and repackaging of national programs by TECs Emphasis on cost-cutting and competitive bidding Passive deregulation of industrial training	Limited scope for local innovation to due contractual and financial restrictions Collapse of apprentice training (and partial subsumption within YT)
Financial structure	Financial planning on basis of anticipated demand for training places Levy-grant system in ITB sectors	Selective and competitive allocation of funds on basis of training outputs and performance measures Abolition of levy-grant system	Output-related and performance-based funding leads to short-termism, quality-cutting, and exclusion of disadvantaged Unregulated poaching
Management culture	Civil service–based and program-driven Bureaucratic and centralist Formally accountable	Increasingly private sector–based management ethos Finance-led and decentralized Elitist and unaccountable	Conflict between ED and TEC management styles Inadequate political control over local decision making
Monitoring and control	Through bureaucratic means and by tripartite interests Largely uncontested powers of central sanction	Through financial means Minimal central monitoring on nonqualitative criteria	Inadequate quality control Evasion and contestation of powers of central sanction

(cont.)

Table 7.4. *(cont.)*

	MSC	TECs	Contradictions
Spatial form	Bureaucratic and political centrism Strong national policy steer Regional and local tiers concerned with low-level delivery issues	Decentralized centrism Strong central financial control coupled with limited (and channeled) policy delegation to TECs Minimal regional and national bureaucratic structures Increasing spatial differentiation	Tension between pressures for local autonomy and imperatives of political and financial control of programs for unemployed Stimulation of inter-TEC competition leads to indiscriminate, short-term cost-cutting

Derived from Emmerich and Peck (1992) and Peck (1991b).

From Peck and Jones (1995), pp. 1382–3. © 1995 Pion Limited. Reprinted by permission.

Employment Department funding (the bulk of which is now committed to TECs) is projected to fall by 32 percent from £4.7 to £3.2 billion per annum, despite the rise in unemployment. The shortfall has been converted into unit funding cuts on TEC programs for the unemployed (Emmerich and Peck, 1992; Jones, 1995), but has yet to translate itself into an exodus of disenchanted TEC directors. The explanation for this apparent paradox lies in the way that funding cuts have been traded for local flexibility in negotiations between central government and the TECs.

When TEC directors from around the country gathered on budget day in November 1993 to hear Employment Secretary David Hunt spell out the financial implications for TECs, they received good news and bad. While continuing to court TEC directors as the "advance guard of the enterprise economy" and "key players in the regeneration of the nation" (quoted in *Working Brief,* January 1994), Hunt also announced a further round of budget cuts impacting mainly on TEC programs for the unemployed (redefined as "jobseekers").[26] Coupled with the imposition of an even stricter welfare-benefit regime, this served to reinforce the immanent workfare dynamic within the TEC system.[27] The good news, however, was that TECs would be granted access to "new" funding for integrated initiatives in urban and regional regeneration (ED, 1994, Annex I; cf. Finn, 1994). This represented a continuation of an established trend: TECs have proved willing to accept budget cuts in exchange either for new opportunities to bid against public funds (for example, in education, career guidance, ethnic minority initiatives, and urban development) or for a relaxation of their internal operating procedures (for example, enlarging the scope for financial flexibility or the accumulation of "surpluses"). While there are those who continue to promote greater program and finance flexibility as the solution to the TECs' problems (Bennett, Wicks, and McCoshan, 1994), that remains politically infeasible given the overriding government objectives of restraining public expenditure and managing mass unemployment.

As the TECs' mainstream program budgets have been cut, they have found some compensation in the accumulation of new functional responsibilities (and funding opportunities), while constantly lobbying for greater financial and policy autonomy. At a time of considerable pressure on public spending, however, financial accountability and stringency have been at a premium. Even as the entrepreneurial TECs find ever more inventive ways to accumulate "surpluses" and program budgets for local priority projects (*Hansard Written Answers*, 30 November 1993: col. 509), government finance officers instigate a crackdown on "overpayments" to TECs (*Hansard Written Answers*, 1 December 1993: col. 623). Through negotiation and adjustment, the rules of the TECs' operating environment have evolved toward a highly politicized pseudomarket system, providing a means by which regulation of an administratively decentralized but politically central-ized system can be secured through a network of what Jessop (1991) terms "market proxies" (p. 151).

In establishing an operating environment for the TECs, the gov-ernment faced a number of dilemmas. Because they have private company status but spend public money, a strict system of financial accountability had to be established. The TECs, however, lobbied for greater local autonomy and financial discretion, necessary (they quite reasonably claimed) if they were to tailor provision to local needs. In addition, the political imperative of managing unemployment through workfare-style programs such as ET and YT had to be reconciled with the TECs' interests in developing provision for those already in employment. These tensions continue to dog the TEC regime, although the Employment Department has sought to respond to them by developing an elaborate operating system around the TECs which itself seeks to mimic market allocation. In the pseudomarket con-structed around them, the necessity to intervene in TECs' day-to-day operations has been avoided by creating contractual parameters and financial measures for regulation at arm's-length (Peck, 1991b).

Under this pseudomarket system, which is strongly reminiscent of the operating environment established around PICs (Anderson, Burkhauser, and Raymond, 1993; King, 1993), the TECs are paid by results. An increasing proportion of budgets is tied to the achievement of training outputs (placing individuals in jobs or obtaining vocational qualifications), while a system of performance bonuses rewards TECs for securing improvements in value-for-money. Thus, cost-based "league tables" are used to reward "efficient" TECs for "success" in driving down unit training costs (ED, 1993). The deliberate objective in the use of competitive league tables, which refer to "areas of greatest public expenditure" (p. 2), is to achieve a reduction in national spending through the stimulation of cost-based competition between TECs. This represents a geographic version of institutional Darwinism; the existence of a spatially uneven cost terrain is used to force down program costs.

Like a real market, this pseudomarket of the TEC operating regime combines the illusion of freedom with the firm hand of coercion. TECs see opportunities to earn performance and output bonuses, but in the very act of striving to achieve them, reproduce the coercive pressures of the operating system by seeking to outperform competing TECs according to criteria set by central government (see ED, 1994, Annex A).[28] The fact that TECs compete for public funds on a national basis, and that these are allocated at a predetermined limit, means that a bonus won by one TEC translates into a cut suffered by another. Consequently, the TEC operating regime represents a sophisticated form of central control; by setting the parameters of the pseudomarket within which the TECs compete, central government is able to dictate the direction of change in training provision and maintain financial control while creating the illusion that the system has been "freed up" and infused with local flexibility.

Thus, while it may be relatively effective in minimizing exchequer costs and maximizing unemployment register effects, the pseudomarket around the TECs produces unintended consequences that work directly against the grain of good training practice. In ways not dissimilar to the market on which it is modeled, the TEC operating regime is beset with degenerative pressures that individual TECs are in no position to resist. Financial penalties are incurred if training anticipates future rather than meeting immediate labor market need; caters to those at a disadvantage in the labor market or with special training needs; or serves areas of the labor market where skill formation is associated with high capital intensity and/or high cost (Peck, 1991a).[29] Consequently, TEC provision is drawn into the secondary sector of the labor market where employment is volatile and pay and formal skill levels typically are low. As a result, the TECs are compounding rather than tackling the problem of Britain's low skills equilibrium (see Finegold and Soskice, 1988). They also are fueling labor market flexibilization (of the defensive kind) by underwriting and restructuring the processes of selection, recruitment, and induction training in the unstable secondary sector (cf. Jessop, 1993, p. 29). The structure and strategic orientation of the TEC initiative, and the massively deregulated private market alongside which it stands powerlessly, seem set to lead Britain down the low road to flexibility, a strategy that is not only socially and politically regressive, but also economically dysfunctional. It is by no means clear that flexibly competitive labor markets can reproduce themselves, as they exhibit a tendency to lurch into crises of skill formation and wage inflation. In encouraging such developments, TECs seem destined to contribute to the problem they were intended to solve.

Hollowing Out

Geographically, the TEC initiative also appears to echo Jessop's observations on the spatial constitution of the SWS. The nation-state, he argues, is being hollowed out by globalizing and localizing forces, the latter associated with the "resurgence of local and regional governance" (Jessop, 1994, p. 271; cf. Mayer, 1992). In its Thatcherite form, Jessop asserts that the new localism, while being circumscribed by "central, executive power" (1991a, p. 150), is associated with a "real proliferation of regional and local economic development initiatives along Schumpeterian workfare lines" (1994, p. 269). The TEC initiative, perhaps the boldest incursion into this arena, is characteristic of this sort of *centralist localism,* representing an alliance between the institutional and financial power of central government, on the one hand, and the legitimacy of local business on the other. Along with parallel developments such as the devolution of "opted-out" schools and hospitals and establishment of Urban Development Corporations, the TECs reflect a central strand in neoliberal thinking: the disaggregation of political structures below the nation-state (see Peck, 1995).

Under the TECs, key functions in the regulation of unemployment have been contracted out. In the process, a measure of *regulatory space* has opened at the local level such that, within a framework set by central government, the TECs have begun to explore new ways of restructuring the local welfare state. Although the degree of central control over TECs remains high (Peck, 1993), there also is substance to their localism. Financially, TECs have been successful in negotiating increased (albeit strictly limited) scope for local flexibility. Organizationally, they have sought increasingly to distance themselves from bureaucratic norms and structures inherited from the civil service. Politically, TEC directors have been reluctant simply to toe the government line, revealing their potential as political opponents rather than silent and feeble allies. Under the TEC initiative, the government has ceded a degree of political power at the local level, albeit only to a select group of central government–vetted business leaders. Reflecting the diverse ways in which the rhetoric of localism has been taken up by neoliberal discourse (Holliday, 1991; Kearns, 1992), appeals to the local have played a definitional role in shaping TEC ideologies, providing a comparatively uncontentious and nondivisive focal point for mobilizing local business coalitions (Peck, 1995). In establishing the TECs as locally based and business-led agencies, the Conservatives sought to realize an opportunity not only to break up the MSC, but also to construct something quite different at the local level: an organizational basis for *local* neoliberalism.

In pursuing this objective, the Conservatives were particularly attracted to U.S. models of work-welfare reform. While a wholesale shift to workfare at the national level was perhaps politically imprudent in the 1980s, the broad direction of change remained consistent with that long-term goal. Moreover, in the deliberate emulation of the PIC initiative, there was an attempt to open up political space for a more uneven, *and less visible* shift toward workfare at the local scale. According to a leading British government adviser, lessons from the PIC experience "served as guideposts for [the Department of Employment] throughout the planning process on TECs" (Stratton, 1990, p. 71).[30] The PIC model was attractive to the Conservatives for a number of reasons.

- It suggested a way in which the MSC could be broken up into a network of locally based bodies which nevertheless would remain under strict central control.
- It provided a mechanism for privatizing public training by contracting out not only the delivery system (an approach the MSC had followed already for over a decade), but also the bulk of the administrative machinery associated with the planning, commissioning, and monitoring of provision.
- It offered an opportunity radically to restructure the terms and conditions of employment of civil servants in the MSC, who could be transferred to a privatized arm of the state.
- It provided a means to shift the burden of funding from the public to the private sector, as anticipated falls in unemployment

would allow the state progressively to withdraw from (or at least redefine) its role in work preparation for the unemployed.
- It represented an alternative, competing delivery system for the local authority sector (for both funds and functions).
- Perhaps most ambitiously, it provided an organizational platform from which to construct a business-led development agenda at the local level.

While the notion of a PIC-style system coupled with local workfare was undoubtedly attractive to the Conservatives, the process of transplantation was by no means straightforward. In contrast to the United States, local politics in the United Kingdom had traditionally been something of a quiet backwater, with little in the way of active, high-level business involvement (see Bulpitt, 1983; Shaw, 1990). Organizationally, the Confederation of British Industry (CBI) was nationally focused with a weak regional network, while the Chambers of Commerce remained resolutely local, and in many cases parochial, with a weak national presence (see Grant, 1987). The 1986 Local Employer Networks (LENs) initiative (which can be seen in retrospect as a would-be forerunner to the TECs) had sought to use Chambers (and, in some cases, other local business organizations) as institutional hosts for a small-scale program of employer networking in labor market intelligence. The initiative foundered on the inability of the Chambers (the membership of which tends to be skewed toward small- and medium-sized firms) to mobilize adequate employer involvement at the local level. Not only was the Chamber network uneven in terms of organizational capacities but many areas of the country simply had no Chamber presence (see Bennett, McCoshan, and Sellgren, 1990). Thus, the British PICs could not be constructed around the Chambers; new organizations would have to be created, staffed if necessary by personnel transferred temporarily from the civil service. By the time the TEC planning stage was under way, the Chambers were effectively outside the project while the CBI was beginning to strike a chord with its plea to involve business leaders from *major* companies, "the real power brokers in their communities" (Stratton, 1990, p. 71).

The material and symbolic role of private-sector directors is central to the government's thinking on TECs. The TEC initiative sought to coopt business leaders onto TEC boards in order to bring private-sector discipline into the public training system and, via this route, into the welfare system. Seen as custodians of market forces, business representatives are believed to have unique insight into the needs of the market. The transposition of an individual logic onto a collective logic is of course a common theme in neoliberal ideology:

the business representatives on TEC boards would speak for themselves *but in so doing* would express the needs of local business in general (see Bennett, Wicks, and McCoshan, 1994). Such a view both denies the existence of cleavages within the business community and overlooks differences between the needs of an individual company and the collective needs of business in a locality (Peck, 1995).

While it would be ill-advised to view private-sector TEC directors as bearers of some logic of the market, it would be equally unwise to cast them as puppets of central government. The very effectiveness of the TEC lobby suggests that that is not an adequate conception; TEC directors have used their access to the media periodically to berate the government over funding levels and civil service bureaucracy (see Peck, 1991b). In this sense, the TEC initiative was something of a political gamble for the Conservatives (Ashby, 1989; Coffield, 1990) and, insofar as a degree of power has been ceded to local employers, it raises the possibility that this regulatory space may be appropriated in rather different ways in different places. The limited evidence thus far suggests that some TECs challenge the central government line, some toe it, and others pursue it with zeal. For example, while London East TEC complains that ET has failed and proposes progressive new schemes tailored to the needs of women in the Bengali community, Norfolk and Waveney TEC announces an explicitly workfare-style scheme in which the adult unemployed are required to contribute toward the costs of their own training (Emmerich and Peck, 1992).

Thus, the "market paternalism" of the TEC regime is associated with a measure of political indeterminacy, which seems to be opening the door in some areas to politically regressive developments—notably, the establishment of what amount to local workfare systems. While some TECs may be proposing more progressive programs, the danger is that they will fall foul of a funding regime geared toward the goals of maximizing value-for-money and unemployment register effects. The result is a geographically uneven drift toward a workfare system, guided by the TEC operating regime. This is being achieved not through a public—hence politically visible—reorientation of national programs, but through incremental, local-level experimentation tacitly encouraged by the national TEC regime. Because it is geographically uneven, effective opposition is likely to be difficult to mobilize. Although national political opposition to workfare remains strong, an incremental drift toward local workfare through the TECs seems set to be achieved with mere ripples of local dissatisfaction rather than waves of national confrontation.

The TECs' private-sector directors, it should be emphasized, are not the agents of change. The motive force behind local workfarism is not a politicized cadre of TEC directors, but the hidden hand of the TEC operating regime. More important than the fact that the TECs have been privatized, or that they are controlled by boards of local business leaders, is that they encapsulate a *reconstruction of central-local relations* within, and on the margins of, the welfare state. As Cochrane (1993) has observed, one of the most important weapons in the neoliberal attack on the welfare state is the constitution of competitive relations between arms of the local state and, more generally, *between places*. Viewed in this light, the TECs are engaged in a process of centrally articulated, local regulatory undercutting. Again, this is strongly reminiscent of the United States, where the regressive undercutting of welfare standards and entitlements by workfare-oriented states has led to a "major change in the landscape of welfare reform" (Wiseman, 1993, p. 18; see also Handler, 1995). For example, Richard Nathan, a leading U.S. policy analyst, argued in 1987 for a "step by step" transition from welfare to workfare building on state-level experiments and demonstration projects.[31] "The states' new-style workfare reforms are very promising. The states are on a roll and making important changes that, in a quiet way, really count for something. . . . So there is a consensus here we can build on. . . . This is a process, to deal with a hard, stubborn social condition" (quoted in Block and Noakes, 1988, p. 53).

Debates on neoliberal labor reform tend to characterize the process as lowering the floor of employment rights and welfare entitlements (see Deakin and Wilkinson, 1991; Deakin and Mückenberger, 1992). Work-welfare reforms in the United Kingdom and United States suggest that the analogy of a regulatory ceiling might be more appropriate. The operating regimes around the TECs and the PICs appear to be more effective in securing a very low ceiling of regulatory standards (above which individual localities cannot go without incurring financial penalties) than in providing a floor upon which progressively to build and innovate. In the United Kingdom, TECs that cut costs, encourage market-selective "creaming" practices among local providers, and subordinate provision to immediate labor market needs will be rewarded under the funding regime. Those that seek to develop provision in high-cost fields or cater to the needs of disadvantaged trainees will be penalized. As a nationally or centrally constituted system of financial and contractual regulation, the TEC regime places a ceiling above the activities of individual TECs *beneath which* different local forms of regulatory restructuring are occurring. While some of the institutional specifics of the U.S. case are rather different, the similarities are undeniably strong and, clearly, the two systems share a tendency toward the same regressive dynamic of workfarism.

In the United Kingdom, the TEC initiative is being used as a rather blunt tool to effect a transition to local workfare. It is producing a more geographically uneven system of labor regulation and, at the margins, is opening up limited possibilities for a new localism. But if this is hollowing out, a resurgence of the local, it is surely its most hollow form. Under the TEC regime, there is *some* scope for local autonomy, but only for *certain kinds* of local autonomy: innovations that run with the grain of the national operating environment are rewarded and funded; those that do not are penalized and not funded. This most certainly does not amount to a "stronger role for regional and local states" (Jessop, 1994, p. 271). Rather, it is a more elaborate form of central control, and to interpret it any other way is to run the risk of confusing the localist rhetoric of neoliberalism with the reality of state restructuring.

THE WORKFARE STATE IN CRISIS

This chapter has explored the political economy of the TEC initiative in the light of Jessop's abstract claims about the hollowed-out SWS. The analysis self-evidently lacks the breadth necessary comprehensively to assess Jessop's claims on their own terms, although it perhaps responds to his plea for "more concrete [work, aimed at specifying] the nature of the SWS in particular cases" (1993, p. 34). Descending from the abstract level of analysis means coming to grips with the complexity and indeterminacy of policy change and institutional restructuring.

Moreover, the regulationist method lays stress on the integral and dialectic relationship between the dynamics of accumulation and processes of social regulation, within the broad ambit of which individual state policies and institutions are likely to play a comparatively modest role (Jessop, 1992c, pp. 3–8; 1995). As Jessop acknowledges, individual Thatcherite policies are the product of conjunctural and contingent conditions such that "we must take care not to treat these policies as the simple products of generic post-Fordist tendencies" (1991a, p. 143). Similarly, when analyzing the Thatcherite policy package, it is important to recognize that "some of the new structural forms and regulatory practices arose from attempts to manage the crisis of Fordism, others from attempts to escape it; some are primarily defensive, others offensive" (1994, pp. 259–260).

As a product of Thatcherism's most proactive phase and as an intervention focused on the crucial regulatory problem of labor reproduction, the TEC initiative tells us something about the integrity and reproducibility of the neoliberal SWS, British-style. It occupied the leading edge of regulatory reform in late Thatcherism and therefore illuminates some of the contradictions and potentialities of the neoliberal project in Britain. Far from resolving contradictions associated with the breakdown of Britain's flawed Fordism or smoothing the way to a post-Fordist regime, the TEC initiative seems *itself* to be fueling crisis. Powerless to regulate private skill formation, the TECs are caught between the government's conflicting objectives to drive down public expenditure, contain mass unemployment, and reform the system of industrial training. As a result, they seem locked on a course that will result (1) in the further degradation of labor-power, as the unemployed are subjected increasingly and remorselessly to the discipline of the market, and (2) in the paralysis of private skill formation, as the unregulated plundering of labor resources undermines the basis on which firms' training investments are made. The TEC experience might be summarized as: workfare, yes; Schumpeter, no.

These tensions are stimulating calls from many quarters for drastic reform, notably for the restoration of some kind of regulated training system lest there be a politically embarrassing exodus of TEC directors or even the collapse of the TEC system itself.[32] After several years of frantic development, the TEC initiative appears to have arrived at the brink of crisis. What is significant about this is that, in the case of TECs, the object of analysis is not the detritus of the Keynesian welfare state, but an ambitious and recent initiative which appears to satisfy virtually all Jessop's taxonomic criteria for hollowed-out, Schumpeterian workfarism. In so many ways, the advent of the TECs represented a radical break with welfare-corporatist labor regulation and the MSC, but as Table 7.4 reveals, while the scale of institutional transformation has undoubtedly been far-reaching, the contradictions aggravated in the process have been just as deep-seated. This should alert us to the dangers of functionalist teleology, which some see lurking in even the most sophisticated regulationist analyses (cf. Jessop, 1995; Lee, 1995).

In retrospect, TECs were the product of excessive political opportunism. In Jessop's terms, they are caught between the contradictions of the economically productivist and politically electoralist strands of Thatcherism (Jessop, Bonnett, Bromley, and Ling, 1988; Jessop, 1995), foundering on the primacy of the political. The fall in unemployment created the political opportunity to dismantle the MSC, and with it, much of the welfare-corporatist system of labor regulation. In its place was created a new set of institutions quite incapable of coping with the problems ahead. Far from being the vanguard of a "skills revolution" (DE, 1989), the TECs inherited responsibility for a new unemployment crisis. Though they speak the language of strategic partnership and local economic regeneration, they are in fact creatures of mass unemployment, a component of Jessop's "integrated social security state." Their attempts to free themselves from the financial restrictions that come with this role are largely futile.

While the credibility and self-confidence of the TECs may have been dented by the untimely arrival of the early 1990s recession,[33] had they been born into a tight labor market, their fate would have been worse still. Real and sustained economic growth would expose the fundamental flaws of the deregulationist program of which the TECs are a part. In the absence of the policing function performed by a training levy, labor poaching would again break out. TECs would find themselves starved of funds, but few could expect to raise significant sums from the private sector, a more likely scenario being that they would pursue more vigorously than ever alternative sources of *public* funds, particularly from Europe. The task of economic regeneration through TECs—that which at the beginning of the initiative "capture[d] the imagination of British businessmen" (Main, 1990)—might well have been even less fulfilling than that of managing programs for the unemployed during a protracted recession. In reconciling themselves to this latter task, however, TEC directors have not only had to lower their sights, but have had to come to terms with close central budgetary control.

Though there may be a future for TECs as arm's-length managers of the unemployment crisis and agents of a faltering workfare state, the fact is that the training crisis must remain unresolved. It is difficult to escape the conclusion that in order to resolve it, distinctly *anti*-neoliberal forms of state intervention will be called for. This suggests a fundamental structural weakness in the Thatcherite project which, as Jessop (1991a) has acknowledged, rests on a "palaeo-liberal conception of a hire-and-fire, flexi-wage labour market and so shows insufficient official concern for educational and vocational training to produce multi-skilled workers" (p. 157).

If this is Thatcherism, then it can last only until the skills run out. Perhaps all along it was little more than a sustained attack on the welfare state and organized labor (cf. Jessop, Bonnett, Bromley, and Ling, 1988), destined in the final analysis to become a prisoner of the same market forces it sought to liberate. Labor reproduction—the failure of which was central to the Fordist crisis (Aglietta, 1979, p. 165)—may prove to be late Thatcherism's Achilles heel.

Since we are still living through a phase of transition, experimentation and strategic intervention, caution is called for in dealing with the likely form and functions of the post-Fordist state. Its final form will only become apparent later and vary from society to society. One general conclusion seems justified, however, even if it seems banal. If the wage form (even in its new, more flexible guise) continues to be the dominant social relation in capitalism, then there will still be a role for the welfare state (suitably flexibilized) in securing the reproduction of wage labour and the wage form. Thus the crucial question is how the welfare state will be restructured and within what limits its role can be reduced (from a neo-liberal viewpoint) or expanded (from a neo-statist or neo-corporatist viewpoint) without seriously undermining structural competitiveness or restraining the transition to post-Fordism. (Jessop, 1994, p. 276)

Insofar as it is possible to advance general claims on the basis of this very specific interrogation of the structure and logic of the Schumpeterian workfare state, the following conclusion may be drawn. The neoliberal SWS—certainly in its British variant and possibly generically—seems to be critically vulnerable to Polanyian crises of labor reproduction. Institutional experiments, such as the TECs, have proved unable to break out of the spiral of crisis. While they may *look like* and even sound like the institutional epitome of the hollowed-out, neoliberal SWS, it is difficult to see how they can dispense the functions necessary for the *reproduction* of this state form and its mode of growth. Instead, they reflect some of the central contradictions of a neoliberal program which must be understood more as a symptom of, not a solution to, the current global jobs crisis.

NOTES

1. For theoretical argument, see Chapter 8 and, in particular, Burawoy (1985).
2. See Johnson, McBride, and Smith (1994); Mizen (1994); King (1995); and Skocpol (1995).
3. See Bailey (1988) and Donahue (1989).
4. For comparative perspectives on TECs and PICs, see Johnstone (1990); Bailey (1993); Bennett (1995); Graham (1995); and King (1995).
5. See also Mead (1986); Ellwood (1988); Kaus (1992); and for an overview, Deacon (1994).
6. On the concept of low skills equilibrium, see Finegold and Soskice (1988). For context and debate, see Albert (1993) and Streeck (1989).
7. For a general argument concerning neoliberalism and the state, see Gamble (1988). For more concrete analyses, see Deaton (1985); Robertson (1986); and Johnson, McBride, and Smith (1994).
8. The remainder of this chapter is a substantially revised version of an

article jointly authored with Martin Jones and published in *Environment and Planning A*, 27 (1995): 1361–1396 (London: Pion Limited). I wish to thank Martin Jones and Pion for permission to adapt and reprint parts of the article.

9. In particular, see Esping-Andersen (1990) and Cochrane and Clarke (1993).

10. See Chapter 5; also Scott and Storper (1992) and Peck and Tickell (1995).

11. See Aglietta (1982); Boyer (1988b); and Leborgne and Lipietz (1992).

12. This is not to say that Jessop is insensitive to contingency and contradiction in the Thatcherite project. "Thatcherism is neither a natural fateful necessity or a wilful contingency. It is the complex, contradictory, unstable, inchoate and provisional product of social forces seeking to make their own history—but doing so in circumstances they have not chosen, cannot fully understand, and cannot hope to master" (Jessop, Bonnett, Bromley, and Ling, 1988, p. 13).

13. Cf. Salvati (1989) and Goodwin (1992).

14. Jessop borrows the term "institutional Darwinism" from Schoenbaum (1967).

15. This point is stressed by Coffield (1990) and Peck (1991b); compare the overly literal interpretation of Bennett, Wicks, and McCoshan (1994).

16. For example, see Stoker (1989); Goodwin (1992); Mayer (1992); Painter (1992); Stoker and Mossberger (1992); Cochrane (1993, 1994); Eisenschitz and Gough (1993); and Geddes (1994).

17. This, too, has been taken up in the business discourse the TECs have adopted. Unemployment programs are viewed as the TECs' "core business."

18. On the wider effects of the TEC funding regime, see Peck (1991a) and Jones (1995).

19. Boyer also calls for a move beyond "exhaustive description" of institutional innovation toward consideration of "relations between the various [institutional] innovations" (1990b, p. 112).

20. Cf. Offe (1984); Block, Cloward, Ehrenreich, and Piven (1987); and Rank (1994).

21. For more general discussion, see Hollands (1990) and Mizen (1994).

22. For example, according to the U.K. Government, "effective training is essential to producing a more flexible labour market [but] imposing new burdens on employers would make training decisions less efficient and break the link between training and competitiveness" (DE, 1994, pp. 11, 12).

23. Perry (1976) and Streeck (1989); cf. Chapter 5.

24. Since the mid-1960s, the network of ITBs had organized training at the sectoral level on the basis of a statutory levy-grant system (Anderson and Fairley, 1983). Although effective lobbying won a reprieve for the construction and engineering construction ITBs, the remainder of the ITB network was stripped of its statutory powers to raise employer levies, leaving in its wake a large but organizationally weak network of nonstatutory training organizations (Berry-Lound, Chaplin, and O'Connell, 1991). These tend to

be based on employers' associations, have little in the way of union involvement, and without exception are seriously underresourced (Rainbird and Smith, 1992).

25. ET and YT deliver only low-level skills and their program rules tie them firmly to the achievement of unemployment register effects, while the level of funding available for customized training is so small (rarely exceeding 5 percent of budget) as to be insignificant in the context of a local economy.

26. The new jobseeker's allowance involves the merger of unemployment benefits (previously administered by the Employment Department) and income support (previously administered by the Department of Social Security). Its introduction in April 1996 will mean a cut in welfare entitlements (means-testing will occur after six months rather than 12). In a jobseeker's agreement, the unemployed will be required "to specify in advance the steps they will take to find work and then take them" (quoted in *Working Brief*, January 1994).

27. The jobseeker's allowance pushes the U.K. system closer to compulsory participation, an element of pure workfare, by continuing to remove alternative sources of support for the unemployed. As Finn (1988) and King (1995) observed of earlier, less stringent reforms, this implies compulsion in all but name.

28. Again, the parallels with PICs are strong (see Anderson, Burkhauser, Raymond, and Russell, 1992; Bailey, 1993; Bennett, 1995).

29. On the PIC experience, see Donahue (1990) and Anderson, Burkhauser, and Raymond (1993).

30. Stratton was recruited from the United States specifically for her experience of the PIC experiment (see Bennett, Wicks, and McCoshan, 1994; Bennett, 1995; King, 1995).

31. For discussion of state-level demonstration projects, see King (1995) and Handler (1995).

32. For evidence and commentary, see *Financial Times* (10 May 1993, 10 May 1995); Peck and Emmerich (1993); Smith (1993); and Taylor (1995). Cf. Jessop (1992b, p. 38).

33. See Kraithman, Wall, Bowles, Adams, and Rainnie (1991) and Smith (1993).

Chapter 8

LOCALIZING LABOR
Geopolitics
of Labor Regulation

The previous chapter examined the uneven and contradictory drift toward workfarism in state regulatory structures. This chapter locates these developments in a broader geopolitical context, focusing on tensions between globalizing capital and localizing labor and on the contemporary geopolitics of labor regulation. It suggests that current changes—for example, workfare, the decentralization of collective bargaining, and the marketization of social protection—are part of a systematic attempt to resubordinate labor and the conditions of its reproduction to despotic control. Such projects extend (and reshape) labor control, understood in its broadest sense.

The process of "putting labor in its place" is intrinsically geographic. Not only are new relations of domination over labor unfolding unevenly across space, but strategies of *localization* (in industrial relations norms and conventions, in welfare entitlements and programs) play an active role in the subordination of labor. Just as the relative immobility of labor vis-à-vis capital—its rootedness in place—is the source of asymmetrical power between labor and capital,[1] so strategies to localize labor are being used to extend managerial dominance and state discipline. Following Burawoy (1985, p. 87), this process can be characterized as restructuring the *political apparatuses of production,* "the institutions that regulate and shape struggles in the workplace" under which the political conditions for a new era of *hegemonic despotism* are being established. It heralds a period in which local communities are coming under attack not only through deindustrialization and job loss, but also through the erosion and commodification of the basic conditions of social reproduction.[2] As the new despotism spreads, the contours of labor control are being reworked.

Under such banners as deregulation, decentralization and localization, new geographies of labor regulation are being forged as state power is deployed to commodify labor and subjugate communities to the market. Following Beynon and Hudson (1993), if *space* is the domain where capital searches for the most profitable sites of accumulation and *place* is that of labor where meaningful and enduring social relationships are constructed, then the shift toward hegemonic despotism may be seen as an attempt to reduce place to space. Places to live seem increasingly to be reduced to spaces in which to earn, or strive to earn, a wage. The driving forces behind this geographical degradation of labor are unfettered global competition and its ally, neoliberalism. Together, they are eroding labor's bargaining strength both from above, as the actual and potential mobility of capital vis-à-vis labor increase, and from below, as local social conditions and regulatory standards are dismantled in attempts to expose labor to the market and to attract or retain mobile capital (see Peck and Tickell, 1994; Sengenberger, 1994). This does not mean that place—as a theoretical category or as a political site—somehow matters less, but is rather to insist on an appreciation of the local in the context of (and in relation to) the global (see Massey, 1993c; Tickell and Peck, 1996).

This chapter proceeds in three parts. The first attempts to outline a geopolitics of production, linking shifts in labor regulation to the historical and geographic reconstitution of capital-labor relations; following Burawoy, it suggests that a tendential shift toward a new despotism in labor regulation is under way. The second discusses the geography of this new despotism, summarized as a double movement toward globalization *and* localization. Both tendencies erode social conditions in general and labor's bargaining position in particular. Third, the chapter concludes by arguing that the prospects for a turn toward social protection in labor regulation will remain distant so long as neoliberal principles continue to dominate relations between regions and nation-states.

*GEO*POLITICS OF PRODUCTION: GLOBAL CAPITAL VERSUS LOCAL LABOR

The contradictory imperative of labor control lies at the heart of the capital-labor relation, constituting one of the central dynamics of restructuring. Problems of labor control not only occur within the narrow parameters of the labor process, but also relate to social reproduction (see Chapter 2). Labor control in its broader, integral sense was the focus of Michael Burawoy's *The Politics of Production,* which sought innovatively to connect power relations in the workplace to those outside it, and to link production and reproduction.[3] For Burawoy (1985), "the act of production is simultaneously an act of reproduction. At the same time that they produce useful things, workers produce the basis of their own existence and that of capital" (p. 123). Focusing on production-reproduction relationships and the wider politics of production in which they are embedded, Burawoy charts an uneven transition in labor control regimes from "market despotism" to "hegemonic" labor regulation, the latter having been dominant in the postwar period but now giving way to a new "hegemonic despotism" (pp. 125–127, 148–151).

The most primitive form of labor regulation, *market despotism,* describes a situation in which workers are absolutely dependent upon wage-labor for subsistence and, as a result, are exposed to both the economic whip of the market and the summary discipline of capitalists. For Burawoy, despotic regimes were progressively though unevenly superseded by *hegemonic regimes,* in which various forms of state intervention rupture the direct link between the reproduction of labor-power and wage-labor (the defining feature of market despotism). The development of labor legislation and evolution of welfare systems partially separated the processes of production and reproduction; workers were no longer *absolutely* dependent on waged employment for their livelihoods nor were they absolutely vulnerable to the arbitrary despotism of the capitalist. Sharing these common functional features, the institutional form of hegemonic regimes varied widely across space. While coercion was the predominant form of labor control under market despotism, politically mediated consent has come to prevail under the currently dominant labor regime, *hegemonic despotism,* in which the bargaining power of capital is enhanced "by virtue of collective labor's vulnerability to capitalism's national and international mobility" (p. 127). Constructed on the foundations of the hegemonic regime, this new despotism is strongly reminiscent of the more antagonistic and asymmetrical capital-labor relations of nineteenth-century capitalism. Again, institutional forms vary geographically; there is no simple and uniform transition.

While Burawoy's account of the three regimes of labor regulation shares commonalities with earlier periodizations of the labor process,[4] there also are important analytical distinctions. In contrast to the production tradition of labor process studies, Burawoy's (1985) approach rests on the crucial distinction between the labour process conceived as a particular organization of tasks, and the political apparatuses of production conceived as its mode of regulation [the latter of which is treated] as analytically distinct from and causally independent of the labour process. . . . Notwithstanding the important variations among despotic regimes and among hegemonic regimes, *the decisive basis for periodization remains the unity/separation of the reproduction of labour power and capitalist production*. . . . [This] periodization . . . from despotic to hegemonic regimes to hegemonic despotism, is rooted in the dynamics of capitalism. In the first period the search for profit led capital to intensify exploitation with the assistance of despotic regimes. This gave rise to crises of underconsumption and resistance from workers, and resolution of these conflicts could be achieved only at the level of collective capital—that is, through state intervention. This took two forms—the constitution of the social wage and the restriction of managerial discretion—which gave rise to the hegemonic regime. . . . [In turn, the] very success of the hegemonic regime in constraining management and establishing a new consumption norm leads to a crisis of profitability. As a result, management attempts to bypass or undermine the strictures of the hegemonic regime. (pp. 125, 127–128, emphasis added)

Burawoy's approach, then, centers on both the dialectical relationship between the labor process and the political apparatus of production and on the shifting relationship between production and reproduction. The contradictory and uneven nature of each labor regime is always afforded due attention, distinguishing his approach from the crude periodization characteristic of much of the labor process literature.

Burawoy also is sensitive to the changing *spatial* constitution of labor regulation, identifying it as a source of unevenness and contradiction. For example, the crisis of profitability associated with the hegemonic regime in the United States was not anchored in international competition pure and simple, but instead in conflicts with other *national systems of labor regulation,* notably Japan, where "the hegemonic regime gave capital greater room for manoeuvre"; Brazil and South Africa, where instead of hegemonic regimes there was a reliance on "a combination of economic and extra-economic means of coercion"; and export-processing zones where "women workers were subjected to an autocratic despotism fostered by the state" (p. 149). In addition, hegemonic regimes are eroded from within in localized enclaves where a new *local despotism* prevails. "Advanced capitalist states have responded to [international competition and the crisis of profitability] by carving out arenas in which labour is stripped of the powers embodied in hegemonic regimes. The urban enterprise zone is one such attempt to return restricted areas to the nineteenth century through the withdrawal of labour protection and the abrogation of minimum wage laws, health and safety regulations, and national labour relations legislation" (p. 149). As global competition has intensified, not only have national systems of labor regulation been thrown into competition with one another, but local regulatory experimentation also has been fostered (see Jessop, 1994; Peck and Tickell, 1994). The implicit spatial metaphor to which Burawoy alludes is that of islands of despotism surrounded, in his view, by a turbulent and increasingly poisoned sea of hegemonic labor relations.

Thus, the crisis of hegemonic labor regulation is geographically constituted.[5] Two transformations in the spatial constitution of labor relations presage the establishment of a "new political order in the workplace."

> First, it is now much easier to move capital from one place to another, as a result of three phenomena: the generation of pools of cheap labour power in both peripheral countries and peripheral regions of advanced capitalist societies; the fragmentation of the labour process, so that different components can be produced and assembled in different places (sometimes at the flick of a switch); and the metamorphoses of the transportation and communications industries. All these changes are connected to the process of capital accumulation on an international scale; a second set of changes is located within the advanced capitalist countries themselves. The rise of hegemonic regimes, tying the interests of workers to the fortunes of their employers, embodying working class power in the factory rather than state apparatuses, and the reinforcement of individualism, have left workers defenceless against recent changes in capital.
> . . .
> The new despotism is founded on the basis of the hegemonic regime it is replacing. It is in fact a *hegemonic despotism*. The interests of capital and labour continue to be concretely co-ordinated, but where labour used to be *granted* concessions on the basis of the expansion of profits, it now *makes* concessions on the basis of the relative profitability of one capitalist vis-à-vis another—that is, the opportunity costs of capital. . . . The new despotism is not the resurgence of the old; it is not the arbitrary tyranny of the overseer over *individual* workers (although this happens too). The new despotism is the "rational" tyranny of capital mobility over the *collective* worker. The reproduction of labour power is bound anew to the production process, but, rather than via the individual, the binding occurs at the level of the firm, region or even nation state. The fear of being fired is replaced by the fear of capital flight, plant closure, transfer of operations, and plant disinvestment. (Burawoy, 1985, p. 150)

In the contemporary period, a *spatial* mode of calculation has displaced a temporal mode of calculation. The "primary point of reference is no longer the firm's success from one year to the next; instead it is the rate of profit that might be earned elsewhere" (p. 150).

The ties that, under the Keynesian welfare state, bound the reproduction of labor power to the medium-term profitability of capital within national spaces seem certainly to have been broken. In the vacuum created by this rupture, widespread degradation of labor standards has been accompanied by localized experimentation in labor regulation.[6] Although it *may* be that these experiments are opening up new possibilities for labor,[7] they are being developed in the context of globalization and the erosion of labor's bargaining position. As Burawoy (1985) puts it, "One can anticipate that the working class will begin to feel their collective impotence and the irreconcilability of their interests with the development of capitalism, understood as an international phenomenon" (p. 152). There are not likely to be any new deals for labor, even *local* deals, within the context of hegemonic despotism.

Thus, the new despotism must be understood as simultaneously global *and* local. The localized degradation of labor standards—described by Burawoy as state-articulated attempts to "return restricted areas to the nineteenth century" (p. 149)—is inextricably linked to the globalization of capital and the extension of its bargaining power. Through globalization, the asymmetrical power relation between capital and labor has been tipped further in favor of capital (see Offe, 1985; Storper and Walker, 1989). The institutionalized, national accommodation between labor and capital of the Fordist-Keynesian era has been broken, and the new despotism is associated with a double movement in the regulation of labor-capital relations. On the one hand, there is an upward swing as globalizing capital is able to use its actual and potential mobility both to extract concessions from labor in production and to evade the costs of social reproduction. On the other hand, there is a downward swing as labor is defensively localized, locality is pitched against locality, labor costs are forced down, and regulatory standards and structures of social reproduction are eroded.

This double movement is related to fundamental shifts in the organization of the state. Nationally constituted welfare regimes, undermined by fiscal crises and the globalization of accumulation, are giving way to hollowed-out workfare regimes (Jessop, 1993). "As capital and companies move ever more freely to where they expect the best returns, and large corporations grow ever bigger and more powerful, national governments and national labour organisations are increasingly deprived of the sovereignty necessary to govern economic behaviour within their borders. These national institutions are losing their autonomy of action. This raises the question of how the institutional vacuum that still exists at the European level will be filled" (Sengenberger, 1992, p. 41).

In the context of the neoliberal vacuum at the European scale, tendencies toward localization of labor market governance are associated with disempowerment rather than empowerment of the regions (see Dunford and Perrons, 1994; Peck and Tickell, 1994). Through localization, neoliberal states are extending rather than ceding central control and, though the phenomena Jessop (1994) describes as hollowing out are real enough (such as the "growing interest among local states in regional labour market policies, education and training, technology transfer, local venture capital, innovation centres, science parks and so forth," p. 272), it is questionable whether they represent regional resurgence. A more plausible explanation is that the current plethora of local employment and inward investment initiatives is part of a frantic attempt to attract or maintain local jobs in the context of the competitive anarchy fostered by neoliberalism (Peck and Tickell, 1994). Rather than a renaissance of the local, these flurries of activity may reflect the increasing subjugation of the local to the global and, the more vigorously localities compete with one another, the more effectively they are subordinated to the national and global—the scales at which the rules for local competition are made.[8]

Increasingly, these rules are being fixed in accordance with the beggar-thy-neighbor logic of neoliberalism. The cutthroat competition of which neoliberalism makes a virtue tends to foster cost-stripping and short-termism, the effects of which are evident not only in the restructuring of capital and markets, but also in the restructuring of the state and social regulation.[9] Neoliberalism promotes regulatory stripping as well as cost-stripping; it creates a climate of undercutting in social and regulatory standards as well as in markets and it breeds short-termism in social reproduction as well as in capitalist production. Reassuring notions of market clearing and equilibrium, derived from the textbooks of neoclassical economics, are transformed into a political program in which inequality, flexibility, and mobility are promoted as virtues. In this sense, neoliberalism represents a direct attack on labor's rootedness in place (cf. Storper and Walker, 1989; Beynon and Hudson, 1993). It is an attempt to reduce place to space.

Thus the new localism of neoliberal rhetoric is regressive rather than progressive, selling the local to the global on terms determined by the imperatives of international competition and neoliberal policy. Suitably packaged, local labor qualities are traded on a global market as localities are forced to turn to a tired repertoire of inward investment promotion, local boosterism, and labor flexibility programs. Local discourses, echoed globally, link economic salvation with competitive relations between workers and between places. Localities trade on their "competitively priced work force" and the "flexible attitudes and skills" of local workers. Globally mobile capital need only pick the most succulent of the fruits on offer.

Thus, just as labor is exposed as never before to the power of global capital, it also must confront the enemy within: competition (see Lebowitz, 1987). What Marx called the "iron laws of supply and demand" are being remobilized under neoliberalism to divide and weaken workers, between and within places. Over and above the anarchy of the market, this is a politically coordinated anarchy, related to Burawoy's (1985) distinction between primitive despotism and hegemonic despotism in labor-capital relations. Hegemonic despotism is a new form

> built on the basis of the erstwhile hegemonic regime—which, rather than creating antagonistic interests (as the early despotic regimes did), begins to construct a coordination of interests around despotic rule. Collective bargaining is now a means of extracting concessions from workers, faced with the threat of plant closures or lay-offs. Fractions of the working class compete with each other to retain capital's "allegiance." Moreover, the intensification of competition is also made possible on the one hand by the erosion of the popular roots of working-class organization through the previous hegemonic regimes, and on the other hand by the withdrawal of the state as an arena in which struggles between capital and labour can be fought out. The possibility of constructing a hegemonic despotism becomes a major attraction to capital as it faces widening struggles in peripheral and semi-peripheral countries. (p. 264)

"Neoliberated" capital returns home as neoliberal policies provide support for the creation of peripheralized enclaves within the core and former core regions of the advanced industrial nations. Neoliberalism creates a framework in which workers and localities are thrown into competition with one another in order to retain capital's "allegiance," by undermining the bases of labor organization, by dismantling the structures through which labor's former hegemonic accommodation with capital was maintained, and by promoting wage and employment inequalities. Such far-reaching programs of deunionization, casualization, and wage polarization, typically packaged in the politically ambiguous language of flexibility, now occupy a new mainstream in labor market policy.[10] An important element in these programs is the *localization of labor*: labor, literally, has to be put in its place.

PUTTING LABOR IN ITS PLACE:
GEOGRAPHIES OF HEGEMONIC DESPOTISM

Conditions of global political and economic instability usually spell hard times for labor. Polanyi's account of the 1920s slump, for example, has a depressingly familiar ring: "Statesmen like Seipel, Francqui, Poincaré, or Brüning eliminated Labour from government, reduced social services, and tried to break the resistance of the unions to wage adjustments" (quoted in Notermans, 1993, p. 138). During periods of crisis, it is common for capital and the state to attempt to reverse the gains in wages and living standards made by labor during an expansionary phase, tipping the balance of power in favor of capital. In the process of restructuring, the contours of labor control are reworked and remade.

This could be said of the 1920s. It also can be said of the current prolonged crisis, one of the first victims of which was the Keynesian system of labor regulation constructed and consolidated during the postwar period. Based on the principle of full (male) employment, this system sought to maintain a balance between the normalization of aggregate demand, containment of class conflict, expansion of social welfare, and regulation of social reproduction. The Keynesian state was above all a *nation*-state, but one predicated on a particular constellation of global financial and trading relationships and operating under the watchful eye of the U.S. hegemon and the Bretton Woods accord.

> [O]nly after World War II did the tendency to transform the system into a world system become a historical reality, as all functions of capital . . . were globalized. However, a basic and determining contradiction arose: although the economic reproduction process was globalized, the political forms of regulation remain national, due to the fact that the capitalist state is by its very origin a nation state. The great achievement of the "Keynesian revolution" was the establishment of the "lender of last resort" and of "big government" on the level of the national economic system in order to avoid crises of the 1929-type. . . . But there was no equivalent institutional network capable of resolving this problem on the level of international economic relations. (Altvater, 1992, p. 30)

By the 1970s, the institutional "solution" to the problems of the 1920s had become a contributor to new problems. The U.S. hegemon exported more than cars during the Fordist period; it also exported Fordist institutions and modes of calculation, not to mention the "American way of life" (see Jessop, 1992a). In the process, its capacity as a national economy to realize superprofits on the basis of exports to a newly constituted global mass market was fundamentally eroded (see Maddison, 1989; Altvater, 1992; Streeck, 1992). In one sense, the Fordist growth dynamic was ruptured by immanent geographic contradictions as the imperatives of globalizing accumulation came into conflict with national systems of social regulation (Peck and Tickell, 1995).

At the heart of the crisis lay the welfare state, the structure and sheer size of which seemed to have fallen fatally out of step with the new realities of mass unemployment ("flexible labor markets"?), on the one hand, and a problematic combination of destabilized production and accelerated financial speculation ("flexible accumulation"?), on the other. The unwanted debris of Fordism, in the form of unemployed and inappropriately skilled labor, had accumulated in and around the welfare state, and the concern of the Atlantic Fordist countries was that the bulging welfare net, designed to pick up only a relatively small proportion of the economically active work force, would bring down the ship of state itself (see Offe, 1985; Esping-Andersen, 1990). Variously justified in terms of the necessity for restraint in public spending, the desire to reconstitute incentives to work, or the imperative for greater labor market flexibility, welfare rights and entitlements have been under attack for almost two decades in most of the advanced capitalist countries. Consequently, the structures of the Keynesian work-welfare regime have been slowly dismantled.

Despite all the post-Fordist speculation, what will emerge in its place is not yet at all clear. While suitably cautious in deploying post-Fordist terminology, Jessop (1992a) nevertheless insists that the logic and, to a certain extent, the institutional shape of the post-Fordist state are becoming apparent.

> State intervention will shift from a Fordist concern with managing national demand through Keynesian and welfare state measures. For the irreversibly international character of post-Fordism has the paradoxical consequence of reinforcing the state's role in promoting competition—not just of individual firms of national champions but of the overall productive system and its sociopolitical supports. If this marginalizes the state's role in managing national demand, it increases its role in the constant and continuous restructuring of the supply side. . . . Welfare policy will be closely integrated into this process. . . . [The] transition to post-Fordism . . . will not only involve rolling back the frontiers of the Fordist type of state but also rolling forward those of a new type of state. The post-Fordist world will be structured through the interaction of national or regional rivalries in the race for societal modernization and the dynamic of a global production system. (p. 64)

There are already indications, he claims, that these new forms of state action are beginning to resolve the problems associated with "the collapse of Fordist labor market institutions" (p. 65). Jessop's vision of the future is centered on a structural shift toward a Schumpeterian workfare state but while that captures many of the current geopolitical realities, it also runs the risk of foreclosing the question of the search for a new institutional fix *after* Fordism (Peck and Tickell, 1994). Certainly, new regularities, patterns and relationships are emerging, many of them consistent with the post-Fordist elements catalogued by Jessop. Still, the possibility must be entertained that their prevalence stems not from their functionality, but from the fact that they represent *typical responses to an enduring crisis*. The same, largely indisputable evidence of their spread (which country, after all, does not have a program for labor market flexibility?) could just as easily be marshaled in support of an argument for widening and deepening crisis, as for Jessop's claim that a regulatory solution is in sight.

The same might be said of Jessop's thesis of hollowing out, his argument that in the midst of great instability and uncertainty, the spatial constitution of the state is being reordered. Again, from the same empirical phenomena (such as the proliferation of local economic initiatives or the emergence of supranational states), one could draw quite different conclusions. Are they indicative of a new spatial order or a continuing *dis*order? Is this the geography of a workable, flexible future or a crumbling Fordist past? In labor regulation, where there has been considerable policy innovation and institutional restructuring (not to mention more than a little post-Fordist speculation and counterspeculation), there seems to be some way to go before any kind of resolution can be identified.[11] True, there has been a substantial global-local realignment, but both globalization and localization are beset with contradictions.

Globalizing Labor Regulation: Deadlock in Detroit

Speaking at the beginning of the first world jobs summit in March 1994 (which, appropriately, took place in Detroit, one of the fallen citadels of the Fordist era), President Bill Clinton sought to impress on the assembled delegates from the world's richest countries that there was "no place to hide" (quoted in *Guardian*, 15 March 1994). For him, prerequisite to a global program of job creation was the task of building "a consensus among these countries [the members of G7] that unemployment in one country affects unemployment in another, that stagnant wages in one country affect stagnant wages in another, that rich countries have common interests in continuing to grow" (*Guardian*, 14 March 1994). Yet, though the United States, Europe, and Japan may have become mutually dependent in economic and regulatory terms, that does not translate readily as mutual interest. Behind Clinton's remarks lay demands for Japan to open her internal markets in order to stimulate global demand and for Europe to cut interest rates while accelerating welfare reform. On the latter issue, he sought to reassure European delegates, "I don't think for a moment they [the Europeans] should relax their commitment to things like health care and family support policies. . . . But they need to focus a little bit on some of their internal policies as they relate to how unemployment works" (*Guardian*, 14 March 1994).

The force behind the summit, U.S. Labor Secretary Robert Reich, argued for a radical new combination of U.S.-style flexibility and European-style education and training, to be supported by an expansionary macroeconomic program. Conscious of the mounting costs of the United States' low-wage path (see Spriggs, 1993), he sought to distinguish U.S.- from U.K.-style flexibility: "Some seem to define flexibility as the freedom to fire workers and lower wages" (quoted in *Financial Times*, 16 March 1994). Although the U.K. government (with its calls for further labor market deregulation and perverse desire to emulate the U.S. low-wage path)[12] was somewhat isolated at the conference, that need not have troubled the British delegates, content in the knowledge that they had not history, but geography on their side.

The conference's inevitable deadlock was tempered only by the ease with which some appearance of consensus could be constructed around platitudinous appeals to flexibility. This might have drawn a few wry smiles from the British delegation, who no doubt predicted the difficulties of attempts to ratchet up labor regulations multilaterally. Geography was on the side of Britain because, in the current competitive climate, the ratchet works in the opposite direction. The continuing global hegemony of neoliberalism—which, even if not the dominant strand of thinking *within* all the advanced industrial nations, defines key relations *between* them—is fostering an environment in which regulatory undercutting is becoming endemic. In competition among labor regimes, the least-cost, most socially regressive options tend to win out.[13] Pushing the ratchet of labor standards downward represents a neoliberalized process of *regime competition* between labor systems.

The liberal justification for allowing agents to choose between alternative [labor] regimes is that a free market for regulations will generate optimum regulations for all. However, to the extent that

> capital is more mobile between regimes than labor, regime competition adds to its bargaining arsenal the threat to exit and move elsewhere, either from one national or subnational jurisdiction to another, or between a national and a supranational jurisdiction. Being less mobile, the only way in which both governments and labor can respond to regime competition is by offering capital positive inducements not to emigrate, which are likely to include assurances or friendly (that is, less demanding) behavior. (Streeck, 1992, p. 326)

Consequently, competition between labor regimes is tipping the balance of power further in favor of capital and, more generally, having a corrosive effect on regulatory standards.[14] Capital is apparently becoming ever more sensitive to the (short-term) competitive advantages to be derived from exploiting geographic differences in labor regulation,[15] while deregulation strategies seem to be fueling spatial as well as social inequality.[16] Paralleling the situation in the 1960s and 1970s, when capital flight from the Atlantic Fordist countries in search of cheap labor had the effect of destabilizing the Fordist regime (Fröbel, Heinrichs, and Kreye, 1980; Lipietz, 1987), the basis for a global market in labor regulations may now be in evidence—a new international division of labor *regulation,* perhaps. As in the original version of the new international division of labor, the lowest bid invariably wins.

The context for this race to the bottom in labor standards is being set by the neoliberal promotion of competition and cost-stripping. For example, the recent GATT deal presages a harsh global environment in which countries will struggle to defend, let alone extend, labor rights and standards. Under the new global trade regime, labor regulations stand to be assessed not in terms of goals such as social justice or health and safety, but according to market criteria. Debates over minimum wage legislation already are being recast in terms of how much the regulations might cost a nation's exporters. Pleas for effective minimum labor standards, to be applied globally, seem ever more futile (see Sengenberger, 1991, 1994), and at the Detroit summit, a bid by the French and Italian governments for a social clause in the GATT agreement was not considered realistic. Not only could the G7 countries not agree on such measures, but it was deemed by "trade experts" to be "extremely unlikely that a social clause could be inserted in the face of strong opposition from many Asian countries" (quoted in *Financial Times,* 16 March 1994). This seemingly outlandish, supposedly anticompetitive proposal concerned basic restrictions on child labor and compulsory prison labor.

In light of this "institutional deadlock" (Streeck, 1992), the overriding tendency seems to be toward a competitively driven bottoming out of labor regulations around the most minimum of minimum standards (see Sengenberger and Campbell, 1994). Given huge variations in regulatory regimes, there clearly is a long way left to go, but globally, regime competition seems to be based on struggle among "American," "Asian," and "European" models, summarized in Table 8.1. Certainly, there remains scope for new development programs, linked perhaps to the most socially progressive model, the European way (see Lipietz, 1992). However, the neoliberal constitution of EU competition policy, and the corrosive presence of neoliberal nation-states (such as the United Kingdom), mean that a "social Europe"—based on a harmonized, trans-European system of social protection and labor regulation—is viewed by many as a rather forlorn hope.[17] Britain's rejection of the social chapter of the treaty of Maastricht, resistance from low-wage countries within the Union, and continued emphasis on trade liberalization in the Single European Market are undermining attempts to raise the floor of employment rights across Europe. As John Major remarked memorably at the time of Britain's "opt-out" from key social policy provisions of the Maastricht treaty, "Europe can have the Social Chapter, we'll have the jobs" (quoted in Lefresne, 1993, p. 11).[18]

The global context for European debate is critical. If the comparatively wealthy European countries cannot reach agreement on common labor standards due to concerns over national economic competitiveness, more serious still is the perceived competitive threat of low-wage countries outside Fortress Europe. Reflecting on the possibility of a socially progressive turn in European industrial relations, Streeck (1992) is pessimistic.

> Whatever its institutional detail, any labor-inclusive European Community industrial relations system will have to respond to the fundamental condition of external interdependence in a global economy and must survive the fierce competition of other systems that do not share its constitutive commitment to a floor of social and industrial citizenship rights for workers and their organisations. In the absence of a global regime that could take labor out of international competition, projects for a European Social Dimension will have to be discussed and evaluated, not just in terms of their political and normative attractions, but also of their contribution to Europe's economic competitiveness. (p. 314)

Even in Europe, then, where there remains the potentially progressive coexistence of a robust regulatory framework, relatively powerful unions, and underlying economic strength, the prospects for extending labor regulations to reconcile employment standards across the Union

Table 8.1. Supranational Modes of Labor Regulation: Some Generic Features

	The American way	The Japanese way	The European way
Economic structures	Low-skilled, price-competitive approach Downward pressure on wage rates resulting from cost sensitivity of international competition Low and transportable skills	Dualistic, flexible system, combining scope and scale economies with selective enskilling High but firm-specific skills	High-skill, high-wage economy, based on non-price-competitive goods and services Extensive and broadly based human capital investment High and transportable skills
Employment practices	Short-term employment relationships Market-driven approach; employment-at-will Rapid, market-led employment adjustment through external labor market Individualized and competitive employment relations	Long-term employment relationships Confinement of (core) workers to internal labor markets Strong dualism in employment rights and experiences Slow, internalized labor market adjustment	Medium-term employment relationships Institutionalized collective rights High standards of employment protection Macroeconomic stabilization of employment levels
Economic and social norms	"Market" work ethic; employment-rather than employer-oriented Increasing working time combined with low productivity growth and falling investments in human capital High rates of labor market inequality	"Corporate" work ethic; company-as community Acceptance of long working hours Submission to corporate authority; implicit socially encoded rules of managerial dominance	"Social" work ethic; strong non-wage-labor attachments Declining working time Egalitarian wage structure; low inequality and basic income Solidarism and universalism

(cont.)

Table 8.1. *(cont.)*

	The American way	The Japanese way	The European way
Industrial relations institutions	Market voluntarism and adversarialism Individualistic ethos binding goals of efficiency and equity to market Deunionized, human resource management approach	Ethos of culturally and institutionally embedded trust, cooperation, and compliance Enterprise unionism and microcorporatism	State-articulated regulation of economic and political relations Institutionalized rights of employment and economic citizenship Labor-inclusive; unions conferred with public status

Derived from Streeck (1992), Albert (1993), and Peck and Miyamachi (1994).

are not good. The anarchy of neoliberalism, which rages outside and threatens to spread further inside the European Union, continues to exert a corrosive influence. Labor regulations are assessed not in terms of their political, social, or even *long-term* economic value, but instead are represented as merely a variable cost.

Consequently, questions of work and welfare are being reformulated. For example, Chancellor Helmut Kohl links the lack of competitiveness in the German economy to its short working hours compared with the United States; "a successful industrial nation ... doesn't allow itself to be organized as a collective amusement park" (quoted in Rosenberg, 1993, p. 2). Welfare reform, too, is being pushed to the top of the Union's agenda (albeit with residual commitments to social protection).

> Once policy-makers realized that welfare spending could not go on indefinitely increasing its share of the cake, the emergence of a widespread political debate on the future of the welfare state became inevitable.
> Up to now the debate has focused on various issues:
> • the importance of controlling the explosive growth in government social spending, in particular on health care;
> • the establishing of incentives for people to work;
> • a possible new mix of public and private schemes, with some attempts to focus public expenditure on those most in need (sometimes called "targeting"), giving the occupational and/or private sector an increased role in particular in pension and in health care;

> • a more decentralized approach through, in some cases, the
> development of the role of local authorities and/or welfare
> organizations.
> It is important to recognize in this respect that in modern
> societies, where labour markets will be required to be more flexible,
> individuals need social protection. (Commission of the European
> Communities, 1993, p. 20)

It remains to be seen whether it will be possible to marry cost-cutting and flexibility with continued commitment to social protection. With European welfare reform already subject to strong neoliberal influences (partly but not exclusively through British pressure), the prospects do not look good.[19] Regime competition, it seems, is rendering workers' rights as production costs. As the British government recently put it, "If the rights of an employee involve excessive costs, they may deny an unemployed person the chance to get back into work. . . . [S]pending on social protection is a significant and growing burden on employers, employees and taxpayers generally" (DE, 1994). With nation-states calling explicitly for the dilution of social protection and measures to "reactivate the reserve army mechanism" (Bosch and Sengenberger, 1989), it is clear that the regressive dynamic of regulatory cutting and undercutting has been established, and moreover is building as a result of internal pressures and external competition.

Lubricated by neoliberalism, the voraciously competitive global environment is producing a situation which might be summarized in the following way. At best, there is a standoff over labor regulation between nation-states, a regulatory stalemate in which proposals to extend labor regulations are met with a de facto veto. At worst, and almost certainly indicative of the direction of change, a climate of regressive regulatory undercutting has been created. The response of many nation-states has been to pass the regulatory buck, but because they cannot or will not pass it upwards to supranational bodies, they are opting to pass it downwards to the local level. It is in this context that moves toward localized labor regulation must be understood.

Localizing Labor Regulation:
Toward Workhouse Regions

From the resurgence of local economic strategies to the revival of union locals, from the decentralization of pay bargaining to the emergence of local cross-class growth coalitions, from the establishment of local workfare experiments to the widening of regional unemployment disparities,[20] a whole host of developments point to a significant localization, of sorts, in structures of labor regulation. This might be seen in some quarters as a welcome grass-roots movement in long-overdue recognition of the diverse needs and aspirations of regions and localities. Under the neoliberal environment in which localities are pitched into competition with one another, however, localization is likely to lead to increased regional disparities and, in turn, heightened *regional* regulatory undercutting. The competitive process of trading away labor standards and social protection is under way within as well as between nation-states. In Europe, still at the crossroad of what Sengenberger and Pyke (1990) term the "high" and "low road" to flexibility; the downward spiral may be about to begin. Competitive pressures liberated by neoliberalism are producing

> high variation of local conditions between firms, sectors and . . .
> nations, some with cooperative or labor-inclusive industrial rela-
> tions and others not, some using high skills and paying high wages
> and others employing low-wage, unskilled labor. . . . In either case,
> political cohesion among workers across enterprises or regions is
> bound to decline, and parochial identifications resisting redistribu-
> tive intervention must proliferate. Where obligations to cooperate
> [between regions] can no longer be politically generated, the social
> base of politics fragments. . . . [This decentralised] voluntary politi-
> cal and industrial order . . . may have all kinds of other attractions,
> to the undiscerning eye, appearing "soft," "communitarian," "flex-
> ible," "culturally rooted," "decentralised" etc. More importantly,
> it may be the only order on offer. But this must not obscure the
> inevitable losses associated with a shift towards voluntaristic "va-
> riety" and "decentralisation," most prominent among them a
> fragmentation of loyalties and a cumulative growth of inequalities.
> (Streeck, 1992, pp. 327–328)

Viewed from this perspective, the durability of socially progressive local experiments must be questioned, given that they are being formulated in the context of local-local relations constituted largely on a competitive basis.[21] Local models of labor regulation should be assessed not only in terms of their *internal integrity* (for example, whether there is a reproducible system of skill formation, a stable social settlement, and sufficient social protection), but also in terms of their *external relations*. In the present highly competitive climate, internally cohesive systems may be vulnerable to undercutting by internally fragile, low-cost, low-protection systems. Following the distinction (described in Chapter 5) between *defensive flexibility* (for example, the U.K. and U.S. models, with their high levels of labor mobility and job insecurity) and *offensive flexibility* (for example, the German model, with its focus on multiskilling and job security), Michon (1992) points ominously to "the risk of huge disparities emerging within the European Community, with islands of offensive flexibility being submerged in a tide a defensive flexibility" (pp. 240–241).[22] Similarly, Streeck (1992) concludes that Europe is suffering "an *excess* of flexible decentralisation" (p. 328, emphasis added).

In light of competitive regulatory undercutting, European debates around "subsidiarity"—decentralizing regulatory control to the most appropriate, and often lowest, geographic scale—take on rather different meanings. To the British government, "The diversity of Member States' institutions, labour market traditions and legislation is as great in the field of employment as in any other sphere of activity. It must be fully respected. Measures of harmonisation which raise costs and damage competitiveness destroy jobs. . . . [T]he future development of social policy must respect . . . the principle of subsidiarity" (DE, 1994, p. 2). By contrast, labor scholars argue,

> Subsidiarity . . . would allow for more firm specific agreements and more regionally diverse development strategies to emerge. . . . In a world where capital is more mobile than labor and labor is, at best, weakly organized across national boundaries, multinational employers have the potential to play one region off against another and one group of workers off against another in, for example, deciding where to locate new investment. Labor standards will ratchet downward, particularly in an environment where high unemployment weakens worker bargaining power. (Rosenberg, 1993, p. 5)

While it may win support from those pushing for greater regional political autonomy within Europe, the decentralization and localization of labor regulation runs the risk of invoking the ratchet of competitively degraded labor standards, compounded by the capacity of multinational corporations to engage in what Leyshon (1992) terms "regulatory arbitrage" (p. 251).[23]

Despite the continuing faith of some in the capacity of "local political actors [to] extract payments and concessions [from] supra-local actors" (Mayer, 1992, p. 269), the reality is that when nation-states and even supranational trading blocs find themselves vulnerable to regulatory arbitrage, localities are more vulnerable still (Peck and Tickell, 1994). While entrepreneurial local states and localized public-private partnerships should not be dismissed, their influence is surely only a factor at the margin; where the local is being sold to the global, it is the buyer who is in the strongest bargaining position and, in the context of a global shortfall in investments and highly mobile capital, localities are hardly in a position to dictate terms. As Sengenberger (1993) has observed, it would be a robust local partnership indeed that was able to shrug off the effects of, say, a devaluation of the U.S. dollar. Despite the seductive rhetoric of the new localism, local fortunes remain immensely vulnerable to macroeconomic forces and many of the determinants of local success or failure continue to be exogenous, not endogenous (see Markusen, 1991).

Thus, localities with high standards of labor regulation and social protection are persistently vulnerable to undercutting by an investment-hungry neighbor. An inherent tendency toward degradation of labor is at work, conditioned fundamentally by competitive relations between places. Neoliberalism is deeply implicated, not only facilitating but programmatically fostering, *as deliberate political-economic objectives,* the localization of labor regulation and the constitution of regime competition between local labor systems. The current acceleration of regional labor market inequalities, and the related rash of local experiments in the de- and re-regulation of labor, are in many senses products of the prevailing neoliberal environment.[24] In other words, neoliberalism is weakening labor by localizing labor.

Not surprisingly, this process has been taken further in the neoliberal nation-states than elsewhere, though by no means is it restricted to those countries. A distinctive feature of the Thatcher and Reagan governments during the 1980s, for example, was the active, as well as passive, decentralization and localization of labor regulation. Both administrations pursued strategies of deregulation, re-regulation, and (centrally orchestrated) decentralization with a view to weakening unions, driving down wages, and ultimately, constituting competitive relations between workers and between regions.[25] One of the most vivid demonstrations of these tactics was the exploitation of regional divides in the British miners' strike, which culminated in the effective destruction of the vanguard National Union of Mineworkers (Beynon, 1985; Sunley, 1990). On a broader scale, while the British government is at the forefront of moves to encourage the international mobility of workers within the Single European Market, it is equally anxious that such "free market" provisions not be extended to welfare recipients, as this "would mean that EEA [European Economic Area] nationals who were unable or unwilling to support themselves could move to any other EEA country and reside at the expense of the host states' taxpayers" (DE, 1994, p. 14).[26]

Neoliberal nation-states have sought to lubricate the dynamic by which labor standards will be competitively downgraded. At the leading edge of these developments have been those deregulated spaces, such as enterprise zones, which play an important role in eroding labor regulation (Burawoy, 1985). "Strong" regions, with extensive social protection and high wages, are rendered vulnerable to "weak" regions. In the context of globalization, this represents an intractable *georegulatory* problem.

> While the economy has grown increasingly international and partly global, labour institutions and labour market regulation remain largely constituted on the national and sub-national level. . . . A freer flow of capital, goods and people across borders can raise awareness of mutual economic and social dependence, and be a catalyst for progressive change. At the same time, it can exert pressures that threaten existing social standards. Workers, and occasionally also employers and governments, are led to raise charges "unfair competition," and "social dumping." It is argued that low wages, the absence of social security provisions and the denial of worker rights are used to gain economic advantages vis-à-vis countries that respect standards. If a country fails to live up to international labour standards, the effect is to force other trading nations to follow suit . . . [leading to] a "race to the bottom," a vicious cycle of social retrogression in all trading nations. (Sengenberger, 1994, pp. 6–7)

Be they extracted from Nissan workers in Sunderland or Hoover workers in Glasgow, at the expense of the unemployed in Manchester or in Norfolk,[27] local concessions are used not so much to set the (regulatory) standard as to undercut it.

Significantly, competitive downgrading also is at work within the state itself, as the progressive though uneven shift toward a workfare state gets under way (Standing, 1992; Jessop, 1993). Part and parcel of this shift is the constitution of competitive relations within the machinery of the state. Just as in the United States, the transition from welfare to workfare has occurred by way of a geographically uneven process of experimentation and emulation,[28] so also in the United Kingdom the process was characterized in the previous chapter as an orchestrated drift toward *local* workfare (see Costello, 1993; Peck, 1994; Finn, 1995). Following public outcry at Prime Minister John Major's attempt to place *national* workfare on the political agenda (*Guardian*, 5 February 1993), less visible local experimentation has been supported. The politically controversial issue of workfare (one never confronted directly by Thatcher or her strident employment ministers during the 1980s) now is being tackled through local experimentation under the Training and Enterprise Council regime.[29] The basic conditions of a workfare system, under which the unemployed are subjected to the discipline of the local labor market through inducements to participate in low-grade schemes or accept low-paid employment, are already substantially in place in Britain (Costello, 1993; Peck, 1994; Finn, 1995). This has been achieved through geographic incrementalism, not with the bang of national political confrontation but with whimpers of local dissatisfaction.

The uneven development of the workfare state has to be seen not as a policy failure but as a policy *goal*. The localization and geographic differentiation of labor regulation is a prerequisite for the constitution of competitive relations between local regulatory systems. It is through such *subnational regime competition* that neoliberal nation-states seek to lower the floor of employment rights, even if unevenly. Indeed, such is this unevenness that the very notion of a floor for labor standards is fast becoming an anachronism. In its place, an uneven and constantly shifting terrain of *variable* labor standards is being established. Regions weakened by mass unemployment are proving particularly vulnerable to a new local despotism, which translates as a regulatory threat to neighboring regions.

Consequently, the economics of the workhouse—the original and most despotic system of labor control—is being imposed on a new set of *workhouse regions*. In addition to exerting a downward pull on regulatory standards, these regions stand as an ever-present reminder of the price to be paid for unemployment. Just as the unemployed of nineteenth-century Britain were subjected to the degrading and punitive conditions of the workhouse, they now are subjected under workfare to the arbitrary despotism of the local labor market. Emphasizing the historical parallels, Costello (1993) refers to the current package of British welfare reform and benefit policing as "workhouse workfare" (p. 2; see also Handler, 1995). The deterrent effect of the workhouse is being applied and experienced in a regionally differentiated way. As Chapter 7 emphasized, workfare is not just about welfare reform (though its effects there are pernicious enough); it also is about adjusting attitudes to and experiences of the labor market.[30] It resubordinates labor reproduction to the market, setting in place a new regime of labor control.

Experimentation with workfare regimes, particularly at the local and regional levels, has been evident for some time in North America, Europe, Australasia, and elsewhere. Local experimentation has been fostered in the United Kingdom with a view to creating a competitive drag on welfare costs and standards; localism in labor regulation contributes to the marketization of work-welfare programs and the uneven development of labor regulation. Such local and regional experiments also play an important part in national policies and programs; in the United States, "the ideas for [national] reform came from the 'demonstration' work-welfare programs implemented by the states, publicized through congressional committees and policy evaluation studies" (King, 1995, p. 169). In Canada, local stories of labor regulation acquire discursive resonance as they are absorbed into wider debates on alternatives in labor market policy. "Through discursive practices, local and particular experiences are represented and transformed into an extra-local 'documentary reality,' thus facilitating the social organization of management and regulation. . . . [These] processes of policy formulation . . . transform people's experiences of work, economic upheaval and political struggle into administrative categories which can be put to work in state institutions" (Dehli, 1993, p. 87).

It would be quite wrong, then, to dismiss local work-welfare experiments as *merely* local. They contribute to the very spatial unevenness of labor regulation that can open the door on extralocal change. They generate just the sort of policy knowledges that can be deployed in framing, channeling and levering wider regulatory reform.[31] These knowledges perform "a particular kind of epistemological and political work, creating rationales for changes in labor market policy formation, and in modes of regulating education and training for future and incumbent workers (Dehli, 1993, p. 106).

The emergence of workhouse regions also reflects the transition, under hegemonic despotism, from a temporal to a spatial mode of calculation. Under the Keynesian welfare regime, workers were granted access to welfare provisions on the basis that such entitlements had been earned by virtue of *temporally prior* tax and social security contributions, referred to by Costello (1993) as the "social security principle." The "workfare principle," on the other hand, denies workers access to such accumulated entitlements, replacing them with a system in which discipline is *locally enforced* by the economic whip of the local labor market (see Block, Cloward, Ehrenreich, and Piven, 1987). Under workfare regimes, the unemployed are compelled to work or undergo training in return for access to income, which has the effect, within local labor markets, of driving down both the reservation wage of the unemployed and the prevailing market wage for low-paid workers. Significantly, then, the shadow of the workhouse falls across the employed as well as the unemployed, as the forced integration of the unemployed into the local labor market acts as a drag on local wages and conditions of employment. The meso-economics of the workhouse region concern not only reducing the "natural rate of unemployment" (see Burton, 1987), but also the casualization of work and flexibilization of the labor market (see

Hudson, 1989; Standing, 1992). They remake the social relations of work at the local level.

RE*PLACING* LABOR REGULATION

Although it may present some progressive possibilities, in the context of neoliberal hegemony the localization of labor regulation must be seen as regressive. Localization is critically connected to the weakening of labor's bargaining strength and erosion of social protection, with implications for local workers and more widely. Viewed from a global perspective, the localization of labor can be seen as prerequisite to the competitive downgrading of regulatory norms, or what the ILO (1995) terms "the debasement of labor standards" (p. 199). Once localized, labor regulation can be degraded through regime competition.[32]

So long as relations between places and labor regimes continue to be cast in neoliberal terms, labor standards will continue to be ratcheted down. Neoliberalism is implicated in what is, in effect, a *crisis of uneven development* in labor regulation. From a regulationist perspective, Dunford and Perrons (1994) situate this within a systemic context.

> The fact that the deep crisis which followed the end of the golden age [of Fordism] is not over is a clear indication that an adequate new mode of regulation does not yet exist. The shape of post-Fordism—understood as a set of rules and strategies that regulate the contradictions of contemporary capitalism and provide the foundations for regular and sustained economic development and social reproduction—is therefore far from clear. Our view is that with globalization there are self-reinforcing trends towards increased economic interdependence, reduced national autonomy and increased economic integration. At present the dominant concept of integration in Europe is neo-liberal: competitive modes of supra-national regulation and adjustment define the rules of the game for regional economies. . . . An important consequence . . . is the coexistence of a deflationary bias and macroeconomic instability on the one hand and greater inequalities on the other. Greater inequality itself is, however, a cause as well as a consequence of the current crisis. (pp. 164–165)

Neoliberalism is concerned to establish a global market in labor regulations within which workers' rights will be rendered dispensable production costs, ripe for cutting. At the local level, there is a desire to see what is constructed as "welfare dependency" superseded by a new "market dependency." This raises the "spectre of a downscaling of labour conditions . . . [caused by] . . . substantial cross-national disparities in labour costs and other terms of employment" (Sengenberger, 1994, p. 7). Thus, the emergence of hegemonic despotism on a global scale is associated with the *downscaling* of labor regulation in both senses of the word; downscaling is occurring in that material *levels* of protection are being eroded and is manifest in the aggressive *localization* of labor.

The tendential new despotism in capital-labor relations is becoming genuinely hegemonic, its spread facilitated by the very unevenness in the landscapes of labor that neoliberalism seeks to exploit. The "tyranny of capital mobility over the collective worker" (Burawoy, 1985, p. 150) is established, while social reproduction is itself subordinated to the market. No longer underwritten by the Keynesian welfare state, the reproduction of labor-power is being reduced anew to a condition of local dependence. The gradual dismantlement of the complex of national institutions which, under the Keynesian welfare regime, secured the reproduction of labor-power, is creating a regulatory vacuum in which labor reproduction is rendered contingent on local labor market conditions. The retrenchment of national institutions of labor regulation is resulting in the subjection of labor to a new global discipline, locally applied. This amounts to "*leaving social regulation to local regulation* . . . [which in turn] leaves labour exposed to the use of labour costs as the means of destructive inter-locality competition" (Sengenberger, 1992, p. 44, emphasis added). Although this process still has a way to go, having repeatedly run up against political opposition and institutional resistance, an uneven transition to workfarist regulation does seem to be under way.

> The experience of the past six decades rather seems to imply that Social Democratic politics of full employment will reappear on the political agenda when the erosion of wage-setting power of trade unions has progressed to the extent where high unemployment and restrictive government policies spark off a severe price deflation. . . . [T]his scenario is not only unattractive but also unlikely as the welfare state of the seventies and eighties seems to have the capacity to marginalize or otherwise eliminate the unemployed from the labor force so that inflationary pressures reappear at ever higher unemployment rates. For the near future, the most likely prospect is prolonged mass unemployment and the creation of an ever larger marginalized section of the labor force alongside prospering islands of successful internationally competitive regions. (Notermans, 1993, p. 161)

The *global* jobs crisis seems to call for global rather than local solutions. While perhaps appealing as a scale at which social mobilization can occur (Amin and Thrift, 1995), local action can be only part of the solution and, uncoordinated, it may remain part of the problem. At the risk of sounding politically naive or theoretically passé, action to "take labor out of international competition" (Streeck, 1992, p. 314) must be organized at the level of the nation-state *and above*.[33] In order to reverse the downward ratchet of labor deregulation, political action must confront the level at which the rules of regime competition are set (the supranational/global) not that at which the rules are carried out (the local). As the ILO (1995) has argued, "a fundamental requirement for restoring full employment is the creation of an institutional framework for cooperative international action" (p. 198). If the resolution to the crisis of the 1920s involved a new deal for labor at the level of the nation-state, the persistent crisis of the 1990s seems to require one at the level of the global economy. Of course, if nation-states are unable to reach agreement on child labor, the realistic must acknowledge that any such new deal remains a distant prospect.

NOTES

1. In particular, see Offe (1985); Storper and Walker (1989); and Gough (1992).
2. On deindustrialization, see Bluestone and Harrison (1982) and Massey and Meegan (1982); and on the erosion and commodification of social reproduction, see Burawoy (1985) and Harrison and Bluestone (1988).
3. For discussion, see Warde (1989) and Jonas (1996).
4. Notably Braverman (1974); Edwards (1979); and Gordon, Edwards, and Reich (1982).
5. For a useful discussion, see Jonas (1996).
6. See Leborgne and Lipietz (1988); Boyer (1992); Salais and Storper (1992); Sengenberger (1993); and Sengenberger and Campbell (1994).
7. For example, this case has been made by Piore and Sabel (1984) and Mathews (1989).
8. For contributions on this theme, see Gertler (1992); Swyngedouw (1992); Dicken (1994); and Dunford and Perrons (1994).
9. The neoliberal path to labor market flexibility has been summarized by Standing (1992) in the following way: first, a "recontractualization" of the labor process on the basis of individualist rather than collectivist principles; second, a shift toward "welfare pluralism" comprising a minimalist safety net for the poor and a voluntarist, privatized system for the middle classes; third, the privatization of social policy; fourth, a shift from welfare

to workfare; fifth, increasingly stringent welfare policing; sixth, a growing police presence to combat increases in crime resulting from socioeconomic exclusion; and seventh, a "neo-corporatist state" based on an alliance between government and business (p. 271).

10. See Robinson (1986); Pollert (1988); Harrison and Bluestone (1987); and Weir (1992). Important counterarguments have been made by the ILO (1995).

11. See Boyer (1987); Leborgne and Lipietz (1988); Storper and Scott (1990); Salais (1992); Sengenberger (1992); Standing (1992); and Lash and Urry (1994).

12. On this point, see Treasury (1993) and DE (1994).

13. For sober (and sobering) analyses of the current situation, see Sengenberger and Campbell (1994) and ILO (1995).

14. Langille (1994) uses the parable of the prisoner's dilemma to illustrate how "*even* in circumstances of equal starting standards, jurisdictions will rationally [from an *individual* point of view] engage in a race to lower labour standards" (p. 336).

15. See Recio (1992); Toft (1992); and Lash and Urry (1994).

16. See Castro, Méhaut, and Rubery (1992a) and Dunford and Kafkalas (1992).

17. See Rhodes (1991); Amin, Charles, and Howells (1992); Castro, Méhaut, and Rubery (1992b); Deakin and Mückenberger (1992); Freire de Souza and Castro (1992); Marsden (1992a); Streeck (1992); Sengenberger (1992); Towers (1992); and Teague (1993).

18. The British government recently threatened to use its opt-out again should the other member states persist in their policies for social convergence. Its grounds were "inhibiting labour market flexibility" (DE, 1994, p. 4), particularly through "extending employment regulation" (p. 6).

19. Responding to the European Commission's green paper, the British government called for measures to hold down wage and welfare costs, deregulate the labor market, and expose the unemployed to competitive pressures. "Europe's over-regulated, inflexible and high cost labour markets have seriously damaged its capacity to create employment. . . . The need now is to reduce the burden of cost and regulation on businesses" (DE, 1994, p. 5).

20. See Walsh and Brown (1991); Persky (1992); Tarullo (1992); Dunford (1993); Hancké (1993); Jackson, Leopold, and Tuck (1993); Perulli (1993); Sengenberger (1993); Peck (1994); and Martin, Sunley, and Wills (1994, 1996).

21. See Dunford and Kafkalas (1992); Amin and Thrift (1995); Sengenberger and Campbell (1994); and Peck and Tickell (1995).

22. See also Leborgne and Lipietz (1988); Boyer (1992); and Standing (1992). For Standing the ascendancy of defensive flexibility approaches to labor regulation (which he refers to as "subordinated flexibility") presage an inexorable drift toward workfare (p. 270).

23. See also Picciotto (1991); Dicken (1992, 1994); and Recio (1992).

24. See Castro, Méhaut, and Rubery (1992b); Rosenberg (1993); Sengenberger (1993); Peck and Tickell (1994); Sengenberger and Campbell (1994); and ILO (1995).

25. See Harrison and Bluestone (1988); Walsh and Brown (1991); Tarullo (1992); and Rosenberg (1989b, 1994).

26. With chilling implications, "the UK considers that the rights of free movement and residence . . . should continue to be subject to the existing conditions that such persons are financially self-sufficient and do not become a burden on the social assistance of the host member state" (DE, 1994, p. 14).

27. See, respectively, Garrahan (1986); Lefresne (1993); Finn and McDonald (1992); and Emmerich and Peck (1992).

28. See Mead (1986); Burghes (1987); Block and Noakes (1988); Walker (1991); and King (1995).

29. This was illustrated in a recent exchange in the House of Commons between the Prime Minister and pro-workfare MP Ralph Howell (see Howell, 1991).

> SIR RALPH HOWELL: May I remind my right hon. Friend the Prime Minister of the excellent and far-sighted speech he made a year ago—[*interruption*]—at the Carlton Club—[*interruption*]—in which he suggested that the unemployed might be offered work or even required to work? May I thank him for setting up the North Norfolk action pilot scheme, which has proved a great success and is already saving £1,500 a year per person engaged in it? If that scheme were introduced throughout the country, would it not save £4 billion? Could I ask him—[*interruption*]—if he will now sanction the Fakenham right-to-work pilot scheme which, if operated throughout the country, would save at least £13 billion?
>
> THE PRIME MINISTER: As far as I could hear, my hon. Friend is welcoming the pilot schemes that were set up some time ago to help unemployed people. We are evaluating those schemes; they show signs of being successful. We shall examine them and decide to what extent they may be extended. (*Hansard,* 1 February 1994, p. 236(38), cols. 734–735)

30. With respect to the German case, Bosch and Sengenberger (1989) summarize the effects of workfare-style programs and labor market flexibilization as "reactivating the reserve army mechanism in the labor market," noting that one consequence is that "the cost of unemployment is increasingly localized" (p. 102). They continue to stress the "mutually reinforcing relationships between flexibilization policies, a reactivated research army with the effect of restoring tight labor market discipline, heightened structural divisions [hence segmentation] in the labor market and power relations changed in favor of capital and at the expense of labor" (p. 104; cf. Standing, 1992).

31. Regulation theory also recognizes the importance of regulatory experimentation and searching in the production of new institutional "fixes" (see Peck and Tickell, 1994; Jessop, 1995).

32. See Castro, Méhaut, and Rubery (1992b); Deakin and Mückenberger (1992); and Streeck (1992); cf. Edwards (1994). According to labor lawyers Deakin and Mückenberger (1992), " 'creeping deregulation' in the social field [is occurring] as companies re-locate to lower wage areas of the [European] Community [while] the spread of labour competition puts pressure on established terms and conditions" (p. 143).

33. See Dunford and Kafkalas (1992); Freire de Souza and Castro (1992); Deakin and Mückenberger (1992); Dunford and Perrons (1994); Sengenberger and Campbell (1994); and Broad (1995).

EPILOGUE
Local Dialectics of Labor

To allow the market mechanism to be sole director of the
fate of human beings . . . would result in the demolition of
society. For the alleged commodity "labour power" cannot
be shoved about, used indiscriminately, or even left unused,
without affecting also the human individual who happens to
be the bearer of this particular commodity. . . . Robbed of
the protective covering of cultural institutions, human beings
would perish from the effects of social exposure . . . no
society could withstand the effects of such a crude system of
fictions even for the shortest stretch of time unless its human
and natural substance as well as its business organisation
was protected from the ravages of this satanic mill.

—Polanyi, *The Great Transformation*

The aim of this book has been to construct, then put to work, a
theoretical framework through which to analyze the local labor market. Starting from first principles, the irreducibly social nature of labor
and the contradictory manner of its incorporation into the labor
market were emphasized and linked to the fundamental dynamics of
the labor market and the process of labor segmentation. Segmentation
theories begin from a root-and-branch rejection of the mythical characterization of the labor market as a self-regulating commodity market; instead, they insist that the labor market must be understood as
an institutionalized and politicized arena which is systematically struc-

261

tured by social relations of production and reproduction and by immanent institutional forces. It has been suggested here that the labor market should be understood as a socially regulated, not wage-regulated, social system. In Polanyi's terms, it *requires* the "protective covering of cultural institutions." The labor market, then, is a complex, discordant, and contradictory social construct, one which bears little resemblance to the idealized, equilibrating world of the orthodox economist's demand-and-supply schedules.

Given the enduring hegemony of neoclassical economics, it would be presumptuous to claim the status of conventional wisdom for this socialized conception of the labor market. While still a minority view, it nevertheless is in accordance with a diverse and sophisticated body of work which not only has taken apart orthodox theory from first principles, but also has sought to construct an alternative (for example, see Wilkinson, 1981b; Marsden, 1986; Purdy, 1988; Picchio, 1992). These writers have argued for an alternative view of the labor market which, in important ways, is grounded in the reality of labor market experience, not deduced from an abstract commodity market. In rejecting monological explanations where market rules are the only rules, these theories construct the labor market as a multilogical and conjuncturally determined phenomenon. From this perspective, the complex dynamics of the labor market are not reducible to a single explanatory variable (say, the requirements of technology or the actions of unions), but rather are the combined outcome of the interplay of many causal processes (Labour Studies Group, 1985). The labor market emerges in this work as a complex, institutionally mediated social conjuncture.

So much is already well established. A central message of this book is that because these theories of the labor market already concede a central role for institutional variability, contingency, and contradiction (as well as path-dependence), they must also take account of the role of geography. This is not simply to make the empirical point that the concrete form of labor markets varies over space, as evidenced by distinctive occupational and industrial profiles, unique local histories, and characteristic social relations (although labor market theory should be able to account for geographic variation). Rather, it is to stake the more ambitious claim that labor market *processes* are themselves transformed by the way that they are, in Massey's (1994) words, stretched out over space. In particular, the distinctiveness of local labor markets can be linked to the geographically variable ways in which their "protective covering of cultural institutions" both reflects and affects their structure, dynamics, and mode of operation. This implies that labor markets function in different ways in different places, and moreover, that the case can be made theoretically for the spatiality of labor markets. Local labor markets are more than data units or study areas. Fundamentally, they represent the scale at which labor markets work on a daily basis, and they must be among the scales at which labor markets are understood.

Such a claim would be uncontroversial if it were made on behalf of history rather than geography. Strong cases have been made for the historical variability of labor market structures and social relations (see Aglietta, 1979; Gordon, Edwards, and Reich, 1982). However, there has been no systematic attempt to construct a parallel argument for the spatiality of labor markets. Geographic differences in the structures and social relations of the labor market may be acknowledged empirically, but a historically centered view of the world, such differences are deemed theoretically irrelevant.

Unless, that is, they happen to coincide with the boundaries of nation-states. Segmentation theories have become increasingly sensitive to the links between labor market forms and national social formations (Rosenberg, 1989b; Gordon, 1990; Castro, Méhaut, and Rubery, 1992b; Rubery, 1994). This form of geographic variation has been ceded a measure of theoretical importance; significant explanatory roles are assigned to the nationally specific institutional framework through which labor markets operate and the nationally specific complex of social relations in which they are embedded. Fundamental political and juridical forces are articulated at the level of the nation-state, forces which exert a nontrivial influence on the institutional form of labor markets within a national space, the *fait salarial* (Michon, 1992). Thus, there is an exploratory recognition of ways in which space shapes the operation of labor markets or, more precisely, that the operation of labor markets is shaped in space.

Yet, the geography of labor markets is much more finely textured. The processes behind the spatially uneven development of labor markets—those which condition their operation in geographically specific ways—do not cease to operate at the boundaries of the nation-state. Labor markets function in locally specific, as well as nationally specific ways. To concede that geography matters (as segmentation theories have rather reluctantly) is to open up the question of the workings of labor markets at *all* spatial scales. It is not to argue that one scale is more or less important than another, but to expose to critical scrutiny the processes through which labor markets are territorially constituted. There is still a strong case for the study of labor markets at the national level (which remains important for institution building and political struggle), but there is an equally strong case for analysis at the local level (the scale at which labor is mobilized on a daily basis and at which some of the more significant reproduction functions are sited), just as there is, for that matter, at the supranational scale (that at which new forms of labor mobility and market regulation are being constituted). Although this book's focus on the local scale is somewhat restrictive, it has touched on and begun to explore interrelationships between the local, national, and global constitution of labor relations.

Needless to say, the spatiality of the labor market is not static. Because labor markets are geopolitically constructed, they also can be geopolitically deconstructed and reconstructed. Recent analyses of globalization have illustrated this only too clearly. Fueled by neoliberalism, globalization has been associated with an onslaught against the regulatory advances made by and conceded to labor during the "golden age" of the Fordist-Keynesian expansion. The increasingly asymmetrical relationship between labor and capital has been insistently respatialized.

> Capital has slipped the moorings of the nation state, but labour has not. In these circumstances, theory predicts and practice bears out the simple idea that the mobile factor will play off the immobile factors against one another. Thus, international regulatory competition is to be expected. . . . By acquiring the option of exit, capital is liberated to participate in and establish an international marketplace in regulatory policy. . . . The old advice not to cede sovereignty over issues such as domestic labour policy regulation to international processes is now best re-evaluated if not ignored. The reality is that sovereignty has already been ceded and policy is being established to an increasing extent internationally. The issue is not whether but how policy will be determined internationally— through the market or through political negotiations. The problem is no longer avoiding a potential loss of sovereignty, but whether to take an opportunity to reclaim some measure of it. (Langille, 1994, pp. 333–334)

The global deregulation of labor markets is a political project requiring political responses. As Sengenberger has recently reminded us, "there is no labour market without rules . . . the critical issue is not whether to have rules but what kind of rules and who creates them" (1994, p. 11). As evidence mounts of the systemic failures of neoliberal deregulation (ILO, 1995), perhaps the time is ripe for building alternatives, and while this must be a political and social process, it must involve theory-building, too.

One of the central arguments of this book has been that theory-building must be sensitive to, and indeed *explain* the complexities of real-world labor markets. In this respect, the local labor market has self-evident importance. While it may be little more than commonsensical to claim that there are real differences in the way that labor markets function for, say, scientist-engineers in Silicon Valley and Britain's M4 corridor, or for industrial homeworkers in Mexico City and New York City, labor market theorists also would want to understand their common underlying dynamics. Common underlying dynamics there certainly are, but it is important also to recognize that even "common" dynamics take on different forms in different places, with the result that they are associated with different concrete outcomes. The particular conjuncture of labor market conditions in each place is unique, also serving to shape the particular local ways in which the labor market works.

Understanding the labor market means coming to terms *theoretically* with its complex geographies, not assuming them away (as might an orthodox economist) or wrongly assigning them to national or sectoral causes (as might a segmentation theorist). The task has been tackled here through the concept of the local labor market, partly in order to demonstrate that coming to terms with (geographic) complexity need not imply an empiricist turn. Endlessly mapping labor market phenomena will not reveal how labor market processes work in a spatially differentiated way. Instead, the act of mapping must be a conceptual one concerned with revealing the spatiality of the processes themselves, not just the unevenness of their outcomes.

Echoing Polanyi (1944), the conception of the local labor market proposed here is one of a locally instituted conjuncture. The "localness" of the local labor market stems from two sources. First, the concrete form of local labor markets is a product of the unique ways in which the causally constitutive bases of the labor market (i.e., the processes generating labor market structures) interact and are reconciled with one another at the local level. For example, labor market segmentation is an outcome of supply-side as well as demand-side causes, and the way in which tendencies toward segmentation are realized in the form of actual labor market structures will vary from place to place, their interaction being contingent. While it is possible through abstraction for these different tendencies toward segmentation to be explored in isolation from one another, concrete forms of segmentation are always codetermined. This requires a focus on the unpredictable ways in which demand and supply, or structures of production and reproduction, interact in time and space in the shaping of concrete labor market outcomes. The way in which labor markets work in reality is contingent on the non-necessary interaction between the social structures and dynamics of production (and the associated structuring of labor demand) and the social structures and dynamics of reproduction (and the associated structuring of labor supply). This first cut at the spatiality of labor markets has been termed here the production-reproduction dialectic.

Second, the social regulatory milieux in which labor markets are embedded are themselves variable over space, in terms of both their nature and their effects. For example, regimes of labor regulation have a tendency to take on distinctive local forms—in part because of their unique position within wider (national and international) regulatory structures, in part because their effects are geographically indeterminate, and in part because they evolve in a reciprocal and mutually constitutive fashion with unevenly developed local labor market structures. This is not merely to say that labor market processes are institutionally mediated in different ways in different places, but also that the continual interplay between regulatory forms and labor market restructuring is differentiated across space. As Figueroa (1994) puts it, "markets need institutions . . . [and this] implies that the way in which labour markets operate depends, among other factors, upon the prevailing institutions" (p. 63). These prevailing institutions of labor regulation have their own geographies that exert a spatially uneven influence on the structure, dynamics, and functioning of labor markets. The process by which labor markets are unevenly instituted has been termed here the regulatory dialectic.

Together, these two sources of spatiality—the production-reproduction dialectic and the regulatory dialectic—illuminate what it is that is *local* about the local labor market. The local labor market is more than a deviation from some national average (itself, obviously, only the sum of local conditions within a national space); instead, it should be understood as a territorially constituted social structure. This is not to say that labor market processes are unique to each local labor market, but rather that in their operation and empirical effects, they work in different ways in different local contexts (see Sayer, 1985b; Duncan, 1989). General processes have socially, institutionally, and geographically variable outcomes. *Work*-Place: *The Social Regulation of Labor Markets* has searched for a systematic way of confronting this question of uniqueness. Local labor markets, it has been argued, are unique not because they are dominated by particular stages or branches of production or by particular classes of worker, but because each represents a *geographically specific institutionalization of labor market structures, conventions, and practices,* providing unique contexts against which the strategies of labor market actors are formulated.

For example, take the process of ethnic segregation. While black workers may find themselves in the lower echelons of the labor market in both Birmingham, England, and Birmingham, Alabama, the nature and consequences of their marginalization in the labor market are quite different in each case. Why the "same" general process has different effects in different places might lie in the distinctive ways the general process of ethnic segregation interacts with local industrial cultures and structures, localized patterns of immigration, and local forms of racism and racial exclusion. Somewhat perversely, existing segmentation theories are reasonably well placed to account for this kind of diversity, because the two local labor markets happen to be in different countries. However, preoccupation with the "big geography" of international variation might lead them to reduce or subsume local to national variability. Explaining the differential operation of labor market processes between, say, Birmingham, Alabama, and Birmingham, Michigan, would be more difficult.

The point is not to do away with the analytical tools of segmentation theory, but to use them with more sensitivity. The segmentation theorist's tool kit—which specifies at an abstract level the key processes at work and provides some rules of thumb concerning their likely interactions—is undeniably well-suited to the task of labor market analysis. The message of this book is that the task itself varies from one local context to another. Consequently, the basic analytical tools of segmentation theory may be used, but should be handled more carefully. Processes of segmentation are not universal, unbending laws of economics, but should be understood as *tendencies,* the realization of which is particularly sensitive to spatial and historical context. "General" processes— such as forms of labor flexibility, the form and course of industrial restructuring, and the reform of regulatory institutions—are variously shaped by the local contexts in which they operate.

Underpinning these claims is a particular epistemological framework, a critical realist rendering of dialectics in which the concrete form of labor market structures is understood, after *Grundrisse,* as the synthesis of multiple determinations. For Marx, the dialectical method offered "a way of outlining a *structure in movement* [and] more fundamentally it enabled him to depict contradiction as the motor of this movement" (Stedman Jones, 1990, p. 126, emphasis added). Given segmentation theories' emphasis on labor market dynamics and on the contingent, contradictory, and path-dependent nature of labor market adjustment, a dialectical conception of a structure in movement seems apposite. In moving from the abstract (process) to the concrete (outcome), segmentation theories have had a tendency to foreclose or overlook the dialectical interaction of processes at the local level. The reconciliation of dialectical forces is governed not only by their mutual interaction, but also by spatiotemporal context. Without an appreciation of local dialectics—the unevenness, if you like, of the structure in movement—segmentation theorists can offer no more than a blunt and truncated explanation of how labor markets actually work. The local labor market is one of the principal arenas in which processes of reconciliation, adjustment, and contradiction *literally* take place, and the concept of the local labor market has a claim to mid-level status within the architecture of segmentation theory.

That said, there remains a lot left to do. Recognition of the reciprocally related and mutually constitutive nature of both the social relations of the labor market and the institutions of social regulation calls for further theoretical and empirical work. Theoretically, there is a need further to explore the dialectics of regulation and of production-reproduction with particular respect to their constitution at different spatial scales. Empirically, there is a need to explore local labor markets, not as untheorized case study areas or as phenomena to be mapped, but as a significant step in the explanation of labor market processes. For both theoretical and empirical reasons, the analytical category of the local labor market needs resurrection. In the process of explanation, then, there must be a place for the local labor market.

REFERENCES

AAWL (Australia Asia Worker Links). (1982). *Outwork: Undermining Union Gains or an Alternative Way of Working?* Case study 6. Melbourne: Australia Asia Worker Links.

ABS (Australian Bureau of Statistics). (1986). *The Labour Force Australia: Historical Summary 1966 to 1984.* Catalogue no. 6204.0. Canberra: Australian Bureau of Statistics.

ABS (Australian Bureau of Statistics). (1988). *Manufacturing Establishments: Summary of Operations, Australia 1986–87.* Catalogue no. 8202.0. Canberra: Australian Bureau of Statistics.

ACAC (Australian Conciliation and Arbitration Commission). (1987). *In the Matter of an Application by the Clothing and Allied Trades Union of Australia to Vary the Clothing Trades Award 1982 in Relation to Contract Work.* Print G6996. Melbourne: Australian Conciliation and Arbitration Commission.

Aglietta, M. (1979). *A Theory of Capitalist Regulation: The US Experience.* Trans. D. Fernbach. London: New Left Books.

Aglietta, M. (1982). World capitalism in the eighties. *New Left Review, 136,* 5–41.

Agnew, J.-C. (1979). The threshold of exchange: Speculations on the market. *Radical History Review, 21,* 99–118.

Akerlof, G. A. (1984). *An Economic Theorist's Book of Tales.* Cambridge: Cambridge University Press.

Albert, M. (1993). *Capitalism vs. Capitalism.* New York: Four Walls Eight Windows.

Albo, G. (1994). "Competitive austerity" and the impasse of capitalist employment policy. In R. Miliband and L. Panitch (Eds.), *Socialist Register 1994: Between Globalism and Nationalism* (pp. 144–170). London: Merlin Press.

Albrecht, S. L. (1982). Industrial homework in the United States: Historical dimensions and contemporary perspective. *Economic and Industrial Democracy, 3,* 413–430.

Alcorso, C. (1989). *Newly Arrived Immigrant Women in the Workforce.* Wollongong, N.S.W., Australia: Centre for Multicultural Studies, University of Wollongong.

Allen, S., & Wolkowitz, C. (1987). *Homeworking: Myths and Realities.* London: Macmillan.

Allen, V. (1977). The differentiation of the working class. In A. Hunt (Ed.), *Class and Class Structure* (pp. 61–79). London: Lawrence and Wishart.

Althauser, R. P., & Kalleberg, A. L. (1981). Firms, occupations and the structure of labor markets: A conceptual analysis. In I. Berg (Ed.), *Sociological Perspectives on Labor Markets* (pp. 119–149). New York: Academic Press.

Altvater, E. (1992). Fordist and post–Fordist international division of labor and monetary regimes. In M. Storper & A. J. Scott (Eds.), *Pathways to Industrialization and Regional Development* (pp. 21–45). London: Routledge.

Amin, A. (1989). Flexible specialisation and small firms in Italy: Myths and realities. *Antipode, 21,* 13–34.

Amin, A. (Ed.). (1994). *Post-Fordism: A Reader.* Oxford: Blackwell.

Amin, A., Charles, D., & Howells, J. (1992). Corporate restructuring and cohesion in the new Europe. *Regional Studies, 26,* 319–331.

Amin, A., & Robins, K. (1990). The re–emergence of regional economies? The mythical geography of flexible accumulation. *Environment and Planning D: Society and Space, 8,* 7–34.

Amin, A., & Thrift, N. (Eds.). (1994). *Globalization, Institutions and Regional Development in Europe.* Oxford: Oxford University Press.

Amin, A., & Thrift, N. (1995). Institutional issues for the European regions: From markets and plans to socioeconomics and powers of association. *Economy and Society, 24,* 41–66.

Anderson, K. H., Burkhauser, R. V., & Raymond, J. E. (1993). The effect of creaming on placement rates under the Job Training Partnership Act. *Industrial and Labor Relations Review, 46,* 613–624.

Anderson, K. H., Burkhauser, R. V., Raymond, J. E., & Russell, C. S. (1992). Mixed signals in the Job Training Partnership Act. *Growth and Change, 22,* 32–48.

Anderson, M., & Fairley, J. (1983). The politics of industrial training in the United Kingdom. *Journal of Public Policy, 3,* 191–208.

Applebaum, E., & Shettkat, R. (1990). The impacts of structural and technological change: An overview. In E. Applebaum & R. Shettkat (Eds.), *Labour Market Adjustments to Structural Change and Technological Progress* (pp. 3–14). New York: Praeger.

APS (Associated Personnel Services). (1989). *Clothing Industry Training Framework: Report of Findings from Victorian Clothing Industry Project.* Melbourne: Associated Personnel Services and Australian Textiles Clothing and Footwear Industry Training Council.

Ashby, P. (1989). Training and Enterprise Councils: Assessing the gamble. *Policy Studies, 10,* 31–40.

Ashton, D. (1986). *Unemployment under Capitalism: The Sociology of British and American Labour Markets.* Brighton, England: Wheatsheaf.

Ashton, D., Green, F., & Hoskins, M. (1989). The training system of British capitalism. In F. Green (Ed.), *The Restructuring of the UK Economy* (pp. 131–154). Hemel Hempstead, England: Harvester.

Ashton, D., Maguire, M., & Spilsbury, M. (1990). *Restructuring the Labour Market: The Implications for Youth.* Basingstoke, England: Macmillan.

Atkinson, J. (1987). Flexibility or fragmentation? The United Kingdom labour market in the eighties. *Labour and Society, 12,* 87–105.

Bagguley, P., Mark-Lawson, J., Shapiro, D., Urry, J., Walby, S., & Warde, A. (1990). *Restructuring: Place, Class and Gender.* London: Sage.

Bailey, T. (1988). Market forces and private sector processes in government policy: The Job Training Partnership Act. *Journal of Policy Analysis and Management, 7,* 300–315.

Bailey, T. (1993). The mission of TECs and private involvement in training: Lessons from Private Industry Councils. *Oxford Studies in Comparative Education, 3,* 7–26.

Baker, L., Flood, M., Meekosha, H., & Jakubowicz, A. (1984). *Outwork in the Clothing Industry.* Wollongong, N.S.W., Australia: Illawara Migrant Resource Centre and the Centre for Multicultural Studies, University of Wollongong.

Ball, R. M. (1980). The use and definition of travel-to-work areas in Great Britain: Some problems. *Regional Studies, 14,* 125–139.

Barnes, T., Hayter, R., & Grass, E. (1990). MacMillan Bloedel: Corporate restructuring and employment change. In M. de Smidt & E. Wever (Eds.), *The Corporate Firm in a Changing World Economy* (pp. 145–165). London: Routledge.

Barnet, R. J., & Cavanagh, J. (1995). *Global Dreams: Imperial Corporations and the New World Order.* New York: Simon and Schuster.

Barrett, M. (1980). *Women's Oppression Today.* London: Verso.

Barrett, M., & McIntosh, M. (1980). The "family wage": Some problems for socialists and feminists. *Capital and Class, 11,* 52–72.

Barron, R. D., & Norris, G. M. (1976). Sexual divisions in the dual labour market. In D. L. Barker & S. Allen (Eds.), *Dependence and Exploitation in Work and Marriage* (pp. 47–69). New York: Longman.

Becker, G. S. (1975). *Human Capital: A Theoretical and Empirical Analysis.* New York: National Bureau of Economic Research.

Becker, G. S. (1981). *A Treatise on the Family.* Cambridge, Mass.: Harvard University Press.

Beechey, V. (1977). Some notes on female labour in capitalist production. *Capital and Class, 3,* 45–66.

Beneria, L. (1979). Reproduction, production and the sexual division of labour. *Cambridge Journal of Economics, 3,* 203–225.

Beneria, L., & Roldan, M. (1987). *The Crossroads of Class and Gender:*

Industrial Homework, Subcontracting and Household Dynamics in Mexico City. Chicago: University of Chicago Press.

Bennett, L. (1986). Job classification and women workers: Institutional practices, technical change and the conciliation and arbitration system, 1907–72. *Labour History, 51,* 11–23.

Bennett, R. J. (1995). PICs, TECs and LECs: Lessons to be learnt from the USA Private Industry Councils and Britain's Training and Enterprise Councils. *British Journal of Education and Work, 7,* 63–83.

Bennett, R. J., & Business in the Cities. (1990). *Leadership in the Community: A Blueprint for Business Involvement in the 1990s.* London: Business in the Community.

Bennett, R. J., McCoshan, A., & Sellgren, J. (1990). TECs and VET: The practical requirements of organization and geography. *Regional Studies, 24,* 65–69.

Bennett, R. J., Wicks, P., & McCoshan, A. (1994). *Local Empowerment and Business Services: Britain's Experiment with Training and Enterprise Councils.* London: UCL Press.

Benton, L. (1989). Homework and industrial development: Gender roles and restructuring in the Spanish shoe industry. *World Development, 17,* 255–266.

Berger, S., & Piore, M. J. (1980). *Dualism and Discontinuity in Industrial Societies.* Cambridge: Cambridge University Press.

Berry-Lound, D., Chaplin, M., & O'Connell, B. (1991). Review of Industry Training Organisations. *Employment Gazette, 99,* 535–542.

Berthoud, R., Lakey, J., & McKay, S. (1993). *The Economic Problems of Disabled People.* London: Policy Studies Institute.

Beynon, H., (Ed.). (1985). *Digging Deeper.* London: Verso.

Beynon, H., & Hudson, R. (1993). Place and space in contemporary Europe: Some lessons and reflections. *Antipode, 25,* 177–190.

Beynon, H., Hudson, R., & Sadler, D. (1994). *A Place Called Teesside: A Locality in a Global Economy.* Edinburgh: Edinburgh University Press.

Bhaskar, R. (1979). *The Possibility of Naturalism: A Philosophical Critique of the Contemporary Human Sciences.* Brighton, England: Harvester.

Bhaskar, R. (1993). *Dialectics: The Pulse of Freedom.* London: Verso.

Blackburn, R. M., & Mann, M. (1979). *The Working Class in the Labour Market.* London: Macmillan.

Block, F. (1990). *Postindustrial Possibilities: A Critique of Economic Discourse.* Berkeley: University of California Press.

Block, F. (1994). The roles of the state in the economy. In N. J. Smelser & R. Swedberg (Eds.), *The Handbook of Economic Sociology* (pp. 691–710). Princeton, N.J.: Princeton University Press.

Block, F., Cloward, R. A., Ehrenreich, B., & Piven, F. F. (1987). *The Mean Season: The Attack on the Welfare State.* New York: Random House.

Block, F., & Noakes, J. (1988). The politics of new–style workfare. *Socialist Review, 88*(3), 31–58.

Bluestone, B. (1970). The tripartite economy: Labor markets and the working poor. *Poverty and Human Resources, 5,* 15–35.

Bluestone, B. (1972). Economic theory, economic reality and the fate of the poor. In H. L. Sheppard, B. Harrison, & W. J. Spring (Eds.), *The Political Economy of Public Service Employment* (pp. 117–128). Lexington, Mass.: D. C. Heath.

Bluestone, B., & Harrison, B. (1982). *The Deindustrialization of America: Plant Closings, Community Abandonment and the Dismantling of Basic Industry.* New York: Basic Books.

Boddy, M., Lovering, J., & Bassett, K. (1986). *Sunbelt City? A Study of Economic Change in Britain's M4 Growth Corridor.* Oxford: Clarendon Press.

Böhle, F., & Sauer, D. (1975). Intensivierung der Arbeit und staatliche Sozialpolitik. *Leviathan, 3,* 123–146.

Boris, E., & Daniels, C. R. (Eds.). (1989). *Homework: Historical and Contemporary Perspectives on Paid Labor at Home.* Urbana: University of Illinois Press.

Bosch, G., & Sengenberger, W. (1989). Employment policy, the state, and the unions in the Federal Republic of Germany. In S. Rosenberg (Ed.), *The State and the Labor Market* (pp. 87–106). New York: Plenum Press.

Bourdieu, P. (1973). Cultural reproduction and social reproduction. In R. Brown (Ed.), *Knowledge, Education and Cultural Change* (pp. 71–112). London: Tavistock.

Bourdieu, P., & Passeron, J.-C. (1977). *Reproduction in Education, Society and Culture.* Trans. R. Nice. London: Sage.

Bowlby, S., Foord, J., & McDowell, L. (1986). The place of gender in locality studies. *Area, 18,* 327–331.

Bowles, S., & Gintis, H. (1976). *Schooling in Capitalist America.* London: Routledge and Kegan Paul.

Boyce, C. (1984). Family Immigration Policy and Migrant Women Workers: A Case Study of the Textile Industry in Brunswick, 1945 to 1960. B.A. honors dissertation, History Department, University of Melbourne, Australia.

Boyer, R. (1986). *La Théorie de la Régulation: Une Analyse Critique.* Paris: La Découverte.

Boyer, R. (1987). Labour flexibilities: Many forms, uncertain effects. *Labour and Society, 12,* 107–127.

Boyer, R. (Ed.). (1988a). *The Search for Labour Market Flexibility: The European Economies in Transition.* Oxford: Clarendon Press.

Boyer, R. (1988b). Wage/labour relations, growth and crisis: A hidden dialectic. In R. Boyer (Ed.), *The Search for Labour Market Flexibility: The European Economies in Transition* (pp. 3–25). Oxford: Clarendon Press.

Boyer, R. (1990a). The impact of the single market on labour and employment: A discussion of macro–economic approaches in the light of research in labour economics. *Labour and Society, 15,* 109–142.

Boyer, R. (1990b). *The Regulation School: A Critical Introduction.* Trans. C. Charney. New York: Columbia University Press.

Boyer, R. (1992). *Labour Institutions and Economic Growth: A Survey and a "Regulationist" Approach.* No. 9218. Paris: CEPREMAP.

Bradley, T. (1984). Segmentation in local labour markets. In T. Bradley & P. Lowe (Eds.), *Locality and Rurality: Economy and Society in Rural Regions* (pp. 65–90). Norwich, England: Geo Books.

Braverman, H. (1974). *Labor and Monopoly Capital: The Degradation of Work in the Twentieth Century.* London: Monthly Review Press.

Bray, M., & Littler, C. R. (1988). The labour process and industrial relations: Review of the literature. *Labour and Society, 1,* 551–587.

Brennan, D., & O'Donnell, C. (1986). *Caring for Australia's Children: Political and Industrial Issues in Childcare.* Sydney: Allen and Unwin.

Brenner, R., & Glick, M. (1991). The regulation approach: Theory and history. *New Left Review, 188,* 45–119.

Breugel, I. (1979). Women as a reserve army of labour: A note on the recent British experience. *Feminist Review, 3,* 12–23.

Broad, D. (1995). Globalization versus labor. *Monthly Review, 47,* 20–31.

Broadbent, T. A. (1977). *Planning and Profit in the Urban Economy.* London: Methuen.

Brunhes, B. (1989). Labour flexibility in enterprises: A comparison of firms in four European countries. In OECD, *Labour Market Flexibility: Trends in Enterprises* (pp. 11–36). Paris: Organization for Economic Co-operation and Development.

Brusco, S. (1990). Small firms and the provision of real services. Paper presented at the conference, Industrial Districts and Local Economic Regeneration, International Institute for Labour Studies, Geneva.

Bulpitt, J. (1983). *Territory and Power in the United Kingdom.* Manchester: Manchester University Press.

Burawoy, M. (1979). *Manufacturing Consent.* Chicago: Chicago University Press.

Burawoy, M. (1985). *The Politics of Production: Factory Regimes under Capitalism and Socialism.* London: Verso.

Burghes, L. (1987). *Made in the USA.* London: Unemployment Unit.

Burnley, I. H. (1989). Settlement distributions of the Vietnam–born population in Sydney. *Australian Geographical Studies, 27,* 129–154.

Burton, J. (1987). *Would Workfare Work?* Employment Research Centre, Buckingham, England: University of Buckingham.

Cain, G. C. (1976). The challenge of segmented labor market theories to orthodox theory: A survey. *Journal of Economic Literature, 14,* 1215–1257.

Camagni, R., & Capello, R. (1988). Italian Success Stories of Local Economic Development: Theoretical Conditions and Practical Experiences. Milan: Instituto di Economia Politica, Universita Luigi Bocconi. Mimeographed.

Capecchi, V. (1989). The informal economy and the development of flexible specialization in Emilia–Romagna. In A. Portes, M. Castells, & L. Benton (Eds.), *The Informal Economy: Studies in Advanced and Less-Developed Countries* (pp. 189–215). Baltimore: Johns Hopkins University Press.

Cartier, K. (1994). The transactions costs and benefits of the incomplete contract of employment. *Cambridge Journal of Economics, 18,* 181–196.

Castells, M. (1977). *The Urban Question: A Marxist Approach.* Trans. A. Sheridan. London: Edward Arnold.

Castro, A., Méhaut, P., & Rubery, J. (Eds.). (1992a). *International Integration and Labour Market Organisation.* London: Academic Press.

Castro, A., Méhaut, P., & Rubery, J. (1992b). Introduction. In A. Castro, P. Méhaut, and J. Rubery (Eds.), *International Integration and Labour Market Organisation* (pp. 1–16). London: Academic Press.

CATU (Clothing and Allied Trades Union). (1986a). *Background Paper on Future Assistance Arrangements for the Textiles, Clothing and Footwear Industries: Response to the IAC Report.* Sydney: Clothing and Allied Trades Union.

CATU (Clothing and Allied Trades Union). (1986b). *Post-1988 Assistance Arrangements for the Textiles, Clothing and Footwear Industries: Implications for the Workforce.* Sydney: Clothing and Allied Trades Union.

CATU (Clothing and Allied Trades Union). (1987). *Outwork in the Australian Clothing Industry.* Sydney: Clothing and Allied Trades Union.

CCCS (Centre for Contemporary Cultural Studies). (1981). *Unpopular Education: Schooling and Social Democracy since 1945.* London: Hutchinson.

Champion, A. G., Green, A. E., Owen, D. W., Ellin, D. J., & Coombes, M. G. (1987). *Changing Places: Britain's Demographic, Economic and Social Complexion.* London: Edward Arnold.

Chouinard, V., Fincher, R., & Webber, M. (1984). Empirical research in scientific human geography. *Progress in Human Geography, 8,* 347–380.

Clark, G. L. (1981). The employment relation and spatial division of labor: A hypothesis. *Annals of the Association of American Geographers, 71,* 412–424.

Clark, G. L. (1983). Government policy and the form of local labor markets. *Urban Geography, 4,* 1–15.

Clark, G. L. (1986). Regional development and policy: The geography of employment. *Progress in Human Geography, 10,* 274–285.

Clark, G. L. (1992). "Real" regulation: The administrative state. *Environment and Planning A, 24,* 615–627.

Clark, G. L., & Gertler, M. S. (1983). Local labor markets: Theories and policies in the U.S. during the 1970s. *Professional Geographer, 35,* 274–285.

Clark, G. L., Gertler, M. S., & Whiteman, J. (1986). *Regional Dynamics: Studies in Adjustment Theory.* Boston: Allen and Unwin.

Coase, R. H. (1937). The nature of the firm. *Economica, 4,* 386–405.

Cochrane, A. (1993). *Whatever Happened to Local Government?* Buckingham, England: Open University Press.

Cochrane, A. (1994). Restructuring the local welfare state. In R. Burrows & B. Loader (Eds.), *Towards a Post-Fordist Welfare State?* (pp. 117–135). London: Routledge.

Cochrane, A., & Clarke, J. (Eds.). (1993). *Comparing Welfare States: Britain in International Context.* London: Sage.

Cockburn, C. (1983). *Brothers: Male Dominance and Technological Change.* London: Pluto Press.

Coffield, F. (1990). From the decade of the enterprise culture to the decade of the TECs. *British Journal of Education and Work, 4,* 59–78.

Collins, J. (1988). *Migrant Hands in a Hidden Land: Australia's Post-War Immigration.* Sydney: Pluto Press.

Collins, R. (1979). *The Credential Society: An Historical Sociology of Education and Stratification.* New York: Academic Press.

Commission of the European Communities. (1993). *Green Paper: European Social Policy—Options for the Union.* Luxembourg: Office for Official Publications of the European Communities.

Cooke, P. (1986). The changing urban and regional system in the United Kingdom. *Regional Studies, 20,* 243–251.

Cooke, P., & Imrie, R. (1989). Little victories: Local economic development in European regions. *Entrepreneurship and Regional Development, 1,* 313–327.

Cooke, P., & Morgan, K. (1990a). *Industry, Training and Technology Transfer: The Baden-Württemburg System in Perspective.* Regional Industrial Research Report 6. Cardiff, Wales: Regional Industrial Research, University of Cardiff.

Cooke, P., & Morgan, K. (1990b). *Learning through Networking: Regional Innovation and the Lessons from Baden-Württemburg.* Regional Industrial Research Report 5. Cardiff, Wales: Regional Industrial Research, University of Cardiff.

Cooke, P., & Morgan, K. (1991). *Industrial and Institutional Innovation in Emilia-Romagna.* Regional Industrial Research Report 7. Cardiff, Wales: Regional Industrial Research, University of Cardiff.

Coombs, R. (1985). Automation, management strategies and labour process change. In D. Knights, H. Willmott, & D. Collinson (Eds.), *Job Redesign: Critical Perspectives on the Labour Process* (pp. 142–170). Aldershot, England: Gower.

Coombes, M. G., Green, A. E., & Owen, D. W. (1988). Substantive issues in the definition of "localities": Evidence from the sub–group local labour market areas in the West Midlands. *Regional Studies, 22,* 303–318.

Cortés, R., & Marshall, A. (1993). State social intervention and labour regulation: The case of the Argentine. *Cambridge Journal of Economics, 17,* 391–408.

Costello, A. (1993). *Workfare in Britain? Some Perspectives on UK Labour Market Policy.* London: Unemployment Unit.

Cox, K. (1991). Questions of abstraction in studies in the new urban politics. *Journal of Urban Affairs, 13,* 267–280.

Cox, K., & Mair, A. (1988). Locality and community in the politics of local economic development. *Annals of the Association of American Geographers, 78,* 307–325.

Coyle, A. (1982). Sex and skill in the organisation of the clothing industry. In J. West (Ed.), *Work, Women and the Labour Market* (pp. 10–26). Andover, England: Routledge, Chapman and Hall.

CPRS (Central Policy Review Staff). (1980). *Education, Training and Industrial Performance.* London: HMSO.

Craig, C., Garnsey, E., & Rubery, J. (1984). *Payment Structures and Smaller Firms: Women's Employment in Segmented Labour Markets.* Department of Employment Research Paper 48. London: Department of Employment.

Craig, C., Garnsey, E., & Rubery, J. (1985). Labour market segmentation and women's employment: A case study from the United Kingdom. *International Labour Review, 124,* 267–280.

Craig, C., Rubery, J., Tarling, R., & Wilkinson, F. (1982). *Labour Market Structure, Industrial Organisation and Low Pay.* Department of Applied Economics Occasional Paper 54. Cambridge: Cambridge University Press.

Crang, P., & Martin, R. (1991). Mrs. Thatcher's vision of the "new Britain" and other sides of the "Cambridge phenomenon." *Environment and Planning D: Society and Space, 9,* 91–116.

Cummings, K. (1986). *Outworkers and Subcontractors: Non-Standard Employment and Industrial Democracy.* Canberra: Australian Government Publishing Service.

Curtain, R. (1987). Skill formation and the enterprise. *Labour and Industry, 1,* 8–38.

Cusack, D., & Dodd, J. (1978). *Outwork: An Alternative Mode of Employment.* Melbourne: Centre for Urban Research and Action.

CWWC (Centre for Working Women Co-operative). (1986). *Women Outworkers: A Report Documenting Sweated Labour in the 1980s.* Melbourne: Centre for Working Women Co-operative.

Dangler, J. F. (1986). Industrial homework in the modern world-economy. *Contemporary Crises, 10,* 257–279.

Davis, M. (1986). *Prisoners of the American Dream.* London: Verso.

Day, G., & Murdoch, J. (1993). Locality and community: Coming to terms with place. *Sociological Review, 41,* 82–111.

DE (Department of Employment). (1988). *Employment for the 1990s.* Cm 540. London: HMSO.

DE (Department of Employment). (1989). *The Challenge to British Business.* London: Department of Employment.

DE (Department of Employment). (1994). *European Commission's Green Paper on European Social Policy: The United Kingdom response.* London: Department of Employment.

Deacon, A. (1994). Justifying "workfare": The historical context of the debate. In M. White (Ed.), *Unemployment and Public Policy in a Changing Labour Market* (pp. 53–63). London: Policy Studies Institute.

Deakin, S., & Mückenberger, U. (1992). Deregulation and European labour markets. In A. Castro, P. Méhaut, & J. Rubery (Eds.), *International Integration and Labour Market Organisation* (pp. 135–149). London: Academic Press.

Deakin, S., & Wilkinson, F. (1991). Labour law, social security and economic inequality. *Cambridge Journal of Economics, 15,* 125–148.

Deaton, D. (1985). The labour market and industrial relations policy of the Thatcher government. In D. S. Bell (Ed.), *The Conservative Government, 1979–1984: An Interim Report* (pp. 33–48). London: Croom Helm.

de Brunhoff, S. (1978). *The State, Capital and Economic Policy*. London: Pluto Press.

de Grazia, R. (1980). Clandestine employment: A problem of our times. *International Labour Review, 119, 549–563.*

Dehli, K. (1993). Subject to the new global economy: Power and positioning in Ontario labour market policy formation. *Studies in Political Economy, 41, 83–110.*

DEIR (Department of Employment and Industrial Relations). (1985). *Submission to the Industries Assistance Commission Inquiry into the Textiles, Clothing and Footwear Industries.* Canberra: Australian Government Publishing Service.

Dex, S. (1984). *Women's Work Histories: An Analysis of the Women and Employment Survey.* Department of Employment Research Paper 46. London: Department of Employment.

Dicken, P. (1992). International production in a volatile regulatory environment: The influence of national regulatory policies on the spatial strategies of transnational corporations. *Geoforum, 23, 303–316.*

Dicken, P. (1994). Global-local tensions: Firms and states in the global space-economy. *Economic Geography, 70, 101–128.*

Dickens, W. T., & Lang, K. (1985). A test of dual labor market theory. *American Economic Review, 75, 792–805.*

Dickens, W. T., & Lang, K. (1988). The reemergence of segmented labor market theory. *American Economic Review Proceedings, 78, 128–134.*

DIRE (Department of Industrial Relations and Employment). (1987). *Self Employed or Employee? A Survey of Women in NSW Doing Paid Work at Home.* Sydney: Women's Directorate, Department of Industrial Relations and Employment and Ethnic Affairs Commission.

Doeringer, P. B., Feldman, P. H., Gordon, D. M., Piore, M. J., & Reich, M. (1969). *Low Income Labor Markets and Urban Manpower Programs: A Critical Assessment.* Washington, D.C.: U.S. Department of Labor.

Doeringer, P. B., & Piore, M. J. (1971). *Internal Labor Markets and Manpower Analysis.* Lexington, Mass.: D. C. Heath.

Doeringer, P. B., & Piore, M. J. (1985). *Internal Labor Markets and Manpower Analysis* (2d ed.). Armonk, N.Y.: M. E. Sharp, Inc.

DoL (Department of Labor). (1991a). *Restructuring of the Passenger Motor Vehicles and Textiles, Clothing and Footwear Industries in Victoria: An Overview of the Impact on Employees.* Melbourne: Employment Policy and Programs Branch, Department of Labour.

DoL (Department of Labor). (1991b). *The Textiles, Clothing and Footwear Industries Plan: The Regional Labour Market Implications.* Working Paper 37. Melbourne: Employment Policy and Programs Branch, Department of Labour.

Donahue, J. D. (1989). *Shortchanging the Workforce: The Job Training*

Partnership Act and the Overselling of Privatized Training. Washington, D.C.: Economic Policy Institute.

Duncan, S. S. (1989). What is locality? In R. Peet & N. Thrift (Eds.), *New Models in Geography* (Vol. 2, pp. 221–252). London: Unwin Hyman.

Dunford, M. (1990). Theories of regulation. *Environment and Planning D: Society and Space, 8,* 297–322.

Dunford, M. (1993). Regional disparities in the European Community: Evidence from the REGIO databank. *Regional Studies, 27,* 727–743.

Dunford, M., & Kafkalas, G. (1992). The global-local interplay, corporate geographies and spatial development strategies in Europe. In M. Dunford & G. Kafkalas (Eds.), *Cities and Regions in the New Europe: The Global-Local Interplay and Spatial Development Strategies* (pp. 3–38). London: Belhaven.

Dunford, M., & Perrons, D. (1994). Regional inequality, regimes of accumulation and economic development in contemporary Europe. *Transactions, Institute of British Geographers,* n.s., *19,* 163–182.

Dunlop, J. T. (1964). Review of Turner. *British Journal of Industrial Relations, 2,* 287–292.

DuRivage, V., & Jacobs, D. (1989). Home-based work: Labor's choices. In E. Boris & C. R. Daniels (Eds.), *Homework: Historical and Contemporary Perspectives on Paid Labor at Home* (pp. 258–271). Urbana: University of Illinois Press.

Eberts, R. W., & Stone, J. A. (1992). *Wage and Employment Adjustment in Local Labor Markets.* Kalamazoo, Mich.: W. E. Upjohn Institute for Employment Research.

ED (Employment Department). (1993). *Inter TEC Comparison Tables of Selected Programme Performance Indicators, 1992/1993 Operational Year.* London: Employment Department.

ED (Employment Department). (1994). *TEC Operating Agreement 1994–95.* London: Employment Department.

Edgley, R. (1990). Dialectical materialism. In J. Eatwell, M. Milgate, & P. Newman (Eds.), *The New Palgrave: Marxian Economics* (pp. 115–120). London: Macmillan.

Edwards, R. (1979). *Contested Terrain: The Transformation of the Workplace in the Twentieth Century.* London: Heinemann.

Edwards, R. (1994). Reshaping employee protections for a global economy. *Challenge,* Jan.–Feb., 34–39.

EIRR. (1990). Survey of homeworking. *European Industrial Relations Review, 200,* 18–23.

Eisenschitz, A., & Gough, J. (1993). *The Politics of Local Economic Policy: The Problems and Possibilities of Local Initiative.* Basingstoke, England: Macmillan.

Elbaum, B., & Wilkinson, F. (1979). Industrial relations and uneven development: A comparative study of American and British steel industries. *Cambridge Journal of Economics, 3,* 275–303.

Elger, T. (1979). Valorisation and deskilling—A critique of Braverman. *Capital and Class, 7,* 58–99.

Ellwood, D. T. (1988). *Poor Support: Poverty in the American Family.* New York: Basic Books.

Emmerich, M., & Peck, J. A. (1992). *Reforming the TECs: Towards a New Training Strategy.* Manchester: Centre for Local Economic Strategies.

Esping-Andersen, G. (1990). *The Three Worlds of Welfare Capitalism.* Cambridge: Polity.

Evans, M. D. R., & Kelley, J. (1986). Immigrants' work: Inequality and discrimination in the Australian labour market. *Australia and New Zealand Journal of Sociology, 22,* 187–207.

Fairley, J., & Grahl, J. (1983). Conservative training policy and the alternatives. In M. Sawyer & K. Scott (Eds.), *Socialist Economic Review 1983* (pp. 137–154). London: Merlin Press.

Felstead, A. (1993). Putting individuals in charge, leaving skills behind? UK training policy in the 1990s. Paper presented at the conference, Decentralisation and Regulation in the Labour Market. Fifteenth conference of the International Working Party on Labour Market Segmentation, July, Universidad Autonoma de Barcelona.

Ferguson, A. (1989). *Blood at the Root.* London: Pandora Press.

Fernández-Kelly, M. P., & García, A. M. (1989). Hispanic women and homework: Women in the informal economy of Miami and Los Angeles. In E. Boris & C. R. Daniels (Eds.), *Homework: Historical and Contemporary Perspectives on Paid Labor at Home* (pp. 165–179). Urbana: University of Illinois Press.

Fevre, R. (1992). *The Sociology of Labour Markets.* Hemel Hempstead, England: Harvester Wheatsheaf.

Figueroa, A. (1994). Labour market theories and labour standards. In W. Sengenberger & D. Campbell (Eds.), *International Labour Standards and Economic Interdependence* (pp. 57–64). Geneva: International Institute for Labour Studies, International Labour Office.

Fincher, R. (1983). The inconsistency of eclecticism. *Environment and Planning A, 15,* 607–622.

Fincher, R. (1989). Class and gender relations in the local labor market and the local state. In J. Wolch & M. Dear (Eds.), *The Power of Geography: How Territory Shapes Social Life* (pp. 93–117). Boston: Unwin Hyman.

Fincher, R. (1991). Caring for workers' dependents: Gender, class and local state practice in Melbourne. *Political Geography Quarterly, 10,* 356–381.

Fine, B. (1987). *Segmented Labour Market Theory: A Critical Assessment.* Birkbeck Discussion Paper 87/12. London: Department of Economics, Birkbeck College.

Finegold, D., & Soskice, D. (1988). The failure of training in Britain: Analysis and prescription. *Oxford Review of Economic Policy, 4,* 21–53.

Finn, D. (1987). *Training without Jobs: New Deals and Broken Promises.* Basingstoke, England: Macmillan.

Finn, D. (1988). Training and employment schemes for the long term unemployed: British government policy for the 1990s. *Work, Employment and Society, 2,* 521–534.

Finn, D. (1994). TECs and the Single Regeneration Budget. *Working Brief*, Jan., 12–13.

Finn, D. (1995). The Job Seeker's Allowance—workfare and the stricter benefit regime. *Capital and Class*, 57, 7–11.

Finn, D., & McDonald, M. (1992). *New Choices for the Unemployed? Training and Employment Schemes for Unemployed People in Manchester*. London: Unemployment Unit.

Finnegan, R. (1985). Working outside formal employment. In R. Deem & G. Salaman (Eds.), *Work, Culture and Society* (pp. 150–178). Milton Keynes, England: Open University Press.

Fisher, L. (1949). The Harvest Labor Market in California. Ph.D. dissertation, Harvard University.

Florida, R., & Jonas, A. E. G. (1991). US urban policy: The postwar state and capitalist regulation. *Antipode*, 23, 349–384.

Fox, A. (1974). *Man Mismanagement*. London: Hutchinson.

Frances, R. (1986). No more "Amazons": Gender and work process in the Victorian clothing trades, 1890–1939. *Labour History*, 50, 95–112.

Freedman, M. (1976). *Labor Markets: Segments and Shelters*. London: Allanheld.

Friedman, A. (1977). *Industry and Labour: Class Struggle at Work and Monopoly Capitalism*. London: Macmillan.

Friere de Souza, F., & Castro, A. (1992). Towards greater European co–operation: A necessary but difficult road. In A. Castro, P. Méhaut, & J. Rubery (Eds.), *International Integration and Labour Market Organisation* (pp. 19–40). London: Academic Press.

Fröbel, F., Heinrichs, J., & Kreye, O. (1980). *The New International Division of Labour*. Trans. P. Burgess. Cambridge: Cambridge University Press.

Gamble, A. (1988). *The Free Economy and the Strong State: The Politics of Thatcherism*. London: Macmillan.

Garnsey, E., Rubery, J., & Wilkinson, F. (1985). Labour market structure and work-force divisions. In R. Deem & G. Salaman (Eds.), *Work, Culture and Society* (pp. 40–75). Milton Keynes, England: Open University Press.

Garrahan, P. (1986). Nissan in the north east of England. *Capital and Class*, 27, 5–13.

Geddes, M. (1994). Public services and local economic regeneration in a post–Fordist economy. In R. Burrows & B. Loader (Eds.), *Towards a Post-Fordist Welfare State?* (pp. 154–174). London: Routledge.

Gershuny, J. I. (1983). *Social Innovation and the Division of Labour*. Oxford: Oxford University Press.

Gertler, M. (1988). The limits to flexibility: Comments on the post-Fordist vision of production and its geography. *Transactions, Institute of British Geographers*, n.s., 13, 419–432.

Gertler, M. (1992). Flexibility revisited: Districts, nation-states, and the forces of production. *Transactions, Institute of British Geographers*, n.s., 17, 259–278.

Giddens, A. (1981). *The Class Structure of the Advanced Societies* (2d ed.). London: Hutchinson.

Giddens, A. (1984). *The Constitution of Society.* Cambridge: Polity.

Glyn, A., Hughes, A., Lipietz, A., & Singh, A. (1991). The rise and fall of the golden age. In S. Marglin & J. B. Schor (Eds.), *The Golden Age of Capitalism* (pp. 39–125). Oxford: Clarendon Press.

Goldstein, N. (1984). The new training initiative: A great leap backward. *Capital and Class, 23,* 83–106.

Goodman, J. F. B. (1970). The definition and analysis of local labour markets: Some empirical problems. *British Journal of Industrial Relations, 8,* 176–196.

Goodwin, M. (1992). The changing local state. In P. Cloke (Ed.), *Policy and Change in Thatcher's Britain* (pp. 77–96). Oxford: Pergamon.

Goodwin, M., Duncan, S., & Halford, S. (1993). Regulation theory, the local state, and the transition in urban politics. *Environment and Planning D: Society and Space, 11,* 67–88.

Gordon, D. M. (1977). Class struggle and the stages of urban development. In D. Perry & A. Watkins (Eds.), *The Rise of the Sunbelt Cities* (pp. 55–82). Beverly Hills, Calif.: Sage.

Gordon, D. M. (1972). *Theories of Poverty and Underemployment.* Lexington, Mass.: D. C. Heath.

Gordon, D. M. (1990). Distribution theories. In J. Eatwell, M. Milgate, & P. Newman (Eds.), *The New Palgrave: Marxian Economics* (pp. 129–140). London: Macmillan.

Gordon, D. M., Edwards, R. C., & Reich, M. (1982). *Segmented Work, Divided Workers: The Historical Transformation of Labor in the United States.* Cambridge: Cambridge University Press.

Gough, I. (1979). *The Political Economy of the Welfare State.* Basingstoke, England: Macmillan.

Gough, J. (1992). Where's the value in post-Fordism? In N. Gilbert, R. Burrows, & A. Pollert (Eds.), *Fordism and Flexibility* (pp. 31–45). Basingstoke, England: Macmillan.

Grabher, G. (Ed.). (1993). *The Embedded Firm: On the Socioeconomics of Interfirm Networks.* London: Routledge.

Graham, J. (1992). Post-Fordism as politics: The political consequences of narratives on the left. *Environment and Planning D: Society and Space, 10,* 393–410.

Graham, G. (1995). Training US style. *Financial Times,* 19 May.

Granovetter, M. (1981). Towards a sociology of income differences. In I. Berg (Ed.), *Sociological Perspectives on Labor Markets* (pp. 11–47). New York: Academic Press.

Granovetter, M. (1985). Economic action and social structure: The problem of embeddedness. *American Journal of Sociology, 91,* 481–510.

Granovetter, M., & Swedberg, R. (Eds.). (1992). *The Sociology of Economic Life.* Boulder, Colo.: Westview Press.

Granovetter, M., & Tilly, C. (1988). Inequality and the labor process. In N. Smelser (Ed.), *Handbook of Sociology* (pp. 175–221). Newbury Park, Calif.: Sage.

Grant, W. (1989). The erosion of intermediary institutions. *Political Quarterly*, 60, 10–21.

Grant, W. with J. Sargeant. (1987). *Business and Politics in Britain*. Basingstoke, England: Macmillan.

Green, F. (1992). On the political economy of skill in the advanced industrial nations. *Review of Political Economy*, 4, 413–435.

Greig, A. W. (1990a). *Retailing is More than Shopkeeping: Manufacturing Interlinkages and Technological Change in the Australian Clothing Industry*. Working Paper 23. Canberra: Urban Research Program, Research School of Social Sciences, Australian National University.

Greig, A. W. (1990b). *Rhetoric and Reality in the Clothing Industry: The Case of Post-Fordism*. Working Paper 26. Canberra: Urban Research Program, Research School of Social Sciences, Australian National University.

Hadjimichalis, C., & Papamichos, N. (1990). "Local" development in southern Europe: Towards a new mythology. *Antipode*, 22, 181–210.

Haig, B. D. (1982). Sex discrimination in the reward for skills and experience in the Australian labour force. *Economic Record*, 58, 1–10.

Hakim, C. (1987). Trends in the flexible workforce. *Employment Gazette*, 95, 549–561.

Hall, R. E. (1975). Review of *Schooling, Experience and Earnings*, by Jacob Mincer. *Journal of Political Economy*, 83, 444–446.

Hall, S. (1993). Thatcherism today. *New Statesman & Society*, 26 November, 14–16.

Hancké, B. (1993). Trade union membership in Europe, 1960–1990: Rediscovering local unions. *British Journal of Industrial Relations*, 31, 593–613.

Handler, J. F. (1995). *The Poverty of Welfare Reform*. New Haven: Yale University Press.

Hanson, S. (1992). Geography and feminism: Worlds in collision? *Annals of the Association of American Geographers*, 82, 569–586.

Hanson, S., & Pratt, G. (1992). Dynamic dependencies: A geographic investigation of local labor markets. *Economic Geography*, 68, 373–405.

Hanson, S., & Pratt, G. (1995). *Gender, Work, and Space*. New York: Routledge.

Harrison, B. (1971). Human capital, black poverty and "radical" economics. *Industrial Relations*, 10, 277–286.

Harrison, B. (1972). *Education, Training, and the Urban Ghetto*. Baltimore: Johns Hopkins University Press.

Harrison, B. (1992). Industrial districts: Old wine in new bottles. *Regional Studies*, 26, 469–485.

Harrison, B. (1994). *Lean and Mean: The Changing Landscape of Corporate Power in the Age of Flexibility*. New York: Basic Books.

Harrison, B., & Bluestone, B. (1987). *The Dark Side of Labour Market Flexibility: Falling Wages and Growing Income Inequality in the United States*. World Employment Programme Working Paper. Geneva: International Labour Organisation.

Harrison, B., & Bluestone, B. (1988). *The Great U-Turn: Corporate Restructuring and the Polarizing of America.* New York: Basic Books.

Hartman, H. I. (1979). The unhappy marriage of Marxism and feminism: Towards a more progressive union. *Capital and Class, 8,* 1–33.

Harvey, D. (1987). Three myths in search of a reality in urban studies. *Environment and Planning D: Society and Space, 5,* 367–376.

Harvey, D. (1989a). *The Condition of Post-Modernity: An Enquiry into the Origins of Cultural Change.* Oxford: Blackwell.

Harvey, D. (1989b). *The Urban Experience.* Oxford: Blackwell.

Haughton, G. (1990). Skills shortage and the demographic timebomb: Labour market segmentation and the geography of labour. *Area, 22,* 339–345.

Haughton, G., Johnson, S., Murphy, L., & Thomas, K. (1993). *Local Geographies of Unemployment: Long-Term Unemployment in Areas of Local Deprivation.* Aldershot, England: Avebury.

Hecksher, C. C. (1988). *The New Unionism.* New York: Basic Books.

Heinelt, H. (1992). Local labour market policy—Limits and potentials. *International Journal of Urban and Regional Research, 16,* 522–528.

Henry, N. (1992). The new industrial spaces: Locational logic of a new production era? *International Journal of Urban and Regional Research, 16,* 375–396.

Herod, A. (1991a). Homeworking and the fragmentation of space: Challenges for the labour movement. *Geoforum, 22,* 173–183.

Herod, A. (1991b). Local practice in response to manufacturing plant closure: How geography complicates class analysis. *Antipode, 23,* 385–402.

Hicks, J. R. (1932). *The Theory of Wages.* London: Macmillan.

Hiebert, D. (1990). Discontinuity and the emergence of flexible production: Garment production in Toronto, 1901–1931. *Economic Geography, 66,* 229–253.

Hiebert, D. (1994). Labour-market segmentation in three Canadian cities. Paper presented at the annual meeting of the Association of American Geographers, March, San Francisco.

Himmelweit, S. (1991). Reproduction and the materialist conception of history: A feminist critique. In T. Carver (Ed.), *The Cambridge Companion to Marx* (pp. 196–221). Cambridge: Cambridge University Press.

Hinrichs, K., Offe, C., & Weisenthal, H. (1988). Time, money and welfare-state capitalism. In J. Keane (Ed.), *Civil Society and the State: New European Perspectives* (pp. 221–243). London: Verso.

Hirst, P., & Zeitlin, J. (1991). Flexible specialisation versus post-Fordism: Theory, evidence and policy implications. *Economy and Society, 20,* 1–56.

Hobbes, T. (1651). *Leviathan, or the Matter, Forme, & Power of a Commonwealth Ecclesiastical and Civill.* London: Andrew Crooke.

Hoch, H.-D. (1988). *The New Industrial Metalworking Occupations.* Berlin: Bundesinstitut fur Berufsbildung.

Hodgson, G. M. (1988). *Economics and Institutions.* Cambridge: Polity.

Hollands, R. (1990). *The Long Transition: Class, Culture and Youth Training.* Basingstoke, England: Macmillan.

Holliday, I. (1991). The new suburban right in British local government—Conservative views of the local. *Local Government Studies*, November/December, 45–62.

Holmes, J. (1986). The organization and locational structure of production subcontracting. In A. J. Scott & M. Storper (Eds.), *Production, Work, Territory: The Geographical Anatomy of Industrial Capitalism* (pp. 80–106). Boston: Allen and Unwin.

Horrell, S., Rubery, J., & Burchell, B. (1990). Gender and skills. *Work, Employment and Society, 4*, 147–168.

Howell, C. (1992). The dilemmas of post-Fordism: Socialists, flexibility and labor market deregulation in France. *Politics and Society, 20*, 71–99.

Howell, R. (1991). *Why Not Work?* London: Adam Smith Institute.

Hudson, R. (1989). Labour market changes and new forms of work in old industrial regions: Maybe flexibility for some, but not flexible accumulation. *Environment and Planning D: Society and Space, 7*, 5–30.

Hugo, G. (1986). *Australia's Changing Population*. Melbourne: Oxford University Press.

Humphries, J. (1976). Women: Scapegoats and safety valves in the Great Depression. *Review of Radical Political Economics, 8*, 98–121.

Humphries, J. (1977). Class struggle and the persistence of the working class family. *Cambridge Journal of Economics, 1*, 241–258.

Humphries, J., & Rubery, J. (1984). The reconstitution of the supply side of the labour market: The relative autonomy of social reproduction. *Cambridge Journal of Economics, 8*, 331–346.

Hutton, W. (1995). *The State We're In*. London: Jonathan Cape.

Hyman, R. (1988). Flexible specialization: Miracle or myth? In R. Hyman & W. Streeck (Eds.), *New Technology and Industrial Relations* (pp. 48–60). Oxford: Blackwell.

IAC (Industries Assistance Commission). (1986). *Report on the Textiles, Clothing and Footwear Industries*. Report 386. Canberra: Industries Assistance Commission, Australian Government Publishing Service.

Iacobacci, M. (1992). The institutionalist approach to segmented labour markets: A realist interpretation. King's College, Cambridge. Mimeographed.

ILO (International Labour Office). (1995). *World Employment 1995*. Geneva: International Labour Office.

IMRC (Illawara Migrant Resource Centre). (1984). *Outwork: A Guide for Community and Welfare Workers*. Wollongong, N.S.W., Australia: Illawara Migrant Resource Centre.

Jackson, R. M. (1984). *The Formation of Craft Labor Markets*. Orlando, Fla.: Academic Press.

Jackson, M. P., Leopold, J. W., & Tuck, K. (1993). *Decentralization of Collective Bargaining: Recent experience in the UK*. London: Macmillan.

Jacoby, S. (1990). The new institutionalism: What can it learn from the old? *Industrial Relations, 29*, 316–359.

Jacques, M., & Hall, S. (Eds.). (1989). *New Times*. London: Lawrence and Wishart.

Jenkins, R. (1986). *Racism and Recruitment*. Cambridge: Cambridge University Press.

Jessop, B. (1989). *Thatcherism: The British Road to Post-Fordism*. Essex Papers in Politics and Government 68. Essex, England: Department of Government, University of Essex.

Jessop, B. (1990a). Regulation theories in retrospect and prospect. *Economy and Society, 19,* 153–216.

Jessop, B. (1990b). *State Theory: Putting Capitalist States in Their Place*. Cambridge: Polity Press.

Jessop, B. (1991a). Thatcherism and flexibility: The white heat of a post-Fordist revolution. In B. Jessop, H. Kastendiek, K. Nielsen, & O. K. Pedersen (Eds.), *The Politics of Flexibility* (pp. 135–161). Aldershot, England: Edward Elgar.

Jessop, B. (1991b). The welfare state in the transition from Fordism to post-Fordism. In B. Jessop, H. Kastendiek, K. Nielsen, & O. K. Pedersen (Eds.), *The Politics of Flexibility* (pp. 82–105). Aldershot, England: Edward Elgar.

Jessop, B. (1992a). Fordism and post-Fordism: A critical reformulation. In M. Storper & A. J. Scott (Eds.), *Pathways to Industrialization and Regional Development* (pp. 46–69). London: Routledge.

Jessop, B. (1992b). From social democracy to Thatcherism: Twenty-five years of British politics. In N. Abercrombie & A. Warde (Eds.), *Social Change in Contemporary Britain* (pp. 14–39). Cambridge: Polity.

Jessop, B. (1992c). Regulation and politics: The integral economy and the integral state. Department of Sociology, University of Lancaster, Lancaster, England. Mimeographed.

Jessop, B. (1993). Towards a Schumpeterian workfare state? Preliminary remarks on post-Fordist political economy. *Studies in Political Economy, 40,* 7–39.

Jessop, B. (1994). Post-Fordism and the state. In A. Amin (Ed.), *Post-Fordism: A Reader* (pp. 251–279). Oxford: Blackwell.

Jessop, B. (1995). Towards a Schumpeterian workfare regime in Britain? Reflections on regulation, governance, and welfare state. *Environment and Planning A, 27,* 1613–1626.

Jessop, B., Bonnett, K., Bromley, S., & Ling, T. (1985). Thatcherism and the politics of hegemony: A reply to Stuart Hall. *New Left Review, 153,* 87–101.

Jessop, B., Bonnett, K., Bromley, S., & Ling, T. (1988). *Thatcherism: A Tale of Two Nations*. Cambridge: Polity.

Johnson, A. F., McBride, S., & Smith, P. J. (Eds.) (1994). *Continuities and Discontinuities: The Political Economy of Social Welfare and Labour Market Policy in Canada*. Toronto: University of Toronto Press.

Johnson, L. (1987). *Gendering Industrial Spaces: Recent Changes in the World and Australian Textile Industries*. Working Paper 24. Melbourne: Department of Geography, Monash University.

Johnstone, D. (1990). Private Industry Councils and the Training Partnership Act. *Local Economy, 4,* 328–335.

Jonas, A. E. G. (1992). Corporate takeover and the politics of community: The case of the Norton Company in Worcester. *Economic Geography, 68,* 348–372.

Jonas, A. E. G. (1996). Local labor control regimes: Uneven development and the social regulation of production. *Regional Studies,* forthcoming.

Jones, E. (1983). Industrial structure and labour force segmentation. *Review of Radical Political Economics, 15,* 24–44.

Jones, M. (1995). TECs' surpluses and output related funding. *Working Brief, 63,* 8–9.

Junankar, P. N. (Ed.). (1987). *From School to Unemployment? The Labour Market for Young People.* Basingstoke, England: Macmillan.

Kahn, L. (1975). *Unions and Labor Market Segmentation.* Ph.D. dissertation, University of California, Berkeley.

Kalachek, E. (1969). *The Youth Labor Market.* Policy Papers in Human Resources and Industrial Relations 12. Ann Arbor: University of Michigan and Wayne State University.

Kaufman, B. E. (1988). *How Labor Markets Work: Reflections on Theory and Practice.* Lexington, Mass.: Lexington Books.

Kaus, M. (1986). The work ethic state. *The New Republic,* July 7, 22–33.

Kaus, M. (1992). *The End of Equality.* New York: Basic Books.

Kearney, M. (1991). Borders and boundaries of state and self at the end of empire. *Journal of Historical Sociology, 4,* 52–74.

Kearns, A. (1992). Active citizenship and urban governance. *Transactions, Institute of British Geographers,* n.s., *17,* 20–34.

Keat, R., & Abercrombie, N. (Eds.). (1991). *Enterprise Culture.* London: Routledge.

Kelly, J. (1985). Management's redesign of work: Labour process, labour markets and product markets. In D. Knights, H. Willmott, & D. Collinson (Eds.), *Job Redesign: Critical Perspectives on the Labour Process* (pp. 30–51). Aldershot, England: Gower.

Kenrick, J. (1981). Politics and the construction of women as second class workers. In F. Wilkinson (Ed.), *The Dynamics of Labour Market Segmentation* (pp. 167–191). London: Academic Press.

Kern, H., & Schuman, M. (1987). The limits of the division of labour. *Economic and Industrial Democracy, 8,* 151–170.

Kerr, C. (1954). The balkanization of labor markets. In E. W. Bakke (Ed.), *Labor Mobility and Economic Opportunity* (pp. 92–110). Cambridge, Mass.: The MIT Press.

King, D. S. (1992). The establishment of work-welfare programs in the United States and Britain: Politics, ideas, and institutions. In S. Steinmo, K. Thelen, & F. Longstreth (Eds.), *Structuring Politics: Historical Institutionalism in Comparative Analysis* (pp. 217–250). Cambridge: Cambridge University Press.

King, D. S. (1993). The Conservatives and training policy, 1979–1992: From a tripartite to a neoliberal regime. *Political Studies, 41,* 214–235.

King, D. S. (1995). *Actively Seeking Work? The Politics of Unemployment and Welfare Policy in the United States and Great Britain.* Chicago: University of Chicago Press.

Konstantinidis, G. (1987). *Textiles, Clothing and Footwear: Inner Melbourne Database.* Working Paper 9. Melbourne: Economic and Employment Division, City of Melbourne Council.

Kraithman, D., Wall, A., Bowles, T., Adams, J., & Rainnie, A. (1991). *Can TECs Cope with Recession?* Economic Report 59. London: Employment Institute.

Kreckel, R. (1980). Unequal opportunity structure and labour market segmentation. *Sociology, 14,* 525–549.

Labour Studies Group. (1985). Economic, social and political factors in the operation of the labour market. In B. Roberts, R. Finnegan, & D. Gallie (Eds.), *New Approaches to Economic Life: Restructuring, Unemployment and the Social Division of Labour* (pp. 105–123). Manchester: Manchester University Press.

Laflamme, G., Murray, G., Belanger, J., & Ferland, G. (Eds.). (1989). *Flexibility and Labour Markets in Canada and the United States.* Geneva: International Labour Organisation.

Lane, T. (1988). The unions: Caught on the ebb tide. In D. Massey & J. Allen (Eds.), *Uneven Re-development: Cities and Regions in Transition* (pp. 188–197). London: Hodder and Stoughton.

Langille, B. A. (1994). Labour standards in the globalized economy and the free trade/fair trade debate. In W. Sengenberger & D. Campbell (Eds.), *International Labour Standards and Economic Interdependence* (pp. 329–338). Geneva: International Institute for Labour Studies, International Labour Office.

Lash, S., & Urry, J. (1987). *The End of Organized Capitalism.* Cambridge: Polity.

Lash, S., & Urry, J. (1994). *Economies of Signs and Space.* London: Sage.

Lawson, T. (1981). Paternalism and labour market segmentation theory. In F. Wilkinson (Ed.), *The Dynamics of Labour Market Segmentation* (pp. 47–66). London: Academic Press.

Lawson, T. (1989). Abstraction, tendencies and stylised facts: A realist approach to economic analysis. *Cambridge Journal of Economics, 13,* 59–78.

Lawson, T. (1994). Philosophical realism. In G. M. Hodgson, W. J. Samuels, & M. Tool (Eds.), *The Elgar Companion to Institutional and Evolutionary Economics* (pp. 219–225). London: Edward Elgar.

Lawson, V. A., & Staeheli, L. A. (1990). Realism and the practice of geography. *Professional Geographer, 42,* 13–20.

Lazonick, W. (1981). Production relations, labour productivity, and choice of technique: British and US cotton spinning. *Journal of Economic History, 41,* 491–516.

Leadbetter, C. (1991). Britain's days of judgement. *Marxism Today,* June, 14–19.

Leborgne, D., & Lipietz, A. (1988). New technologies, new modes of regulation: Some spatial implications. *Environment and Planning D: Society and Space, 6,* 263–280.

Leborgne, D., & Lipietz, A. (1990). How to avoid a two-tier Europe. *Labour and Society, 15,* 177–199.

Leborgne, D., & Lipietz, A. (1992). Conceptual fallacies and open questions on post-Fordism. In M. Storper & A. J. Scott (Eds.), *Pathways to Industrialization and Regional Development* (pp. 332–348). London: Routledge.

Lebowitz, M. (1987). The political economy of wage labour. *Science and Society, 51,* 262–286.

Lee, D. (1982). Beyond deskilling: Skill, craft and class. In S. Wood (Ed.), *The Degradation of Work* (pp. 146–162). London: Hutchinson.

Lee, D. (1989). The transformation of training and the transformation of work in Britain. In S. Wood (Ed.), *The Transformation of Work? Skill, Flexibility and the Labour Process* (pp. 156–170). London: Unwin Hyman.

Lee, D. (1991). Poor work and poor institutions: Training and the youth labour market. In P. Brown & R. Scace (Eds.), *Poor Work: Disadvantage and the Division of Labour* (pp. 88–102). Buckingham, England: Open University Press.

Lee, J., & Fahey, C. (1986). A boom for whom? Some developments in the Australian labour market, 1879–1891. *Labour History, 50,* 1–27.

Lee, R. (1995). Look after the pounds and the people will look after themselves: Economic relations, social reproduction, and social exclusion in western Europe. *Environment and Planning A, 27,* 1577–1594.

Lefresne, F. (1993). Hoover's relocation: Towards the development of a social space within Europe? Paper presented at the conference, Decentralisation and Regulation in the Labour Market. Fifteenth conference of the International Working Party on Labour Market Segmentation, July, Universidad Autonoma de Barcelona.

Lerner, G. (1986). *The Creation of Patriarchy.* New York: Oxford University Press.

Lever, W. (1979). Industry and labour markets in Great Britain. In F. E. I. Hamilton & G. J. R. Linge (Eds.), *Spatial Analysis, Industry and the Industrial Environment: Progress in Research and Applications* (Vol. 1, pp. 89–114). Chichester, England: John Wiley.

Lever-Tracy, C. (1983). Review of *Segmented Work, Divided Workers* by D. M. Gordon, R. C. Edwards, & M. Reich, and *The Dynamics of Labour Market Segmentation,* edited by F. Wilkinson. *Australia and New Zealand Journal of Sociology, 19,* 354–358.

Lever-Tracy, C. (1984). The paradigm crisis of dualism: Decay or regeneration? *Politics and Society, 13,* 59–89.

Lever-Tracy, C., & Quinlan, M. (1988). *A Divided Working Class: Ethnic Segmentation and Industrial Conflict in Australia.* London: Routledge and Kegan Paul.

Leyshon, A. (1992). The transformation of regulatory order: Regulating the global economy and environment. *Geoforum, 23,* 249–268.

Lipietz, A. (1986). New tendencies in the international division of labour:

Regimes of accumulation and modes of social regulation. In A. J. Scott & M. Storper (Eds.), *Production, Work, Territory: The Geographical Anatomy of Industrial Capitalism* (pp. 16–40). Boston: Allen and Unwin.

Lipietz, A. (1987). *Mirages and Miracles: The Crises of Global Fordism.* Trans. D. Macey. London: New Left Books.

Lipietz, A. (1988). Reflections on a tale: The Marxist foundations of the concepts of regulation and accumulation. *Studies in Political Economy, 26,* 7–36.

Lipietz, A. (1992). The regulation approach and capitalist crisis: An alternative compromise for the 1990s. In M. Dunford & G. Kafkalas (Eds.), *Cities and Regions in the New Europe: The Global-Local Interplay and Spatial Development Strategies* (pp. 309–334). London: Belhaven.

Lipsig-Mumme, C. (1983). The renaissance of homeworking in developed countries. *Relations Industrielles/Industrial Relations, 38,* 545–567.

Littler, C. R., & Salaman, G. (1984). *Class at Work: The Design, Allocation and Control of Jobs.* London: Batsford Academic.

Lo Bianco, J., & Boland, A. (1980). *The Rag Trade in Brunswick: Its Problems and Potential.* Melbourne: Brunswick Secondary Education Council.

Loh, M. (1988). Vietnamese community life in Australia. In J. Jupp (Ed.), *The Australian People* (pp. 836–840). Sydney: Angus and Robertson.

Lorenz, E. (1984). Labour supply and the employment strategies of French and British shipbuilders, 1890 to 1970. Paper presented at the conference of the International Working Party on Labour Market Segmentation, July, Budapest.

Lorenz, E. (1992). Trust, community, and cooperation: Toward a theory of industrial districts. In M. Storper & A. J. Scott (Eds.), *Pathways to Industrialization and Regional Development* (pp. 195–204). London: Routledge.

Loveridge, R., & Mok, A. L. (1979). *Theories of Labour Market Segmentation: A Critique.* The Hague: Martinus Nijhoff.

Lovering, J. (1989). The restructuring debate. In R. Peet & N. Thrift (Eds.), *New Models in Geography: The Political Economy Perspective* (Vol. 1, pp. 198–223). London: Unwin Hyman.

Lovering, J. (1990). Fordism's unknown successor: A comment on Scott's theory of flexible accumulation and the re-emergence of regional economies. *International Journal of Urban and Regional Research, 14,* 159–174.

Lovering, J. (1991). Theorizing postfordism: Why contingency matters (a further response to Scott). *International Journal of Urban and Regional Research, 15,* 298–230.

Luria, D. (1990). Automation, markets, and scale: Can flexible niching modernize US manufacturing? *International Review of Applied Economics, 4,* 27–65.

MacKay, D. I., Boddy, D., Brack, J., Diack, J. A., & Jones, N. (1971). *Labour Markets under Different Employment Conditions.* London: George Allen and Unwin.

Maddison, A. (1989). *The World Economy in the 20th Century.* Paris: Organization for Economic Co-operation and Development.

Mahnkopf, B. (1992). The "skill-oriented" strategies of German trade unions: Their impact on efficiency and equality objectives. *British Journal of Industrial Relations, 30,* 61–81.

Mahon, R. (1987). From Fordism to ?: New technology, labour markets and unions. *Economic and Industrial Democracy, 8,* 5–60.

Main, D. (1990). Local economic development and TECs. In R. J. Bennett, G. Krebs, & H. Zimmerman (Eds.), *Local Economic Development in Britain and Germany* (pp. 85–89). London: Anglo-German Foundation.

Manwaring, T. (1984). The extended internal labour market. *Cambridge Journal of Economics, 8,* 161–187.

Manwaring, T., & Wood, S. (1985). The ghost in the labour process. In D. Knights, H. Willmott, & D. Collinson (Eds.), *Job Redesign: Critical Perspectives on the Labour Process* (pp. 171–196). Aldershot, England: Gower.

Marden, P. (1992). "Real" regulation reconsidered. *Environment and Planning A, 24,* 751–767.

Markusen, A. (1991). The military-industrial divide. *Environment and Planning D: Society and Space, 9,* 391–416.

Markusen, A. (1993). Classics in human geography revisited: Commentary 2. *Progress in Human Geography, 17,* 70–71.

Marsden, D. (1986). *The End of Economic Man? Custom and Competition in Labour Markets.* Brighton, England: Wheatsheaf.

Marsden, D. (1992a). The transition to the Single Market and the pressures on European industrial relations systems. Paper presented at the fourteenth conference of the International Working Party on Labour Market Segmentation, July, Cambridge University.

Marsden, D. (1992b). Trade union action and labour market structure. In A. Castro, P. Méhaut, & J. Rubery (Eds.), *International Integration and Labour Market Organisation* (pp. 150–161). London: Academic Press.

Marshall, A. (1890). *Principles of Economics.* London: Macmillan.

Marshall, B. L. (1994). *Engendering Modernity: Feminism, Social Theory and Social Change.* Cambridge: Polity Press.

Martin, R. (1988). Industrial capitalism in transition: The contemporary reorganization of the British space-economy. In D. Massey & J. Allen (Eds.), *Uneven Re-development: Cities and Regions in Transition* (pp. 202–231). London: Hodder and Stoughton.

Martin, R. (1993). Classics in human geography revisited: Commentary 2. *Progress in Human Geography, 17,* 69–70.

Martin, R., Sunley, P., & Wills, J. (1994). The decentralization of industrial relations? New institutional spaces and the role of local context in British engineering. *Transactions, Institute of British Geographers,* n.s., *19,* 457–481.

Martin, R., Sunley, P., & Wills, J. (1996). *Union Retreat and the Regions: The Shrinking Landscape and Organized Labour.* London: Jessica Kingsley.

Marx, K. (1973). *Grundrisse: Foundations of the Critique of Political Economy.* Trans. B. Fowkes. Harmondsworth: Penguin.

Marx, K. (1976). *Capital: A Critique of Political Economy* (Vol.1). Trans. B. Fowkes. Harmondsworth: Penguin.

Massey, D. (1979). In what sense a regional problem? *Regional Studies, 13,* 233–243.

Massey, D. (1984). *Spatial Divisions of Labour: Social Structures and the Geography of Production.* Basingstoke, England: Macmillan.

Massey, D. (1985). New directions in space. In D. Gregory & J. Urry (Eds.), *Social Relations and Spatial Structures* (pp. 9–19). Basingstoke, England: Macmillan.

Massey, D. (1991). The political place of locality studies. *Environment and Planning A, 23,* 267–281.

Massey, D. (1993a). Classics in human geography revisited: Author's response. *Progress in Human Geography, 17,* 71–72.

Massey, D. (1993b). *Geography, Gender and High Technology.* South East Programme Working Paper 7. Milton Keynes, England: Open University Press.

Massey, D. (1993c). Power-geometry and a progressive sense of place. In J. Baird, B. Curtis, T. Putnam, G. Robertson, & L. Tickner (Eds.), *Mapping the Futures: Local Cultures, Global Change* (pp. 59–69). London: Routledge.

Massey, D. (1994). *Space, Place and Gender.* Cambridge: Polity.

Massey, D., & Meegan, R. (1982). *The Anatomy of Job Loss: The How, Why and Where of Employment Decline.* London: Methuen.

Massey, D., & Meegan, R. (1989). Spatial divisions of labour in Britain. In D. Gregory & R. Walford (Eds.), *Horizons in Human Geography* (pp. 244–257). London: Macmillan.

Massey, D., & Painter, J. (1989). The changing geography of trade unions. In J. Mohan (Ed.), *The Political Geography of Contemporary Britain* (pp. 130–150). London: Macmillan.

Mathews, J. (1989). *Age of Democracy: The Politics of Post-Fordism.* Melbourne: Oxford University Press.

Maurice, M., Sellier, F., & Silvestre, J.-J. (1984). The search for a societal effect in the production of company hierarchy: A comparison of France and Germany. In P. Osterman (Ed.), *Internal Labor Markets* (pp. 231–270). Cambridge, Mass.: The MIT Press.

Maurice, M., Sellier, F., & Silvestre, J.-J. (1986). *The Social Foundations of Industrial Power.* Cambridge, Mass.: The MIT Press.

Mayer, M. (1992). The shifting local political system in European cities. In M. Dunford & G. Kafkalas (Eds.), *Cities and Regions in the New Europe: The Global-Local Interplay and Spatial Development Strategies* (pp. 255–278). London: Belhaven.

McCreadie, S. (1990). Protection racket? *Australian Left Review, 116,* 16–19.

McDowell, L. (1991). Life without father and Ford: The new gender order of postfordism. *Transactions, Institute of British Geographers,* n.s., *16,* 400–419.

McDowell, L., & Court, G. (1994). Missing subjects: Gender, power and sexuality in merchant banking. *Economic Geography, 70,* 229–251.

McDowell, L., & Massey, D. (1984). A woman's place? In D. Massey & J. Allen (Eds.), *Geography Matters: A Reader* (pp. 128–147). Cambridge: Cambridge University Press.

Mead, L. M. (1986). *Beyond Entitlement: The Social Obligations of Citizenship.* New York: The Free Press.

Méhaut, P. (1992). Further education, vocational training and the labour market: The French and German systems compared. In A. Castro, P. Méhaut, & J. Rubery (Eds.), *International Integration and Labour Market Organisation* (pp. 162–174). London: Academic Press.

Meillassoux, C. (1981). *Maidens, Meal and Money: Capitalism and the Domestic Community.* Cambridge: Cambridge University Press.

Meissner, M., Humphreys, E. W., Meis, S. M., & Scheu, W. J. (1988). No exit for wives: Sexual division of labour and the cumulation of household demands in Canada. In R. Pahl (Ed.), *On Work* (pp. 476–495). Oxford: Blackwell.

Mendell, M., & Salee, D. (Eds.). (1991). *The Legacy of Karl Polanyi: Market, State and Society at the End of the Twentieth Century.* Basingstoke, England: Macmillan.

Meulders, D., & Wilkin, L. (1987). Labour market flexibility: Critical introduction to an analysis of a concept. *Labour and Society, 12,* 3–17.

Michon, F. (1987). Segmentation, employment structures and productive structures. In R. Tarling (Ed.), *Flexibility in Labour Markets* (pp. 23–55). London: Academic Press.

Michon, F. (1990). The "European Social Community," a common model and its national variations? Segmentation effects, societal effects. *Labour and Society, 15,* 215–236.

Michon, F. (1992). The institutional forms of work and employment: Towards the construction of an international historical and comparative approach. In A. Castro, P. Méhaut, & J. Rubery (Eds.), *International Integration and Labour Market Organisation* (pp. 222–243). London: Academic Press.

Milkman, R. (1976). Women's work and economic crisis. *Review of Radical Political Economics, 8,* 73–97.

Miller, J. (1988). Jobs and work. In N. Smelser (Ed.), *Handbook of Sociology* (pp. 327–359). Newbury Park, Calif.: Sage.

Mingione, E. (1991). *Fragmented Societies: A Sociology of Economic Life Beyond the Market Paradigm.* Trans. P. Goodrick. Oxford: Blackwell.

Mitter, S. (1986). Industrial restructuring and manufacturing homework: Immigrant women in the UK clothing industry. *Capital and Class, 27,* 37–80.

Mitter, S., & van Luijken, A. (1983). A woman's home is her factory. In W. Chapkis & C. Enloe (Eds.), *Of Common Cloth: Women in the Global Textile Industry* (pp. 61–67). Amsterdam: Transnational Institute.

Mizen, P. (1994). In and against the training state. *Capital and Class, 53,* 99–122.

Moore, B., & Townroe, P. (1990). *Urban Labour Markets.* London: HMSO.

Morales, R. (1984). Transitional labor: Undocumented workers in the Los Angeles automobile industry. *International Migration Review, 17, 570–596.*

More, C. (1980). *Skill and the English Working Class.* London: Croom Helm.

Morgan, K., & Sayer, A. (1988). A "modern" industry in a "mature" region: The remaking of management-labour relations. *International Journal of Urban and Regional Research, 9,* 383–404.

Morrison, P. S. (1990). Migrants, manufacturing and metropolitan labour markets in Australia. *Australian Geographer, 21,* 151–163.

Moulaert, F. (1987). An institutional revisit to the Storper-Walker theory of labour. *International Journal of Urban and Regional Research, 11,* 309–330.

Murgatroyd, L. (1983). The production of people and domestic labour revisited. In M. Sawyer & K. Schott (Eds.), *Socialist Economic Review 1983* (pp. 85–98). London: Merlin.

Murray, R. (1989). *Crowding Out: Boom and Crisis in the South East.* Stevenage, England: South East Economic Development Strategy.

Murray, R. (1991). *Local Space: Europe and the New Regionalism.* Manchester and Stevenage: Centre for Local Economic Strategies and South East Economic Development Strategy.

Nelson, K. (1986). Labor demand, labor supply, and the suburbanization of low-wage office work. In A. J. Scott & M. Storper (Eds.), *Production, Work, Territory: The Geographical Anatomy of Industrial Capitalism* (pp. 149–171). Boston: Allen and Unwin.

Neumark, N., & Eldestin, K. (1982). The hidden workers: Migrant women outworkers in Australia. *Refractory Girl, 24,* 6–8.

Nohara, H., & Silvestre, J.-J. (1987). Industrial structures, employment trends and the economic crisis: The case of France and Japan in the late 1970s. In R. Tarling (Ed.), *Flexibility in the Labour Market* (pp. 147–176). London: Academic Press.

Notermans, T. (1993). The abdication from national policy autonomy: Why the macroeconomic policy regime has become so unfavourable to labor. *Politics and Society, 21,* 133–167.

O'Donnell, C. (1984). Major theories of the labour market and women's place within it. *Journal of Industrial Relations, 26,* 147–165.

O'Donnell, C. (1988). Research into the situation of clothing outworkers in NSW. *Journal of Occupational Health and Safety, 4,* 29–34.

OECD (Organization for Economic Co-operation and Development). (1986a). *Flexibility in the Labour Market: The Current Debate.* Paris: Organization for Economic Co-operation and Development.

OECD (Organization for Economic Co-operation and Development). (1986b). *Labour Market Flexibility: Report of a High-Level-Group of Experts to the Secretary General.* Paris: Organization for Economic Co-operation and Development.

OECD (Organization for Economic Co-operation and Development). (1989). *Labour Market Flexibility: Trends in Enterprises.* Paris: Organization for Economic Co-operation and Development.

Offe, C. (Ed.). (1984). *Contradictions of the Welfare State*. London: Hutchinson.

Offe, C. (1985). *Disorganized Capitalism: Contemporary Transformations of Work and Politics*. Cambridge: Polity.

Offe, C., & Berger, J. (1985). The future of the labour market. In C. Offe, *Disorganized Capitalism: Contemporary Transformations of Work and Politics* (pp. 52–79). Cambridge: Polity.

Offe, C., & Hinrichs, K. (1977). Sozialokonomie des arbeitsmarktes und die lage "benachteiligter" gruppen von arbeitnehmern. In C. Offe (Ed.), *Opfer des Arbeitsmarktes: zur theorie der strukturierten arbeitslosigkeit* (pp. 3–61). Neuwied-Darmstadt: Luchterhand.

Offe, C., & Hinrichs, K. (1985). The political economy of the labour market. In C. Offe, *Disorganized Capitalism: Contemporary Transformations of Work and Politics* (pp. 10–51). Cambridge: Polity.

Offe, C., & G. Lenhardt. (1984). Social policy and the theory of the state. In C. Offe (Ed.), *Contradictions of the Welfare State* (pp. 88–118). London: Hutchinson.

Offe, C., & Weisenthal, H. (1980). Two logics of collective action: Theoretical notes on social class and organizational form. *Political Power and Social Theory, 1,* 67–115.

Oi, W. (1962). Labour as a quasi-fixed factor. *Journal of Political Economy, 70,* 538–555.

O'Neill, P. M. (1991). Plants on stand by: The textiles and clothing industry in non-metropolitan areas of New South Wales and Victoria, Australia. *Australian Geographer, 22,* 108–112.

Osterman, P. (1980). *Getting Started: The Youth Labor Market*. Cambridge, Mass.: The MIT Press.

Osterman, P. (1984). Introduction: The nature and importance of internal labor markets. In P. Osterman (Ed.), *Internal Labor Markets* (pp. 1–22). Cambridge, Mass.: The MIT Press.

Painter, J. (1992). Changing modes of regulation: Production and consumption relations in the British local state. Paper presented at the conference, Towards a Post-Fordist Welfare State? September, University of Teesside, Middlesbrough, England.

Parkin, F. (1974). Strategies of social closure in class formation. In F. Parkin (Ed.), *The Social Analysis of Class Structure* (pp. 1–18). London: Tavistock.

Pateman, C. (1989). *The Disorder of Women*. Cambridge: Polity Press.

Peck, J. A. (1989). Reconceptualizing the local labour market: Space, segmentation and the state. *Progress in Human Geography, 13,* 42–61.

Peck, J. A. (1990a). Circuits of capital and industrial restructuring: Adjustment in the Australian clothing industry. *Australian Geographer, 21,* 33–52.

Peck, J. A. (1990b). Outwork and restructuring processes in the Australian clothing industry. *Labour and Industry, 3,* 302–329.

Peck, J. A. (1990c). The Youth Training Scheme: Regional policy in reverse? *Policy and Politics, 18,* 135–143.

Peck, J. A. (1991a). Letting the market decide (with public money): Training and Enterprise Councils and the future of labour market programmes. *Critical Social Policy, 31*, 4–17.

Peck, J. A. (1991b). The politics of training in Britain: Contradictions of the TEC initiative. *Capital and Class, 44*, 23–34.

Peck, J. A. (1992a). "Invisible threads": Homeworking, labour-market relations, and industrial restructuring in the Australian clothing trade. *Environment and Planning D: Society and Space, 10*, 671–690.

Peck, J. A. (1992b). Labor and agglomeration: Control and flexibility in local labor markets. *Economic Geography, 68*, 325–347.

Peck, J. A. (1992c). TECs and the local politics of training. *Political Geography, 11*, 335–354.

Peck, J. A. (1993). The trouble with TECs . . . A critique of the Training and Enterprise Councils initiative. *Policy and Politics, 21*, 289–305.

Peck, J. A. (1994). From corporatism to localism, from MSC to TECs: Developing neoliberal labour regulation in Britain. *Economies et Sociétés, 17*, 99–119.

Peck, J. A. (1995). Moving and shaking: Business elites, state localism and urban privatism. *Progress in Human Geography, 19*, 16–46.

Peck, J. A., & Emmerich, M. (1991). *Challenging the TECs.* Manchester: Centre for Local Economic Strategies.

Peck, J. A., & Emmerich, M. (1993). Training and Enterprise Councils: Time for change. *Local Economy, 8*, 4–21.

Peck, J. A., & Haughton, G. F. (1991). Youth training and the local reconstruction of skill: Evidence from the engineering industry of North West England, 1981–88. *Environment and Planning A, 23*, 813–832.

Peck, J. A., & Jones, M. R. (1995). Training and Enterprize Councils: Schumpeterian workfare state, or what? *Environment and Planning A, 27*, 1361–1396.

Peck, J. A., & Lloyd, P. E. (1989). Conceptualizing processes of skill change: A local labour market approach. In G. J. R. Linge & G. A. van der Knaap (Eds.), *Labour, Environment and Industrial Change* (pp. 107–127). London: Routledge.

Peck, J. A., & Miyamachi, Y. (1994). Regulating Japan? Regulation theory *versus* the Japanese experience. *Environment and Planning D: Society and Space, 12*, 639–674.

Peck, J. A., & Tickell, A. (1992). Local modes of social regulation? Regulation theory, Thatcherism and uneven development. *Geoforum, 23*, 347–364.

Peck, J. A., & Tickell, A. (1994). Searching for a new institutional fix: The *after* Fordist crisis and global-local disorder. In A. Amin (Ed.), *Post-Fordism: A Reader* (pp. 280–316). Oxford: Blackwell.

Peck, J. A., & Tickell, A. (1995). The social regulation of uneven development: "Regulatory deficit," England's South East and the collapse of Thatcherism. *Environment and Planning A, 27*, 15–40.

Peet, R. (1983). The geography of class struggle and the relocation of United States manufacturing. *Economic Geography, 59*, 112–143.

Peet, R. (1989). Conceptual problems in neo-Marxist industrial geography: A critique of themes from Scott and Storper's *Production, Work, Territory.* *Antipode, 21,* 35–50.

Penn, R. (1985). *Skilled Workers and the Class Structure.* Cambridge: Cambridge University Press.

Pennington, S., & Westover, B. (1989). *A Hidden Workforce: Homeworkers in England, 1859–1985.* Basingstoke, England: Macmillan.

Perry, P. J. C. (1976). *The Evolution of British Manpower Policy: From the Statute of Artificers of 1563 to the Industrial Training Act of 1964.* London: British Association for Commercial and Industrial Education.

Persky, J. (1992). Regional competition, convergence and social welfare—The US case. In A. Castro, P. Méhaut, & J. Rubery (Eds.), *International Integration and Labour Market Organisation* (pp. 88–98). London: Academic Press.

Perulli, P. (1990). Industrial flexibility and small firm districts: The Italian case. *Economic and Industrial Democracy, 11,* 337–353.

Perulli, P. (1993). Towards a regionalization of industrial relations. *International Journal of Urban and Regional Research, 17,* 98–113.

Pettman, B. O. (1975). External and personal determinants of labour turnover. In B. O. Pettman (Ed.), *Labour Turnover and Retention* (pp. 31–50). Aldershot, England: Gower.

Phillips, A. (1983). *Hidden Hands: Women and Economic Policies.* London: Pluto Press.

Phillips, A., & Taylor, B. (1980). Sex and skill: Notes towards a feminist economics. *Feminist Review, 6,* 79–88.

Picchio, A. (1992). *Social Reproduction: The Political Economy of the Labour Market.* Cambridge: Cambridge University Press.

Picchio del Mercato, A. (1981). Social reproduction and the basic structure of labour markets. In F. Wilkinson (Ed.), *The Dynamics of Labour Market Segmentation* (pp. 193–209). London: Academic Press.

Picciotto, S. (1991). The internationalisation of the state. *Capital and Class, 43,* 43–63.

Piore, M. J. (1978). Dualism in the labor market: A response to uncertainty and flux—The case of France. *Revue Economique, 26,* 26–50.

Piore, M. J. (1983). Labor market segmentation: To what paradigm does it belong? *American Economic Review Proceedings, 73,* 249–253.

Piore, M. J., & Sabel, C. (1984). *The Second Industrial Divide: Possibilities for Prosperity.* New York: Basic Books.

Piven, F. F., & Cloward, R. A. (1971). *Regulating the Poor: The Functions of Public Welfare.* London: Tavistock.

Piven, F. F., & Cloward, R. A. (1993). *Regulating the Poor: The Functions of Public Welfare,* (Updated ed.). New York: Vintage.

Polanyi, K. (1944). *The Great Transformation: The Political and Economic Origins of our Time.* Boston: Beacon Press.

Polanyi, K. (1957). The economy as instituted process. In K. Polanyi, C. M. Arensberg, & H. W. Pearson (Eds.), *Trade and Market in the Early Empires* (pp. 243–269). Glencoe, Ill.: The Free Press.

Pollert, A. (1988). Dismantling flexibility. *Capital and Class, 34*, 42–75.

Prais, S. J., & Wagner, K. (1988). Productivity and management: The training of foremen in Britain and Germany. *National Institute Economic Review, 123*, 34–47.

Pratt, A. (1995). Putting critical realism to work: The practical implications for geographical research. *Progress in Human Geography, 19*, 61–74.

Purdy, D. L. (1988). *Social Power and the Labour Market.* Basingstoke, England: Macmillan.

Ragmag. (1988). Outwork: New rights for workers, new rules for employers. *Ragmag,* April. Sydney: Clothing and Allied Trades Union.

Rainbird, H., & Smith, J. (1992). *The Role of the Social Partners in Vocational Training in Great Britain.* Coventry: Industrial Relations Research Unit, University of Warwick.

Rainnie, A. (1984). Combined and uneven development in the clothing industry: The effects of competition on accumulation. *Capital and Class, 22*, 141–156.

Rank, M. R. (1994). *Living on the Edge: The Realities of Welfare in America.* New York: Columbia University Press.

Recio, A. (1992). Economic internationalisation and the labour market in Spain. In A. Castro, P. Méhaut, & J. Rubery (Eds.), *International Integration and Labour Market Organisation* (pp. 69–87). London: Academic Press.

Reder, M. (1989). Review of *How Labor Markets Work: Reflections on Theory and Practice,* edited by B. E. Kaufman. *Industrial and Labor Relations Review, 42*, 456–459.

Rees, A., & Schultz, G. P. (1970). *Workers and Wages in an Urban Labor Market.* Chicago: University of Chicago Press.

Rees, G. (1990). *Vocational Education and Training Systems: The Challenge of the 1990s.* Cardiff, Wales: School of Social and Administrative Studies, University of Cardiff.

Reich, M., Gordon, D. M., & Edwards, R. C. (1973). A theory of labor market segmentation. *American Economic Review, 63*, 359–365.

Rhodes, M. (1991). The social dimension of the Single European Market: National versus transnational regulation. *European Journal of Political Research, 19*, 245–280.

Robertson, D. (1986). Mrs. Thatcher's employment prescription: An active neo–liberal labour market policy. *Journal of Public Policy, 6*, 275–296.

Robinson, D. (1970). External and internal labour markets. In D. Robinson (Ed.), *Local Labour Markets and Wage Structures* (pp. 28–67). London: Gower Press.

Robinson, D. (1986). *Monetarism and the Labour Market.* Oxford: Clarendon Press.

Robinson, J. (1979). History versus equilibrium. In *Collected Economic Papers of Joan Robinson* (Vol. 5, pp. 48–58). Oxford: Blackwell.

Rodgers, G., & Rodgers, J. (Eds.). (1989). *Precarious Jobs in Labour Market Regulation: The Growth of Atypical Employment in Western Europe.* Geneva: International Labour Organisation.

Rojot, J. (1989). National experiences of labour market flexibility. In OECD, *Labour Market Flexibility: Trends in Enterprises* (pp. 37–60). Paris: Organization for Economic Co–operation and Development.

Rosenberg, S. (1989a). From segmentation to flexibility. *Labour and Society, 14, 363–407.*

Rosenberg, S. (1989b). Labor market restructuring in Europe and the United States: The search for flexibility. In S. Rosenberg (Ed.), *The State and the Labor Market* (pp. 3–16). New York: Plenum Press.

Rosenberg, S. (Ed.). (1989c). *The State and the Labor Market.* New York: Plenum Press.

Rosenberg, S. (1989d). The state and the labor market: An evaluation. In S. Rosenberg (Ed.), *The State and the Labor Market* (pp. 235–249). New York: Plenum Press.

Rosenberg, S. (1993). The more decentralized mode of labor market regulation in the United States in the 1980s: Lessons for policy in the 1990s. Paper presented at Decentralisation and Regulation in the Labour Market. Fifteenth conference of the International Working Party on Labour Market Segmentation, July, Universidad Autonoma de Barcelona.

Rosenberg, S. (1994). The more decentralized mode of labor market regulation in the United States. *Economies et Sociétés, 18, 35–58.*

Rosewarne, S. (1983). The political economy of retailing into the eighties. *Journal of Australian Political Economy, 15, 18–38.*

Rowbotham, S. (1993). *Homeworkers Worldwide.* London: Merlin Press.

Rubery, J. (1978). Structured labour markets, worker organisation and low pay. *Cambridge Journal of Economics, 2, 17–36.*

Rubery, J. (Ed.). (1988). *Women and Recession.* London: Routledge and Kegan Paul.

Rubery, J. (1989). Precarious forms of work in the United Kingdom. In G. Rodgers & J. Rodgers (Eds.), *Precarious Jobs in Labour Market Regulation: The Growth of Atypical Employment in Western Europe* (pp. 49–74). Geneva: International Institute for Labour Studies, International Labour Office.

Rubery, J. (1992). Productive systems, international integration and the single European market. In A. Castro, P. Méhaut, & J. Rubery (Eds.), *International Integration and Labour Market Organisation* (pp. 244–261). London: Academic Press.

Rubery, J. (1994). The British production regime: A societal-specific system? *Economy and Society, 23, 335–354.*

Rubery, J., & Tarling, R. (1982). Women in the recession. In D. Currie & M. Sawyer (Ed.), *Socialist Economic Review 1982* (pp. 47–76). London: Merlin Press.

Rubery, J., Tarling, R. & Wilkinson, F. (1987). Flexibility, marketing and the organisation of production. *Labour and Society, 12, 131–151.*

Rubery, J., & Wilkinson, F. (1981). Outwork and segmented labour markets. In F. Wilkinson (Ed.), *The Dynamics of Labour Market Segmentation* (pp. 115–132). London: Academic Press.

Rubery, J., Wilkinson, F. & Tarling, R. (1989). Government policy and the labor market: The case of the United Kingdom. In S. Rosenberg (Ed.), *The State and the Labor Market* (pp. 23–45). New York: Plenum Press.

Rueschemeyer, D. (1986). *Power and the Division of Labor.* Stanford, Calif.: Stanford University Press.

Ryan, T. (1981). Segmentation, duality and the internal labour market. In F. Wilkinson (Ed.), *The Dynamics of Labour Market Segmentation* (pp. 3–20). London: Academic Press.

Salais, R. (1992). Labor conventions, economic fluctuations, and flexibility. In M. Storper & A. J. Scott (Eds.), *Pathways to Industrialization and Regional Development* (pp. 276–299). London: Routledge.

Salais, R., & Storper, M. (1992). The four "worlds" of contemporary industry. *Cambridge Journal of Economics, 16,* 169–193.

Salvati, M. (1989). A long cycle in industrial relations, or: Regulation theory and political economy. *Labour, 3,* 41–72.

Sassen, S. (1988). *The Mobility of Capital and Labor: A Study in International Investment and Labor Flow.* New York: Cambridge University Press.

Sassen, S. (1991). *The Global City: New York, London, Tokyo.* Princeton, N.J.: Princeton University Press.

Saxenian, A. (1983). The urban contradictions of Silicon Valley: Regional growth and the restructuring of the semiconductor industry. *International Journal of Urban and Regional Research, 7,* 237–262.

Sayer, A. (1981). Abstraction: A realist interpretation. *Radical Philosophy, 28,* 6–15.

Sayer, A. (1984). *Method in Social Science.* London: Hutchinson.

Sayer, A. (1985a). Industry and space: A sympathetic critique of radical research. *Environment and Planning D: Society and Space, 3,* 3–29.

Sayer, A. (1985b). The difference that space makes. In D. Gregory & J. Urry (Eds.), *Social Relations and Spatial Structures* (pp. 49–66). Basingstoke, England: Macmillan.

Sayer, A. (1989). Postfordism in question. *International Journal of Urban and Regional Research, 13,* 666–696.

Sayer, A., & Walker, R. (1992). *The New Social Economy.* Oxford: Blackwell.

Schneider de Villegas, G. (1990). Home work: A case for social protection. *International Labour Review, 129,* 423–439.

Schoenbaum, D. (1967). *Hitler's Social Revolution.* London: Lawrence and Wishart.

Scott, A. J. (1984). Industrial organization and the logic of intra-metropolitan location III: A case study of the women's dress industry in the Greater Los Angeles region. *Economic Geography, 60,* 3–27.

Scott, A. J. (1986). Industrial organization and location: Division of labor, the firm and spatial process. *Economic Geography, 62,* 215–231.

Scott, A. J. (1988a). Flexible production systems and regional development: The rise of new industrial spaces in North America and western Europe. *International Journal of Urban and Regional Research, 12,* 171–186.

Scott, A. J. (1988b). *Metropolis: From the Division of Labor to Urban Form.* Berkeley: University of California Press.

Scott, A. J. (1988c). *New Industrial Spaces: Flexible Production Organization and Regional Development in North America and Western Europe.* London: Pion.

Scott, A. J. (1991a). Flexible production systems: Analytical tasks and theoretical horizons—A reply to Lovering. *International Journal of Urban and Regional Research, 15,* 130–134.

Scott, A. J. (1991b). A further rejoinder to Lovering. *International Journal of Urban and Regional Research, 15,* 231.

Scott, A. J. (1992). The role of large producers in industrial districts: A case study of high technology systems in Southern California. *Regional Studies, 26,* 265–276.

Scott, A. J., & Cooke, P. (1988). The new geography and sociology of production. *Environment and Planning D: Society and Space, 6,* 241–244.

Scott, A. J., & Paul, A. (1990). Collective order and economic coordination in industrial agglomerations: The technopoles of southern California. *Environment and Planning C: Government and Policy, 8,* 179–193.

Scott, A. J., & Storper, M. (Eds.). (1986). *Production, Work, Territory: The Geographical Anatomy of Industrial Capitalism.* Boston: Allen and Unwin.

Scott, A. J., & Storper, M. (1990). *Regional Development Reconsidered.* Lewis Center for Regional Policy Studies Working Paper 1. Los Angeles: University of California.

Scott, A. J., & Storper, M. (1992). Industrialization and regional development. In M. Storper & A. J. Scott (Eds.), *Pathways to Industrialization and Regional Development* (pp. 3–17). London: Routledge.

Scott, B. (1987). Outworking and Restructuring in the Australian Clothing Industry: A Geographical Perspective. B.A. honours dissertation, School of Earth Sciences, Macquarie University, Sydney.

Seccareccia, M. (1991). An alternative to labour market orthodoxy: The post-Keynesian/institutionalist policy view. *Review of Political Economy, 3,* 43–61.

Selznick, P. (1985). Focusing organisational research on regulation. In R. Noll (Ed.), *Regulation and the Social Sciences* (pp. 363–369). Berkeley: University of California Press.

Sen, A. (1982). *Choice, Welfare, and Measurement.* Cambridge, Mass.: The MIT Press.

Sengenberger, W. (1981). Labour market segmentation and the business cycle. In F. Wilkinson (Ed.), *The Dynamics of Labour Market Segmentation* (pp. 243–259). London: Academic Press.

Sengenberger, W. (1991). Labour standards in the international economy: Challenges and perspectives. Paper presented at the symposium, Production Strategies and Industrial Relations in the Process of Internationalisation, October, Tôhoko University, Japan.

Sengenberger, W. (1992). Future prospects for the European labour market: Visions and nightmares. In A. Castro, P. Méhaut, & J. Rubery (Eds.), *International Integration and Labour Market Organisation* (pp. 41–52). London: Academic Press.

Sengenberger, W. (1993). Local development and international economic competition. *International Labour Review, 132,* 313–329.

Sengenberger, W. (1994). International labour standards in a globalized economy: The issues. In W. Sengenberger & D. Campbell (Eds.), *International Labour Standards and Economic Interdependence* (pp. 3–15). Geneva: International Institute for Labour Studies, International Labour Office.

Sengenberger, W., & Campbell, D. (Eds.). (1994). *International Labour Standards and Economic Interdependence.* Geneva: International Institute for Labour Studies, International Labour Office.

Sengenberger, W., & Pyke, F. (1990). Small firm industrial districts and local economic development: Research and policy issues. *Labour and Society, 16,* 1–24.

Shaw, K. (1990). The lost world of local politics revisited: In search of the non-elected local state. *Regional Studies, 24,* 180–184.

Shergold, P. R. (1982). *Working-Class Life: The "American Standard" in Comparative Perspective.* Pittsburgh: University of Pittsburgh Press.

Shields, R. (1991). *Places on the Margin.* London: Routledge.

Shutt, J., & Whittington, R. (1987). Fragmentation strategies and the rise of small units: Cases from the North West. *Regional Studies, 21,* 13–23.

Singh, A. M., & Kelles-Viitanen, A. (Eds.). (1987). *Invisible Hands: Women in Home-Based Production.* New Delhi: Sage.

Skocpol, T. (1995). *Social Policy in the United States: Future Possibilities in Historical Perspective.* Princeton, N.J.: Princeton University Press.

Sloan, J., Baker, M., McGavin, P., Ryan, J., & Wooden, M. (1985). *The Employment Consequences of Economic Changes on Australian Textiles, Clothing and Footwear Industries: The Regional Dimensions.* Adelaide: National Institute of Labour Studies.

Smith, A. (1976). *An Inquiry into the Nature and Causes of the Wealth of Nations.* Vol. 1. Oxford: Clarendon Press.

Smith, D. (1981). *Unemployment and Racial Minorities.* London: Policy Studies Institute.

Smith, N. (1984). *Uneven Development.* Oxford: Blackwell.

Smith, P. (1993). TECs: A Growing Disillusion. *Training Officer, 29,* 38–43.

Solow, R. (1990). *The Labor Market as a Social Institution.* Cambridge: Blackwell.

Sorensen, A. B., & Kalleberg, A. L. (1981). An outline of a theory of matching persons to jobs. In I. Berg (Ed.), *Sociological Perspectives on Labor Markets* (pp. 49–74). New York: Academic Press.

Spriggs, W. E. (1993). Labor market regulation and the low-wage path in the U.S. Paper presented at the conference, Decentralisation and Regulation in the Labour Market. Fifteenth conference of the International Working Party on Labour Market Segmentation, July, Universidad Autonoma de Barcelona.

Standing, G. (1986). *Unemployment and Labour Market Flexibility: The United Kingdom.* Geneva: International Labour Organisation.

Standing, G. (1989). Labour market flexibility in Western European labour markets. In G. Laflamme, G. Murray, J. Belanger, & G. Ferland (Eds.), *Flexibility and Labour Markets in Canada and the United States* (pp. 37–60). Geneva: International Labour Organisation.

Standing, G. (1992). Alternative routes to labor flexibility. In M. Storper & A. J. Scott (Eds.), *Pathways to Industrialization and Regional Development* (pp. 255–275). London: Routledge.

Stedman Jones, G. (1990). Dialectical reasoning. In J. Eatwell, M. Milgate, & P. Newman (Eds.), *The New Palgrave: Marxian Economics* (pp. 121–128). London: Macmillan.

Steedman, H., & K. Wagner. (1987). A second look at productivity, machinery and skills in Britain and Germany. *National Institute Economic Review, 122,* 84–95.

Stein, B. (1976). *Work and Welfare in Britain and the USA.* London: Macmillan.

Stoker, G. (1989). Creating a local government for a post-Fordist society. In J. Stewart & G. Stoker (Eds.), *The Future of Local Government* (pp. 141–171). Basingstoke, England: Macmillan.

Stoker, G., & Mossberger, K. (1992). The post-Fordist local state: The dynamics of its development. Paper presented at the conference, Towards a post-Fordist Welfare State? September, University of Teesside, Middlesbrough, England.

Storer, D. (1976). *But I Wouldn't Want My Wife to Work Here . . . A Study of Migrant Women in Melbourne Industry.* Melbourne: Centre for Urban Research and Action.

Storper, M. (1990). Responses to Amin and Robins: Michael Storper replies. In F. Pyke, G. Beccatini, & W. Sengenberger (Eds.), *Industrial Districts and Inter-Firm Cooperation* (pp. 228–237). Geneva: International Labour Organisation.

Storper, M. (1995). The resurgence of regional economies, ten years later: The region as a nexus of untraded interdependencies. *European Urban and Regional Studies, 2,* 191–222.

Storper, M., & Harrison, B. (1991). Flexibility, hierarchy and regional development: The changing structure of industrial production systems and their forms of governance in the 1990s. *Research Policy, 20,* 407–422.

Storper, M., & Scott, A. J. (1989). The geographical foundations and social regulation of flexible production complexes. In J. Wolch & M. Dear (Eds.), *The Power of Geography: How Territory Shapes Social Life* (pp. 21–40). Boston: Unwin Hyman.

Storper, M., & Scott, A. J. (1990). Work organisation and local labour markets in an era of flexible production. *International Labour Review, 129,* 573–591.

Storper, M., & Walker, R. (1983). The theory of labour and the theory of location. *International Journal of Urban and Regional Research, 7,* 1–41.

Storper, M., & Walker, R. (1984). The spatial division of labor: Labor and the location of industries. In L. Sawyers & W. K. Tabb (Eds.), *Sunbelt/Snow-*

belt: Urban Development and Regional Restructuring (pp. 19–47). New York: Oxford University Press.

Storper, M., & Walker, R. (1989). *The Capitalist Imperative: Territory, Technology and Industrial Growth.* Oxford: Blackwell.

Stratton, C. N. (1990). TECs and PICs: The key issues which lie ahead. *Regional Studies, 24,* 71–74.

Streeck, W. (1989). Skills and the limits of neo–liberalism: The enterprise of the future as a place of learning. *Work, Employment and Society, 3,* 89–104.

Streeck, W. (1992). National diversity, regime competition and institutional deadlock: Problems in forming a European industrial relations system. *Journal of Public Policy, 12,* 301–330.

Sunley, P. (1990). Striking parallels: A comparison of the geographies of the 1926 and 1984–85 coalmining disputes. *Environment and Planning D: Society and Space, 8,* 35–53.

Swyngedouw, E. A. (1992). The Mammon quest. "Glocalization," interspatial competition and the monetary order: The construction of new spatial scales. In M. Dunford & G. Kafkalas (Eds.), *Cities and Regions in the New Europe: The Global-Local Interplay and Spatial Development Strategies* (pp. 39–67). London: Belhaven.

Tait, D., & Gibson, K. (1987). Economic restructuring: An analysis of migrant labour in Sydney. *Journal of Intercultural Studies, 8,* 1–26.

Tarling, R. (Ed.). (1987). *Flexibility in the Labour Market.* London: Academic Press.

Tarullo, D. (1992). Federalism issues in United States labour market policies and employment law. In A. Castro, P. Méhaut, & J. Rubery (Eds.), *International Integration and Labour Market Organisation* (pp. 99–111). London: Academic Press.

Tassie, J. (1989). *Out of Sight—Out of Mind: Outwork in South Australia.* Adelaide: Working Women's Centre.

Tate, J. (1993). *Homeworking in the EC: Report of the Ad Hoc Working Group.* Brussels: Employment, Industrial Relations and Social Affairs Directorate, European Commission.

Taubman, P., & Wachter, M. L. (1986). Segmented labor markets. In O. Ashenfelter and R. Layard (Eds.), *Handbook of Labor Economics* (Vol. 2, pp. 1183–1217). Amsterdam: Elsevier Science Publishers.

Taylor, R. (1995). Red tape tangle for TECs. *Financial Times,* 3 May.

TCF Council (Textiles, Clothing, and Footwear Council). (1987). *Submission to the Prices Surveillance Authority Inquiry into Retail Prices of Clothing.* Melbourne: Textiles, Clothing and Footwear Council.

TCF Council (Textiles, Clothing, and Footwear Council). (1991). *Industry Implications of March 12 Statement.* Melbourne: Textiles, Clothing and Footwear Council.

TCFUA (Textiles, Clothing and Footwear Union of Australia). (1995). *The Hidden Cost of Fashion: Report on the National Outwork Information Campaign.* Sydney: Textiles, Clothing and Footwear Union of Australia.

Teague, P. (1990). The political economy of the regulation school and the flexible specialisation scenario. *Journal of Economic Studies, 17,* 32–54.

Teague, P. (1993). Between convergence and divergence: Possibilities for a European Community system of labour market regulation. *International Labour Review, 132,* 391–406.

Théret, B. (1994). To have or to be: On the problem of the interaction between state and economy and its "solidarist" mode of regulation. *Economy and Society, 23,* 1–46.

Thurow, L. C. (1969). *Poverty and Discrimination.* Washington, D.C.: Brookings Institution.

Thurow, L. C. (1975). *Generating Inequality.* New York: Basic Books.

Tickell, A., & Peck, J. A. (1992). Accumulation, regulation and the geographies of post-Fordism: Missing links in regulationist research. *Progress in Human Geography, 16,* 190–218.

Tickell, A., & Peck, J. A. (1996). Neoliberalism and localism: A reply to Gough. *Area, 28,* forthcoming.

TNC Workers Research. (1985). *Anti-Union Employment Practices.* Sydney: Printers Devil.

Toffler, A. (1981). *The Third Wave.* London: Pan Books.

Tomlins, C. L. (1984). Long swings and spatial yardsticks: Directions in American labour history (2). *Labour History, 46,* 128–141.

Toft, C. (1992). The regulation of social protection in the European Community: The case of unemployment compensation. In A. Castro, P. Méhaut, & J. Rubery (Eds.), *International Integration and Labour Market Organisation* (pp. 190–202). London: Academic Press.

Towers, B. (1992). Two speed ahead: Social Europe and the UK after Maastricht. *Industrial Relations Journal, 23,* 83–89.

Training Agency. (1989). *Training and Enterprise Councils: A Prospectus for the 1990s.* Sheffield: Training Agency.

Training Agency. (1989b). *Training in Britain.* Sheffield: Training Agency.

TransNational Brief. (1980). The invisible workers. *TransNational Brief, 3,* 1–6.

Treasury. (1993). *Competitiveness and Employment.* London: HMSO.

Trigilia, C. (1991). The paradox of the region: Economic regulation and the representation of interests. *Economy and Society, 20,* 306–327.

Turner, H. A. (1962). *Trade Union Growth, Structure and Policy: A Comparative Study of the Cotton Unions.* London: Allen and Unwin.

Urry, J. (1981). Localities, regions and social class. *International Journal of Urban and Regional Research, 5,* 456–474.

Urry, J. (1985). Social relations, space and time. In D. Gregory & J. Urry (Eds.), *Social Relations and Spatial Structures* (pp. 20–48). Basingstoke, England: Macmillan.

van Luijken, A., & Mitter, S. (1989). *Unseen Phenomenon: The Rise of Homeworking.* London: Change.

Vietorisz, T., & Harrison, B. (1973). Labour market segmentation: Positive feedback and divergent development. *American Economic Review, 63,* 366–376.

Villa, P. (1986). *The Structuring of Labour Markets: A Comparative Analysis of the Steel and Construction Industries in Italy.* Oxford: Clarendon Press.

Viviani, N. (1984). *The Long Journey: Vietnamese Migration and Settlement in Australia.* Melbourne: Melbourne University Press.

Wachter, M. L. (1974). Primary and secondary labor markets: A critique of the dual approach. *Brookings Papers on Economic Activity, 3,* 637–680.

Walby, S. (1990). *Theorizing Patriarchy.* Oxford: Blackwell.

Walker, A. (1982). *Unqualified and Underemployed: Handicapped Young People in the Labour Market.* London: Macmillan.

Walker, J. (1987). *Home-Based Working in Australia: Issues and Evidence.* Working Paper 1. Canberra: Urban Research Unit, Australian National University.

Walker, J. (1989). Production of exchange-values in the home. *Environment and Planning A, 21,* 685–688.

Walker, R. (1988). The geographical organization of production–systems. *Environment and Planning D: Society and Space, 6,* 377–408.

Walker, R. (1991). *Thinking about Workfare: Evidence from the USA.* London: HMSO.

Wallace, M., & Kalleberg, A. L. (1981). Economic organization of firms and labor market consequences: toward a specification of dual economy theory. In I. Berg (Ed.), *Sociological Perspectives on Labor Markets* (pp. 77–117). New York: Academic Press.

Walsh, J., & Brown, W. (1991). Regional earnings and pay flexibility. In A. Bowen & K. Mayhew (Eds.), *Reducing Regional Inequalities* (pp. 185–215). London: Kogan Page and National Economic Development Office.

Warde, A. (1982). *Comparability in Local Studies: The Case of the Deindustrialization of Lancaster.* Lancaster Regionalism Working Paper 4. Lancaster, England: Department of Sociology, University of Lancaster.

Warde, A. (1985). Spatial change, politics, and the division of labour. In D. Gregory & J. Urry (Eds.), *Social Relations and Spatial Structures* (pp. 190–212). London: Macmillan.

Warde, A. (1989). Industrial discipline: Factory regime and politics in Lancaster. *Work, Employment and Society, 3,* 49–63.

Webber, M. J. (1982). Agglomeration and the regional question. *Antipode, 14,* 1–11.

Webber, M. J. (1986). Regional production and the production of regions: The case of Steeltown. In A. J. Scott & M. Storper (Eds.), *Production, Work, Territory: The Geographical Anatomy of Industrial Capitalism* (pp. 197–224). Boston: Allen and Unwin.

Weir, M. (1992). *Politics and Jobs: The Boundaries of Employment Policy in the United States.* Princeton, N.J.: Princeton University Press.

Wilde, L. (1991). Logic: Dialectic and contradiction. In T. Carver (Ed.), *The Cambridge Companion to Marx* (pp. 275–295). Cambridge: Cambridge University Press.

Wilkinson, F. (1981a). Preface. In F. Wilkinson (Ed.), *The Dynamics of Labour Market Segmentation.* London: Academic Press.

Wilkinson, F. (Ed.). (1981b). *The Dynamics of Labour Market Segmentation.* London: Academic Press.

Wilkinson, F. (1983). Productive systems. *Cambridge Journal of Economics, 7,* 413–429.

Wilkinson, F. (1988). Deregulation, structured labour markets and unemployment. In P. J. Pedersen & R. Lund (Eds.), *Unemployment: Theory, Policy, Structure* (pp. 167–185). Berlin: Walter de Gruyter.

Williams, F. (1986). The changing labour markets. *European Trends, 2,* 60–66.

Williams, G. (1981). Reflections on the responses of employers to educational qualifications. *Policy Studies, 2,* 107–115.

Williamson, O. E. (1975). *Markets and Hierarchies: Analysis and Antitrust Implications.* New York: The Free Press.

Williamson, O. E. (1985). *The Economic Institutions of Capitalism.* New York: The The Free Press.

Willis, P. (1977). *Learning to Labour: How Working Class Kids Get Working Class Jobs.* Aldershot, England: Gower.

Wilson, E. (1977). *Women and the Welfare State.* London: Tavistock.

Wiseman, M. (1993). Welfare reform in the States: The Bush legacy. *Focus, 15,* 18–36.

Wood, S. (Ed.). (1982). *The Degradation of Work.* London: Hutchinson.

Wood, S. (Ed.). (1989). *The Transformation of Work? Skill, Flexibility and the Labour Process.* London: Unwin Hyman.

Woodbury, S. (1987). Power in the labor market: Institutionalist approaches to labor problems. *Journal of Economic Issues, 21,* 1781–1807.

Wootton, B. (1955). *The Social Foundations of Wage Policy.* London: George Allen and Unwin.

Wright, G. (1987). Labour history and labour economics. In A. J. Field (Ed.), *The Future of Economic History* (pp. 313–348). Boston: Kluwer Nijhoff.

You, J.-I., & Wilkinson, F. (1994). Competition and co-operation: Toward understanding industrial districts. *Review of Political Economy, 6,* 259–278.

Young, D. (1982). Worried about unemployment? How you can help . . . *The Director,* August, 34–35.

Zeitlin, J. (1979). Craft control and the division of labour: Engineers and compositors in Britain, 1890–1930. *Cambridge Journal of Economics, 3,* 263–274.

Zuscovitch, E., Heraud, J.-A., & Cohendet, P. (1988). Innovation diffusion from a qualitative standpoint: Technology networks and economic evolution through case studies. *Futures, 20,* 266–306.

Zukin, S., & DiMaggio, P. (Eds.). (1990). *Structures of Capital: The Social Organisation of the Economy.* Cambridge: Cambridge University Press.

INDEX

Fox, A.: 33–34
Functional flexibility: 63; *64*

G

G7 countries, jobs conference of: 242–248
García, A. M.: 162–163
Garment industry
  in Australia, homework in: 154–155; 163–179; 182–183n.20; 183nn. 21, 25, and 26; 184n.31
  controlling labor in: 180–181
  exploitation in: 96
GATT (General Agreement on Tariffs and Trade): 244
Gender issues: 38; 44–45n.21 (*See also* Men; Women)
  in division of labor: 65; 66–67
  and domestic labor: 37
  and income-sharing: 67
  and skill formation: 135–136
General Agreement on Tariffs and Trade (GATT): 244
Geography of labor markets: 11–16; 20n.9; 78–79; 262–267 (*See also* Europe; Local labor markets; Spatial divisions of labor; *specific cities, states, and countries*)
  and flexibility: 119–120
  and labor regulation: 106–109
  and nation-states: 263
  and new industrial spaces: 132–134
  and occupational socialization: 81n.30
  and *rapport salarial* vs. *fait salarial*: 109
  and segmentation theory: 86
  and social undercutting: 43n.3
  and uneven development: 102–105
Geopolitics
  of labor regulation: 232–257
    and geographies of hegemonic despotism: 240–248
    and global capital vs. local labor: 233–239
    and localization of labor regulation: 248–257
  of production: 233–239
Germany
  training system in: 143–145; 147
  workfare in: 259n.30

Ghettos, labor markets in: 6–8
Gordon, D. M.: 6; 62; 137
Green, A. E.: 88

H

Hall, R. E.: 19n.1
Hanson, S.: 43n.5; 89–90
Harrison, B.: 19n.4; 130
Harvey, D.: 15; 88–89; 113n.15; 150
Hegemonic despotism in labor regulation: 234–248; 256
Hegemonic regimes in labor regulation: 36; 44n.16; 233–248; 255–257
Hicks, J. R.: 3
Hiebert, D.: 95; 114n.22
Hinrichs, K.: 27; 30; 31; 34; 35; 44n.8; 70; 71
Hispanics, homework by: 162
Historical analysis: 77–78; 84
Hobbes, T.: 1
Holland Report (U.K.): 212
"Hollowing out" of nation-states: 190–191; *197*; 197–198; 221–226; 238; 242
Homework: 153–181 (*See also* Domestic labor)
  in Australian garment industry: 154–155; 163–179182–183n.20; 183nn. 21, 25, and 26; 184n.31
  costs of: 168
  and deregulation: 165
  economic rationale of: 166–173
  and flexibility: 66
  as global phenomenon: 161
  and industrial competition: 168
  and industrial structure: 161–175
  and labor competition: 168
  and labor process: 167
  and labor unions: 166–167
  and local imperatives of labor control: 180–181
  social construction of: 153–154
  and state regulation of labor markets: 165–166
  in U.S.: 162
  and vertical disintegration: 168
Housework (*See* Domestic labor)
Howell, Ralph: 259n.29
Hudson, R.: 15; 126
"Human capital": 3